B(8 ou B6   1055   542

Autographs

A KEY TO COLLECTING

by

MARY A. BENJAMIN

DOVER PUBLICATIONS, INC., NEW YORK

Published in Canada by General Publishing Company, Ltd., 30 Lesmill Road, Don Mills, Toronto, Ontario.

Published in the United Kingdom by Constable and Company, Ltd., 10 Orange Street, London WC2H 7EG.

This Dover edition, first published in 1986, is an unabridged and further corrected republication of the 1963 corrected and revised edition as published by Walter R. Benjamin Autographs, New York (first edition, R.R. Bowker, New York, 1946). A new preface has been written by the author specially for the Dover edition.

Manufactured in the United States of America.
Dover Publications, Inc., 31 East 2nd Street, Mineola, N.Y. 11501

Library of Congress Cataloging-in-Publication Data

Benjamin, Mary A.
   Autographs: a key to collecting.

   Reprint. Originally published: New York : W.R. Benjamin Autographs, 1963.
   Bibliography: p.
   Includes index.
   1. Autographs—Collectors and collecting. I. Title.
Z41.B4 1986   929.8'8'075   85-20571
ISBN 0-486-25035-0

To the Memory

OF

Walter Romeyn Benjamin

Preface to the Dover Edition

WHEN Walter R. Benjamin, my father, established his firm of autographs one hundred years ago in September 1887, he was the only dealer in America who specialized strictly in old letters and manuscripts.

In 1946, when the present book was first published, the situation had changed markedly. The number of autograph collectors, as well as the number of dealers, had increased and continued to do so, and the book was reissued in 1963 and 1966.

My father died in 1943 and I followed in his footsteps, becoming the firm's second generation. In 1986 it is difficult to realize how great the development of the interest has grown these past forty years. Autograph and book dealers abound throughout the country and auction houses offer material constantly.

It seems an appropriate time, therefore, to reissue the book, not only as an introductory guide to newcomers, but to mark the firm's centennial.

Needless to say, I have taken the opportunity to make several changes in the text in the interest of bringing prices mentioned more up-to-date and revising some of the historical information given.

Few people today have had the privilege, as I have had since joining my father in 1925, of being meticulously trained in the field and of working with old letters. Today the third generation is represented by my nephew, Christopher C. Jaeckel, a member of the firm since 1971. I am indebted to him for his help in updating values mentioned.

For her invaluable suggestions with this revision, I am particularly grateful to my colleague and dear friend, Miss Rosejeanne Slifer, without whose generous help and encouragement I might not have attempted this reissue.

MARY A. BENJAMIN

Preface to the 1963 Edition

THIS book first appeared sixteen years ago, and the original printing has long since been exhausted. It is, of course, gratifying to realize that the available copies are still fulfilling the purpose for which the book was intended: to serve as a handbook for the constantly increasing group of history-loving autograph collectors. Yet the demand for additional copies continues. A reissue seems appropriate at this time which marks the completion of the 75th year of the firm originally founded by my father, Walter Romeyn Benjamin, in 1887.

It is questionable whether any book has ever appeared in print that did not cause its author anguished moments over its errors and omissions. Mine is no exception. And in addition to errors and omissions there are inevitable changes brought about by time. The errors have been corrected in the text itself, but among the omissions the first I would mention was my failure to identify specifically the facsimile of the Lincoln letter referred to on page 157. This was an A.L.S., one-page quarto, Executive Mansion, Washington, March 20, 1865, addressed to Mrs. Amanda Hall.

Not mentioned in my warning chapter on Facsimiles, for at the time they did not or were not known to exist, are many facsimiles of such noted figures as Sir Winston Churchill, Hitler, Presidents Hoover, Truman, Eisenhower, Kennedy, and others. Of special danger to the unwary are the signatures of these same persons, executed by members of their staffs. The number of these facsimiles and "professional forgeries" are too many to enumerate, but they exist and may prove costly if purchased in the belief that they are genuine.

A second omission pertains to the forged checks of Washington by Robert Spring. I failed to note that when Spring's supply of printed checks gave out he carefully wrote them entirely by hand, drawing the funds on the same Cashier of the Office of Discount and Deposit at Baltimore. These written checks appear more frequently on the market than the filled out printed forms. Most books dealing with autographs either refer to or reproduce examples of this most common of all American forgeries.

Again, I notice that I made no mention of a troublesome Constitution Signer, Nicholas Gilman of New Hampshire, who lived from 1755 to 1814. His father, Nicholas Gilman, Treasurer of New Hampshire, who died in 1783, all too often appears in Constitution sets in lieu of his more famous son.

Where changes are concerned, I can only touch upon a few most worthy of comment. To attempt to include all would involve my writing a new book, a venture which at this time is quite impossible.

First among the changes must be noted a sad one: the death of many of the great collectors mentioned in these pages, not the least of whom were Oliver Barrett, Dr. Frederick M. Dearborn, and Dr. Max Thorek. Some of their enviable collections now grace our major institutions; others have been dispersed at public auction or privately for the enjoyment and instruction of a younger and no less ardent group of collectors.

The most marked change is, of course, in valuations. I cannot give revised figures for all prices quoted in my book, but by referring to a few, these few may perhaps serve as a gauge by which to measure others. On page 35, I mentioned a Lincoln signature as being worth $25. Today, $75 to $100 would be more correct. A Pasteur letter is valued on page 41 at $85; today, $150 to $250 would be the price. And a Washington A.L.S., page 42, valued at $150 in 1946, could hardly be purchased for less than $350 in the present market. The increase in values is not surprising. It is the normal result of inflationary times and scarcity.

The new location of the fifth and last privately owned copy of Lincoln's handwritten Gettysburg Address, known as the Bliss copy, is another change worthy of note. Collectors of autographs are as interested in learning of the exact whereabouts of great autographs as are artists and lovers of art in knowing where great paintings are to be found. The Bliss copy was sold at the Parke-Bernet Galleries on April 27, 1949, to Oscar B. Cintas for $54,000. Upon his death, according to the terms of his will, it was presented to the White House for permanent display in the Lincoln Room. It is comforting to know that today, with the first and second drafts of this great document being housed in the Library of Congress; the Bancroft copy, presented by Mrs. Nicholas H. Noyes to Cornell University; and the Everett copy owned by the Illinois State Historical Library: all five copies are now safely preserved in permanent collections.

On pages 227 and 228, I referred to the possibility that the as yet unstudied and unopened Lincoln papers presented to the Library of Congress by the President's son, Robert Todd Lincoln, might reveal sensational information. Though when finally made available nothing sensational was discovered in them, they did, according to Dr. Paul Angle, Director of the Chicago Historical Society and a leading authority on Lincoln, turn out to be valuable source material and to contain many drafts and copies of Lincoln's own writings, some hitherto unknown, as well as the great bulk of his incoming correspondence.

In the chapter on Confused Identities I mentioned there having been two contemporary John Harts, one of whom was the New Jersey Signer of the Declaration of Independence. Later research on this subject, published in *The Collector* for April, 1956, disclosed that there were no less than seven contemporary John Harts, of varying ages, with five of them from Hopewell, New Jersey!

Again, on page 66, I spoke of the existence of the one and only known franked signature of Martha Washington which it was my good fortune to discover. Since then, hidden in a miscellaneous lot of material acquired at public auction, I came upon the second.

Out of existence, into the limbo of useful-in-their-day books has gone the *U. S. Cumulative Book Prices Current*, now survived by its only predecessor and contemporary, the invaluable *American Book Prices Current*, ably edited by the bookman's friend, Edward Lazare.

No doubt other important new facts should be incorporated in this preface. I can only plead that no one book can hope to cover all angles of the absorbing and intricate subject of autographs. To compensate for my own inadequacies, I have included in this reissue, omitted in the original printing, a selected list of reference books. In addition to books on autographs and autograph collecting, I have listed a few useful biographical and historical volumes which have proved indispensable in my work.

In conclusion, I wish to express my sincere appreciation of the good will shown by those true friends who, upon the first appearance of this book, drew my attention to its errors which I have now endeavored to correct.

MARY A. BENJAMIN

New York, N. Y., December 1, 1962.

Foreword (1946)

FOR *many years, librarians and autograph dealers have been besieged with inquiries from collectors and those tentatively interested in the subject of autographs. Too often the questioner has been turned away because the answer was not readily known or because information sought could not be supplied without going into great detail. The published books dealing with autographs provided a few answers but were more essentially memoirs or lightly written anecdotes. No one work could be recommended. During the lifetime of my father, Walter Romeyn Benjamin, dean of autograph collectors, I contemplated the writing of a book to satisfy this need but for various reasons could not carry through the necessary and laborious research that must provide the fundamental basis of such a task. The need remained, and at every turn of the twenty odd years during which I have followed in his footsteps, I have been made acutely aware of it through personal experience.*

In undertaking to meet it, I have sought to establish a balance between the things which the confirmed autograph collector on the one hand and the beginner-collector on the other would wish to know. For those active in the field there may be much in Autographs: A Key to Collecting *with which they have long since been familiar, but I hope there will be sufficient to refresh their memories as to facts they may once have known but have perhaps forgotten, and enough new information to reward their reading. For those who have decided, or are debating a decision, to take up autograph collecting, I have tried to make the book as comprehensive as possible, yet I make no pretense to cover the entire field. The book is only an introduction to the subject. Where more detailed information on special phases of the study is desired, the quoted sources will provide the answers.*

To beginners, then, among American collectors, whose tastes are naturally more familiar to me than the interests of those abroad, this book is primarily addressed. I have aimed to introduce them to those points which are of immediate and essential importance as well as to the problems their newly acquired knowledge should help them to solve. I have deliberately tried to avoid the mention of specific values of autographs since, as shown in the chapter on Evaluation, these are dependent on too many varying factors and are only representative of current prices. Certain statements regarding the autograph situation in Europe, it should be noted, apply of course to conditions prior to the recent war. At the time of this book's writing it was impossible to ascertain what plans there were for reopening autograph markets on the continent.

In writing the book I have been constantly benefited by the advice of many, who, whether friends or business or correspondence acquaintances, have cheered me on by their ready willingness to help. This help has been forthcoming repeatedly no matter what work was entailed in verifying facts, revealing new facets of knowledge and supplying elusive information. In particular, the invaluable assistance and sympathetic understanding of librarians has demonstrated anew the asset the world of scholarship has in them.

To all who have aided me, I here offer both my thanks and tribute. I am especially grateful to officials of The New York Public Library — F. I. D. Avelino of the American History Room; Lewis Stark of the Reserve Division; G. William Bergquist, Chief of the Preparation Room; Wilmer R. Leech and his assistant, Edward B. Morrison, of the Manuscript Division, and, above all, Robert W. Hill, Keeper of Manuscripts.

The latter's unfailing generosity in locating concealed facts, pursuing clues and assisting me "on call" has been both a great contribution and an incentive to my efforts.

To R. W. G. Vail of The New York Historical Society, and to the Reverend John J. O'Rourke, S.J., of America, I am deeply indebted for their suggestions and other aids. Dr. St. George L. Sioussat, Chief of the Manuscript Division of the Library of Congress, and Thomas P. Martin, Assistant Chief of the same Division, were untiring in obtaining information available only in their files. I am also keenly appreciative of the fact that many passages of this book could not have been written had there not stood figuratively at my elbow Adelaide E. Minogue, Chief of the Repairing and Cleaning Division of the National Archives of Washington; William J. Barrow, Restorer of Documents at the State Library, Richmond, Virginia; Dr. Dard Hunter, Curator of the Dard Hunter Paper Museum of the Massachusetts Institute of Technology; Dr. William R. Van Lennep of the Harvard Theatre Collection, and Eric Morrell, son of W. T. Morrell, noted London bookbinder, and formerly with The New York Public Library.

My gratitude is also extended to Gertrude Hess, Assistant Librarian of the American Philosophical Society; Louise Savage, Librarian of the Alderman Library; Ella May Thornton, State Librarian of Georgia; Harriet S. Tapley, Librarian of The Essex Institute; Virginia N. Lawrence, expert repairer of manuscripts, of New York City; Paul M. Angle, Director of the Chicago Historical Society; Oliver Barrett of Kenilworth, Illinois; Frederick S. Peck of Providence, Rhode Island; Dr. Randolph G. Adams of the William L. Clements Library; Dr. Lawrence C. Wroth, Librarian of The John Carter Brown Library; Dr. Leon de Valinger, Jr., State Archivist of Delaware; Charles Francis Jenkins, President of the Historical Society of

Pennsylvania; Dr. Leslie Bliss, Librarian of the Huntington Library; Dr. John J. Meng, President of the American Catholic Historical Society; Richard Breaden of the Pierpont Morgan Library; E. G. Millar, Keeper of Manuscripts at the British Museum; Dr. James G. McManaway of the Folger Shakespeare Memorial Library; Louis C. Karpinski of Ann Arbor, Michigan; Albert S. Osborn, Examiner of Questioned Documents; Abigail Davidson, Manager of The Carthage Republican *of Carthage, Illinois, and William P. Rogan, attorney-at-law, of New York City. To Arthur C. Pforzheimer, Edmond C. Bonaventure, Ernest Bissegger and, above all, to Forest G. Sweet of New York City, my colleagues and friends, I extend my thanks for their interest and their efforts to make "straight the road." My friend of many years, Mary Stamps Gaillard, has also contributed immeasurably with her helpful suggestions and valuable advice. And I cannot omit a grateful mention of the tireless work of my assistants, Maura Dillon, A. Margery Storrs and, in particular, the able and competent help of Ellen C. Ahern in proofreading the galleys.*

Dr. Julian Boyd, Librarian of Princeton University, has most generously consented to write the Introduction to this book, and in so doing has augmented my previous obligation to him for his guidance and counsel.

Lastly, to John Gilland Brunini, Editor of Spirit, *a Magazine of Poetry, is due the greatest debt of gratitude. Without his understanding and invaluable editorial assistance, this book could never have been completed. His keen interest and constant encouragement helped me to overcome obstacles that at times seemed insurmountable.*

To these and many others whom it is impossible to list but to whom I am further indebted, I sincerely give my thanks.

MARY A. BENJAMIN

New York, N. Y., January 9, 1946

Contents

The Illustrations section appears at the end of Part One, following page 238.

Illustrations

(section follows page 238)

Introduction

"A Little Key," wrote Roger Williams in 1643, "may open a Box, Where lies a Bunch of Keyes." Thus the great advocate of religious toleration explained his choice of title for *A Key into the Language of America*, one of the rarest and earliest of the publications about New England that sought to unlock the doors to knowledge, experience and opportunity in America. Language, as Williams knew, was one of the most important of keys.

Miss Benjamin, in her first book, has chosen a similarly appropriate title. The bunch of keys that she holds forth is intended primarily for the use of that fortunate and growing group of people who have just become infected, or are blissfully unaware that they are about to become infected, by the pleasant and useful virus which arouses the collecting instinct. Once the symptoms have become unmistakable—that is, once the victim's family and friends have begun to comment upon his condition, an indication likely to precede his own awareness—his first action, if he is prudent, will be to learn how to use the keys here proffered. But one of the insidious effects of the virus is that it often builds up an immunization to all counsels of prudence. The victim, unaware of any tendency toward imprudence and carried away by the exhilaration of his new enthusiasm, will reject the advice of experience. He will make a game of his mistakes, reciting them with the same gusto that enlivens his anecdotes of victories achieved, and his frustrations will only enlarge his determination. He will not be bored by the tedious process of charting the pitfalls and closed alleys, nor will he at first regard the centuries-old tradition that has built both an ethic and an opportunity around this ancient human trait of collecting—an ethic calling for honor, urbanity and civilized practices and an opportunity evoking, too often, fraud and avarice in the path of the uncritical novice. But wisdom will come soon or late, and the inexperienced collector will take hold of the keys here offered, using them for his pleasure and often for his profit. He will find not all, perhaps, but some of the best answers to some of the most important questions—how, what, where and how much. He has no need of the answer to "Why?" because he would not be susceptible to the virus if that question had not been effectively answered already.

Even the seasoned collector, scarred by many a battle in the auction market and enriched as well by many a rewarding experience there, will neglect this "Bunch of Keyes" at his own peril. Collecting is an exacting task as well as a useful indulgence, and the collector who does not know at first hand the latest information about paper, ink, water-marks, methods of repair and protection and tests of authenticity would do well to ponder Miss Benjamin's chapters on these subjects. Before me as I write there lies a letter that would delight any collector—if only it were authentic: a letter from John Paul Jones to Thomas Jefferson, in which Jones presents to Jefferson a bust of himself by Houdon. The paper is genuine eighteenth-century paper, the color of the ink appears right, the handwriting looks as genuine as anything John Paul Jones ever wrote. A very distinguished American collector, who was a scholar who knew American history extremely well, apparently thought it was genuine. But the simplest of Miss Benjamin's tests would have proved it otherwise. The chapter on forgeries is itself a whole bunch of keys, and very valuable keys they are.

Scholars and librarians will also find these keys useful, though they possess one of the most important of all keys and one that neither Miss Benjamin nor anyone else can give away. It is one that must be earned by assiduous effort: the key represented by a critical understanding of history. It is well to know the chemistry of ink and the history of paper, but it is also essential to know history. It is a fact worth noting that all of the really great forgeries and hoaxes—those of Ireland, Chatterton, Bertram and Cunningham—were exposed by scholars who knew their subject. No one familiar with eighteenth-century American history would need to see the manuscripts of the letters printed by Miss Benjamin on pages 101-102 to know that they are not genuine.

But all forgers are not so unlettered as to assume that Patrick Henry would close a letter with the phrase "Yours very sincerely," and the collector therefore ought to know ink and paper and handwriting as well as history.

Thus scholars, librarians, collectors and dealers in historical manuscripts will find valuable uses for Miss Benjamin's keys. There will be — and should be, for it is a large part of the excitement of studying history— debate over questions of importance or utility. Questions of responsibility will also be raised. Where, for example, lies the responsibility for the permanent violation of the historical integrity of a group of family papers that are dispersed at auction or by a dealer—with the family, with the dealer, with the librarian or with the collector who wants not a corpus of manuscripts but an example? What is to be done, in fairness to the dealers who have preserved against destruction great quantities of archival documents that were abstracted, borrowed or given away by official custodians in the nineteenth century? These are questions that, if raised in the past, would have caused recriminations to be passed among scholars, collectors, dealers and librarians. But to raise them now is only to evoke a mutual respect for what each has done in a single cause — the preservation of our common heritage. It is also to bring forth mutual efforts to solve difficulties that in the past were ignored. Collectors and dealers have played a tremendously important part in the preservation of much of the record of our history, and the light thrown on that history would be the dimmer if it had not been for the materials they protected. Scholars and librarians have played a rôle no less important, for without them the history could not have been written. One of the chief answers to our questions, then, is a mutual understanding of the community of interest that is shared. With this understanding, perhaps we can jointly protect the integrity of a collection that is threatened with dispersal by calling in the aid of science and by using microphotography. This is one of the few instances in which science makes it possible for the collector, the dealer, the scholar and the librarian each to have his cake and eat it too. With such a mutuality of respect and interest, we can also see that collectors and dealers have their interests protected in the matter of archival estrays that they have acquired in good faith and protected with admirable zeal. Indeed, the beginning has already been made in this direction.

By the valuable information that she has presented, by the responsibility that she places squarely upon collectors, dealers and librarians, by the clear recognition of the scope and importance of her profession and by the hope she holds forth that problems formerly dividing the collector from the scholar and the librarian from the dealer may no longer evoke recriminations but solutions and mutually helpful answers, Miss Benjamin has produced a volume of the first importance to all of these groups of useful citizens.

JULIAN P. BOYD.

PART ONE

CHAPTER I

A Historical Summary

MAN'S interest in autographs is of ancient origin. It may seem a paradox to state that the impulse to collect antedated the existence of autographs, at least as they are known today. Yet man cherished his written records from the earliest days, long before the alphabet came out of the East. His interest began when ideas were first expressed in visible form, and persisted, deepened and widened through various stages of development.

Anyone who has even casually dipped into the ancient histories of the world is familiar with the picture-writing of the first men and how this method of recording gradually evolved into that of Egyptian hieroglyphics and cuneiform. The latter form of writing was extensively used during most of the pre-Christian centuries and was devised by the Sumerians in a period so remote that it is idle to speculate concerning the time of its origin. It was first known to have been adopted by the Semitic Babylonians, who wrote their inscriptions in cuneiform from *circa* 4500 B.C. to the first century B.C. Following the discovery of the Tel-el-Amarna tablets in upper Egypt in 1887, scholars demonstrated that the same script was in use for purposes of correspondence in the fifteenth century B.C. from Elam to the Mediterranean and from Armenia to the Persian Gulf.

Cuneiform, from the Latin, meaning "wedge shape," may be described as a modified method of picture-writing and was variously transformed as it was perfected and made more flexible. In its first uses, it was probably reserved for public inscriptions, but as man sought to conquer distance and to communicate with his absent fellows, "letters" in cuneiform began to appear. These were written on wet clay tablets, with the message being pressed in or inscribed by a stylus; the tablet was then dried by baking and dispatched.

A collection of cuneiform letters would not have been easy for an individual to preserve privately, and it is extremely doubtful that an Assyrian Juliet saved the love letters of her Babylonian Romeo even on the unlikely assumption that he wrote any. Yet cuneiform letters were definitely preserved and were in many instances as closely guarded as the Ark of the Covenant in which the Israelites treasured the tables of the Ten Commandments. Many museums throughout the world today display cuneiforms discovered in the ruins of cities in what is now known as the Middle East. Translated, they often include accounts of merchants and temples and correspondences between chieftains and rulers.

In libraries, the history of which dates far back into the cuneiform era, such records were preserved, and a large portion of one of the earliest libraries known to scholars is today housed in the British Museum. It formed part of the library of Sardanapalus, who was not only one of the most powerful monarchs of the Assyrians, but one of their greatest patrons of literature. It is estimated that Sardanapalus had amassed ten thousand distinct works, some of which extended over several tablets. The collection was discovered at Nineveh and appeared then to have been methodically arranged and catalogued and open to the general use of the king's subjects.*

Knowledge of the libraries of ancient Egypt is incomplete, but there are many references to their existence. At an early date, Heliopolis was a literary center of great importance, and more than six thousand years ago there flourished numerous scribes of many classes whose duties were to record official events in the lives of their royal masters or details of their domestic affairs and business transactions. Each temple included professional scribes on its staff, and these devoted themselves both to religion and science. Records show that Khufu, a monarch of the Fourth Dynasty, and Khafra, the builder of the second pyramid both possessed libraries. The most famous of the Egyptian libraries was that of King Osymandyas, who has been identified as the great King Rameses II. Located at western Thebes, its directors, among whom the name of one,

* Menant, *Bibliothèque du palais de Ninive*, Paris, 1880.

Amen-en-hant, is known, had responsibilities similar to such officials in our own times.

When material more easily handled than clay was discovered, a new impetus was given to writing, and a new solicitude to collect and preserve immediately followed. Man invents out of his necessities, and it was the Egyptians who first produced a new and more convenient medium. Their introduction of papyrus, which was one of the ancient monopolies, was a long journey forward in man's instinctive effort to convey his thoughts to those contemporaries with whom he could not speak directly, and perhaps even to project himself into the future and make himself known to others who would come after him. In the centuries before Christ, the practice of writing greatly increased through the exportation of papyrus from Egypt itself.

The various books of the Hebrew writers, which later were to be assembled into the Old Testament of the Bible, were preserved on thick rolls of closely written papyrus in the Temple at Jerusalem and the synagogues. The Athenians, who considered the manuscripts of the Greek classical writers as the most precious possessions of their city, jealously guarded them, and only under compulsion surrendered them to the great library at Alexandria. Ptolemy Philadelphus is reputed to have refused to supply wheat to Athens, then in the midst of a famine, unless he was allowed to borrow the original manuscripts of Aeschylus, Euripides, Homer and Sophocles. His stated purpose was to have copies made, but, once he had obtained the originals, it was the copies, supposedly, which were returned to Athens. Ptolemy also fostered the translation from Hebrew into Greek of the biblical religious books now called the Septuagint. It is so known because seventy Hebrew scholars accepted the king's invitation, journeyed to Alexandria, eventually completed their work and made the library the first beneficiary of their labors.

Strabo, the Greek geographer who died during the lifetime of Christ, declares that Aristotle was the first person who collected a library in Greece, and that it was he who communicated the taste for collecting to the Egyptian sovereigns. It is certain, in any event, that the libraries of Alexandria were the most important in the ancient world. They enjoyed widespread fame. Ptolemy sent his emissaries into every part of Greece and Asia to acquire the most prized works, and his successor is said to have used more drastic methods—he seized all books brought into Egypt and gave copies to their owners in recompense.

However questionable these methods, the fact remains that only in Egypt did there seem to be climatic conditions favorable for papyrus preservation. But the Ptolemies' ambition to bequeath their collections forever to posterity was not to be realized. Over the centuries, the Alexandrian libraries were visited by one catastrophe after another until their vast accumulations of books and manuscripts were almost entirely lost. The first of these disasters occurred accidentally, when Caesar burned his fleet in the harbor, and the larger of the two libraries in the path of the wind took fire and was completely destroyed. Vandalism, invasions, wars, floods and earthquakes took terrific toll of other ancient papyrus libraries. From them, however, the world today possesses—besides official literature—examples of many commentaries on the sacerdotal books, historical treatises, works of moral philosophy and proverbial wisdom, collections of medical prescriptions and even a great variety of popular "novels" and humorous pieces.

Of the papyri which have been saved until now, a few are of the highest significance. Foremost among them is a small fragment of a Biblical codex, the earliest extant from the New Testament. Containing parts of the Gospel of St. John and dating back to the first half of the second century, it is now in the John Rylands Library at Manchester, England. The British Museum also possesses portions of three leaves of a papyrus codex whose author is unidentified, but whose "Gospel" bears close similarities in phrasings to those of St. John and the Synoptics. These fragments also date from the first half of the second century.* A. Chester Beatty, an American collector residing in England, possesses a greater number of papyri, which date from the early third century. Of the papyrus codex of the Pauline Epistles, one group of thirty leaves from an original one hundred and four is

* Frederic Kenyon, *The Story of the Bible*, J. Murray, London, 1936.

at the University of Michigan, and numerous others are in England.

It may surprise some to learn that Cicero and Pliny are known to have been deeply interested in their collections. Any collector who today bewails an incomplete set of Signers of the Declaration of Independence, because he cannot acquire a rare Button Gwinnett or a Thomas Lynch, Jr., will sympathize with Pliny's complaint that letters of Julius Caesar were very scarce even in his time. Other Romans, too, were collectors of the writings of their famous predecessors and contemporaries.

When, in the early centuries of the Christian era, the Egyptians shut off the exportation of papyrus, a new writing material came into use and soon displaced all others. This was the skin of animals—parchment or vellum. Although parchment is generally identified as sheepskin, it also can be the skin of a goat or other animal. Parchment includes vellum, which—finer than sheepskin—is specifically the skin of a lamb, kid or calf. Despite the obvious disadvantages attached to the preservation of parchment, every great library in Europe and many in America possess such manuscripts of considerable antiquity. The Codex Vaticanus and the Codex Sinaiticus are preëminent among these. The former, carefully treasured in the Vatican Library, is a copy of the Scriptures, made about the fourth century; the latter, housed for many centuries in a monastery atop Mount Sinai, is now in the British Museum.

It is true that, although these ancient manuscripts on parchment once existed in quantity, few of the collections of libraries and individuals of this period are known to have survived the ravages of time. Among the earliest parchment manuscripts ever offered on the American market was a group of documents—three of Pepin le Bref, King of the Francs, dated 753, June 760, and July 766; three of Charlemagne, dated 781, August 1, 786, and September 15, 802; and two of Arnulf, King of Germany, dated February 9, 888, and September 15, 896. The relatively few remaining afford plentiful and definite evidence that shortly after people commenced to write they also began to preserve autographs.

Some insight into the causes of the loss of many manuscripts is incidentally, yet graphically, stated by Francis Cardinal Gasquet, writing on the Vulgate in the *Catholic Encylopaedia*. The Cardinal headed the Papal Commission established by Leo XIII to restore the Latin Bible in accordance with the authentic version which St. Jerome wrote in the third century. The Commission over many years was embarked on one of the most extensive tasks of scholarly research ever undertaken, and the Cardinal indicates a few of the many difficulties.

"From time to time," he wrote, "the Commission has come across fragments of Bibles in the course of researches in libraries which show how precious manuscripts have been destroyed. When other and newer texts had been made for the use of some church or monastery, there appears to have been little hesitation in using the older copies for binding purposes or, for the sake of the parchment, obliterating the original writing and putting some other text upon it. Thus, in the bindings of books at Durham and at Worcester, some precious fragments of very old Bibles have been found. At Worcester, the fragments recovered in this way may not impossibly be leaves of a Bible presented to Worcester by King Ethelred in the tenth century. Perhaps the most curious fragment of a Gospel book that has come to the Commission's notice is a portion of a fine Spanish manuscript of large size. This, which contained the whole of the Gospel of St. John, had been torn out of a volume in such a way that several fragments of the Gospel of St. Luke had been left on torn leaves of fine parchment. The Commission has endeavored in vain to locate the rest of the text from which this excellent Visigothic fragment had been so ruthlessly torn away."

A shortage of parchment itself apparently caused the destruction of an indefinite number of irreplaceable documents and manuscripts. With the invention of paper, obviously less expensive, less bulky and easier to store, great changes occurred. Paper, although it had these and other advantages over previous mediums and was first known as early as A.D. 105, was not produced on the European continent until 1150, in Spain.* The manufactur-

* Julius Grant, *Books and Documents,* Grafton & Co., London, 1937.

ing process was shortly afterwards extended to other countries. The earliest documents on paper, practically in their entirety, have been absorbed by libraries, and it is an exception when any come on the market. The year 1400, approximately, is the earliest date for the small number which have in recent years been offered for sale.

With the invention of printing, paper definitely and finally supplanted vellum, save on special occasions. Italy, France, Switzerland and Germany, following the lead of Spain, established new and larger paper mills, and England, which had probably first relied on importing her supplies, followed in 1490. Education inevitably became more widespread as the presses made the printed word familiar to the people. The art of writing, which up to that time had been infrequently acquired, and only, for the most part, by members of religious orders, became more and more common. The utilitarian value of the alphabet was more acutely recognized. And so also was penmanship, as an essential and easy skill to acquire — a skill which was necessary if one was to participate in the new and accelerated exchange of ideas which was so notable in the Europe of that day.

Almost simultaneously with this increased interest in writing, the serious collecting of documents, letters and papers of distinguished and not-so-distinguished people appears to have begun in earnest. The great universities, which had then been established at Paris, Oxford, and Salamanca, among other cities, were centers for a practice comparable to the seed from which has grown the entire family tree of modern autograph collecting. Students, anxious to preserve the memories of days which would always be unique in their lives, took up the assembling of *alba amicorum*. These were small albums or notebooks in which they would themselves jot down quotations from the classroom and notes of events which interested them personally. Often they enlisted their professors and friends to write some saying or sentiment or good wish. Complying, the royal, the noble, the theologian, the historian penned quotations in Latin and Greek or proverbs from the Scriptures or earlier philosophers.

The comparative few of these old albums now extant in whole, or more often in part, are usually owned by libraries, but at infrequent intervals they appear on the market. They point to the fact that the eminence of the individuals whose writings they contain is higher, on the whole, than in similar collections which are assembled today. Education in the Renaissance period, despite its rapid increase, still remained a luxury, and only those of outstanding qualities of mind were encouraged to undertake the severe training then demanded of students. Both the faculty member and the student were either already men of unusual achievements or, by position in life and ability, were destined to play leading roles in the history of their times. It was these men who greatly furthered the practice of letter-writing.

Gradually, correspondence, which had heretofore been confined almost exclusively to the wealthy and the talented, was attempted more generally. Side by side with official communications and papers concerned exclusively with scholarship, there grew up personal and private correspondence. The costs of dispatching a message at a time when there was no postman to knock or ring at the door, and the courier provided the only equivalent to a postal service, were high. It was an event to write or to receive letters, and, in consequence, letters were carefully worded and painstakingly penned. Since paper was still expensive, it was fully used, and the pages were often covered with closely written lines. Particularly because such writers played so important a part as the chroniclers of their times, their letters were often detailed and of tremendous historic importance. The senders knew that, when no other method of communication of news—save that of word of mouth—was available to their contemporaries, those they favored with letters would receive them with grateful appreciation.

Inherent in the whole procedure were certain elements which prompted men and women to save carefully any missive they received. In this they gave a further impetus to autograph collecting. By the sixteenth century it had become general throughout Europe, especially in Germany. Collectors broadened their interests—from acquiring letters personal in their contents, they went on to assemble first the notables of their own localities, then of their nations and, finally, all writings which they could obtain by purchase or by trade.

Frequent wars and other vicissitudes which are still familiar today dissipated the majority of Renaissance collections, but a fair proportion were preserved, and certain groups, as well as single items, are now exhibited in the Vatican Library, the British Museum, the Bibliothèque Nationale and in smaller libraries all over Europe. These collections are altogether distinct from the great stores of historical papers of official nature which are contained in the archives of European governments. Some, privately owned, have occasionally been dispersed at auctions in London, Paris and Berlin. As knowledge concerning them has become more general, many who take up autograph collecting for the first time are startled to find that letters written by the famous of the Renaissance era are occasionally offered at very reasonable prices.

Documents and letters of St. Francis of Assisi, Michelangelo, Luther, Machiavelli, Amerigo Vespucci, Galileo Galilei, Molière, Racine, Beethoven, Bach and countless others of equal rarity and desirability are not uncommonly listed in the catalogues of great firms of autograph dealers. The lists of auctions in all countries also demonstrate the amazing variety and value of manuscripts that are now purchasable on the market. With such inducements, it is not surprising that the interest in autograph collecting has not only continued through the centuries but has actually been intensified in the present one.

Recent years, particularly, have seen the number of collectors increase by leaps and bounds, and this has been further prompted by librarians who, within the past thirty or forty years, have shown a new and impelling interest in the possibilities and significance of acquiring manuscript collections. In America, with few exceptions, credit for preserving the records of the nation's past must go to private collectors. "About the deadest thing in this country is the average Historical Society," Walter R. Benjamin editorially observed in an 1890 issue of *The Collector,* the still-existing publication founded by him in 1887.

"Not one in a dozen has the slightest sign of life about it."* Librarians at that time were not, as a rule, of the calibre of those in charge of America's great institutions today.

The Mauve Decade developed such far-sighted and historically minded private collectors as J. Pierpont Morgan, Henry E. Huntington, Thomas Addis Emmet, Ferdinand Dreer, Simon Gratz, Charles F. Gunther and John Boyd Thacher. The material which they collected now forms the enviable nuclei of the many magnificent manuscript libraries of which America can boast. The traditions established by early collectors have in more modern times been well and faithfully carried on by Alfred Meyer, Jerome Kern, William Randolph Hearst, John Gribbel, Frederick S. Peck, Cardinal Mundelein, Frank J. Hogan, W. T. H. Howe and numerous others.

The story of why these men individually embarked on collecting has never been written. For some, the accidental acquisition of a single item—the letter of a favorite writer, statesman, philosopher or poet—drew them, as it still draws new collectors to the field. Whatever the cause, once embarked on this absorbing pursuit, they have shown their own individualities in the various roads they have taken. One is impartial in collecting any letters or papers of interest, another concentrates on some specialized subject. The Hogan collection, which was sold at auction in 1945, showed a bewildering variety of taste, whereas that of Boyd B. Stutler has one common denominator. He possesses over seven thousand letters, manuscripts, clippings and books devoted to John Brown of Osawatomie, whom the poet, Stephen Vincent Benét, so popularized in his *John Brown's Body*. One collector specializes in Dickens, another in Theodore Roosevelt and a third in Robert Louis Stevenson.

Collections have mushroomed all over the country in institutions whose work, because of more ample resources, has naturally reached far more substantial proportions than it would be possible for private individuals to duplicate. Fortunately, the interests of neither conflict. Chiefly, the fact that their approaches are from different angles encourages them to work happily together.

* Volume IV, November 1890, p. 27.

The librarian, in particular, is always cognizant of the existence of the collector, and it is not at all to the former's discredit if he nurses the silent hope that some particular major collection will eventually find its permanent home in his institution. Yet, if there is naturally such an ulterior motive in his consideration of the collector, a more immediate one governs. He is frequently eager to profit by the specialized knowledge of the private collector.

Mutual advantage, then, leads the two to work hand in hand, and, especially through consultation, to contribute each from his knowledge and experience to the advancement of the other. Both at heart desire the preservation of old records. The individual collector is more often primarily interested in single items, whereas libraries and institutions, covering a wider scope and range, share not only this interest but go further.

They, in their recognition of how important it is to have full knowledge of the events, places and people that figure in the lives of great men, have branched out and sought far and wide any correspondences which may contribute to better comprehension. Many letters have been written by persons not at all historically notable—schoolteachers, clergymen, shopkeepers, artisans, farmers and housewives—who have a flair for vividly describing details of everyday existence. They reveal the hardships of pioneer life, the scarcity or abundance of food, the success or failure of crops, the men who have wielded political influences, the progress of religion, conditions of climate, customs long since outmoded and now-forgotten medical formulae. Such bits of information, singly of not too much importance, collectively take on great value. Written by men and women who, unlike their contemporary famous brothers and sisters, were not too busy to write at length and in detail, they focus a clearer light on many given periods of history and point up the drama of the times. They are often full of local color and incident. The important contributions they offer cannot wisely be disregarded by any student or writer of their times.

Due to limitations of his facilities for housing documents, the private collector, naturally, is seldom in a position to undertake the ownership of such continuous correspondences of little-known men and women. Few, it is certain, could parallel such a wholesale collection as that of Mr. Stutler, and even fewer would be prepared to give room to the collection which is one of the prides of the George Washington Flowers Memorial Library of Duke University—the complete correspondence of the Socialist Party of the United States from 1895 to 1938. On the other hand, Mr. Benjamin, who acquired the papers of William Lloyd Garrison, the famous publisher and abolitionist editor of *The Liberator*, two car-loads in all, could find no one purchaser for them and was obliged to sell the items individually. They included many letters and manuscripts which forcefully and revealingly stated the position of Lincoln, John Brown and others active in the anti-slavery movement before the Civil War and covered the events of the Reconstruction Period.

Of similar importance are the correspondences of the noted families of America, many of which are to be found in libraries throughout the country. Obviously, for the student it is fortunate when these collections are preserved not only intact but in one place. In the majority of instances, however, family papers appear on the market and are immediately broken up. The Biddle family papers and the James McHenry papers, sold at public auction in 1943 and 1944, were divided among many purchasers. Should an attempt now or later be made to reassemble them, the task would be as impossible as the gathering of goose feathers scattered in a high wind. Collectors prize individual pieces too greatly to give them up lightly or altruistically.

The Biddle papers comprised countless letters of most remarkable historic content, written by many who were famous in the annals of America, including Washington, Jefferson, John Adams and Benjamin Rush, the Philadelphia physician and Signer of the Declaration of Independence. The importance of the McHenry papers is possibly even greater than that of the Biddle papers. McHenry, who had served as an aide to General Washington at Valley Forge, was Secretary of War both under the first President and the second, John Adams. This fact must be coupled with another—a severe fire in the War Department building in 1800 caused the loss of all official papers. The extensive McHenry correspondence, covering his terms of office, which he had chosen to keep in his own possession, therefore represents the only extant record of many events which governed or affected the War Department in the formative years of America's nationhood.

The breaking up of the Biddle and McHenry collections, which had been coveted by many libraries and which most appropriately might have been housed in the Library of Congress, at least provided a field day for private collectors. Out of this, unquestionably, came new stimulation no less to those established members of this class but to others who were interested in joining it. If the acquisition of really important papers becomes too impossible, through scarcity or any other cause, the individual collector is apt to be discouraged, as was the uncle in the Mark Twain story who, since he could not complete his collections of stamps, coins, cowbells and clocks because some crowning item was unobtainable, successively abandoned each and finally set about collecting echoes.

New opportunities to aid in the preservation of historically valuable letters, either in a small or large way, may in themselves be a spur to the beginner. It is not at first likely that he will be moved by more than the desire to possess, but as he progresses he will wish to share knowledge of the contents of what he possesses with librarians and others. And as he gradually realizes the good that can be achieved through his efforts, his autograph collecting will take on that more serious, more responsible, and more idealistic purpose which has been so noticeably characteristic in recent years.

CHAPTER II

The A. B. C.'s of Terminology

ANYONE who decides to collect autographs in a serious way must recognize immediately that to be successful he needs not only to exercise patience but through study to acquire certain very necessary knowledge and balanced judgment. He will first turn to the terms used in the professional field. Among collectors there is definitely shop-talk as incomprehensible to the layman as the shop-talk of the electrical engineer, the doctor or the pilot. Fortunately, in autograph collecting this basic language, often expressed in abbreviations, is not difficult to learn, and one quickly comes to use *M. O. C.* and *A. L. S.* as readily as Americans today refer to the *W. P. B.* or the *O. P. A.*

The tyro might count as his first lesson the practice of using the word "autograph" to designate the entire body of a letter or document in a person's handwriting. He will avoid limiting it to the mere signature. Only the uninitiated look upon the word "autograph" as meaning signature alone. In the professional sense an autograph is the writing itself on the document, letter or manuscript, which may or may not bear a signature. It is an example of a person's writing, and its interest and value are more than sentiment or the curiosity of learning how a Patrick Henry or an Andrew Jackson, a Wordsworth or a Napoleon, signed his name. The importance lies in the contents and the light that is thrown on the writer's personality or on the history or the customs of his day. The word "autograph" is frequently used interchangeably with "holograph." Both actually mean the same thing. Americans customarily use the former, and in England, where once "holograph" was preferred, "autograph" has also now largely supplanted it. By adjusting his ideas to these facts the new collector at once raises himself above the level of so-called "autograph fiends" who lurk in theatre alleyways to pounce upon the star with notebook and pen, or who doggedly write a plea designed to wheedle a signature from the latest Hollywood success, or who are ubiquitous wherever men and women, even fleetingly in the limelight, may be corralled.

Autograph collecting, in its professional sense, cannot be visualized as bound within the small compass which the handling of signed scraps of paper would imply. Signatures in themselves, or the brief letters which usually accompany answers to requests for them, are of no serious value to the student, biographer, historian, novelist or librarian. This does not imply that their collecting affords no pleasure or that many who would unjustly be characterized as "autograph fiends" are to be read out of court. Like the collecting of many other things, the hobby has by-products of merit. The signature collector, for instance, may well arrive at an increased appreciation of history and be prompted to widen his interest and become a real collector of autographs. But this is rather the exception than the rule.

The collector of signatures needs little help from the dealers, although occasionally he may enter their doors to acquire the signature of one long since dead or otherwise inaccessible. By and large, he will add to his store by other methods somewhat more dignified than ambushing a celebrity. He may attempt to obtain signatures by writing his prospects directly, enclosing stamps and return envelope, proffering words of praise, or making some ingenious plea which he hopes will win special treatment of his request. The theory might be advanced that people who have been hounded by such pleas may have coined the term "autograph fiend." There is nothing very modern or novel about this situation to which various of the hounded have had their own individual reactions.

Longfellow, who did not have to court a public as many stage, radio and screen stars feel they must, gladly responded to all requests, despite the fact that to do so made serious demands on his time. There were days when he had to devote an hour to one of the penalties of being famous. On the other hand, James Russell Lowell, not only deplored this type of victimizing, but is said to have remarked that an autograph album was "an instrument of torture unknown even to the Inquisition." At another time he wrote protestingly to a friend, "I am thinking seriously of getting a good forger from the state's prison to do my autographs, but I suppose the unconvicted followers of the same calling would raise the cry of convict labor." Alexander Dumas, Jr., held the signature collector also in low esteem, for once he replied to a request: "I prefer the wicked to fools, because the former can sometimes be rebuffed."

To meet the increasing demand for presidential signatures, Ulysses S. Grant had small cards engraved simply "Executive Mansion." Prior to his day, any slip of paper was used. The Grant innovation, with the heading change to "The White House" in the time of Theodore Roosevelt, was continued into the administration of the second Roosevelt. Since extremely few signed by the latter have appeared on the market, it seems probable that early in his tenure he may have been forced by pressure of duties to deny signature requests. Another more elaborate card, with an engraving of the White House itself, was introduced by Chester B. Arthur and selectively distributed until the time of Warren G. Harding.*

Lowell indicated one very dominant reason why signatures are not too seriously considered by the collector and the autograph profession when he jokingly proposed hiring a forger. In effect, that is precisely what many respected figures in public life actually do. The practice, in fact, has become so widespread that it is generally impossible to guarantee the authenticity of a signature when it stands alone. This is a problem which is almost entirely modern, although it spottily existed in other days.

The pace at which people live today makes it impossible for many men and women of note to fill their numerous duties and public obligations and simultaneously follow their generous instinct to oblige those who ask for their signature. They have recourse to a secretary, or even to a professional—but honest—forger, whose existence would probably have scandalized their forebears. Principals whose signatures are duplicated, in some cases, have been forced into this practice by the very demands of their office. Formerly the presidents of the United States, to cite one example, were legally compelled to sign all commissions

---

*This was before the introduction of the autopen, not in use by the Presidents in 1946.

of army and navy officers. Normally, this would be an assignment that could not be filled without serious neglect of other and more vital duties. In war time, it becomes an impossibility.

The majority of long-popular stage, radio and cinema stars employs someone who accepts the duty of filling requests for autographs and signing many other letters. These favorites must keep an eye on box-office appeal, if not for personal considerations, at least in fairness to their employers, and they cannot afford to offend admirers by disregarding their interest—no matter how burdensome it may be. Politicians, statesmen, business men and many other leaders frequently are also aided by a person expert in duplicating a signature on letters and documents of all kinds. The signatures of Presidents Buchanan and Pierce, of the first President Harrison and General Anthony Wayne, were almost perfectly imitated by their secretaries; less perfect but very good were similar "duplications" of Garfield and Arthur. In recent years the story is told of a prominent New Yorker whose check, which he had signed on an occasion when he faced an emergency shortage of money, was returned as a forgery by his bank, habituated to recognize his name only when it was signed by his personal secretary.

Only under special circumstances, and then after due caution, will dealers consider a guarantee on a signature that appears alone. The authenticity of a signature on a document or letter may be substantiated or refuted by additional factors not possible when the signature is by itself. The quality of the paper, the contents and character of the letter and the character of both the writer and the source of the item contribute each its own degree of certainty or doubtfulness. Any one of these, and other similar factors, may point to validity or indicate the possibility of forgery.

Unlike certain "autograph fiends," the serious collector of autographs, when the term is used in its special sense, has no desire to meet celebrities in order to cajole them for a mere signature. He finds his fascination in what the celebrity in a more thoughtful mood has to record, and his adventure lies in locating such material. He sets about acquiring his new vocabulary and learns that the distinctive and professional terms for describing letters and manuscripts will present problems unless he quickly learns them. These he will encounter as soon as he enters the field either in conversation with other collectors, auctioneers or dealers and, possibly even more mystifying, in catalogues. Once fully grasped, however, either the oral or written references are actually simple.

The new collector soon discovers that to know a paper is old and pertains to some famous person is but the starting point in any proper consideration of it. Other definite details must be ascertained. Is a letter entirely handwritten and signed? Is it written by the person but not signed by him at all? Is it written by one person and signed by another? Upon the answers to these questions any adequate appreciation and evaluation depends.

The collector, therefore, as so many have done before him, resorts to the alphabet to give him a ready means to describe in full and explicitly the nature of the paper under consideration. Initially, *A*, or *Auto*, stands for autograph, meaning handwritten. This symbol does not, however, imply that there is any signature. Rather it refers solely to the fact that the body of the document is in the handwriting of the individual. When *A*, then, precedes any description, that is, begins any series of alphabetical designations, it clearly asserts that the item is entirely handwritten.

L, the abbreviation for letter, denotes that the paper includes a formal salutation and ending, such as "Dear Sir" and "your obedient humble servant." When *L* is preceded by *A*, becoming *A. L.*, the combination specifies that the missive is entirely handwritten, but states nothing concerning a signature. Indeed the letter may, in fact, never have been signed, due to one cause or another, including absent-mindedness, or may have been, as frequently happened and still does, the draft of a letter kept for filing. Or, once signed, the signature may have been cut off. But when the letter is signed and the signature is on it, this fact is indicated by adding *S*.

S always signifies that an item is personally signed with the name of the individual. If he signed only with his initials, this fact must always be further indicated by cataloguers. An *A. L. S.*, then, is definitely a full autographed letter, written and signed by the individual with his full name. An *L. S.* states that he signed but did not write the letter itself.

N stands for note. An *A. N. S.* is occasionally used interchangeably with *A. L. S.* when the latter is very brief—only a line or two in length—and the contents of little significance. Strictly speaking, an *A. N. S.* differs from the *A. L. S.* in that the salutation and ending are omitted. An original telegram, for example, which bears the name of the recipient and his address, as well as the sender's name, is classed as an *A. N. S.* It may be referred to as an *A. D. S.* *D*, indicating document, and *N* for note are at times interchangeable, when representing a brief communication.

The general public is apt to call a poem anything that is not prose, and in a certain sense, the autograph collector uses the word "document" to distinguish anything which is not a letter. Documents may be printed or handwritten, of legal or military nature, a bank-note or a receipt or a telegram—actually, any formal item that does not fall into the letter category.

Like the term "document," "manuscript"—abbreviated to *Ms.* —embraces a wide class. A manuscript may be a complete or incomplete page of writing from a book, one of its chapters or an entire book, a sheet of music or a poem. But the symbol *Ms.* seldom stands alone, for it needs further description. Combined with *A* or *Auto*—*A. Ms.* or *Auto. Ms.*—the declaration is that this is an autograph or handwritten manuscript. Adding, as in the case of an *A. L.*, the letter *S* to *A. Ms.*—thus *A. Ms. S.*—further declares that the manuscript is signed. It is then easy to deduce that *Ms. S.* means that this is a manuscript which is not handwritten but signed, as would be the case with a page from a book of printed poems which the poet had signed. More frequently, of course, such manuscripts are typewritten and signed, and in such instances, these facts are mentioned—"Typewritten *Ms. S.*"

In other days, when formality characterized practically all social life, letter-writing often took on the same aspect. This formality still prevails today in certain circles where etiquette strictly governs. The Emily Posts insist that a formal invitation should always be answered in the third person—"The President of the United States regrets his inability to be present at..." or "Mr. Paul Edward Jamison accepts with pleasure the kind invitation of..." The title or name in such cases is always considered a full signature. All letters which carry a signature in the body rather than at the end are customarily designated "*A. L. S.* 3d person, name (or title) in body." Either "*A. N. S.* 3d person, title in body" or "*A. L. S.* 3d person, title in body," therefore, could be used to describe the following message, as provocative of sympathy as was the occasion which prompted its sending: "Field Marshal, the Duke of Wellington, begs to inform William Harris that his toad is alive and well." Wellington, on a country stroll, had encountered a little boy who, leaving the next day for school, was weeping over a pet toad which he feared might be neglected and starve. The Field Marshal not only took on the responsibility for the toad, but subsequently dispatched this health bulletin in proof of his good faith.

There is another letter of the alphabet to be added to those used by the autograph collector. This is *Q*, and it indicates any type of quotation. In the *alba amicorum*, which were assembled by students in the Renaissance universities, and which are not too infrequently assembled by the sentimental in modern times, friends very often jotted down appropriate messages remembered from some author, and then signed them. The same practice is still to be observed today by people who want to respond with something more when asked for a signature. An author may write out a pertinent quotation from his book on its flyleaf, following with his signature, or a musician may quote Shelley's "Music, when soft voices die, vibrates in the memory," or a painter may write Goldsmith's "A flattering painter who made it his care to draw men as they ought to be, not as they are." Following out the procedure of alphabetical combinations, an *A. Q. S.*—Autograph Quotation Signed—would indicate that the quotation is in the handwriting of a particular person and signed by him.

Standing somewhat alone by its nature is another class of items handled by the collector. This is the broadside, incidentally not denoted by a symbol, a printed one-page form whose contents are a declaration of a public nature. From the first days of printing, well before the introduction of newspapers, the broadside, occasionally termed a broadsheet, was employed for royal proclamations, papal indulgences and similar notices to the people. In England, its chief home, it was used for ballads, particularly in the sixteenth century. More often it was a means to instigate political agitation. Individuals resorted to the broadside for personal statements of all kinds, and, oddly enough, so did criminals to publicize their gallows confessions or protestations of innocence.

The autograph usages heretofore explained are fundamentally concerned with contents, but there are other designations which apply to size and length. It is as important that the collector know these facts as that he distinguish between an *A. L. S.* and an *Ms. S.*, for they also control value and desirability. A man who wants a painting for a particularly large space above a mantel would not buy a miniature for it. Similarly, many autograph collectors definitely consider size before buying. One will confine himself to single-page letters suitable for framing, and another to small letters which will readily find a place in an album.

Perhaps the most common descriptive term used in this connection is *folio*, which is abbreviated to *fol.* Unless otherwise qualified, *folio* describes a sheet roughly twelve by sixteen inches, and when the word *giant* precedes it, the size is four to eight times as large. *Quarto*, shortened to *4to*, is used in reference to a sheet measuring eight by twelve inches, and an *octavo*, or *8vo*, to one approximately six by eight. *Duodecimo* and *sextodecimo*, Latin words reduced to the more easily used *12mo* and *16mo*—*twelve-mo* and *sixteen-mo*—are respectively one half and one quarter *octavo*. Actually, they are little differentiated from one another and are often used interchangeably.

The physical characteristics of a manuscript, document or letter are also further described by the word *oblong*, or *obl.*, which denotes any long narrow sheet, regardless of size. On occasions, a description is made more explicit by stating that an item is either *oblong quarto* or *oblong folio*.

The use of abbreviations, *p.* and *pp.*, to indicate *page* and *pages* is familiar even to the layman. In the autograph profession, however, it must be noted that customarily it is the pages, not sheets, that are counted. If a sheet is written on both sides, each side is considered a page, and 5pp. would indicate either that there are five sheets, each written on one side, or that there are two sheets written on both sides and a third with only one side used.

There are three indications which apply to certain omissions in autographs—*n. d.*, *n. y.* and *n. p.* The first, which stands for "no date," means that the paper has no date whatsoever; *n. y.*—"no year"— that it bears the month and the day but not the year; and *n. p.*—"no place"—which says nothing about the date, but means that the letter does not show the place where it was written. In these days, when the general practice of letter-writers is to have printed or engraved stationery, it is not often that the place-designation is omitted, but some writers, still as formerly, attach little or no importance to a date or, if they do, often content themselves with noting "Monday" or another day of the week.

Once the novice collector has familiarized himself with these terms and their abbreviations, he can turn with some confidence to an autograph catalogue. He will next need to know the special meaning which is attached to the parentheses and brackets in this type of listing. The procedure observed can best be explained by considering a typical portion of a dealer's catalogue, like the following, minus the prefatory numbering:

1. Madison, James. A. L. S., 1p., 8vo, Washington City, 3 p.m., Feb. 24, 1811. To Washington Irving.
2. Madison. A. D. S., 2pp., fol., Philadelphia [1780].
3. (Madison). Auto. Ms. S., 3pp., 4to, 1810, of John Doe.
4. Madison, Dolly. A. L. S., 4pp., 8vo, Washington, Mar. 3, 1807. To Henry Dearborn.
5. Madison. A. Q. S., on card.

In reading this example, it will be noted that it is customary for the cataloguer to list first the individual's name with the surname first, next the description of the item, its length, from what place written, the hour (when given, as it occasionally was) and full date. The name of the addressee is also of importance, and it follows last.

Example number two shows the date in brackets. This indicates that Madison himself did not include the year 1780 but that it had been added subsequently. It may have been affixed by some previous owner after he had completed research which discovered probable, if not final, proof that the letter must have been written at that time. Occasionally, the one to whom the letter was addressed docketed the letter on the date of receipt, endorsing it, perhaps with his name or initials. In such cases, the cataloguer accepts the date without question as authentic and omits the brackets in his description. But where no date is specifically given, the brackets must be used to indicate that probability—and no more than probability—exists in such instances. Someone in the course of time may have written "1848" in pencil on the letter, and the present owner may not understand why. The cataloguer, too, may have no clearer knowledge, but he would always append the date and enclose it in brackets. Should the latter find only the year endorsed by the letter's original recipient, and thereafter specifies the month and day in his catalogue, brackets must be used around the month and day.

In example number three—"(Madison). Auto. Ms. S., 3pp., 4to, 1810, of John Doe."—the parentheses invariably mean that the manuscript in question was neither written nor signed by Madison, but it is *about* him. It may have been written by a contemporary, or possibly by a historian who discusses the President during the War of 1812, or a manuscript copy of one of Madison's speeches in an unknown hand. The parentheses here plainly declare that the manuscript concerns or refers to Madison, but definitely does not carry his handwriting, and no claim whatsoever is made to that effect. Here the ever-recurring John Doe, therefore, has written and signed a three-page manuscript (not a letter) on sheets roughly eight by twelve inches, which he has dated 1810 and which deals with James Madison.

Each of the other five cataloguer's items may then be translated. Number one—"Madison, James. A. L. S., 1p., 8vo, Washington City, 3 p. m., Feb. 24, 1811, to Washington Irving."—states that Madison, while president and residing in the Capital, himself wrote and signed a one-page letter, on a sheet approximately six by eight inches, to Washington Irving, on February 24, 1811, at three in the afternoon. Item number two—"Madison. A. D. S., 2pp., fol., Philadelphia [1780]."—explains that this is a document written and signed by James Madison, on a sheet about twelve by sixteen inches, in Philadelphia, probably in 1780. It is James and not any other Madison by virtue of the fact that the surname follows item number one. Cataloguing practice has established this rule. Some cataloguers, instead of repeating the surname, use instead a triple dash to indicate that the item must be referred to the one listed immediately above.

"Madison, Dolly. A. L. S., 4pp., 8vo, Washington, Mar. 3, 1807. To Henry Adams," which is item number four, states that Dolly Madison herself wrote and signed a four-page letter addressed to Henry Adams from Washington on March 3, 1807, on sheets of octavo size. Finally, item number five, which again, because it follows number four, is of Dolly and not James Madison—"Madison. A. Q. S., on card."—states that Dolly, at a time in her career which is unknown, but possibly when as mistress of the White House she was approached by some admirer, wrote out a quotation on a card and signed it.

These examples obviously illustrate that the system of cataloguing has been devised primarily to economize on space. And collectors of long standing have added over the years a few other shorthand methods of references. One repeatedly comes across mention of letters stated to be by an *M. O. C.* This alphabetical grouping indicates that the letter, if it is an *A. L. S.*, was written and signed by a Member of the Old Congress, better known to students of American Colonial history as the Continental Congress which sat from September 1774, to March 4, 1789. The addition of an "*s*"—*M. O. C.s*—forms the plural, as it does in the other forms of autograph abbreviations. Collecting a full autograph set of these congressmen—there were over four hundred—was once very popular, but the undertaking is now very difficult, for many of the names were scarce even in their own day. When in 1787 the Constitution of the United States was adopted and the new Houses of Congress established, the titles of Senators and Representatives came into use in America. *M.C.s* in autograph circles denotes these members of subsequent congresses. The term, *M.O.C.*, is strictly and exclusively limited to members of the Continental Congress.

When the word Signer, or Signers, is capitalized, it invariably refers to one or several of those who, heeding Franklin's pun, "We must all hang together, or assuredly we shall all hang separately," affixed their signatures to the American Declaration of Independence. Signer, when the word ·is applied to those who signed the Constitution in the next decade, is also capitalized, but the phrase "of the Constitution" is always added. Signers of anything else, no matter how important, are described by the word written with a small "s." Such abbreviations as *C.S.A.* for Confederate States of America and the usual abbreviations for the States of the Union are as obvious as U.S.A., Eng., Switz., It. or Sp.

The collector needs to understand the meaning of two other words which are never formally abbreviated, but which are frequently encountered in autograph shop-talk. The first is "provenance" or "provenience." This term has somewhat the same relationship to a letter, a document or a manuscript as genealogy has to a person. It refers to the history of a paper in question and the identification of all those who have previously owned it. In cases of very rare and important items, a prospective purchaser advisedly ascertains the validity of title, just as one who proposes to buy land. And as land titles are traced back, from registered deed to registered deed, so the title to papers may be traced back, as far as possible, from generation to generation. This is rarely feasible, save when the item is really a sensational one, and indeed scarcely necessary when the purchaser follows the usual caution—*caveat emptor.*

The second word is "sleeper," which refers neither to a person nor to a Pullman car. It is properly an autograph which has gone undiscovered, whether as one of a large miscellaneous lot or in a smaller group whose owner did not recognize its value. There are occasions, for instance, when some manuscript has a particular feature that lifts it out of the average, and this feature is overlooked. Again, certain papers require translation or a deciphering of script to reveal their true value. Many other factors may account for circumstances under which a particular sleeper has failed to attract attention. It goes without saying that in autograph circles, the majority of collectors entertain the hope that some day they may encounter one.

A noteworthy incident of a sleeper occurred at the auction of the Gideon Welles papers at Philadelphia in 1927. Welles had been Lincoln's Secretary of the Navy. His papers and correspondence covering a period of many years comprised thousands of items, some of which were routine in nature, but others of great importance. Accordingly they had been catalogued both singly and in lots, and, for the most part, the sale had gone swiftly. The procedure had stalled, however, when the auctioneer could not obtain a bid on a particular lot briefly described in the catalogue. Mr. Benjamin, no more interested than any other present but anxious to have the sale continue, spoke up, and the lot was knocked down to him for $1.

When, after a month, Mr. Benjamin took time to examine his purchase, he found it on the whole of little value except for a bound notebook, entirely handwritten by the Secretary, partly in ink, partly in pencil. In no time at all he disposed of it to Emanuel Hertz, the well-known Lincoln collector, for $1,000. Still later that same year the notebook, after having been extensively and dramatically catalogued, was auctioned at the Anderson Galleries. The spirited bidding reached $1,500, a fact that proved too much for a dealer who rose, and, shaking his head in disbelief, was heard to exclaim, "And Benjamin only paid $1 for it!" The notebook went for $1,500. Mr. Hertz never forgave the dealer, for he always maintained that the remark had immediately short-circuited the bidding, which otherwise might have gone considerably higher.

This belief was not unjustified. The notebook contained a seventy-page presentation of the Reconstruction policies of President Lincoln and Vice-President Andrew Johnson. In addition, thirty-seven pages written between the years 1846 and 1877 comprised an account Welles had kept of his departmental work. These set forth the proclamation to close the ports of the South, gave vivid pictures of the closing scenes of the War, told of Lincoln's desire to have the Confederate leaders escape from the country, his request to Welles to do nothing to prevent this, his visit to Grant and Sherman—particularly to see that they granted merciful terms to the enemy—and accounts of other equally important matters.

But possibly of greatest interest to the majority of people was the description Welles included of Lincoln's last Cabinet meeting. " ... When I went to the Cabinet meeting on Friday, the 14th of April," he wrote, "General Grant was with the President, and one or two members had already arrived. General Grant said he was expecting hourly to hear from General Sherman, and had a good deal of anxiety on the subject. The President remarked that the news would come soon and come favorably, he had no doubt, for he had last night his usual dream which had preceded nearly every important event of the War. I enquired the peculiarities of this remarkable dream. He said: 'It is in your department.' It related to water. That he seemed to be in a singular and indescribable vessel, but always the same, and that he was moving with great rapidity toward a dark and indefinite shore. That he had had this dream preceding the firing on Sumter, the Battles of Bull Run, Antietam, Gettysburg, Stone River, Vicksburg, Wilmington, etc. Victory did not always follow, but the event and results were important." In tribute to Lincoln, Welles continued: "Great events did indeed follow. Within a few hours, the good and gentle as well as truly great man who narrated his dream was assassinated, and the murder which closed forever his earthly career affected for years and perhaps forever the welfare of his country."

The term, sleeper—some use "find" instead—recurs time and time again in autograph stories and conversation. So, too, does the word "date," but in no special interpretation. Yet there are certain irregularities concerning dates with which those who propose to deal in autographs, written before the eighteenth century or written in countries other than America, should be familiar. The simplest of these arises from the practice of using numerals to designate the month in a date. This fact was brought to the fore in the spring of 1945 by Major Randolph Churchill, M. P., son of the former Prime Minister. In the House of Commons, he inquired of his father if anything was being done to bring uniformity to the disparate systems of dating letters and documents and cited that in America 10/1/45 referred to October 1, 1945, whereas in England (and this is true also in France) it referred to January 10, 1945. The British and French put the numeral designating the month second instead of first and would note October 1, 1945, as 1/10/45. "Uniformity of notation and nomenclature," Winston Churchill replied, "is, of course, of high value between allies in war, and progress has been made in many directions. I am not aware of any serious difficulty that has arisen in this particular instance, but inquiries will be made."

Perhaps in the not too distant future such uniformity will be agreed to in consultation among the nations of the world, but this does not change the discrepancies which, occurring in the past, may puzzle the autograph collector. He will repeatedly come across certain practices of double dating, as January 25, 1752/3, or July 12/23, 1701, or he will find dates with months listed as Thermidor and Brumaire. Very few Americans who rejoice in the fact that February twenty-second is a national holiday know that Washington originally celebrated his birthday on February eleventh and that its date is sometimes—and quite properly—noted February 11, 1731/2 (Old Style) and February 22, 1732 (New Style).

It is not often recalled, in the first place, that the calendar most universally used today, the Gregorian, is not precisely ancient. Preceding it was the Julian, which Caesar established and which was thereafter used throughout the entire Roman dominions. As century followed century, it became apparent that the calendar actually was lagging more and more behind solar time. A year is not precisely three hundred and sixty-five days—no more, no less. It was increasingly recognized that, to avoid the difference, which the later use of leap years almost reconciled, a new system must first be devised and thereafter adjustments made to inaugurate it. In consequence, Pope Gregory XIII commissioned astronomers and other experts to undertake a complete study, and, on the basis of their report, he promulgated the calendar now known and used, the Gregorian, which was adopted October 1582, in Rome, and was introduced into Spain, Portugal and parts of Italy on the same day.

Any student who wishes to familiarize himself with the intricacies of this calendar, which some reformers hold should now again be revised, will find sufficient reference books. But it is important for the autograph collector to know that when the Gregorian Calendar was adopted, it stipulated that the year should begin on January first. Prior to that time, it began much later.

The pattern of the adoption of the new calendar was largely shaped by the religious history of Europe. France officially took it up in the December after its announcement in Rome. So did the Catholic states in Germany in 1583, but the Protestant states there remained aloof until 1700, when Denmark and Sweden, both Protestant states, followed. England, probably because the very government was then predicated on a monarch who was the head of a nationally established church, refused a calendar which came from Rome, and it was not until the adoption of a parliamentary act in 1750 that the "New Style" calendar was finally accepted. Her American colonies followed suit.

At that time, the difference of the two styles, aside from the fact that the English New Year's Day was then on March twenty-fifth, amounted to eleven days. The discrepancy was removed by the parliamentary order that the day following the second of September of the year 1752 should be accounted the fourteenth of that month, and the year 1753 should begin on January first. Oddly enough, this act of Parliament created terrific furore in England, where the ignorant were aroused—in some instances to violence—by their belief that their lives had been shortened by eleven days. Meanwhile, in Scotland, January first had been adopted as New Year's Day from 1600, according to an act of the Privy Council in December 1599. The fact was of immediate practical importance in reference to the dating of legal deeds executed in Scotland between that period and 1751, when the change was effected in England. It was necessary in such cases if parties to the deed had any English connection, to use both the Scottish and English method of dating.

There were then periods in the past when the confusion caused by two calendar systems existing side-by-side required double-dating. A person, writing in England at the stage when there was some uncertainty concerning which calendar should be used, may have written the date February 8, 1752/3. This implied that, according to the officially abandoned Julian Calendar, the year 1753 did not begin until March twenty-fifth. For him who refused to accept the new timing, February eighth that year was really 1752; but for those who did accept, February eighth was in the year 1753.

Russia actually continued to use the Julian Calendar until February 14, 1918, when the Union of Soviet Socialist Republics, dropping thirteen days, adopted the Gregorian Calendar by official decree. The French Revolutionists had also adopted a calendar of their own by a constitutional act on November 24, 1793. This French era was computed from the previous year, the birth date of the Republic, and the calendar, therefore, was back dated. The best-known versions accordingly begin with September 22, 1793, the Second Year, and end with September 1805. They list the usual twelve months, but to each was assigned thirty days. The remaining five were called "Sans-culottides," or, as Carlyle with sly humor translated the phrase, "Days without breeches." These days, placed at the year's end, were observed as "Festivals" of Virtue, of Genius, of Labor, of Opinion and of Rewards. A greater poetic imagination was used in renaming the months: In order from January through December they were Nivôse, Pluviôse, Ventôse, Germinal, Floréal, Prairial, Messidor, Thermidor, Fructidor, Vendémiaire, Brumaire and

Frimaire. In English these names would be translated as month of snow, of rain, of wind, of seed, of flower, of meadow, of harvest, of heat, of fruit, of vintage, of fog and of hoar frost.*

The autograph collector obviously need not study the histories of the French Revolutionary or any other world calendar, since it will suffice him to know why differences in dates occur. Should he be confronted with some specific example of this, it will not then be too difficult for him to find the proper explanation. The same is true of the other calendar departures—the Jewish, the Masonic and the liturgical calendar of the Catholic Church.

Further, those who devote a few hours to the study of autograph catalogues, after a very small amount of application, soon find little or no difficulty in interpreting the symbols. As in the past he has painlessly learned to pick up such words as "movies," "broadcasts" or "internees," so in short order the neophyte will glibly talk about *quarto*, *A. N. S.*, and *D. S.*

* See Appendix, p. 277.

CHAPTER III

Evaluation

WERE there as few and fixed guides to the price of autographs as there are to its terminology, the collector's study would be much simplified. But such guides do not exist in the autograph market. The law of supply and demand applies, and certain general rules affecting price fluctuations can be traced to it. A broker dealing in cotton or tobacco might well begin his training of an inexperienced assistant by teaching him quality and grades. The same factors are important in the selling and buying of autographs. It is when the latter refuse to fit readily into standard categories of quality or desirability that marketing becomes complex.

Evaluating autographs is a process which requires long experience and study. For the autograph dealer, it is more than a business. It is a profession. In addition to the intimate knowledge he must have of a market, which is governed by numerous known and unforeseen causes, he must also be familiar with many allied fields that come under the heading of general culture. He must, above all, know history. Otherwise he is apt to fall into the mistake of a certain appraiser who was called on to evaluate household furnishings which included two Sèvres vases. These he listed as First Empire and priced accordingly. He overlooked the fact that the authenticity of his period was open to question since on each vase there were four medallions, and one of them pictured the Empress Eugénie, born several decades later.

It may come as a surprise to some to learn that there are autograph dealers, but this surprise is due solely to their ignorance of the existence of autograph markets. Markets and dealers are like smoke and fire. The collector, once he has begun his noviceship, sooner or later recognizes that the very existence of the dealer is his greatest protection. He can discover this fact for himself, but the proof of it is in the reliance on such dealers constantly shown by the librarians, the long-standing collectors and others engaged in related endeavors.

Of the many problems the dealer faces, the proper and accurate evaluation of material requires a broader background and more expert judgment than possibly any other. How he handles this involved procedure is the test of his success. It may often appear that values are purely arbitrary, as indeed they are when demand itself is arbitrary. In the majority of cases, however, the value of a particular autograph item must be given special study and the problem attacked by breaking it down into its component parts and solving each individually. The dealer never plucks a figure out of the air and places it on a letter of Thomas Jefferson or Richard Wagner or Rudyard Kipling. Instead he prices the item only after careful consideration of its various merits. There are very definite and controlling reasons why a letter written by one whose name is barely known will be at the top of the price list at the same time that items by Clay or Webster or Calhoun command no more than nominal sums.

The unusual is always certain to make the news columns, and an autograph letter or manuscript which is bid in for thousands of dollars is more the exception than the rule. The wide publicity attached to these sales incorrectly leads the uninitiate to believe that autograph collecting must be left to the wealthy. Actually, the facts are otherwise. The vast majority of autograph letters sell for under $350. Signatures, documents or letters of such outstanding Americans as Edison, Madison, Monroe and Lindbergh, or of such men of achievements as Darwin, Disraeli, Longfellow and Holmes, or of many of the kings and queens of France, England and Germany may be purchased today for a comparable figure.

There are standard values in autographs just as there are in other commodities. Supply and demand, rarity, contents, length, condition, date and association are all factors which cause autograph prices to go above or below the level of fairly fixed evaluations. Autographs of a particular person, rare today, may become so common tomorrow that the demand is over met and disappears. A formal letter accepting a dinner invitation is very much less desirable than another by the same writer in which he discusses the issues of his day. If he discusses these briefly or lengthily, either has its bearing on value. The special market of autographs is also affected by conditions in the general market. Inevitably prices mount during periods of prosperity, mount higher still in boom times and sink to very low levels in depressions. From decade to decade, autograph prices fluctuate, but usually with a gradual, perhaps almost imperceptible, upward trend.

The conscientious dealer, who has had long experience in his profession, always looks below the surface market indices and recognizes the bases for values which are more or less stable. By studying the catalogues of all countries and by consulting his own records and those of other dealers and auction houses, he is equipped to judge the innate merit of the items that come to his attention. Not swept away in the current, he will always make the long-range appraisal. He keeps a middle road, regardless of the times, and advises his customers as to what he believes are honest rather than arbitrary, lasting rather than fleeting, values. He is quick to recognize that there are fads in collecting, as there are in other fields, and is cautious when autographs of certain persons, particularly of contemporaries, suddenly gain wide popularity among collectors. Experience has demonstrated that tastes of succeeding generations differ greatly, that the admired persons of one era are quickly forgotten in another, and that certain demands which once mushroomed soon disappear.

Among the more stable and general rules which the dealer, and after him the majority of collectors, has learned, is a simple one applying to letters and documents considered as average. Among this type there is to be noted what can be called a relationship or ratio of values. The A. L. S., which is normally the most highly valued, is used as the basis in this comparison. If an A. L. S., for example, is worth $4, the following values will govern: an A. D. S. or an A. N. S. will be worth $3; an L. S., $2, and a D. S., $1.

The rule can more safely be used as a guide in valuing letters written before than during this century. The typewriter has brought about many changes in letter-writing. Today there are prolific writers of letters who very rarely use longhand for more than their signatures. In the case of such an individual, the price of his A. L. S. in relation to a typewritten letter which he has only signed is entirely disproportionate. This is particularly true of those written by American presidents after the typewriter was introduced into the White House. Since the chief executive rarely has time to write messages by hand, whether they be of an official or personal nature, a president's L. S., typed, dated and signed by him while in office is quite common and his A. L. S. extremely rare. Demand for the latter has forced its price very high, whereas the L. S.s are nominally valued. This situation is not logical from the historical point of view, since the importance of the letter's statement remains unchanged irrespective of whether it is typed or handwritten. It is more often sentiment, rather than logic, which causes the majority of collectors to prefer the A. L. S.

Like the typewriter, the telegram first and then the telephone have affected the autograph field, since these two inventions not only reduced the number of handwritten letters but eliminated the necessity to write in many instances. Before their advent, letter-writing was considered an art. The writer composed in more leisurely fashion and with considerable care. Good penmanship was more definitely encouraged in the schools of our forefathers, and their letters were normally written more clearly. When the writer had the advantage of a fair degree of education, mistakes in spelling and grammar were rare. He took pride in his own correspondence and looked upon it as an index to his character, his position and his attainments.

Washington, who like many of his own times, seldom availed himself of the services of a secretary, wrote almost all of his letters. He did this whether they were of a personal or business nature and whether or not they were single-page or ran to five or six double-written sheets. In addition, he made and kept drafts of all his letters. Only during the war, when it was not always possible for him to conduct correspondence of the greatest urgency, did he permit some of his aides to assist him. Nevertheless, many of his war letters, written entirely in his characteristic copper-plate hand, have survived and can be found on the market. Communications written by secretaries or aides or clerks of Washington are actually scarcer than his handwritten letters. This same fact is true of Jefferson, John Adams, Monroe, Madison, John Q. Adams and others of the earlier presidents. Yet, since collectors prefer the full A. L. S.s, the price of these early L. S.s has not risen in proportion to their scarcity.

To the general rule governing early presidential L.S.s, Jefferson very understandably made one exception during that period when he served as Minister to France. He was aware of his inexpertness with the French language, so, according to Professor Gilbert Chinard of Princeton University, he turned for assistance to William Short, the Secretary of the Legation. Jefferson's L. S.s written by Short are not common, but his A. L. S.s in French, being extremely few, have a correspondingly high value.

Lincoln only rarely signed a letter which he had not himself written. A curious sidelight on "the simple backwoodsman" is that on his inauguration he first introduced formal stationery headed "Executive Mansion," which was standard until Theodore Roosevelt changed it to the still current "The White House." Lincoln apparently assumed full responsibility for all save a very small percentage of both his official and personal correspondence. Both professional autograph dealers and experts among the collectors, in consequence, were startled some years ago when Dr. Nicholas Murray Butler in his book, *Across the Busy Years*,* stated the following: "As a matter of fact, Abraham Lincoln wrote very few of the letters that bore his signature. John G. Nicolay wrote almost all of those which were official, while John Hay wrote almost all of those which were personal. Hay was able to imitate Lincoln's handwriting and signature in well-nigh perfect fashion!"

Countless letters of both Nicolay and Hay have been handled since, and their own handwritings are therefore decidedly familiar to those who, in the autograph profession, must have expert knowledge of calligraphy [Plate II]. They show that Lincoln generally used a rather thick pen, Hay and Nicolay finer ones,

* Charles Scribner's Sons, New York, 1939-1940. Volume II, p. 392.

in comparison. Lincoln's hand is irregular, and yet characteristically as rugged and strong as his own nature. Hay has a fine, slightly pointed, neat hand, which shows that he was well schooled in good penmanship; Nicolay also revealed a pen-style markedly different from that of the President. To copy another's signature so perfectly that it cannot be spotted as an imitation is extremely difficult; to copy another's handwriting undetectably through one letter after another is a definite impossibility [Plate I].

It is axiomatic to state that prices must be based on the genuineness of an item. It is further axiomatic that the purchaser of a collector's item, if he has any doubt about its authenticity, logically consults someone on whose judgment he can rely. There are indeed few collectors who buy important autographs without professional advice. For letters of minor significance whose valuations are familiar, they may, however, apply the rule of ratios between the A. L. S., L. S. and D. S.

The law of supply and demand, as it controls the autograph market, cannot easily be assayed. Often very special circumstances enter. If there are a great many A. L. S.s by some particular person on the market, obviously the demand will shrink and the price will drop. On occasion a dealer, who has a large number of these A. L. S.s on hand with no wish to hold them indefinitely, will cut his price in order to dispose of them. The opposite set of conditions has governed in sales of autographs of Button Gwinnett and Thomas Lynch, Jr., so often publicized. The two Signers left very few autographs, and the prices of these are so high that they are above all reason. The dominant factor is not the historical importance of either man—both died in early manhood, and their chief claim to fame is that they signed the Declaration of Independence—but that their autographs are very scarce in proportion to the many collectors who wish to complete sets of the Signers.

When prices, like the extreme ones which Gwinnett and Lynch autographs commanded in past markets, get so thoroughly out of hand, inevitably a corrective reaction follows. The unavailability of two Signers was detrimental to the entire market in Signers. The one-time interest of serious collectors of moderate means, who wished to assemble sets of the Signers, was very definitely discouraged by the over-eager and stubborn sufferer of auction fever. Prices, in consequence, fell drastically. Once the boom-day hysteria, which pushed Gwinnett to $28,000 and $51,000, had passed, the more sane valuations of recent years generally prevailed. These, at $5,000 to $10,000, more properly reflect his autograph value. With this restored soundness of evaluation to the market, lowered prices revived the latent interest of collectors in this group. Their values hereafter may rise normally and reasonably or again may be pushed to unjustified peaks.*

The rarity of an item, or indeed its uniqueness, does not spell a soaring price, for the demand may be negligible, and the price accordingly remain normal or possibly below normal. Colonial material before the 1700's, which is rare, has been so affected. The theory of Thomas F. Madigan, well-known dealer in manuscript letters, may accurately report the reason for this lack of demand. In his book, *Word Shadows of the Great,*† he suggests that collectors, if their interest is to be kept active, must add to their collections from time to time or find that their avocation will quickly pall. Those who specialized in early Americana were too often baffled by the fact that little or no material was offered them. The situation could not have been otherwise because what was wanted was scarce. The very scarcity probably discouraged collectors from attempting to find what remained after the destruction over the years and the major absorption by libraries of that which is still extant.

No popular demand for certain other categories of letters— letters of artists and foreign material—exists in America. There is no ready explanation for the fact, save in the case of foreign autographs. Formerly being difficult to move, they were infrequently handled by dealers who found that Americans, for the most part not linguists, preferred to collect that which they could read and understand. American dealers, in consequence, specialize chiefly in Americana.

*A document signed by Button Gwinnett was sold at auction for $100,000 in 1980.

†Frederick A. Stokes Co., New York, 1930.

The same situation holds true with autograph dealers in other countries. Their catalogues indicate that the majority of their customers collect autographs of their own countrymen, and their listings are largely limited to this class of items. The catalogues of French or German dealers, before the war, offered very little material which the American collector would have wished. However, in America today, due primarily to the great influx of refugees from Europe, consequent upon the war, there can be noted a newly awakened interest in foreign items. The bounds of national interests have always been surmounted by one category—music. At all times, coming from all countries which can be said to have a common language in music, there has been a demand for letters of the great composers and musicians irrespective of their national origins.

The limelight today is focused with new brilliance on science and medicine. Items in these classifications, which not long ago aroused little interest, now command great attention, and their prices have suddenly been carried to new high levels. Thus, a Louis Pasteur A. L. S., which in 1900 sold for from \$3 to \$5, would be priced today at \$750; an A. L. S. of Edward Jenner, the father of inoculation, sold recently at \$2,500, whereas it could have been had for from \$10 to \$12 in 1900. Again, the former value of a Benjamin Rush A. L. S., which, because he was a Signer, was not inconsiderable, has today been very much augmented because he was also a physician. In 1891, a Robert Fulton, describing his steam engine, priced today from \$750 to \$1,000, brought only \$15; and in the same year, an Audubon sold for \$4, when today it could not be bought for less than \$1,000. Most probably, such material will have its own cycles produced by supply and demand and other causes affecting both.

Oversupply, in particular, has always kept the market for letters of living actors and authors depressed. Such letters, by the very nature of the profession of those who wrote them, are extremely common. Actors are constantly in the public eye, and their popularity is built and sustained upon the generosity with which they give of themselves. The demand for their A. L. S.s is, in a sense, stifled by the existence far and wide of so many of their signatures.

When a person gets his first insight into the autograph world, he is apt to be startled by the fact that a letter written by a truly major figure may occasionally be purchased for a relatively small sum. He cannot initially understand why the letters of so great a man should command so low a price because he does not know, as do those in the field, that the person in question wrote many thousands of them. Napoleon is said to have over twenty-two thousand to his credit, despite the fact that he customarily left his correspondence unanswered for six weeks, by which time he expected events themselves would have taken care of the bulk of it. The practice, however discourteous, is not altogether unknown today.

The new inquirer into autographs may also note a seeming discrepancy between the prices of Confederate material and items by the generals who led the armies of the North. He may argue that there is usually more romance in a lost cause, but this sentimentality is not the explanation of the higher costs of the Confederate. The reason is quite practical. The North was not visited by the devastation and destruction which so denuded the South both during the war and in the Reconstruction days. While the letters of Grant, Sherman, Porter and other Union army officers were sent to those who could easily preserve them and are today to be found literally by the hundreds, the papers of Lee, Jackson, Stuart, Hood and their brothers in arms were addressed to those whose homes were frequently in the path of the invader and the pillager.

It must also be recognized that people have received and destroyed letters from some friend who at the time of their correspondence was obscure and years later became famous. Both Washington and Napoleon, for instance, became distinguished early in life. Those who received letters from either had an incentive to preserve them, and this fact partially explains why there are so many that at times the market in them becomes bearish. It is logical to conclude that the available quantity of letters written by men who reached fame in their mature years was drastically reduced because their earlier correspondence was valued only in terms of the immediate day.

Where demand for all the letters of such men is strong, those written at the start of their careers frequently command higher prices. The finest writing of many authors was done in their youth, and letters written by them during that more exuberant period are more desirable than those written in later life. Longfellow's early correspondence, for instance, is markedly higher in value than any of his later letters. The first, letters on quarto sheets, are extremely rare, and their contents, generally speaking, are more interesting. They bring four times the price of letters which Longfellow, advanced in years, wrote on octavo sheets, and which are very common. For no other reason than that they are rare, collectors prize Lincoln quartos, irrespective of dates, more than the commoner octavos.

The fact that there are few letters of John Paul Jones or Daniel Boone on the market does not necessarily indicate that there are few of their letters extant. It sometimes happens that a certain man's autographs have been scarce and high-priced because one or more collectors have specialized in these and withdrawn them from the market. Later, upon a specialist's death, a mass of material comes back on the market, and a sharp drop in value inevitably follows until the unexpected supply can be absorbed. Of course, if the specializing has been done by a library or a historical institution, there is little likelihood of a break in prices, because their collections are very rarely dispersed.

The possibility of a sudden market-flooding is among one of the important reasons why most modern material is low-priced. Abundance is, of course, another. Letters of distinguished persons who are still living are evaluated always with an eye to the probability that upon their deaths an even greater quantity of their autographs will come into the market. Those who own a letter from a noted living contemporary are frequently surprised, even indignant, at the small price offered for it. Dealers occasionally have a difficult time explaining that they really do know how very prominent the personage is, that they are not antagonistic to him, and that they are *sure* he will be even more famous after death than he is in his own generation.

But the owner of such a letter, and probably there are many others who reason as he does, goes away determined not to sell but to keep his possession. His correspondent some day will die, and then indeed his letter will skyrocket in value. The argument, however common, is not as a rule true. The very commonness of the hope should demonstrate that others also will combine to glut the market. They will be joined by the many who possess letters from the same writer and who hestitated to market them while he was alive for fear that he would learn and disapprove their action. This very rarely, if ever, happens, but the mere remote possibility serves as a definite restraint. Immediately upon the writer's death, this restraint is removed, and the flood follows.

The market, of course, may find a strong demand which will prevent prices from falling. But then, fame is fragile, and collectors, who sometimes are no less fickle than the general public, often want the autograph of a living celebrity. They are definitely indifferent if there is no assurance that interest in him will not disappear on his death. This does not mean to imply that the historical value of letters by such people may not exist and even subsequently increase. Yet an accurate and proper evaluation may not come about for years or decades. Meanwhile, the sales value must be realistically gauged in terms of the present market. There are infrequent instances when the value of a letter may substantially increase after its writer's death, since the work of an individual who has lived and labored obscurely may be recognized and fittingly acclaimed only posthumously. The bulk of his letters will not normally have been saved, and the few remaining will command prices based in greater part on scarcity.

Next to rarity, one of the most important features of a letter or document is its contents. The letter of a person, whose name has absolutely no significance today and which ordinarily would be of little financial value, may be worth several hundred dollars or even more if the subject matter is unusual or treats of facts not generally known. Revolutionary and Civil War diaries of enlisted men, when sufficiently detailed, legible and well written, attract considerable competition at sales. A letter of an unknown person, if its contents are good, may bring far more than an uninteresting one written by a figure prominent in historical textbooks. Similarly, no matter how famous the individual or how old the document, if the contents are unimportant, the value is relatively low. Contents, likewise, are often responsible for the wide disparity in the prices of letters written by the same person. The three following John Adams' A. L. S.s, partially quoted, will serve as an example.

President Adams wrote the first of the three to James McHenry, then serving in his cabinet as Secretary of War, on October 5, 1798: "Inclosed are Recommendations of Rufus Graves and Joseph Dunham, from Mr. Freeman, and Letters from themselves requesting appointment in the Army. And some notes of Observation made to me verbally and put down on paper at my desire, which you may consider at present and return to me when I meet you again, if ever."

On June 12, 1812, Adams wrote to Benjamin Rush: "The Similitude between 1773 and 1774 and 1811 and 1812, is obvious. It is now said by the Tories that we were unanimous in 1774. Nothing can be further from the Truth. We were more divided in 74 than We are now. The Majorities in Congress in 74 on all the essential points and Principles of the Declaration of Rights were, only one, two or three. Indeed all the great critical questions about Men and Measures from 1774 to 1778 were divided by the vote of a Single State, and that vote was often decided by a Single Individual . . . I have heard much of Washington's impatience under the lash of Scribblers. Some of it from his own mouth... He knew there to be an opposition to him at the next Election [had Washington stood in this it would have been his third campaign] and he feared he should not come in unanimously . . . The Times were critical, the labour fatiguing . . . and he felt weary and longed for Retirement... The great Eulogium 'First in War, first in Peace, and first in the Affections of His Country' was suspected by him and all his Friends to be in some danger... I believe he expected to be called in again after a four years respite...I heartily wished he might live or had lived for that very purpose."*

The third letter Adams wrote to William Plummer from Quincy on March 28, 1813, when, a man of seventy-nine, he was again looking back on the notable events in which he had participated:

"You enquire in your kind Letter of the 19th whether 'every Member of Congress did on the 4th of July, 1776, in fact cordially approve of the Declaration of Independence?'

"They who were then Members all Signed it, and, as I could not see their hearts, it would be hard for me to say that they did not approve it. But as far as I could penetrate the intricate internal foldings of their Souls, I then believed, and have not since altered my opinion, that there were Several who Signed with regret and Several others with many doubts and much luke-warmness.

"The Measure had been upon the Carpet for Months and obstinately opposed from day to day. Majorities were constantly against it. For many days the Majority depended on Mr. [Joseph] Hews of North Carolina. While a Member one day was Speaking and reading documents from all the Colonies to prove that the Public Opinion, the general Sense of all was in favour of the Measure, when he came to North Carolina and produced Letters and public Proceedings which demonstrated that the Majority of that Colony were in favour of it, Mr. Hews, who had hitherto constantly voted against it, started suddenly upright and lifting up both his Hands to Heaven as if he had been in a trance, cry'd out: 'It is done! and I will abide by it.' I would give more for a perfect painting of the terror and Horror upon the Faces of the Old Majority at that critical moment than for the best Piece of Raphaelle.

"The Question, however, was eluded by an immediate Motion of Adjournment. The Struggle in Congress was long known abroad. Some Members, who foresaw that the Point would be carried, left the House and went home to avoid voting in the Affirmative or Negative. Pennsilvania and New Jersey recalled

* *The Collector*, Volume LVIII, December 1944-January 1945.

all their Delegates who had voted against Independence and Sent new ones expressly to vote for it.

"The Last Debate but one was the most copious and most animated; but the question was not evaded by a Motion to postpone it to another day, some Members however declaring that if the Question Should be now demanded they Should now vote for it, but they wished for a day or two more to consider of it. When that day arrived Some of the New Members desired to hear the Arguments for and against the Measure. When these were Summarily recapitulated the Question was put and carried. There were no Yeas and Nays in those times. A Committee was appointed to draw a Declaration, when reported, underwent an Abundance of Criticism and Alteration, but when finally accepted all those Members who had voted against Independence now declared they would Sign it and Support it..."*

A person need not be a Sherlock Holmes in economics to appraise the Adams letters to Rush and Plummer as ones of very much more value than that to McHenry. It is true that the latter was written during Adams' tenure as President, which is not the case with the others, and that it would be higher priced than a routine letter he wrote out of office. But the unusualness of the contents of the Rush and Plummer letters lift them far above the price level of the McHenry. Other factors immediately enter into the appraisal of these two A. L. S.s, and their contents constitute a dominant one in explaining the great difference of value between them. The Rush letter takes on added significance because of association, since Rush was a Signer. But the importance of the Plummer letter is outstanding and unique, and this A. L. S. takes place accordingly in the very high price brackets.

Nor does one need to have gone far in economic studies to know how to value from the standpoint of contents these two A. L. S.s of Dickens—the first written from Folkestone, Kent, to Samuel Brown, on July 18, 1855: "Your letter has been forwarded to me here. I do not consider myself at liberty to disclose the sources from which the information to which you

* *The Collector*, Volume LIV, March 1940, p. 49.

refer is derived, or it would have been a pleasure to me to have complied with your request." The second, written to Henry Casey, on August 24, 1854, from Boulogne, reads in part:

"I think it possible that I may have considered the powers and purposes of fiction a little longer and a little more anxiously and attentively, than your lady friend. To interest and affect the general mind in behalf of anything that is clearly wrong, to stimulate and rouse the public soul to a compassionate or indignant feeling that it *must not be*—without obtruding any pet theory of cause or cure, and so throwing off allies as they spring up—I believe to be one of Fictions highest uses. And this is the use to which I try to turn it."

Always if there are two A. L. S.s of an author under consideration, that in which he expounds his literary theories is more highly prized than one in which he arranges a luncheon engagement or announces that he will arrive on the 6:26 train. Similarly, were a composer at the time of the full flowering of his genius to have written a profound letter on musical technique, this would far over-balance the value of another of his letters, which, dispatched in his obscure years, does not mention music.

It can always be properly deduced, then, that the date of a letter carries its own importance and greatly influences value. A letter written by a Civil War general and dated in 1875 would be cheaply priced, but, were the letter dated between 1861 and 1865, its value would be considerably increased. This is a rule which applies almost universally to all autographs of men who have "gone to the wars," and frequently the cataloguer lists letters of such men as "peace letters" to indicate that they were not written during their days of combat activities. Yet, always the value of a war-dated letter is gauged simultaneously by its contents. An army officer, who won distinction on the battlefield, may have written on the day of an engagement an order for military supplies for his horse. In after years, he may also have written a penetrating tactical analysis of the same engagement. His "peace letter" would then be valued severalfold more than his war-dated one. The process of evaluating based on dates extends to the Signers, and their autographs dated 1776, as a matter of course, are the prize items of their output. Even a document, dated 1776, and signed by one of these early patriots, may sometimes exceed in value their A. L. S.s of an earlier or later date. Also, when Signers' autographs are dated 1776, those written nearest July 4 of that year have a very much enhanced value.

In the autograph world nothing, incidentally, is seriously considered as old unless it dates back to the fifteenth century or earlier. The term "old letters" or "old papers" is, however, frequently used in ordinary parlance. Material of the sixteenth and seventeenth centuries is always considered as modern from the collector's viewpoint, despite the fact that items of seventeenth-century America are fairly rare. Those of the same century which originated abroad are common, particularly in Europe. Oldness, however, is not always a criterion of value. Vellum deeds of the fifteenth century are repeatedly sold at $150, although only in instances when the signer is not well known. If such items are dated earlier, they are normally priced slightly higher.

Irrespective of dates, autograph manuscripts, signed or unsigned, which unquestionably constitute the most important category in the autograph field, vary so greatly in the many factors which must be considered for proper evaluation, that it is impossible to include them in any general discussion of autograph prices. When an Auto. Ms. of Edgar Allan Poe's "Murders of the Rue Morgue" was bid in at $34,000, of Robert Louis Stevenson's "The Plague Cellar," at $185 or an Auto. Ms. of Charles Lamb's acrostic poem for Grace Joanne Williams, at $130, the variations in prices show the lack of a common denominator.

Concerning such manuscripts and letters certain associational values are responsible for higher prices. The letter of John Adams addressed to a fellow Signer, Benjamin Rush, is by association more to be coveted than another Adams letter addressed to Senator Henry Tazewell of Virginia. A letter written by Whittier to a fellow poet, or one written by Queen Elizabeth to Mary, Queen of Scots, would also follow this pattern, and both would be inestimably more valuable than Whittier to a tradesman or Elizabeth to the Keeper of her Wardrobe. The letter of one president to another, one Signer to another, one scientist to another, further illustrates the same pattern, and values are always augmented by both the prominence of the letter's writer and the one addressed.

Again, when frequent references to notable men and women occur in the letter's contents, value is definitely advanced. This rule operates in the case of a very revealing letter written by the great tragedian, Edwin Booth, to Nahum Capen on July 28, 1881. Despite his eminence in the theatre, he had been forced into retirement following the notoriety that fastened on him when it was quickly publicized that the assassin of Lincoln was his younger brother, John Wilkes Booth. About the latter, fantastic stories were told, and legend soon turned him into a monster of iniquity and evil. Capen, a wealthy Boston historian, who seemingly went to primary sources for his information, had obviously written Edwin Booth for factual material on his brother, and Edwin replied:

"I can give you very little information regarding my brother John. I seldom saw him since his early boyhood in Baltimore. He was a rattle-pated fellow, filled with Quixotic notions. While at the farm in Maryland he would charge on horseback through the woods, 'spouting' heroic speeches, with a lance in his hand—a relic of the Mexican War, given to father by some soldier who had served under Taylor. We regarded him as a good-hearted, harmless, though wild-brained boy, and used to laugh at his patriotic froth whenever secession was discussed. That he was insane on that point no one who knew him well can doubt. When I told him that I had voted for Lincoln's re-election he expressed deep regret and declared his belief that Lincoln would be made King of America—and this, I believe, was the idea that drove him beyond the limit of reason. I asked him once why he did not join the Confederate Army, to which he replied: 'I promised Mother I would keep out of the quarrel if possible, and I'm sorry that I did so.' Knowing my sentiments he avoided me, rarely visiting my house, except to see his mother, when political topics were not touched upon—at least in my presence.

"He was of a gentle, loving disposition, very boyish and 'full of fun'—his mother's darling, and his deed and death crushed her spirit. He possessed rare dramatic talent and would have made a brilliant mark in the theatrical world.

"This is positively all I know about him; having left him a mere schoolboy when I went with my father to California in 1852, and on my return in '56 we were separated by professional engagements which kept him mostly in the South while I was employed in the Eastern and Northern States.

"I do not believe any of the wild, romantic stories published in the papers concerning him—but, of course, he may have been engaged in political matters of which I knew nothing. All his theatrical friends speak of him as a poor crazy boy, and as such his family think of him . . ."

It is not difficult to understand why a collector will willingly pay many times the price for this Booth letter than he will for one of the ordinary, more routine type frequently written by the actor. Should such a letter be unpublished, its value would be further enhanced, although this feature may not be of importance in the eyes of the average collector. He does not usually take note of such a detail unless he is specializing in autographs of some particular man or period, and it is doubtful that in the majority of instances he would be willing to pay more for a letter that was unpublished than for one which had appeared in print. Actually, some collectors prefer to own published items. They enjoy the opportunity they have to refer friends to book, chapter and page in which their possession is mentioned.

On the other hand, librarians and those who specialize, because they wish their material to be used for research purposes, definitely prefer the unpublished manuscripts. They are partial to manuscripts whose existence is not a matter of general knowledge. A few collectors and institutions even refuse to buy items which have appeared in print despite the fact that they are offered at nominal figures. Dealers, except in the case of a very rare item in the top-price brackets, cannot assume the task of ascertaining if a given item is published or unpublished. This fact, if the letter is by someone with a well-known name, can definitely be determined by its owner or prospective purchaser through reference books to be found in all great libraries. It is generally safe to assume that family papers in an omnibus group are usually unpublished, but, otherwise, no rule of thumb can be followed.

Among the remaining elements which govern values of autographs, there is length, which obviously ties in with content. A long communication, because the writer was in a more expansive mood, with much to note or express, is normally assured of greater interest. The exception comes, naturally enough, when the letter imparts very little but inconsequentially rattles along in the boresome manner of the prattler. Letters written in the past by clergymen are not always augmented in value because of length. This does not faintly imply that clergymen are to be classed with the bores and the garrulous. At the same time, wordy and pious exhortations do not make good general reading nor attract autograph seekers because such messages were designed to bring spiritual advice, consolation or support to the correspondent, and are therefore too private in nature to appeal to any but the one so individually and exclusively addressed.

Like length, there is the factor of a letter's condition which must always be considered. With few exceptions, autograph collectors, as do philatelists, seek material which is in good condition. They are not so enamoured of history that they are willing to buy documents which are badly damaged, mildewed or faded. When they are so marred, dealers are usually obliged to cut prices sharply. Yet, if the item can be neatly repaired, the sales value is restored to some extent. Librarians, for the greater part, are more tolerant of the poor condition of autographs if their contents are worth while. This, among other reasons, may possibly be due to the fact that libraries are equipped with more readily available facilities for restoring manuscripts to a state in which they can be handled without fear of causing greater damage and may be safely used for all desired purposes.

Librarians also depart slightly from the American private collectors' predilections concerning the manner in which letters are signed. The average collector in this country, although not in Europe, objects to initialed letters. He wants his A. L. S. signed James Whitcomb Riley, not J. W. R. He will not find it too difficult to compromise on James W. Riley or even J. W. Riley, but Riley would disaffect him almost as much as J. W. R.

Americans also draw the line between a letter written in ink and one written in pencil. The latter is apt to smudge or become erased, whereas ink used in modern times, although it may smear if subjected to moisture, will last fairly well when it is not exposed to direct sunlight and is otherwise properly safeguarded. The mere juxtaposition of a penciled item in a collection, however, may cause it and its neighbor to smudge. Modern methods of spraying such an item with a fixative* can prevent serious damage, and make the pencilings more lasting than other items in ink. Logically, the value of such a treated manuscript will be greater than the untreated.

There is a practical aspect to the proper evaluation of autograph material which is over and above that of selling and buying. This arises because of insurance and mailing requirements. When insuring autographs, the private collector must establish to the satisfaction of the underwriting company precise and sound values. The same is true of dealers when they insure either their full stock or autographs in transit. No insurance company, it need scarcely be said, will assume liability unless it is convinced of the justness of the appraisal, the reliability of the dealer, and his right, which comes from his recognized ability and accurate judgment, to establish his evaluations. Insurance companies will guarantee against loss in mailing, and it is possible to send autographs by registered mail. The U.S. postal authorities rule that a letter or document bearing any handwriting, no matter what the date, may be accepted only as first-class mail. Manuscripts, even though they are five hundred or more years old, are classed no differently from a letter fresh from a present-day pen, pencil or typewriter, and may not be forwarded

* *Cf.* Chapter XIII, p. 248.

by dealers, or anyone else, as merchandise. It is a violation of postal laws, subject to the usual penalties, to send autographs by parcel post or third-class mail. Express company regulations, however, permit the acceptance of letters and manuscripts whether they are old or currently written.

Whereas the collector rarely has reason to entrust any of his autographs to the mails, he does have an object lesson in the care the dealer takes in such matters. In particular, he learns to insure at least the most valuable papers in his collection, if not all, meanwhile taking all possible precautions for their preservation. Carefulness, even in minor details, ideally becomes one of the new collector's prime characteristics, as it already is that of most others who have preceded him as established private collectors, librarians or dealers. Certainly, the evaluation of autographs demands careful study. Its procedures, like those of any other profession or business, are guided by certain common-sense rules. To disregard any of them may prove very costly. Considering all the factors which determine autograph values, the collector who deals with a reliable autograph firm will not go far afield in quality or in the prices he pays.

Individually, he will come to realize that he has little to do with the establishment of prices for specific items, and he soon learns that collectors as a class play a very dominant role. Demand, through the aggregate, comes into action. If there are prices which appear to be governed more by whim than by logic, it is actually the collectors, not the dealer, who basically are responsible for precipitous rises or drops. The dealer's function is to consider painstakingly all the elements which weigh in value determination. His reputation stands or falls in accordance with his customers' acceptance or non-acceptance of his decisions. In the final analysis, then, it is not the dealer who sets values on autographs. The collectors themselves do this. If runaway prices develop, the final responsibility for them must ultimately be put at the door of one or two rather than at that of collectors as a whole.

CHAPTER IV

What to Collect

IN the ranks of autograph collectors, not a very numerous class but larger than many people realize, there are men and women with purses of all sizes. Among all collectors who have basically in common only the acquisition of items in a specific category—stamps, coins, old glass, first editions or autographs—may be found many of moderate means. Indeed, in the group which collects only signatures, there are some of no means at all. At the other pole are those who can afford even the top-flight prices of the rarest manuscripts. In between are the vast majority, people in widely separated walks of life—people of the professions, of business, of labor, people of high scholarly attainments, school children, people reaching out for knowledge and anxious to broaden their cultural activities.

Recognizably, among such a diverse class, there must be some inner drive that is shared by all. The cynic might attribute this urge solely to that acquisitive instinct inherent in man's nature which often finds an early outlet as in the activity of a boy who fills his pockets, *à la* Tom Sawyer, with fishhooks, marbles, cards, string and other incomprehensibly valued odds and ends. But the explanation is not so simple. Actually, it is impossible to "type" each autograph collector on the basis of what impels him to take up his pursuit. Children, for example, begin the collecting of signatures for a variety of reasons, and one need not ascertain more than that they enjoy themselves. This, the most popular form of collecting, is a simple and easy matter. It only becomes complicated when the collector has a definite pattern and is insistent on completing it, as would be the case if he were determined to obtain the signatures of living statesmen and women and be unhappy if he did not acquire every one.

Generally, however, the signature collector is entirely catholic in his taste and will be found to have gathered in random fashion anything from screen, radio or stage stars and opera singers to examples from outstanding figures in the world of sports. One name will follow another, sometimes in bewildering succession and in amusing juxtapositions. A few collectors assemble albums and arrange their contents in orderly fashion—a series of pages will be devoted to cabinet members, a second series to authors, a third to supreme court judges, a fourth to musicians and on through all the divisions. The care they have taken in their arrangements denotes a deeper interest and a more sincere appreciation of what they own. Other collectors have inherited the hobby on coming into possession of albums of signatures that have been preserved in their families for two, three or more generations. In most instances no flexible plan of arrangement was originally set for these albums, and the new recruit to collecting, who wishes to have order in his collection as he makes his own additions, is generally baffled because he cannot systematize without breaking up and reassembling the album's contents. Sentiment, at least, forbids him to do this.

Were the signature collector willing to add through purchase, he would discover that no great outlay is required. Necessarily, he would consult the dealer, whose catalogues list signatures that are for the most part reasonably priced, ranging from five dollars to twenty-five dollars. They include many "cut signatures," an expression applied when signatures are clipped from documents or letters. Like the omnibus offers of "one hundred selected stamps from all countries," such a collector will often find it possible to obtain at a cost of fifty to one hundred dollars a collection of one hundred signatures of congressmen, governors, politicians, writers, composers or actors. Many of these signers may be unknown to him, but he will be able thereby to enjoy the process of identifying them through a little research.

That the majority of signature collectors content themselves with specimens personally secured, either through the mail or in direct meetings, is obvious. When they turn to the dealer, they show a greater seriousness. In purchasing items in the $50 to $100 range they give first evidence of passing from the dilettante stage to the status of serious autograph collectors. At these prices there are apt to be fewer signatures and many more

A.L.S.s, L.S.s or D.S.s. In the price range from $50 to $100, the signature alone will very seldom be found.*

Meanwhile, the random collector of signatures should guard himself against false hopes, especially the belief that on some day, near or distant, he will be able to realize a handsome sum on his collection. He must not overlook the fact that essentially it possesses a high sentimental value for him which is not too readily shared by another. From time to time, such albums are brought to the dealer. Of these collections those of men who are prominent on Capitol Hill in Washington sprout up almost weekly. Formerly it was a popular custom for visitors there to seek a memento in the form of signatures from such personages. The Senate and House of Representative page boys opportunistically came forward and for two dollars saw to it that a modest-sized album was filled. Senators and congressmen, frequently the vice-president, and occasionally the chief executive, obliged. President Harry S. Truman, on the day following that dramatic April 12 on which he had hurriedly taken the oath of office while Franklin D. Roosevelt lay dead in Georgia, made an unprecedented and unheralded visit to the Capitol. Reporters covering the event described the long procession of hand-shaking legislators, building employees and "page boys with their albums!" Today these albums, so carefully preserved by their owners, fetch little more on the market than the page boys' charge.

The dealer is normally not at all interested in such signature collections, since they provide few problems that cannot be solved without his help. As a matter of fact, he and the collectors of these signatures focus attention on different things. But the serious autograph collector finds it imperative to turn to the dealer for very necessary advice. The relationship between the two is close and requires trust in each other at the outset. On the one hand, it becomes the responsibility of the dealer to guard and guide the newcomer to the field as best he can, and on the other the collector must have confidence in the honesty and sound judgment of the person from whom he obtains his material. He must acquaint the dealer with the details of

*Exceptions do occur. A simple signature of Thomas Lynch, Jr., the rare Signer of the Declaration of Independence, sold for $3,600 in 1980. Presidential signatures go from $50 to over $1,000.

his interests and the purposes and aims toward which he proposes directing his activity. Only under these circumstances can the two work best together. An individual collector may have the greater knowledge of a period of history or literature, but the dealer possesses the complementary knowledge—an understanding of autographs and the problems relating to their acquisition. The specialized knowledge of the one added to that of the other makes the two an excellent working team.

Often the collector does not begin with any definite idea of what he wishes, because, although he has proved to himself his interest in collecting, he is not at first equipped to specialize. Until the dealer is well acquainted with his fellow-worker's background, education and personal tastes, he can only suggest those areas which are particularly rich in material and colorful in contents, meanwhile warning against those that will prove discouraging because of their difficulties. If the new collector is indifferent to literature, music and history, if he has no special bent, then it is not simple to advise him. Usually he must follow his own inclinations, add to his collection whatever may from time to time attract him, and have no concern, being impartial about categories, whether there is a relationship or none between the items he accumulates. The heterogeneous collection has its own engrossing aspects and in a sense is often of greater appeal for the collector's friends than a specialized collection of letters.

Gradually, as the newcomer gains greater experience, his ideas inevitably become more formulated through reading and study, and he will find himself developing his taste and narrowing it to a specific type of material. He may embark on acquiring autographs of each of the presidents or of American poets or cabinet officers or Mexican War army officers. By selecting a particular subject, he obviously excludes much of interest, but at the same time he experiences a concurrent pleasure and satisfaction when he finds among a limited number of pieces those he needs to compose the picture he is assembling. This is what collectors mean by specializing, and, when carried out successfully, it has resulted in some of the greatest collections in the country—collections that have contributed notably to the writing of history.

Eventually, the collector who has not determined his own preference will gravitate deliberately or unconsciously to what will enlist his deepest interest. The dealer can provide some of the helpful short cuts and post red lights on those roads which he knows are dead ends. He can cite the fascination which Oliver Barrett of Kenilworth, Illinois, has had from his remarkable and still growing Lincolniana; the enthusiasm of Lieutenant Thomas L. Shattuck in his magnificent set of foreign kings and queens; the hours of study given by Dr. Frederick M. Dearborn of New York City to his comprehensive collections of Civil War and Revolutionary material, or the joy derived by Dr. Max Thorek and William M. Spencer, both of Chicago, in their immense collections of Napoleonana. Thomas J. Acheson of California, writes: "My collection of British prime ministers is fascinating; the complete file of 'also rans' arouses much interest among my friends." Suggesting collections "of inventors, of great women, of secretaries of state, of American ministers and ambassadors to England," he adds, "the more specialists that get started, the wilder the dance!" These will be indices. The collector will settle on his own choice first by his predilections and secondly by the factors which prevail and of which he has been made acquainted by the dealer.

There is practically no period within the past four centuries which does not provide the real collector with definite rewards. Since each new addition to a collection is in itself an incentive to continue, it is always wise to select a special type of material whose representative items may be obtained without facing impossible or very formidable hurdles. To seek today a complete set of Signers is a difficult assignment. The American Colonial period has many but somewhat more surmountable obstacles. Always the fact that some one field is poverty stricken, another is mediumly productive and a third is extremely rich can easily be ascertained by consulting a dealer.

In the United States, American, rather than foreign, material is more readily available with certain already-noted exceptions.

Its abundance is doubtless due to the unique history of a young country, which, in its rapid growth to nationhood, developed dramatically and colorfully. There are her statesmen and officers and soldiers and naval heroes of the wars of America, her poets and constantly growing list of men of letters, her missionaries and pioneers, her abolitionists, her legislators, her jurists and her many other men and women of eminence. These provide wide variety awaiting the choice of all who care to explore. In addition, such manuscript records are available in quantity and include a predominance of unpublished material which at once provides the delight of discovery for the collector and the sought-after source of the historian.

In ordinary times, foreign manuscripts are plentiful if the collector does not too much restrict his choice. This situation is abruptly changed on the advent of war, since American dealers are chiefly dependent on their colleagues abroad for their supply. When transatlantic communications are once more resumed, catalogues again present a fair assortment of interesting foreign material. Yet it is very seldom that at any time the average American dealer, who generally does offer attractive European selections, will list more foreign than American items. The American usually far outnumber all others both because they are more desired and more available.

The most popular form of collecting autographs is that limited to sets or to a given period. Strictly speaking, American historical periods are themselves few. But there is boundless opportunity for sets, of which that of the presidents undoubtedly leads all others in popularity. It has a lasting, never flagging appeal and can be assembled either in the narrowed and more costly range of A. L. S.s written by the presidents while in office, or in the broadest and least expensive form of mere signatures of America's chief executives. Other collectors are staunchly in favor of less obvious sets. It was particularly for their benefit that Madigan published in 1916 his helpful *Biographical Index of American Public Men,** a book which, although now out of print, may still be obtained by advertising for it. It includes lists

---

* Privately printed by Thomas F. Madigan, New York, 1916.

of Aides to General Washington, Members of the Federal Convention, Justices of the United States Supreme Court, the Officials of the Confederate States, Colonial Governors, Delegates to the Stamp Act Congress, Signers of the Articles of Confederation and other similar historical categories. Equally good lists may be obtained through other sources, such as the *World Almanac*. Were one undecided on what he should collect, some examination of lists of this nature might give him a clue to his choice.

A variation of the set type of collection recommends itself highly to many. This confines interest to material which has its source in a native state, or even in a native county, city or community. The importance and permanent interest of such collections can scarcely be overestimated. Those who acquire them are in a true sense pathfinders. The beaten track for collectors is the Signers of the Constitution, the Generals of the Revolution and Colonial Governors and other equally obvious groups. To follow each of these through to completion requires time and patience.

But to round out a state collection, particularly one which has not before been attempted, to acquire autographs of its patriots, the three or four Signers—if the state was one of the original thirteen—its twenty or thirty senators, its congressmen, authors, poets, jurists and other outstanding men and women is not unduly difficult. It provides its own excitement of discovery and its joys of acquisition. The by-products of such a collection, aside from its historical value, include the opportunity to make the state better known and admired. More interest, too, is evoked in the collector's immediate circle of friends and acquaintances, who will be more appreciative of his work if he has devoted himself to the local. The latter fact may explain to some extent why many collectors have followed this course, since the respect of one's associates provides both a recompense and an incentive.

Whereas emphasis has rightly been given systematized collecting of letters that are for the most part signed by men and women who have notably or in minor fashion contributed to America's history, there are other areas of collecting that invite and repay the collector. These embrace autographs which, irrespective of the writer's prominence or his obscurity, deal with the mores of America's past. Collections of such autographs, besides possessing their own entertainment opportunities, are of great practical value to present and future students of history. They, above all, offer a tremendous variety of selection. Collectively, they recreate in vivid fashion the life of our forefathers. This life is illuminated by individual items, such as early ships' papers, land grants, apprenticeship indentures, sales deeds of slaves, emancipation papers, insurance documents, broadsides, trade cards and other written matter which describe foods, medicines, clothing and all that was available to the American consumer of those times.

The early ships' papers, for instance, were all signed by the president, and no ship could sail without this properly authorized "passport." Were such papers, for every ship that left an American port today, to be signed by the chief executive, he could not fulfill the task if he devoted every minute of his time to it. Formerly this was part of the daily presidential routine. The fact in itself demonstrates the small beginnings of our merchant marine. Again, the first presidents signed countless land grants which were in many cases the forerunners of the War Veterans' bonus. Land, being plentiful in the early years of a nation constantly expanding westward, comprised the nation's show of gratitude to her valiant, and acres in pioneer states served instead of dollars and cents.

The fledgling days of America's great corporations are fascinatingly written in many documents. Among these, the policies of insurance companies are of unusual interest. They are not the present-day cold printed forms, with their long and tedious stipulations, but simple and clear statements easily interpreted by the inexpert. At a time when pirates and buccaneers flourished, the cargoes of schooners and four-masters and other wooden and sailing vessels were insured clearly and specifically against "the adventures and perils of the Seas, Men of War, Fires, Enemies, Pirates, Rovers, Thieves, Jettisons, Letters of Mart and Counter Mart, Supprisals, Takings at Sea, Arrests, Restraints and

Detainments, of all Kings, Princes of People of what Nation, Condition or Quality soever, Barratry of the Masters or Mariners, and all other perils, losses and misfortunes... ."

Individual persons signed their names to a policy stating forthrightly to what extent each was willing to underwrite the merchandise. Some could risk small sums, others larger, but everywhere the personal element entered. It would not be easy to imagine the confusion which would result were such procedure followed today in insuring any luxury liner.

"This Indenture made this 6th day of January A.D. 1776... That we Roger Sterry, John Tyler, Jonathan Brewster, Ezra Kinne, Aaron Crary, do put out & Bind an Apprentice unto ye sd. James Hopkins one Phoenix Ellis, *a Poor Child of ye town of Preston* of about Seven Years of Age. Ye Sd. Select Men on our Part Promise that ye Sd. Apprentice, his Sd. Master Shall faithfully serve, His Secrets keep & his Lawfull Commands Obey from ye Date hereof Untill he Shall Arrive to ye Age of Twenty one years—& the Sd. James Hopkins doth on his Part Promise that he will Provide Suitable Meat Drink Clothing Washing and Lodging for ye Sd. Apprentice & also to Instruct Sd. Apprentice to Read, Write & Cypher Sufficient for Proper Book keeping & also when ye Sd. Apprentice Shall Arrive to ye Age of Twenty One Years ye Sd. Master is to Give to ye Sd. Apprentice two Good Suits of Apparel, One Suitable to wear at Common Labour & ye other Decent to wear on Sundays & also one Bible... ." This apprentice indenture reveals an early American practice which was much more common than is today realized, nor are many of the factual details of such transactions well known.

"I CERTIFY, That the bearer hereof, Lucy Slain, a black Woman about 40 years old living in the first Ward hath produced to me, satisfactory evidence of the legality of her title to freedom, pursuant to an act of the Corporation in the City of Washington... passed on the thirty-first day of May in the year eighteen hundred and twenty seven...." "Stark Sims of Union S. C., on Jan. 26, 1852, made a deed of gift to his son William Sims 'in appreciation of his many acts of faithful duty,' gives him thirty male and female slaves, their children 'together with and singular their increase ... to have and to hold' ... ." Such quotations pertaining to transactions covering slavery are from documents many of which today are moderately priced. The same is true of the following quotations from other documents which carry their own individual flavor and interest.

"ONE CENT REWARD: Run away from the Subscriber, on the 3rd inst. an indented lad named JONAS LAMB, aged 16. Whoever will return said runaway shall receive the above reward—all persons are forbid harboring or trusting him on my account." "Rachel Wilson having removed with her parents within the limits of your Meeting [Quaker], hath requested our Certificate thereto. We hereby inform you that her conduct hath been in a good measure orderly. She frequently attended our religious Meetings, and is clear of Marriage engagements as far as appears. We therefore recommend her to your Christian care, desiring her Growth in the Truth ... ." "A LOAF CAKE: 5 pounds of flour, Two of sugar, Three quarters of lard, five and three quarters of butter, a pint of yeast, one tablespoon of ginger, and one of pearl ash." Mrs. Cornelia Livingston, whose recipe this was, noted "Too much pearl ash," and the modern housewife today is apt to rejoin "Too much of everything." And how modern are today's perfumeries when contrasted with "A scarlet Lip Salve: Take an ounce of oil of sweet almond, cold drawn, a drachm of fresh mutton, and a little bruised alkanet root. Simmer the lot together. Instead of oil of sweet almond you may use oil of jessamine or the oil of any flower you choose. The lip salve should have a fragrant scent."

Real estate transactions in the metropolis of New York would be at a standstill if sales were conducted in accordance with the following: "On this day the 25th of January A.D. 1656 is Consented and Agreed Between William Peters de Groot on the one and Dirck Claesen von Leewarden on the other side Concerning the sale of a Certain House and parcel of Land Lying Next to the House of Harry Brasher on the East Side which aforesaid House and Land the aforesaid Dirck Claesen acknowledgeth to have bought of the aforesaid William Peters for the sum of four hundred and twenty five Guilder to be paid in the following terms to witt the one half in Beavers and the other half in wampum. N.B. If ye buyer could not get any beavers the purchasers shall pay to ye Grantor ten Guilders for one beaver."

Many such papers reveal on one hand the seamy side—practices which then were considered routine but now are regarded as inhumane—of earlier American customs, and on the other that sense of neighborliness and responsibility to one's fellows which has always been so characteristic of this country. Above all they reveal the warmth that goes with immediate and human, rather than the impersonal, business transactions—a warmth that has too often been lost today. All such items constitute a most productive area for autograph collectors, and there are few fences around it. The catalogue of every dealer lists a few or more samples, and frequently they are obtainable in many unexpected and out-of-the-way places.

This is also true of franks which, although generally considered to lie within the province of the stamp dealer since they appear on envelopes or address sheets of letters, also fall into the autograph category. Naturally this is true only when the frank includes a signature and not when the name of the franker is printed, stamped or otherwise reproduced. The right to send letters by mail without having to pay postal charges was formerly, and even today, granted to specially privileged persons. To exercise this right necessitated only the signing of the individual's name immediately above or below the printed, handwritten or handstamped word "Free." Benjamin Franklin, who was the first postmaster of the Colonies, occasionally wrote "Free B. Franklin." At other times, he varied this with "B. Free Franklin," recording, perhaps, his long devotion to the cause of American Independence.

In earlier days the franking privilege was limited to higher officers who served during the Revolution, to postmasters, to the presidents, senators and congressmen. A precedent was set during World War II when the privilege was extended to all in the armed forces. Formerly the frank was supposedly only to be used for letters of an official business nature and was not authorized for the wives of living presidents. Nevertheless, the majority of the chief executives permitted their wives to abuse the franking privilege. Apparently these ladies were not above petty economies, and a "newsy" letter of the popular Dolly Madison, or a motherly epistle by Abigail Adams, or an order for ribbons from a tradesman by Mary Lincoln, all bearing the free franks of their husbands, have been known on the market.

Widows of the presidents of the United States, however, customarily have enjoyed the franking privilege. This was not theirs automatically. The right to it is a special courtesy voted each by Congress. It may be remembered that, immediately after the death of President Franklin D. Roosevelt in 1945, Congress unanimously granted Mrs. Roosevelt the privilege. Naturally, in the case of the presidential widows, the frank's use is not limited to official letters, but extends to all their mail. She who was the first First Lady, and the first to enjoy the privilege, survived her husband by only two years. Martha Washington's frank, accordingly, is almost "as scarce as snakes in Ireland." Only one is known to be in existence, and, curiously, this was narrowly saved from miscataloguing. The item could have been listed as a letter of Tobias Lear, one of General Washington's less-known secretaries, since it was his A. L. S. The dealer was puzzled because it had been found in a large collection purchased from the estate of a collector noted for his autograph knowledge and discrimination. The Lear message, definitely of no significance, simply did not "belong." His letters were common, and no importance could be attached to the fact that he had also served briefly as secretary to the widowed Mrs. Washington. On the fourth examination, the dealer solved the puzzle. In the left-hand corner of the address sheet was the small irregular signature, "M. Washington," that saved Lear the postage.

Like franks, telegrams are dealt with on the autograph market. The original messages written in longhand and signed by their senders are always listed as either A. D. S.s or A. N. S.s. From these, the copies—the messages fully machine- or handwritten by the telegraph operator on the receiving end—must be distinguished. Such copies are valued only if the contents are of unusual importance—for example, if the message was sent in war time and refers to outstanding events. In cataloguing such an item, the simple term "War Telegram" tells the story. "A. D. S., War Telegram" or "A. N. S., War Telegram" would refer to the original, not the copy.

Those who plan to enter the field of autograph collecting, after surveying all its many divisions, have a tremendous variety from which to select. Even if they do not decide to specialize, they will find the services of an autograph firm both advisable and valuable. Unless he can devote his full time to his collecting, these services become almost imperative if the collector does determine to specialize. It is seldom possible, as an example, for the collector to keep posted on the material which he needs to carry on and which may be put on sale in a market of whose existence he is not even aware. He may need a letter of Mendelssohn, and there is none listed in any catalogue which has come his way, but a dealer might be able to tell him that the very letter for which he has long searched could have been purchased at that time from a French dealer. Or another collector for years may have sought a Thomas Jefferson to complete his A. L. S. collection of the presidents, when a dealer could have quickly told him where and for what amount it could have been obtained.

Actually, the dealer's daily business includes his familiarization with all American autograph markets and many in other countries. He works most happily with the collector when he knows what the latter seeks. It may be that the desired item is not presently available, but in such cases the dealer becomes the watchdog not only prepared to note if, and when, and where it is offered, but to track down any rumor that it may come upon the market. Frequently, the dealer becomes the clearing house between seller and purchaser, and he can serve the latter much more effectively if he can carry on his list of "wanted" those items which his client specially desires. Even more conveniently, the dealer is prepared to advise the collector of American admirals that a particularly fine letter of Admiral Farragut may be obtained; the collector of Illinois autographs that the Stephen

Douglas A. L. S. he has wanted for years will be sold on the liquidation of an estate; the collector of ships' papers that his collection will be enriched by the addition of a newly discovered document on the *Alabama,* which figured so conspicuously during the Civil War in the serious friction between the United States and England. Collectors may not even suspect the existence of many items which the dealer may discover.

For these reasons, the maintenance of extensive listings of his collector-clients is an important part of the dealer's day-to-day work. He carefully notes the gaps in a particular collector's set or the partiality of another for the odd and unusual in documents. He is equipped and alert to channel items to particular customers, and this he normally does in a personal communication without waiting for the publication of his monthly, bimonthly or quarterly catalogues. So accustomed have many collectors become to this service that, urgent in their desire for some particular autograph, some will even consider it a personal affront if the dealer forgets their interests and fails to advise and quote wanted material.

The chagrin of a collector, who has missed a long-sought item through what he considers to be the dealer's negligence, is intensified if the item was sold at a lower than estimated cost. The collector shares the human delight in a bargain, even if he realizes that autographs themselves are not to be considered as sure investments. This is a fact which the conscientious dealer will emphasize for any new collector who consults him. That is not to say that one who acquires an autograph in 1985 may not eventually find it marketable years later for a profitable figure. The vagaries of purchasers cannot be anticipated. But only the long-schooled collector may safely buy, hold and sell autographs consistently on the same terms as the dealer. Trading in autographs is a dangerous gamble for any but the expert.

In many instances, the collector by his very nature is not equipped for such activity. He is the lover of history, the true appraiser of human values and the virtues that go to make up the great among men. He is the man whose education is never complete and who has developed through intensive habits of reading a mind that innately seeks wider and wider knowledge. Very often culture and profit-seeking do not make happy bedfellows. There may be exceptions, and the successful collector-trader need not necessarily be as non-existent as the unicorn. Yet essentially the collector who enters the field seeking to invest in autographs as he would in diamonds is almost certain to be a failure as an investor, and very apt to make a poor showing as a collector. His vision immediately becomes limited, and his desire for bargains will frequently cause him to ignore the very historically valuable items he should have. He passes them by because their purchase would seem financially unsound.

Actually, when the average collector attempts to sell his autographs, he stands little chance of obtaining the prices for which he purchased them. In the first place, he usually has entered the field in a haphazard manner and often without consultation with those who could guide him to proper valuations. Too many collectors have acquired sizable collections before it occurs to them that they should have been expertly advised in regard to proper procedures, the open roads and the cul-de-sacs of collecting. Once their interest has been seriously and more or less permanently engaged they move to correct this situation, and soon thereafter, with goals established, they become completely indifferent to the miscellaneous items acquired in their salad days as collectors.

That such a collector, seeing his past experience in a new light, would wish to dispose of unwanted items if not at a profit at least not at a loss is certainly natural. But he, and others like him, are fairly certain to be as disappointed as the camera amateur and enthusiast who seeks to market his favorite shots. It is well, then, in order to avoid unnecessary disappointment and to be realistic about autograph collecting itself, for anyone who begins to collect to understand fully that the profit motive should prohibit, rather than encourage, their entrance into the field. At the same time, these facts do not rule out the further fact that there are occasions when, the autographs being of fine or unusual content and the market strong, the collector can hope to realize the full value—and more—of autographs he has looked upon as treasures.

The average A. L. S. of a person who enjoys only minor fame is practically never bought from anyone but a dealer. Auctions will not handle these items singly. It does not pay them to do so. They deal in such items collectively. An "omnibus" of hundreds of cheap items is prepared, and the whole put on the block. Only when the collector offers an autograph of unusual rarity or worth would it be auctioned singly, or a number of such autographs auctioned item by item.

The dealer habitually will buy such "omnibuses" at auctions, whereas the collector would not usually wish to acquire the lot in order to obtain only one or two desired letters. The dealer, however, buys with the specific intention of splitting up the group. To compensate himself for his work in sorting, appraising and listing, he will catalogue the individual items thus obtained at a substantial increase. His experience demonstrates that the sale of a cheap or an expensive item requires equal effort. Because he always has on hand a very considerable stock of lower-priced autographs, which are the more common ones, and because he can always augment this number by the purchase of new lots offered at auctions, the dealer logically is not interested in purchasing the miscellanies of the inexperienced collector. The latter must then take his chances that his minor items will be accepted by some auction house and simultaneously hope that the eventual sale of them will be handled apart from the usual routine.

Among the other lessons taught them by experience is the very important rule that the collector should relate his autograph purchases at all times to his means. The rule is obviously sound for everyone no matter what he buys, but the continual spectacle of people in debt because they are "keeping up with the Joneses" indicates that it needs to be repeated and emphasized. The collector's enthusiasm can be a very moving force, and, if it is not kept within bounds, he is certain to covet what he could acquire only by going into debt. No psychologist need be consulted to advise him that the pleasure of owning an item which he obtained by paying what was for him an extravagant price will be over-balanced by the realization that he is in debt. This fact will also prevent him from acquiring other items necessary to keep his interest alive. A number of people, so burned, have abandoned autograph collecting entirely because they did not early learn to keep within properly set limits of expenditures and to curb desires for high-priced letters they could not afford.

Caution in buying, if he is to be successful, is a virtue the collector can place alongside that of patience. Should the autograph he has long desired come on the market at a time of booming prices, he needs restraint. Similarly, patience must operate in those instances when what he wants is not even on the market horizon. It may not appear for years. The impatient who wish to begin and complete a collection in short order are likely to be disappointed. On the other hand, those prepared to bide their time are fairly well assured that sooner or later what they seek will be available and at a price they can safely meet.

The acquiring of autographs and shaping them into a really fine collection, though it may be a long-time process, is not the difficult and bewildering task that it may at first seem. Nor need it require the outlay of exaggerated sums. The beginner may have to feel his way for some time, but in comparatively short order he will be at home with his acquisitions and can warm with pleasure during the hours he spends with them and those of his friends and acquaintances. He will soon learn also that many things, and most particularly the dealer's and auction catalogues, will take on new meanings, and that the bond between himself, the dealer and other collectors is close and strong.

CHAPTER V

Where to Buy

THE fewness of those who regularly deal in autographs reduces to simple terms the question of where to buy. The two major sources are the dealer and the auction house. Each serves its special purpose, and, being to a large extent dependent on each other, they are less competitors than friendly rivals.

The dealer may be described as a channel into whose offices pours a vast and steady stream of autographs and documents of all kinds originating in cellars, attics, warehouses and even in rubbish heaps. Through him they find their outlet into the permanent archives of public institutions or private collections. Without his aid many of the finest autograph collections in America could not have been assembled. The dealer's enterprise and interest are largely responsible for many prized items in the Albert Berg, George Arents, and W. T. H. Howe collections of the New York Public Library, for others in the Morgan and Huntington Libraries, and for yet others in the state, city and university libraries scattered throughout the country.

Of all in the field, the dealer perhaps more than others is in a position to prevent the destruction of material which is not generally recognized as having value. He is acutely aware that records are repeatedly lost through ignorance, carelessness or stupidity. Stories are relayed to him of family papers, rich in historical information, that he would gladly have bought, but which have been tossed out while the heirs concentrated on carefully made inventories of jewelry, stocks, bonds, bank accounts, real estate and other assets. The "worthless" manuscripts are left for disposal to lawyers and executors who also may ignore their intrinsic value and call in the junkman or simply order them destroyed.

In many cases, informed in advance, the dealer is able to prevent the proposed destruction. By advertising his interests widely he invites offers from varied sources. Again by traveling and following up information, whether specific or merely tips, he manages to save unwanted accumulations and single fine items that might otherwise be destroyed. As his work is publicized, discarded business correspondences, files of magazines, publishers, charitable organizations and other societies, come to him without any direct effort or solicitation on his part.

The heterogeneous nature of many of these lots renders them of doubtful interest for either libraries or collectors. The mere reading and examination, not to speak of the sorting, appraising and evaluation, of such papers is to the busy librarian an almost prohibitive task. Equally few collectors wish to undertake it. Properly arranged by the dealer, however, individual items which were lost in the shuffle are brought to light, and their importance accentuated. On the other hand, the less important are grouped for disposition in lots. The material is arranged and labeled according to period or subject—here the Signers and the Revolutionary patriots, there the men and women of the Civil War, here the literary figures of the world, there the musicians. In addition, individual letters and documents in the groups must be alphabetically arranged so that any given name or subject may be instantly located upon demand. At a moment's notice, the dealer can produce an A. L. S. of Stephen Decatur or Mozart or Queen Victoria, an L. S. of Woodrow Wilson or Ethan Allen or Mahatma Gandhi, a D. S. of Cardinal Bellarmine or William Penn or Jefferson Davis.

Since autographs from all parts of the world, covering many centuries and in many languages and in an almost bewildering variety of scripts, come to the dealer, he obviously must be able to read them. He can neither appreciate nor evaluate them unless he first understands them and their references. To do this properly in many cases involves considerable research and accurate checking. Few can appreciate the tremendous range of subject matter that may be found in even one group of family papers or in one bundle caught on its way to destruction.

Whereas collectors, and especially beginners, may enjoy a visit to a dealer's office, the majority for one cause or another, chiefly distance, are unable to have such direct contact. Their association with dealers is necessarily restricted to the mails or the telephone. With those who cannot come to him specifically in mind, the dealer periodically issues catalogues in which he painstakingly lists at least some items of unusual, and many of more general, appeal. These catalogues in which he not only describes but quotes freely from autographs merit close reading. This is true even if the collector is not immediately interested in any of the offerings. He can never foresee when odd bits of information acquired may be of later use to him in evaluating his own autographs.

Methods of cataloguing vary in America and in Europe, although certain generalities may safely be applied to both. In Europe it is customary to list all offerings together in alphabetical order; in America a division is first made according to subject, and then the alphabetical arrangement within each category is followed. The European dealer claims that his system obliges collectors to read the entire catalogue carefully, thereby enticing them into buying letters which might not otherwise have come to their attention. The American appreciates the specialized interests of some of his customers. These include librarians whose time is limited yet who must read hundreds of catalogues each month. He prefers to aid them by identifying their particular interests for them. He knows that the private collector of greater leisure will read his lists in their entirety, regardless of the arrangement.

In addition, he undertakes to school his customers to know that if there is anything they wish, and it is not found in his catalogue, they may send in their lists, together with some idea of the price they prefer to pay. This practice is always encouraged, and the American dealer at least is happy when it is followed. He is at all times willing to keep such customers' lists on file and to communicate with them when he locates anything that checks. He also is customarily willing to submit material on approval if a client well known to him requests that it be mailed him for inspection. The request is not made, it is generally understood, unless the client is fairly certain that he wishes to purchase. In the first place, the item will have been adequately catalogued by the dealer or carefully described by letter. The material, if not bought, must be returned at once since delay may result in the loss of its sale to someone else. Many reasons, including the fact that frequent handling of autographs cumulatively damages them and that postal employees are not noted for gentleness with the mails, cause the dealer whenever possible to hold mailings on approval down to the minimum. In this matter he relies on the consideration and judgment of his clients. *

He also relies on the recipient, whether private collector or librarian, to observe fully the well-defined ethics of approval shipments. This forbids the copying, photographing, photostating, microfilming or in any manner reproducing the whole or any part of the manuscript. Material sent on approval is often unpublished, and, in certain cases where contents have been copied, others of the dealer's prospective purchasers have refused to buy. The physical ownership of an autograph and its contents, where the latter are not reserved by the writer or his accredited representatives or executors, resides in the owner of the document. A person who temporarily holds an autograph which he considers buying has no more right to use its contents, most particularly if they are unpublished, than he has to steal his neighbor's wallet. The procedure followed when a dealer submits autograph material on approval is based and carried through entirely on trust. If it is violated the dealer at the very least can penalize the guilty by eliminating him from any mailings and consideration.

Generally every autograph listed in both American and European catalogues bears the dealer's guarantee, a fact which is customarily explicitly stated. If at any time, then, the authenticity of an autograph can be authoritatively challenged, it may at once be returned to the dealer. He acts to the best of his ability, but he would not be human if he never blundered. Despite the greatest caution, the most careful examination and the application of a long-proved expertness, he is not infallible in his judgment.

There are, however, definite chemical tests to which the dealer or collector may turn as a final resort in determining the authenticity of manuscripts. Because these methods of testing, applied to all autographs, would be prohibitively expensive and

*Today there exists a prevalent use of photocopies submitted on approval in place of sending original letters for inspection.

complicated, the dealer must rely in most cases on his own expertness as a specialist or consult with others in the particular line of work or particular field. His own experience, through which over a long period of years he has developed a sixth and uncanny sense, stands him in good stead, and in the majority of cases is his own best, safest and most adequate protection against mistakes.

Because the price range of letters varies from one dealer's catalogue to another's, it cannot be assumed that one is correct and the other wrong. The differences are inevitable and are due to the very nature of autographs and the uniqueness of their contents. The similarity of price range, apparent in the bulk of average material listed by the dealers, proves the existence of generally accepted standard valuations. Contents, more than any other cause, is responsible for sharp variations from the norm. These differences in value are to be expected and are largely dependent upon the individual cataloguer's judgment. The collector, then, must select that dealer in whose opinion and knowledge he has most confidence and whose reputation he decides is soundest.

The new collector who wishes to inform himself concerning the reliability of an autograph firm or firms should take the trouble, as a matter of self-protection, to consult those who may not be in but are thoroughly conversant with the profession. If the university librarian or the director of the county or local historical society is unable to give such recommendations, the State Librarian or the Librarian of Congress in Washington will furnish him with the information. The average local public librarian, having small interest in manuscripts, is not always able to provide such assistance. But any larger institution, particularly if it owns autograph collections, may be trusted to suggest and recommend the better-known and trusted firms. The small dealers throughout the country, if they cannot provide the collector with what he needs, will often recommend a metropolitan autograph professional.

There are few librarians who would not counsel a novice collector that a reputable dealer can best protect him from two recurring dangers. The first is the risk either of being unmercifully trimmed by deliberately unscrupulous persons or of being woefully taken in by those who like himself are ignorant of actual market values. In the enthusiasm of his newborn interest, he may easily be persuaded by smooth salesmanship to pay exorbitant prices. His understandable anger when he eventually learns how he has been overcharged may result in a distrust of all dealers and failure to differentiate among them.

The second risk to confront collectors is that of purchasing either stolen material or facsimiles or forgeries. There are uncommon thieves who have been known to specialize in antique silver or masterpieces of art. It is generally recognized that articles of high value will inevitably attract thieves. Autographs are no exception, and from time to time thefts from great libraries and institutions have occurred, and the stolen articles been offered to unwary private individuals. The dealer is constantly prepared for such eventualities. He may either have been put on the alert by advices from the pilfered library or been warned by police inquiries. When purchasing material, of any nature, he makes a point of carefully questioning the would-be seller about his source either through directly sought answers or by adroitly manoeuvred conversation. Evasive replies will quickly arouse his suspicions. Forgeries and facsimiles present no serious problem for him, as he can generally recognize them with little difficulty.

Collectors will also encounter other hazards, but these two alone are sufficient to indicate that, whatever autographs are collected, it is safest to deal with specialists. There are other markets which may be depended on, however. These have been established by a number of old book firms whose long service to the public has proved their soundness of reputation and ability. Their special departments devoted to autograph letters are thoroughly reliable. This is not true of all book dealers. There are some who carry autographs as a minor side-line, and, because they cannot pretend to the practical experience which is part and parcel of the specialist's equipment, they, however honest and well intentioned, are seldom in a position to guarantee authenticity. Such a guarantee obviously should accompany every autograph sold but is often worthless unless backed by years of training.

The stock of many book dealers is often limited to the handling of items whose fairly quick sale they can anticipate with some sureness. The autograph dealer, on the other hand, has a department-store stock to meet the demands of a steady clientele, with tastes as varied as they are numerous. In consequence, everything is grist for his mill. Much of the material he has accumulated may remain unsold for years, but he is confident both of its inherent merit and its ultimate sale. A quick turn-over has its points, but he has long since known that his results will be obtained over a broader range of time. He knows that like the slow wheeling of the centuries the librarian or collector, who is seldom in a rush to reach his objective, will eventually arrive to select a long-held autograph.

The autograph dealers and book firms are the first major source of supply; the second, which is more accurately considered as supplementary, is the auction galleries or auction houses. In America there are a number of these which specialize in book and manuscript sales, particularly in New York and Philadelphia.* They repeatedly offer fine collections, and such auctions deserve the attendance and patronage of collectors. The reputation of these firms is well founded, and they will, as do the reliable dealers, accept full responsibility for any mistakes in their listings. The same care, which should be shown in the selection of a dealer, should ideally govern in the case of auctions. Yet not every auction house provides safe hunting for the autograph collector. Those which deal in furniture and antiques almost exclusively are best avoided. To them autographs are a little-known field, and, because they do not have experienced cataloguers to present such material, all too often lots are inaccurately listed.

The reputable auction houses are invaluable in supplementing the careful and studied work of dealers. Their sales are perforce not designed to maintain the sustained interest of collectors since the type and quality of material offered at them is unpredictable, nor do sales occur with any degree of regularity. On the other hand, material frequently appears that is otherwise

*Today few sales are held in Philadelphia. They have occurred in Chicago and Los Angeles. Small auction galleries have sprouted throughout New England and the South, especially in New England.

hard to procure, and therefore not only collectors but also the dealers are among their constant patrons. At times, too, dealers turn to the auction house and put on the block certain autographs for which they wish to find a ready market. They keep a close watch on all auction sales, for at them they are seeking special items either for their customers or to add to their own stock. The collector, although he is often able to secure excellent autographs at auction, soon finds that he cannot limit himself entirely to such a source. What he needs may appear infrequently or not at all, or, when offered, may go at a prohibitive figure. Or when the sale occurs, he may not be in a position to buy. Credit is of course not extended to private collectors.

Again, the very letters he wishes may be found grouped with several hundred others, and he cannot purchase the two or three he really wants without obtaining the entire lot. The practice of offering letters in such lots is forced upon them, auction houses maintain, because they cannot afford the cost of issuing catalogues in large numbers and with detailed listings of each item. Letters that individually sell for 100 dollars or less, they hold, can profitably be sold only in groups of two or three pieces, five or ten, or at times a hundred or a thousand. Private collectors or librarians generally prefer to let the dealer handle such lots first and then later, after these have been sorted and rearranged and guaranteed, to acquire singly the desired items from him. In the long run they find it much less costly in time and work, and generally in money. *

The collector of experience recognizes that prices at auction are no sure criteria of actual standard autograph values. Very desirable items may at times be obtained at unusually low figures, whereas indifferent ones may go fantastically high. Inflation may control an autograph market as it does all others. Again, there are bidders determined to acquire an autograph no matter what they may have to pay for it and without any particular regard for its true worth. Certain auction values, however, are important. This is so in those cases when an exceptionally rare item, whose previous sale is unrecorded in any auction or dealer catalogue, is being sold for the first time. The price that it then

*The author has been informed in a letter that one major auction house claims they do not handle letters that are valued at less than $500 to $1,000 individually. Other auction houses say $50 to $100.

commands both points to the demand for it and, because it constitutes the first known sale, serves as a standard for future comparisons.

Collectors who wish to familiarize themselves with auction prices may secure the yearly copies of *American Book-Prices Current*—familiarly referred to in shop talk as A. B. C. —or the *United States Cumulative Book Auction Records*. In both, the auction prices commanded by books and autographs each year are listed. These compilations are reference guides which are helpful but with very definite limitations. Auction values may or may not reflect true values accurately. Further, the listings are in abridged form, and it is difficult to make any final judgment regarding contents, condition and other factors controlling autograph prices. Likewise, proper evaluation cannot be made because of the lack of information concerning the conditions of sales which, in their particular histories, may have been so unusual that prices at them deviated far from real values. Lastly, there are items sometimes listed at extremely low figures quite out of proportion with previous records. Not infrequently this may be due to the fact that dealers refrained from bidding because they recognized the item to be unauthentic, merely a copy or not as described in the catalogue.

These two series also cannot be considered as unfailing guides, since too many factors influence auction values for a summarized report to tell the whole story. There are in the first place the circumstances of the particular sale itself. The attendance on that day may have been small, or, if large, those in attendance may have been predominantly the curious rather than the buyers. The sale may not have been sufficiently well advertised. It may have been held on an afternoon when only dealers were certain to be present, rather than at the more popular and convenient evening session. Stormy weather may have kept indoors many who planned to attend. Others may have stayed away because autographs were not to be sold singly but in lots, or because the material was not attractively catalogued. The reflection of Wall Street may or may not have been favorable. Any one of these causes would have definite results at the sale. The auctioneer who attempts to gauge what may develop on a given date is sometimes a far worse prophet than the weather man.

This dependence on personal and other elements, which makes the results of auctions so uncertain, indicates that the collector is well advised when he secures the services of a reliable dealer to represent him on such occasions. This advice when followed does not forbid his attendance. It is not unusual to find the dealer and his collector-client sitting side-by-side at sales with the dealer doing the actual bidding.

Obviously, when the dealer is to represent a client at an auction sale, the two should confer in advance to determine the maximum amount the latter is willing to pay. This advance limitation is a safeguard, and, whereas the customer may occasionally be inclined to state that "the sky's the limit," most responsible dealers would strongly advise against such an attitude. Successful bidders at certain sales in the past have in many instances deplored their payments, since the same items today would bring only a fraction of the old price (although the pendulum has been known to swing back again). A limit, even if a high one, set after due consideration and discussion between dealer and client, is the sounder policy. And always if the dealer is able to buy below the maximum set, he will do so and save his customer.

It may occasionally happen that both the collector and the dealer are interested in acquiring a particular item. In such a situation, if the collector's declared maximum is higher than that of the dealer, the latter, accepting the collector's bid, will not compete. And should he, representing the collector at the sale, find it possible to bid in the desired item at a figure less than the one he himself would have paid, still he would turn over the item to his client. If, on the other hand, the dealer's intended bid exceeds that of the collector, the latter is expected to withdraw his bid in turn, permitting the dealer to obtain it, regardless of the low price at which the auctioneer may close the sale. It is a case of fair give and take.

This procedure guards against the possibility of the dealer's becoming the collector's keenest competitor, as often otherwise happens at auctions. The dealer's fee, as collector's representative, is customarily ten per cent of the sales price. For this charge, he must examine the autograph carefully, convince himself that it agrees in all details with the catalogue description, evaluate it in terms of current market values and state unequivocally whether it is in his opinion genuine or spurious. If he has any suspicions concerning authenticity, he must warn the buyer, who can determine whether he wishes to take the risk or not. It is in this matter of guarantee that one finds the most important reason why the collector needs the protection of the expert at auction sales. In America it is not the custom of auction houses to guarantee the authenticity of the autographs for sale. Those who have studied auction catalogues in recent years will not discover any mention of guarantee in their forewords covering the terms that govern sales.

In France the procedure for auctions is radically different. There, when an auction house obtains a large collection of manuscripts, the services of a recognized expert are enlisted. It is he who catalogues or supervises the listing of all individual items, and for this work is paid a certain commission based on the prices they bring. At the time of the actual sale, this same expert is present and actively participates. He is not the auctioneer, but, as each item is brought forward, he either guarantees its genuineness or unmistakably declares that this is to be sold without guarantee. Further, he names the value and places his own bid. The auctioneer then carries on and takes other bids from the floor. Should the buyer, on examining his purchase, be dissatisfied with it, he may return it, but only within twenty-four hours. By this method, the auction buyers are obviously protected. They do not need the services of an intermediary since the expert at the time of sale himself guarantees each item or separate lot. The guarantee, of course, is not necessarily infallible, since infallibility is not lodged in the best expert, but, at least, there is assurance that the auction house has secured the soundest judgment available.

In other European countries an expertized appraisal is printed in parentheses opposite each item listed in the auction catalogues.

In America no such printed appraisals are made available nor does the auction house provide an expert to represent it and to attend sales where at that time he vouches for authenticity or places an evaluation on all listings. American auction houses, on request—a fact which is not well known—will, however, give an approximate evaluation of a specific item in advance of its sale. Unfortunately, these estimates often reflect the inexpertness of the appraiser. Yet the novice collector is inclined to accept them as finally authoritative, and in doing so he may not only himself overbid but force others who are interested to do likewise.*

Experience has shown that often a recommended "fair price" will at times be so low that the bidder, who is eager to obtain a catalogued item, misses out completely. On the other hand, swayed perhaps by inflationary trends, the auction appraisals will be ridiculously high and scare off the prospective buyer. On many occasions autographs so overestimated have sold for a fraction of their reputed valuation. A collector hesitates to hand in a $25 bid on a manuscript appraised at $250. And yet, when he has done so, he has been known to secure the coveted autograph. It is the duty of the dealer, who is constantly fighting the causes of inflation, to protect the private buyer against inflated prices, to point out possible discrepancies and to encourage the collector to put in whatever bid he feels he can afford. The latter's insurance premium is the ten per cent charge the dealer sets for his services.

The American auction house conditions would require very much less circumspection on the part of the buyer if there were more assurance that the catalogues of even responsible firms contained only a minute number of errors. But errors are not infrequent. That they do not occur in even larger numbers is surprising. The auction cataloguer, in the first place, cannot pretend to be an expert. In the course of a day's work, he must describe hundreds of varieties of objects—books, maps, autographs, broadsides and other papers—and any one of these is a study in itself. This situation probably explains a somewhat humorous mistake by which a dealer recently profited. He bid in

*Today most auction houses print estimates of value, which serve as a helpful guide. The exception abroad appears to be the French auction houses, which makes it difficult to bid at their sales.

a lot which the cataloguer had listed under the heading "Prominent American Women," all letters which had been addressed to Dolly Madison. On examination, it was found to contain an invitation to Mrs. Madison, written on behalf of President Jefferson. The note requested the pleasure of her company and that of whatever ladies she might care to bring to spend the evening at the then "White House." The handwriting was rather feminine and the note was signed "M. Lewis." Doubtless some unknown "female," the cataloguer concluded, and, on that assumption, decided the item was next to worthless despite the association value in linking the names of Jefferson and Madison. Actually, however, the writer was recognized as being Meriwether Lewis, the famous explorer who with William Clark blazed a trail across the Rockies to the Columbia River and opened up the West, and certainly one of the most masculine of men. Lewis' letters are of the greatest rarity, and unusual interest is attached to any written while he was briefly private secretary to Jefferson.

Such "accidents" may not infrequently occur in a cataloguer's work. Lack of time plays a contributory part, and errors inevitably creep in. Facsimiles are offered instead of originals, forgeries go undetected, mistakes in identity are made and other inaccuracies appear. That these are definitely inadvertences will prove of little comfort to one who has suffered from them and discovered the fact too late.

Of course, if the purchaser discovers the error, the reliable auction house, despite its lack of guarantee, will accept the return of the item within a reasonable period of time. It is extremely improbable that such a house would make redress five or ten years later. This, the autograph dealer, who values his reputation, must and would do irrespective of the interval of time between his sale and the discovery of his error. All too often this interval is too long for the customer reasonably to take back to the galleries the autograph he has found to be other than as represented at the time of his purchase. It must be remembered that the material offered for sale at auction belongs, not to the house, but to one or more consignors. Dealers, when they buy at such sales, are permitted a limited period of credit, but other buyers are requested to pay at the time of purchase.

Consignors must be paid within thirty days. The auction purchaser must act then before the house has made its settlement with the consignor, although in some cases exceptions are made. Were any other procedure followed, there would be untold confusion, especially since many auction firms conduct weekly sales, and during certain periods, even more.

The collector who chooses to buy personally at auction may unquestionably save the ten per cent commission charge of a dealer although that same dealer may have been the very competitor who has run the price up. But he simultaneously gambles on incurring serious loss because he is not protected against unauthenticity. It is possible, when he has procured an autograph at a very low price and a great saving, to secure a guarantee later from some dealer. If the latter can honestly give such a guarantee, he can scarcely be expected to provide this professional service gratis. One does not take a legal tangle to a lawyer, even if he is a friend, and not expect to receive a bill. So the dealer who guarantees an autograph bought at auction charges ten per cent of the sale price, the same amount he would have been paid had he originally represented the collector at the sale itself.

The procedures followed in American auction houses, whatever they may require of caution on the part of the autograph buyer, contribute definite benefits to the autograph field. The latter are uppermost in the case of very great family correspondences for the handling of which the auction house is particularly well equipped. Such large accumulations may require a greater expenditure than the dealer wishes to undertake since they generally cover only one period in history and include large quantities of unimportant and duplicated items written by a small group of people. It does not usually pay the dealer to overstock nor does he care to tie up his capital in this type of material. What he has to offer his customers must always be representative of all periods and all countries, must comprise as many individually significant names as possible and must include letters the contents of which are somewhat above the average in their importance.

Neither in such stock nor in auction rooms is the collector likely to run across the ever-hoped-for "find." Yet this is unquestionably the ambition of practically every collector. The dealer's stock and the auction house material have been too carefully examined for hope in this quarter to be more than a pleasant and elusive dream. Those who entertain the dream may possibly realize it. To work toward such an eventuality, however, they must venture off the beaten track and explore the other odd, minor and innumerable sources of autograph supply.

These, by their very number, evade ready classification. At the top of the list would be the many small bookshops, antique stores, junk establishments and nondescript shops usually dealing in curios which are scattered across the country in likely and unlikely spots. Many show a very catholic taste in what they handle, and from time to time certain of them may display autographs. To browse in musty and little-known places, situated attractively or pseudo-picturesquely in back alleys or streets, is in itself a pleasant method of passing a few hours. For such scouting expeditions, the collector must not only possess leisure, but patience, since he may spend months and years before he finds an autograph of real significance.

In addition, on such explorations he must be equipped with incredulity and caution, for he may not possess the required technical knowledge by which he can detect the fraudulent. However vociferously the statement "absolutely as represented" is made, the seller is himself more often than not entirely ignorant of autographs. If, then, the collector will be satisfied with visits, which may be rich only in potentialities of autograph discoveries, he will at least invite other rewarding experiences. Should he happen on what he decides is a "find," the gamble, for this is inescapable under the circumstances, may be well worth taking.

CHAPTER VI

The Forger and his Work

THE newcomer cannot go far into the field of autograph collecting before he learns that its "big, bad wolf" is the forger, or the forgery itself. He also learns that the wolf is not to be sneered at, but really to be feared and watched for at all times. Nor can the cry, "wolf, wolf," be raised too often. Forgers, however clever they may be, rarely escape detection in the long run, a truth which affords little comfort to the collector who has been sadly penalized by them, excepting the doubtful satisfaction that justice has eventually been served.

For centuries forgers have played important, if disgraceful, roles in the autograph world. This is pointed up by the fact that many notorious among them have earned places in biographical dictionaries, and a few have been made the subjects of books and treatises. So ancient are their activities that it is impossible to determine at what point in history the forger first appeared. In *Literary Forgeries,** J. A. Farrer suggests that he flourished long before the Christian era and possibly began when the Ptolemies, anxious to elaborate their libraries, employed many copyists. The Egyptian monarchs offered such tempting prices that individuals of literary propensities, but of doubtful honesty, were encouraged to "adopt" the names of the then-distinguished writers of Greece.

In later centuries further confusion was brought into literature by a practice prevalent in the schools of the Sophists. This involved the writing of exercises, in which the student used his imagination to compose a speech or letter as though he himself were the celebrated man he imitated. Parenthetically, it might be stated that the practice is somewhat paralleled today by the army of ghost writers which stands behind many of the world's notable figures. With the Sophists, the sheer excellence of their "exercises" caused later students to accept them as original works of the one imitated. Such "forgers," who had no intention to

* Longmans, Green & Co., London, 1907.

deceive, wrote with great skill and often with high artistry, and their work accordingly justified what high praise it received.

The intentional forger, however, acts from different motives, some more blameworthy than others. The most reprehensible is that which, as in the instances of "Antique" Smith, Denis-Lucas, Alberti, Spring, von Gerstenbergk, Byron, Cosey, and Weisberg, arose from a desire for financial gain. Other forgers, such as Chatterton and Ireland, were prompted by personal ambition; and still others, among whom are Bertram and Cunningham, by that curious form of arrested maturity which leads adults to perpetrate hoaxes. Those in the latter two classes are more the problem of the scholar and historian, but those of the first are the particular concern and worry of experts, dealers, criminologists and the law itself.

There is a saying that if a man is worth while, time will discover him; if he is no good, time will uncover him. The same applies to those who try to counterfeit autographs. Anachronisms are the rock on which the forger generally founders. Today the knowledge of paper, ink, water-marks, scripts and other factors has become so perfected that the expert need not rely solely on such time errors to detect a forgery. By means of many newly discovered methods, he is able to date the materials used with surprising accuracy and to give their source and origin. Nevertheless, the field has continuously proved lucrative for the forger, since there are always those who are unequipped to recognize his work. It is for them that he floods the market with spurious Washingtons and Franklins, Longfellows and Blakes, Shelleys and Byrons, Lincolns and Marshalls, Scotts and Dickens, Poes, Fields and Burns.

The Chattertons, Irelands, Bertrams and Cunninghams resembled the Sophists, at least in the fact that they possessed great literary talent. None of them copied authentic manuscripts word for word in an assumed hand. They did not need, in a sense, to imitate script, nor was special ink or quality of paper too much their concern, since there were few authorities in their day to question these. The renown of Thomas Chatterton, who committed suicide in 1770 at the pathetic age of seventeen, is based on more than the tragic story of his desire for a short cut to fame. Coleridge, Wordsworth, Keats and Rossetti wrote poems which greatly lament his untimely death and extol his poetic genius. The forgeries of which Chatterton stood guilty would have had little chance of success had they been produced today. Even in his own time, the period in which they were considered authentic was very brief.

What he wrote, and what the centuries still regard as exceptionally good, were poems in an antique hand on old parchment. These were attributed to a fifteenth-century monk, Rowley, whom Chatterton invented. Actually, they were his own brilliant compositions, and, when later they had attained their own fame, it was his full intention to acknowledge his authorship. Meanwhile, his father "discovered" the planted manuscripts in an old chest at St. Mary Radcliffe Church in Chatterton's native Bristol, and they were given to the world as Rowley's poetry. When their intrinsic merit eventually attracted considerable favorable attention in Bristol, the youth was delighted and appealed to Horace Walpole to further the publication of Rowley. Walpole, who at first accepted the fictitious monk, took the precaution of consulting others more expert than he. They detected the fraud, Walpole rebuked Chatterton and the latter found his scheme had died aborning. The story of his attempt, however, did not spread sufficiently rapidly throughout literary England to prevent one further step. His *Elinoure and Juga*, with authorship credited to Rowley, which Walpole had not seen, was later published in *Town and Country Magazine*. This hoax, too, did not go long unrevealed. Today Chatterton's Rowley manuscripts, as well as others which he initially designated as his own, are preserved in the British Museum.

The eighteenth century in England proved fertile for literary forgeries, and in its last decade William Henry Ireland, inspired perhaps by Chatterton's scheme, believed he could succeed where his predecessor had failed. In any event, he had an even more ambitious plan which carried further. Ireland's father was a Shakespearean authority, and, when the boy was approaching eighteen, after a childhood during which the great poet's work and style had become thoroughly familiar, he often amused himself by forging documents purporting to be connected with Shakespeare. He was so remarkably clever at this that the elder Ireland was completely deceived and, in 1795, despite protests of the son, who feared exposure, published a collection of Shakespeare's works in facsimile, entitled *Miscellaneous Papers and Legal Instruments under the Hand and Seal of William Shakespeare*. The seemingly blind acceptance of the work by his contemporaries encouraged the boy, who, with boundless imagination and apparently motivated by no hope of great financial profit, was next responsible for a "recently discovered" drama of Shakespeare, *Vortigern and Rowena*. The play actually was produced at London's Drury Lane Theatre by Richard Brinsley Sheridan with a prominent acting cast, including John Philip Kemble who played the lead. But the first-night audience was not remotely fooled, as it indicated very quickly by its jeers.

Such details may seem remote to the present-day collector who feels that at best they offer no more than academic interest for him. This may be. Yet, it is a fact that many of Ireland's forgeries are extant, and the most important of them are today in America. In addition to the entirely invented *Vortigern and Rowena*, Ireland put out what he announced were the original manuscripts of *Hamlet* and *King Lear*. These three forged dramas were later owned by the rare-book dealer, Dr. A. S. W. Rosenbach, according to a letter from his office dated March 1945. When the Drury Lane episode exposed Ireland, he fully confessed to his frauds, and later, with continued frankness and doubtless with a determination to realize what profit he could, published his *Confessions*. In fact, he went further and blandly sold imitations of his forgeries, many of which, in addition to some of his originals, are still in the British Museum.

With both Ireland and Chatterton, the hoax was a means to another end, but with Charles Julius Bertram and Allan Cunningham it was perpetrated solely for the sake of the hoax itself. Cunningham not only brazenly labeled as ancient Scottish ballads work he had himself composed but succeeded in convincing the anthologist, R. H. Cronek, that they were as represented.

They were, accordingly, embodied in *Select Scottish Songs* which Cronek proudly published in 1810. Cunningham hugely enjoyed his later revelation of authorship and took particular pleasure in the thought that among the authorities on Scottish literature he had fooled was his old friend, Sir Walter Scott.

Bertram's hoax, which still does not seem clearly motivated, was in the historical and not the literary world. For this reason, it proved very much more serious, and its after effects can still be traced today. A man of distinguished talents and honorable reputation, Bertram was a professor of English in the Royal Marine Academy at Copenhagen and the author of several books of considerable and recognized scholarship, including a good Danish-English grammar. These facts doubtless at the time forestalled any questions concerning his veracity, and, since he did not apparently wish any to admire his cleverness, his hoax was not discovered until after his death.

Briefly, in 1747, he wrote to Dr. William Stukeley, a celebrated English antiquarian, mentioning that he had seen in the hands of a friend an extract from a "curious manuscript history of Roman Britain by Richard of Westminster." His correspondent, greatly excited by such a marvelous discovery and its potentialities for historians, soon "persuaded" Bertram to send, letter by letter, a transcript of the work, together with a copy of the map that purportedly went with it. Dr. Stukeley, after consulting a prominent librarian, who only saw the transcripts but stated his belief that the original would be four centuries old, sought and obtained permission to print. Accordingly, in 1757, the book appeared with the elaborate title, *Britanicarum Gentium Historiae Antiquae Scriptores Tres: Ricardus Corinensis, Gildas, Badonicus, Nennius Banchorensis*. Its publication caused a sensation in British academic circles, and Dr. Stukeley, who long enjoyed the thrill of his "discovery," was repeatedly called upon to lecture on the newly revealed British author, "Richard of Westminster."

The latter's supposed history gave innumerable details about England under the Roman Empire, mentioned customs heretofore unknown and startling, and furnished elaborate descriptions of the Island's geography as it was then mapped. Dr. Stukeley's reputation, together with the endorsements of the librarian he had first consulted and of other authorities, was sufficient to head off any doubts. Scholars and historians innocently and happily quoted Bertram's "history," and references to it can even be found in Gibbon's classic *Decline and Fall of the Roman Empire*. The search for the original manuscript, which had begun almost immediately on Stukeley's announcement, was renewed with full vigor in 1845, eighty years after Bertram's death, and the fact that it was totally unsuccessful added proof to a charge then made that the manuscript never existed. This charge was brought by Karl Wex, a German writer. He, by a mass of evidence, particularly based on anachronisms, demonstrated without question that Bertram's success as a hoaxer was as amazing as was his knowledge of ancient Britain.

The work of these and similar other forgers and hoaxers, all of whom were backed by extensive knowledge, was not properly in the field of autographs, for it was literature and history rather than handwriting which was foisted on the public. In the case of Bertram, who, despite his anachronisms, did know history profoundly, no original manuscript ever came into the picture. Had one done so, the story might have been entirely different. Yet however short or long lived was the success of a Chatterton or an Ireland, a Cunningham or a Bertram, each suggests possibilities which, if translated into action, become of more immediate interest and concern to the autograph collector.

From the time that autograph collecting became popular, it can be said with assurance that forgers have been active. Their operations, until interest in autographs became rooted in America, were first confined to Europe, where alone their dishonesty could be made profitable. One of the more notorious of those who devoted themselves to autograph imitations was Count Mariano Alberti, a captain in the Swiss Guard, who operated in the middle of the past century in Rome. He marketed many books which he claimed came from the library of Torquato Tasso, and which were profusely annotated in the "handwriting" of this great sixteenth-century Italian poet.

So cleverly was his work done, in regard to the imitation of ink and script and the selection of the proper edition of the particular book, that the fraud would have gone undetected had it not been for the inquisitiveness of scholars thoroughly familiar with Tasso's literary period. It was soon demonstrated that Alberti had liberally borrowed appropriate comments from literary criticisms by obscure writers, who had not only published years after Tasso's death but who lacked Tasso's mastery and perfection of language, particularly that of Latin.* He believed none would bother to search out their identity, but he forgot that research is routine to scholars. Their revelations were quickly forthcoming, and Alberti went to jail.

Alberti's forgeries concerned only Tasso, but not many years later, in France, his example was followed in wholesale fashion by Vrain-Denis Lucas, an even more unscrupulous but much less competent forger. Lucas acquired a victim in M. Michel Chasles, a mathematician and astronomer of note, whose unbounded trust caused him to accept the wildest fabrications. Chasles, beginning in 1861, blinded by his enthusiasms and overjoyed at the acquisition of one startling rarity after another, purchased no less than twenty-seven thousand forged letters from Lucas. He demonstrated that a specialist in one field may be a dunce in another, and Lucas did not need to take special pains with his counterfeits. Nor was the forger interested in other aspects of the truth. He produced a series of letters supposedly written by Pascal to Robert Boyle, the English chemist and physicist, which indicated that Pascal had anticipated Newton in the discovery of the law of gravitation.

Since scientists, among whom Chasles had a recognized place, would unquestionably be keenly interested in such a supposition, Chasles determined to share his discovery with the world. Before embarking on the publication, he presented two of the forged Pascal letters to the Academy of Science, and the storm broke. National pride was uppermost in the controversy which continued for two years, and Chasles (and of course Lucas) was fiercely attacked from across the English Channel and as fiercely

* Cf. Rudolph Altrocchi, *Sleuthing in the Stacks*, Harvard University Press, Cambridge, Massachusetts, 1944.

supported in France. To the credit of the French, two of their scholars aided in the demonstration of fraud, and the whole story of Lucas' duplicity was exposed in 1870, when he was brought before a Paris criminal court.

His career had been a most astounding one. So completely catholic was he in his forgeries that he had sold letters, all written in French and on paper made in France, of Julius Caesar, Cleopatra, Mary Magdalen and even of Lazarus—after his resurrection. The prosecution produced one exhibit after another—examples of the private correspondence of Sappho, Herod, Pompey, Judas Iscariot, Pontius Pilate, Charles Martel and Joan of Arc, six letters of Alexander the Great to Aristotle, five from Alcibiades to Pericles and one of Attila to a Gallic general. The trial did not bring out the quirk in Chasles' character which made him one of the greatest dupes in history. The court gave Lucas a light sentence. After he had paid the imposed fine of $100 and served two years in prison, the question as to whether he resumed his career of forgery has remained unanswered.

Approximately at the same time that Lucas was being brought to scant justice in France, Robert Spring, one of the better-known American forgers, was flourishing. By that time the popularity of autograph collecting had grown in America, and values were increasing. Spring, however, employed great care with his frauds, which included spurious letters of Washington—one of which actually hung in Philadelphia's Independence Hall—Franklin, Stonewall Jackson and other famous Americans. Only experts are able to distinguish them from the originals. For all his pains, Spring, who had a list of aliases—Robert Speering, Harriet Copley, William Emerson, Samuel R. Hampton, M.D., Samuel Hawley, M.D., Emma Harding and Fannie Jackson (supposed to have been Stonewall Jackson's daughter)—was uncovered, served a jail term and, penniless, ended his days in 1876 in a Philadelphia hospital.

Spring did not confine himself to one victim but instead used the mails to approach his prey, choosing for this purpose mostly those who were known to have very fine private libraries. He most frequently represented himself as a widow seriously reduced in circumstances and forced to market letters with which otherwise "she" would not consent to part. In advance he would have obtained, by some unrevealed means, genuine letters and then traced these on sheets of paper which he had stained with coffee grounds to simulate the appearance of age. One of the duplications would always go forward with his pity-appealing letter, which bore the implication "Give what you think it is worth." To cover his trail, particularly after he had been arrested and had jumped bail in Philadelphia, Spring mailed his offers far and wide and from many different post offices. Remittances were sent to the "widow" in care of one of the many aliases he assumed.

Letters forged by Spring do not often appear on the market today, but the many checks of Washington he forged do. He had found a large supply of blank checks belonging to the cashier of the Office of Discount and Deposit at Baltimore. These are always canceled with an incised cross bank stamp as was then customary, and, curiously enough, such forgeries sell readily for $50 or more. Other Spring forgeries, including his letters of Washington written from Valley Forge and Mount Vernon, also have a value of their own.

Spring obviously realized no extravagant sum for any one of his forgeries, but it would have been impossible, by the time he was apprehended, to trace what inflationary values may have been obtained for them subsequently. Unfortunately, once autograph forgeries have entered into the stream, it is not always possible to determine precisely where they will be washed ashore. If over the years one has repeatedly been sold, only the last and most unsuspecting purchaser may be financially victimized when he becomes the first in a chain of owners to have the fraud proved.

The forger is often as shrewd in covering his trail as he is in perpetrating his "originals." Among the nineteenth-century German forgers was Baron Georg Heinrich von Gerstenbergk, specializer in spurious Schiller A. L. S.s, who repeatedly drew red herrings over the trail. He unloosed a flood of these letters in 1852, and was prepared with authentic ones by the German poet and playwright when experts were sent to investigate him. The latter, in consequence, were understandably convinced that he was not the source of the fraud. Von Gerstenbergk's sales of the bogus were profitable, and he soon released more of the forged variety. His greed, however, betrayed him into excessive production, and eventually he was trapped. Had he marketed in the America of his time, his detection might have been an even slower process. Even today, in this country more than in Europe, fabricated foreign autographs are more apt to escape investigation. Not many years ago, an Italian returned to his native country after having made a rich haul by means of finely executed examples of Galileo, Luther, Vespucci, Tasso, Haydn and others. He was ultimately arrested, but his products have since appeared on the markets at fairly regular intervals.

The procedure of this Italian was reversed in a sense by George Gordon Byron, who largely operated in this country but marketed in England. Originally an Englishman, he had roved about the world and later, after buying a farm in Wilkes-Barre, Pennsylvania, wrote extensively to friends, including the publisher, of Lord Byron. He claimed to be the latter's illegitimate son—a claim which was given plausibility by his astonishing resemblance to the poet and the likeness of their handwritings. He was first heard from when, threatened with the loss of his land, his letters appealed for financial assistance. He also moved to meet this emergency, which incidentally was not forestalled, by the publication of a life of his "father."

The career of this self-proclaimed bastard, which was later completely revealed, involved many people in London, and, had not certain forgeries been detected, important—although false—biographical data would have been perpetuated. To lend credence to his tales Byron stated that he had publicized his desire to receive any letters which would help him in his projected biography of Lord Byron, and he maintained that this public appeal had netted him approximately one thousand returns. He made a mistake in announcing in England, as apparently he had done in America, that his *Life* would contain many unpublished letters to which he had been given access by Mrs. Augusta Leigh, the poet's half-sister. When this statement was brought to Mrs. Leigh's attention, she not only vigorously denied it but also challenged in no uncertain terms his alleged family relationship.

Prudently, Byron abandoned his idea of publishing his biography in England, but actually he published two installments of the work in this country before he was forced, probably by lack of means, to drop this project. Thereafter the story becomes more and more complex. Letters of Lord Byron, Keats and Shelley appeared in 1848 in London, and some were bought by a reputable London dealer who had obtained them from a seemingly artless and naïve young woman. She had a most plausible story of how she had come by them. After there had been considerable trading in the letters, she was months later discovered to be George Gordon Byron's wife.

The Lord Byron letters were next bought by the poet's publisher, who, thoroughly familiar with the style, tone and writing of his own author, accepted them as authentic. The fact that they were later proved beyond doubt to be spurious testifies to the extreme skill with which they had been forged. The letters bore foreign postmarks as well as seals, and the addressees, the creases and the faded color of their paper pointed strongly to genuineness. Despite arguments to the contrary, Byron's "son's" subsequently notorious career* makes it highly probable that the latter was responsible for many, if not all, of them.

The authenticity of the Byron letters was not questioned until much later, and, possibly, they would never have been doubted had the Shelley letters not been auctioned at Puttick & Simpson's and Sotheby & Wilkinson's. Once challenged as forgeries, suspicion followed the trail back to the dealer who had purchased them from the "artless" young lady, and, wisely, everything she had sold him was minutely investigated. The Shelley letters, also bought by a publisher, were issued in book form before an astonishing chain of coincidences led to discovery. A review copy was sent to Tennyson, and when it arrived the poet was entertaining a friend who casually turned its leaves, and from

* Robert Metcalf Smith, *The Shelley Legend*, Charles Scribner's Sons, New York, 1945, pt. III, pp. 50-133.

them there "leaped out" sentences which he immediately recognized had been lifted verbatim from a magazine article by his father Lord Palgrave, the English anthologist. Advance copies were recalled, and publication abandoned. The Shelley forgeries were in almost all other details as singularly well executed as the Byron forgeries. So also were the Keats forgeries, some of which were addressed to "My dear Woodhouse," who was well known as this poet's intimate, and they had excellent imitations of Keats' motto and seal with clasped hands. Next, in fairly short order, the majority of this considerable body of letters of the three English poets, many of them now in the safekeeping of the British Museum, was incontestably proved to be spurious. Considering George Gordon Byron's career in England, it is not impossible and more likely probable that he may have channeled additional false material into the hands of private collectors in America.

Although Lord Byron, Shelley and Keats manuscripts should always be sharply examined, for no one can tell when and where doubtful ones may appear, other forgeries are equally important to the American autograph collector. Among these must be mentioned the work of Alexander Howland Smith, Joseph Cosey and Charles Weisberg. The first, at one time a clerk in Scotland, operated in the 1890's and began with a fraudulent Robert Burns A. L. S. Later, from an apparently unlimited supply, he sold autographs of such historic personages as Mary, Queen of Scots, Darnley, Bothwell, the Stuart Kings, Prince Charles, Oliver Cromwell, Edmund Burke and William Pitt. Although he was overtaken and sentenced to a year's imprisonment, irreparable harm had been done, and his forgeries, of which a number had been auctioned off at Dowell's in Edinburgh, took a high toll of victims. Among the victims was the distinguished and generous patron of arts, John S. Kennedy, Trustee of the New York Public Library, who had bought and later presented these unauthenticities to that and other American institutions. The Library on request will still show over two hundred Smith-forged letters and manuscripts obtained from its Trustee. The *Annual Burns Chronicle** also states that the

* Series 2, Vol. XVI, 1941, Article by John S. Clarke, pp. 24-30.

Earl of Rosebery and the late John Gribbel, whose magnificent collections of autographs have been auctioned off in recent years, were both fooled by the same forger.

For his time, Smith, who was quickly dubbed "Antique" Smith, probably reached a high-water mark in the forger's skill, depending more on accurate caligraphy than on the cruder methods of tracing or drawing. He moreover carefully chose the paper he used, selecting that of the proper period correctly water-marked. This he obtained from genuine quartos and folios, theological books and similar works. He frequently stained his sheets with weak tea, coffee or tobacco juice, and also doctored the ink. In these attempts at simulation he was careless, and, inevitably, they proved his downfall. Only those who ignored the missing testimony of naturally aged paper and ink and who judged entirely by script could have been duped. That he was, however, one of the most able script forgers is indisputable, a fact to which many an unsuspecting collector can sadly testify.

Cosey and Weisberg, who both were extremely skilled in their shady occupation, have cast their shadows even further over the modern scene. Examples of old forgeries are still occasionally offered for sale, but the work of these two criminals, who were operating in the last decade, have literally flooded the market. It is not positively known that they have ceased operation, and for this reason, if no other, it is well for American collectors especially to become acquainted in more detail with their activities.

Cosey, the name by which he is generally referred to, according to an article in the New York *Sun*, November 13, 1941, has a career checkered with jail terms and convictions—nine in all, for grand larceny, carrying concealed weapons, forging checks and various other crimes. He is known, like "Antique" Smith, for his great skill, and, in addition, for the inordinate pride he took in his forgeries. He began, as he admitted to Mr. G. William Bergquist, Special Investigator of the New York Public Library, whose tact and patience were largely responsible for the full exposure of both Cosey and Weisberg, with stealing from the Congressional Library a pay warrant signed by Benjamin Franklin. This he offered to a book dealer, who scornfully refused it as unauthentic. Cosey, he himself explained, was angered to the point of taking up diligent practice in handwriting imitations and succeeded so well that, to quote Mr. Bergquist's lecture before the Bibliographical Society in January 1943, "A year later, he had the satisfaction of selling a forged Lincoln to this same store."

Soon he began a series of experiments in the making of ink, at first using Waterman's brown correspondence ink, and, later, one that was more accurate. He obtained paper from various sources and was lucky in unearthing a supply bearing Monnier's 1851 water-mark and of a blue color identical with the paper on which many of Lincoln's authentic legal documents were written. He claimed he had acquired this paper in an old ledger which he had bought in Peoria. Cosey's vanity led him to boast untruthfully that he himself had manufactured another supply of long white paper which bore the water-mark, "T. Edmonds, 1824," but this stock Mr. Bergquist eventually traced to its right source.

Cosey, who had good reason to be proud of his Lincoln forgeries on the Monnier paper, had mastered Lincoln's writing in an astonishing manner. Once his supply of this paper gave out, and he could not obtain proper substitutes, his subsequent forgeries were more easily detectable. For the most part, he did not attempt Lincoln A. L. S.s but rather devoted himself to the production of lengthy legal manuscripts and pleadings of the Civil War President. With these he was singularly generous for a forger. Many of them covered three or four folio pages. Regardless of whether he wrote a one- or four-page item, he sold each at a fairly uniform price. Originally, it is said, this ran as high as $20 to $50, but he later disposed of them at approximately $2 each.

The Lincoln forgeries were only a small fraction of Cosey's output. Items of Francis Bacon, John Marshall, Patrick Henry, Richard Henry Lee, Thomas Lynch, Jr., Button Gwinnett, Aaron Burr, John Adams, Samuel Adams, Alexander Hamilton, Rudyard Kipling, Mark Twain, Mary Baker Eddy and others were believed to have been put on the market by him at various times. And, sadly enough, a goodly number of them still appear at sales. His best work was with his Franklins, Poes and Lincolns, and, of the latter, the most irritatingly acceptable of his forgeries are Lincoln endorsements, which he wrote on authentic Civil War records. These he docketed with three or four lines signed in the President's hand. So perfectly were they executed that only experts, by sharp examination of the ink, which alone provided the clue, could detect them.

In his work Cosey resorted to many stratagems. For example, knowing that a certain famous man used a particular color of stationery, he dyed his own paper with Tintex to the required shade. This device was, however, among his less successful. Even more clever was his custom of composing a letter on old paper and then writing a modern letter to authenticate the forgery. Again, a great number of his forgeries carry endorsements in blue or red pencil or in ink different in color from that used in the body of the document. Such endorsements, written obliquely across some portion of the paper, appear quite frequently on authentic manuscripts, and Cosey was quick to catch on and use this subtle imitation.

Nor was he averse to piling up his effects through association, as is illustrated by the following item, dated Mount Vernon, June 12, 1779, which, were it genuine, would command a substantial price. Owned by the New York Public Library, it begins:

To the
    Hon. P. Henry,
    House of Burgesses
Dear Sir:
        Thank you for submitting this map of ancient symbols. I am sure that John Marshall will find in it just what he seeks for his new book.
                Cordially yours,
                Richard Henry Lee

This was purportedly in the handwriting of Lee, the Virginia Signer, with his signature, and, below it, dated on the same day, appears "Endorsed by me Th. Jefferson," presumably written by that patriot. Then follows:

> My dear Mr. Henry:
>   There remains nothing for me to do but add my approval, since Mr. Lee and yourself have endorsed the drawings therein.
>   As ever,
>   G. Washington

Next comes, dated June 16, 1779, from Washington City:

> Hon. John Marshall,
> Richmond in Virginia
> Sir:
>   Here is a map which was kindly given to me by Doctor Priestly. If you will examine figures 1 to 9 and all of them with the exception of 11, 12 & 13 you will see the various periods represented of which we are speaking. I showed this to the Continental General, and he expressed a desire to use it when you have finished with it.
>   Mr. Adams of Boston has promised to send me some maps showing old money and coins used in the period of which you are writing. These are very fine steel engravings, and I hope they will be of some aid to you in your book.
>   Yours very sincerely,
>   P. Henry

Cool craft also characterized Cosey's methods of marketing. For instance, he never stated that he was offering a Lincoln, or a Poe or a Franklin. He simply presented a paper with the remark that he had found it in an attic or cellar and knew nothing of its value, adding "Do you think it is anything of interest?" His carefully chosen victim, seeing an excellently executed forgery and perhaps thinking he knew sufficient of the signer's writing to judge properly, not unnaturally jumped to the conclusion intended. If he considered the letter authentic under the circumstances, Cosey unselfishly shunted the responsibility over to him.

Equal to the work of Cosey as a menace is that of Charles Weisberg, but, on the whole, the latter was in no way as shrewd, deft or prolific. His work as a forger was far from good. Only Cosey in the more recent past is distinguished for that painstaking care which characterized many of his predecessors. Weisberg, unlike Cosey, regarded his victims as thoroughly credulous. A graduate of the University of Pennsylvania, where he had an excellent record as a student of American history and literature, he executed forgeries of Washington, Walt Whitman, Heinrich Heine and others, but in the *Publishers' Weekly* of August 11, 1934, his arrest was announced. At that time the New York post office revealed that he, operating under the name of Kane, had victimized a number of book dealers. Kane was only one of his aliases—he has bobbed up as Dr. Charles Levitt and Brand Storm, and probably under many other names. A personable man in his forties, his associates dubbed him "Baron" because of his pleasant and agreeable manner.

The records show that in 1933 Weisberg served a three-months sentence for forging a postal money-order, and in 1935 he was given a year and a half for using the mails to defraud. For the same offense he received two and a half years in 1941. Released, he resumed his interrupted career under the alias Brand Storm, was apprehended and indicted, but jumped bail. Once more arrested in February 1945, he was again sentenced to a two-and-a-half-year stretch. Auction houses, autograph collectors and dealers alike rejoice over the event, their only regret being that his sojourn behind bars is not permanent.

The modern forgeries of these two men, Cosey and Weisberg, as well as of others less notorious, doubtless netted them a fairly comfortable income if one can judge by the number of spurious items which appear in out-of-the-way small auction houses and antique shops and at stamp auctions. So common have such frauds become that many who actually handle them frequently do not bother to call attention to them. Whereas genuine Washingtons and Lincolns admittedly are not rare, still they are not so plentiful that, when they are included in a miscellaneous collection of stamps, they merit no mention at all.

The collector who, on purchasing such a collection, concludes that he has made a "discovery" which had unwittingly slipped through the seller's hands, is in almost all instances due for an awakening, whose only value is that of experience. "I appealed to the vendor," wrote a man who had bought a collection in which all the important pieces were later revealed as forgeries, "to at least make a concession for part of the purchase price; his reply was that the spurious items had simply been added as models for future comparison."

Dealers and collectors who are market wise not only know the areas where they may stumble on a mine planted by a forger but occasionally are able to look ahead and determine some of the traps that may be set tomorrow. They literally or mentally pigeon-hole all small pieces of information which may point to the possibility that a new forgery is being prepared for the future. Such a clue was provided by Dr. Julian Boyd, Librarian of Princeton University, when, writing about a sale of Philadelphia Custom House papers,* he added: "One interesting sidelight of this episode was the fact that a very competent forger ...secured a large quantity of [these] documents and salted away among them some fine specimens of his penmanship, involving the names of John Paul Jones and James Buchanan (the Postmaster of Baltimore)." It is possible on some fine day that the forger will come into unwarned markets with collections of Jones and Buchanan papers composed entirely of faked autographs or one or two authentic items included for bait with a lot of fabrications.

An amusing story in this connection was recently told by a Boston collector, who found in a New England shop window an example of a Lincoln signature. "Seventeen dollars," said the owner to an inquiry about its price, "but to you twelve dollars cash." The collector, who was readily shown the item, examined it and turned to the dealer, saying, "I cannot take advantage of this generous offer. I would be robbing you. This is a unique piece. It is worth one thousand dollars." "You don't say!" the dealer gasped in his horror at the mistake he had apparently

* See Chapter XII, pp. 231-232.

made, "Why is it worth so much? What is there about it?" "This is a most rare manuscript," the visitor explained, "President Lincoln apparently signed this document three years after he was assassinated." And with that he left the great bargain on the counter.

It would be a happy circumstance if autograph collectors in general could spot a fraud as readily as the collector in this story. But they are continually being taken in not only by forged letters and documents but also by presentation or association copies of books. The most common type of forgery in recent markets concerns such books, which rightly take on a greater value if their flyleaves bear some sentiment written and signed by the author. It is a far simpler matter for the forger to give this type of personal touch than to undertake an entire A. L. S., which necessitates the locating of correct paper, ink and other items required to make it appear authentic. An old book of the indicated period is not difficult to acquire, nor is the further claim that it originated from the library of some well-known person easily contestable. If the latter's name is written in the book, the claim may be demonstrably true. It will be even more seemingly true if the author himself is represented as having given a copy of his work to some friend.

Experts and dealers are wearily familiar with many of those individuals who have prepared spurious association items. But positive proof must be available before criminal charges can safely be brought. In such matters, the law is justly strict. For this reason, although certain in his knowledge of the identities of some forgers, an expert or a dealer can do little more than keep his guard and hope that at some time these malefactors will overextend themselves and be duly arrested.

The most flagrant examples of forged association items were those which came out of Chicago. They consisted of authentic pamphlets and a few books which had been in Lincoln's possession. To increase their valuation, Lincoln's signature had been forged on various pages. Parenthetically it might be said that the forgers in this manner offer their own inverted tribute to "Honest Abe." Although experts quickly did their own detective work, it is almost certain that many of the inexperienced paid handsome prices for these doctored books.

Not very many are as wise immediately after purchase of such items as was a collector who in recent years bought what he considered a once-in-a-life-time bargain. His acquisition, which had the makings of a sleeper, certainly seemed to be remarkable. He had obtained it from an auction house, which was not ordinarily reputed to conduct sales of books and autographs. This fact encouraged him to believe that he had made a find which no one else had recognized up to the time it had been auctioned together with all kinds of miscellanies. It was a small hard-back account book, bearing the seal of a stationer whom Edgar Allan Poe might easily have patronized. To judge by the book itself, without very expert study, there could be little doubt that it was unique. On the first few leaves were carefully written out petty accounts of Poe with his friends. The next few pages were devoted to an analysis of "The Raven," and towards the center of the book were several verses of this, his most famous poem. All of these were executed in a hand that closely resembled that of the poet.

The collector readily gave $150 for the account book, a price somewhat underslung in proportion to the $19,000 at which other Poe manuscripts had at times hovered. In addition, here was a treasure which apparently outshone all other Poe items. It would have, in fact, had the handwriting been that of the poet, but this was forged and very probably by Cosey. The collector's story, however, did have a happy ending. He approached an expert and, being quickly advised of what he actually had bought, was able to return the forgery to the auction house and obtain a full refund.

Had the supposed Poe account book been authentic, it would unquestionably have caused as much excitement as is caused even now by rumors that a hitherto undiscovered Shakespeare document or signature has come to light. Such rumors periodically fly about, and, when Shakespearean items are mentioned, our present day is almost as well prepared to welcome them as were Ireland's dupes. Queried as to the number of known authentic examples of Shakespeare's writing now extant, E. G. Millar, Keeper of Manuscripts in the British Museum, on October 5, 1944, advised: "I cannot do better than give you the following extract from p. 300 of Volume I of *Shakespeare's England*, Oxford, 1916 (actually from Chapter X, 'Handwriting,' by Sir E. Maunde Thompson)."

The quoted passage reads: "The only known examples, of undisputed authenticity, of Shakespeare's handwriting are six signatures attached to the following documents: 1. The poet's deposition in a suit brought by Stephen Bellott against his father-in-law, Christopher Montjoy, of Silver Street, Wood Street, in the city of London, recently discovered by Dr. C. W. Wallace in the Public Record Office: May 11, 1612;* 2. The conveyance of a house in Blackfriars, London, purchased by Shakespeare: March 10, 1613 (now in the Guildhall Library); 3. A mortgage-deed of the same property: March 11, 1613 (now in the British Museum [Egerton MS. 1787]);† 4. The poet's Will, written on three sheets of paper, and with his signature at the foot of each one: executed March 25, 1616 (now in Somerset House)."

Mr. Millar further advised that Thompson accepts all three signatures in the Will as written by Shakespeare, and quotes him as stating: "We have here an unusual instance of a writer spelling his name in two different ways. It is well known that in Shakespeare's time people were not consistent in their signatures and that they exercised considerable freedom of spelling in subscribing their names. But it is remarkable that two differently spelt signatures should be employed in one and the same document. The inconsistency may be attributable to the writer's state of health; or it may even be taken as further evidence that Shakespeare was so much in the habit of abbreviating his signature, that he was indifferent to the form of the conclusion of the name when he was required to write it in full."‡

It is not illogical to argue that, since Mr. Millar in 1944 still appealed to a book published in 1916, the British Museum and

* Purchased by the City of London in 1843 for £145.
† Purchased by British Museum in 1858 for £315.
‡ *Op. cit.*, p. 306.

other authorities—indeed practically all—are convinced that no genuine examples of Shakespeare's handwriting have appeared in the intervening years.* Very probably, few among them anticipate that the future will produce new Shakespearean items. Almost comparable to Shakespeare in rarity are Gwinnett and Lynch signatures in America. When, therefore, in 1927 a document, dated 1776 and signed by Gwinnett and other Signers, was sold for $51,000, it was to be expected that forgers would greedily scent profits. They not only did but proceeded to their kill. Even before 1927, individual examples and complete sets of the Signers had been forged and sold. In *The Collector* Mr. Benjamin editorially had denounced the sets of Signers' signatures which in 1909 were appearing on the market.

"There is a...man who lives somewhere near Amesbury, Mass.," he wrote, "[whose] specialty is forging complete sets of signatures of the Signers of the Declaration of Independence. I have seen two of these sets. The signatures are pasted side by side on a strip of grey linen about a foot wide. They are careful copies of the originals and written on old linen paper. Some, like John Hancock, are well done, but the majority are poor and would deceive no expert. One set was sold to a bookseller in Albany, another to a collector in Maine, and a third appeared at an auction sale in Philadelphia, where Mr. Simon Gratz and myself denounced it as a forgery, and it was withdrawn from the sale."†

* Numerous articles and books have been published in recent years about disputed Shakespeare manuscripts. For an interesting discussion of a signature found on the title-page of a book in the Folger Shakespeare Memorial Library in Washington, the reader is referred to an article by Dr. Joseph Quincy Adams, Director of the Library, "A New Signature of Shakespeare?" in the Bulletin of The John Rylands Library, Manchester, England, Vol. xxvii, No. 2 (June 1943), pp. 256-259. This signature, after being subjected to exhaustive microscopic, chemical, photographic and other tests available to modern science, and to a careful paleographical study, would appear to be the autograph of the poet. Authorities, however, recognizing the fact that it is practically impossible to guarantee unequivocally a signature which stands alone on a fly-leaf or blank slip of paper, hesitate under such circumstances to make any positive statement. It has not been ascertained whether, due to the war, experts at the British Museum have had the opportunity to pass judgment.

† Vol. xxiii, December 1909, p. 17.

Two years later *The Collector* reported more explicitly: "A few years ago I had some correspondence with Frank H. Percy, of Bath, Maine, in regard to a complete set of signatures of the Signers. . . . They turned out to be bold forgeries and the matter ended. . . . One of them has now turned up again. It was offered to Mrs. Garret A. Hobart, the wife of the late Vice-president. It was as usual on a brown linen roll, and several of the signatures were very fine copies, and this time one was genuine, Oliver Wolcott. It was accompanied by a letter addressed to Frank H. Percy, of Bath, Maine, stating that it had been found in an old attic, and that the writer wished to sell, and had sent it to Mr. Percy, knowing he dealt in antiquities. This was signed B. D. Wadleigh, of 479 Main St., Amesbury, Mass. I would be glad to learn if there is any such person as Wadleigh at the address specified."[*]

Probably it was one of these sets, mentioned by *The Collector*, that a dealer recently examined at the request of its owner, a well-known Eastern collector. Several of the signatures were unquestionably genuine, but for the far greater part they were forgeries. In a different category, but also spurious, have been papers bearing upon the New England witchcraft trials of the late seventeenth century, and purporting to be original depositions, which have repeatedly appeared for about the past fifteen years. Certain indications lead to the belief that they were forged in Chicago and peddled to private collectors throughout the Middle West for prices ranging from $100 to $1,000. The idea has been further advanced that the forger, or forgers, attempted to imitate a series of authentic witchcraft documents reproduced in Charles W. Upham's *Salem Witchcraft*. [†] These forgeries are very clumsy. They give themselves away in the first place by the fact that the language in the body of the document is illiterate while those who were associated with the trials were educated men. The paper used was treated to make it look age worn and was probably soaked in coffee or some similar liquid that accentuated the dark markings of the creases. The paper itself

[*] Vol. xxv, November 1911, p. 2.
[†] Wiggin and Lunt, Boston, 1867.

bears no resemblance to that used in the many authentic 1692 documents owned by the Essex Institute of Salem, Massachusetts. The handwriting on these is unusually plain but is very dim on the forgeries. Lastly, the forgers in many cases invented names for their signers with complete disregard for history. Actually one of these ineptitudes absurdly included the name of King Philip, the Indian chief, who had died in 1675 and who probably had very different ideas about witchcraft and what should be done with witches.

Many similar episodes are not infrequently encountered in the shop-talk of the autograph world. They can be told extremely entertainingly when leisure permits the introduction of full details plus related "asides." For the beginner, they may possibly have their frightening aspects, but the fear need not exist if ordinary care and common sense are shown in the proper placing of confidence. The autograph collector and forgeries might be compared to the child and fire. He is not sent from the room because the fireplace logs are lighted; instead he is cautioned and either is amenable to the words of those he trusts or else must learn by being burned. Fire, of course, has its marvelously good uses; forgeries have none. The dealer, like the child-cautioning parent when himself careless, may also be caught napping and be burned. Should this occur, however, his clients never suffer with him, for he will always make good his mistake.

CHAPTER VII

Facsimiles, Reproductions and Manuscript Copies

WITH the invention of lithographing, electroplating, photostating, photo-offsetting and other methods of reproducing handwriting, the use of facsimiles has become as popular as it is common. There are few today who are not acquainted with advertisements, charity appeals, bank and industrial statements which include a letter with the facsimile signature of some prominent chairman or high official. The custom in itself is an implicit recognition of public interest, however small, in autographs. The duplicated signature is believed to carry an appeal which the printed name lacks. Similarly, a completely reproduced A. L. S. is considered an even more effective, although more expensive, circulation item.

Since early English dictionaries define a facsimile as "an exact copy or likeness," obviously facsimiles existed long before many of the currently used processes of reproduction were known. And whereas a facsimile is always a reproduction, the reverse is not strictly true. A facsimile of a letter is accurately an exact copy of it in size and contents. The color of ink and type of paper are at rare intervals approximated. One that is smaller than the original should be more specifically defined as a printed, photographic or lithographic reproduction. Facsimile, however, is a generic word, and it is as often used loosely as strictly.

Facsimiles and reproductions, whether these be of handwritten, typed or printed copies or drafts of manuscripts, documents and letters, have always been the concern of the autograph expert. Newspapers occasionally publish some notable letter in full, either duplicating the handwriting throughout or printing the text and concluding with a signature facsimile. Books and magazines of historical interest freely enliven their pages with reproduced letters and maps. Compilers of biographical dictionaries quite often include the subject's picture and an example of his signature. This practice has resulted in the mistaken purchase of many prints, etchings and steel engravings, which are accompanied by the properly duplicated signature of the famous.

Although it should be apparent that these facsimile signatures are not original autographs, the autograph expert is repeatedly puzzled by the fact that many of the public seemingly make no distinction. Time after time sheets, torn from some book in which A.L.S.s were reproduced, are offered as originals to dealers. Those who offer them for sale are at least unrealistic in not arriving at the simple conclusion that, had many prominent men and women undertaken such wholesale signing, it would have had to be a full-time job for them.

In the majority of cases, facsimile reproductions can easily be recognized. There remain many others which present problems and difficulties to librarians, autograph collectors and dealers alike. Whereas an original letter can never be mistaken for a facsimile, the latter can be, and often is, passed off as the original. At times reproductions have reached such a degree of perfection in simulating color, ink, type of paper and other details that only the sharpest scrutiny will reveal their true nature. The craft of the forger in such instances provides no more pitfalls than the zeal of a good printer to perfect his handiwork. That the latter should get a rating of "Excellent" for his work and the honesty of his intentions is a fact which will not cheer collectors who years after pay handsome sums for his items and then learn they do not own genuine originals.

A number of clever facsimiles of famous letters turn up with unfailing regularity and are offered for sale. Not at all infrequently some are eagerly bought. One of the most common is Lord Byron's letter, April 27, 1819, to Galignani, editor of *Galignani's Messenger*, 18 Rue Vivienne, Paris, an example of which was at one time purchased at auction for $42 by a man who definitely thought it was the original. Chancellor Bismarck's letters, acknowledging birthday greetings, which he received by the hundreds, are almost invariably facsimile. The famous German statesman could hardly have been expected, in his advanced years, to have written out these notes in longhand. Facsimiles of Schiller, Walter Scott, Admiral Nelson, Robert Burns and others have all been sources of trouble in this manner. Washingtons are also common and repeatedly come on the market, especially pages, running into many folio sheets, from his expense account with the United States Government.

Another facsimile of an interesting and unusual letter occasionally crops up. The original, owned by the Library of Congress, was written by Benjamin Franklin from Philadelphia, July 5, 1775, and addressed but never sent to his friend of many years, William Strahan, English printer and publisher of Samuel Johnson's *Dictionary*. Word that Strahan had been elected to Parliament reached America not long before the battles of Lexington and Bunker Hill and provoked Franklin to write Strahan in an outburst of indignation and anger: "You are a member of Parliament, and one of that Majority which has doomed my Country to Destruction. You have begun to burn our towns and murder our People. Look upon your Hands! They are stained with the Blood of your Relations. You and I were long Friends. You are now my Enemy, and I am Yours, B. Franklin." This dramatic letter, not surprisingly, has also attracted the forger, who has succeeded in fooling collectors with varying degrees of success.

The Chicago Historical Society owns the original octavo, six-line note, dated Charlestown, Virginia, December 2, 1859, which John Brown, a few hours before he was hanged, handed to his prison guard, Hiram O. Bannon, and which reads: "I John Brown am now quite *certain* that the crimes of this *guilty land will* never be purged *away*, but with Blood. I had *as I now think vainly* flattered myself that without *very much* bloodshed it might be done." This note, together with his entire collection, was presented to the Society by Frank G. Logan. In 1890 these Brown facsimiles were appearing on the market, a fact which caused *The Collector** to issue an immediate and appropriate warning. It is impossible to estimate the number of collectors who since that time have bought them. Could the purchasers compare experiences with one another they would be forced to conclude either that their items are spurious or,

* Vol. IV, October 1890, p. 14.

which is preposterous, that Brown spent the short time before the gallows duplicating his own note. Another facsimile of Brown that often appears is the two-page A. L. S., quarto size, addressed to the Reverend Luther Humphrey and dated from Charlestown, Jefferson County, Virginia, November 13, 1859. Stating that he has no regrets, shame or fear of being hanged, it is a letter of extraordinary courage, written with obvious disregard of the death he faced.

"I am in bed and in the least gallant and the least grateful frame of mind conceivable," Robert Louis Stevenson began a letter to a Mrs. Ehrich. The original of this A. L. S. was formerly owned by Elmer Adler, who presented it to the Stevenson Society of Saranac, in New York. Before he did so, he had struck off for his friends a number of excellent facsimiles which so skillfully imitate shading, ink, paper and other qualities that the facsimile items, offered on the market, have trapped many, including a few dealers. One of the latter paid $35 for an example at an auction sale in 1931.

The most common of all facsimiles which has appeared recently is a one-page A. L. S. of Thomas Jefferson, which begins: "If my note for D. 558.14 paiable the 15th of Dec. is still in your hands, I should be very glad if it could be either postponed a while or paid by monthly portions... ." Jefferson dated this letter Washington, November 27, 1803, and addressed it to his agent, Craven Peyton, at Stumpisland, near Milton, Virginia. The frequency with which this item is offered for sale is not surprising in view of the fact that some years ago a Staunton, Virginia, bank issued as an advertisement a splendid and realistic reproduction that includes even the franked Jefferson signature with postal markings.

A letter of King George V of England, which constituted a handwritten address of welcome to American soldiers en route to the battlefronts of the First World War, was reproduced, and copies still plague many of the unwary. Signed "George R. I." and dated at Windsor Castle, April 1918, the message reads as follows: "Soldiers of the United States, the people of the British Isles welcome you on your way to your stand beside the Armies of many Nations now fighting in the Old World the great battle for human freedom. The Allies will gain new heart and spirit in your company. I wish that I could shake the hand of each one of you and bid you God speed on your mission." At the top of the page, which is an octavo sheet, appears the monarch's crest, but on ordinary reproductions both the crest and the type are flush with the paper. Some facsimiles sport an embossed crest which adds a touch of verisimilitude and another point for confusion. Such items are generally offered for sale by American veterans of the last war.

Some of these men unquestionably realize what they possess, and this is likewise true of those who own facsimile copies of the Declaration of Independence. Facsimiles of this most important of all American documents, believed to be genuine originals by their owners, are offered for sale more often perhaps than any others. Dr. John Franklin Jamieson, former Chief of the Manuscript Division of the Library of Congress, once ruefully declared that the weekly mail included at least one letter offering such "originals." In most cases the letters reported that the "manuscript" had been rummaged out of an old trunk or chest of drawers, and very likely it had, for the age of the facsimile need not be questioned. Its owner, being informed that a Button Gwinnett was found in a Bible long stored in an attic and was sold at auction for $51,000, is convinced that he can make his fortune with his "original." In reality, the true one can be seen by any visitor to the Library of Congress who cares to ascend to the second floor where the document is carefully guarded and displayed.

Records show that throughout the years many facsimiles and reproductions of the Declaration of Independence have been made. Congress in 1823 authorized the first, a lot of two hundred, which was engraved by W. J. Stone of Washington, D. C. This was identical in all respects save for the ink and the material on which it was reproduced—paper instead of parchment. Two copies were presented to each of the surviving Signers, two each to the then President and Vice-President and two each to former President Madison and General Lafayette. The balance were given to governors of states and various officials, and twenty went to the two houses of Congress itself. At widely spaced intervals, one of these true facsimiles, occasionally signed by its original owner, appears on the market. The first reproductions, not exact facsimiles as was the Stone edition, were made by Benjamin O. Tyler in 1818. In the same year John Binns issued another and at the time criticized Tyler's work in comparison with his own. Neither, however, could be classed as true facsimiles. These and other subsequent reproductions, including some with decorative borders in color or with patriotic scenes, generally carry either the mark of the printer or other notation which shows clearly the commemorative or advertising purpose that was being served.

A puzzling point about the Stone first facsimiles is explained by Dr. St. George L. Sioussat, Chief of the Division of Manuscripts at the Library of Congress, who wrote in 1945: "...the early Stone facsimiles bear the name of the engraver and authorization of the Department of State at the top of the reproduction; while the later ones carry only the name of Stone as engraver (and no authorization) on the lower part of the document. This was apparently to permit Stone to reproduce *ad libitum* .... From personal inspection of the copper-plate, I am convinced that the suggestion of Dr. [Roscoe R.] Hill of The National Archives is correct, viz: that the older line at the top was obliterated and the new line on the lower part engraved *on the same plate;* but I know of no contemporary documentary proof." On a page of a copy of John H. Hazelton's comprehensive book, *The Declaration of Independence, Its History,** preserved by the New York Public Library in its "American History Room," Dr. Wilberforce Eames, the Library's former Bibliographer, initialed a penciled note stating that he had seen a facsimile similar to Stone's bearing the inscription "Anastatic Fac-simile."

Although original *manuscript* copies of the Declaration of Independence exist, there is only the one original with authentic signatures of all the Signers. These signatures were not, as

* Dodd, Mead & Co., New York, 1906.

is generally supposed, appended to the document on July 4, 1776. James Truslow Adams, in the *Dictionary of American History*, explains that the copy included in the Journal of Congress for that date bears only the name of John Hancock. On July 19, Congress resolved that the Declaration be "fairly engrossed," and on August 2, it "being engrossed and compared at the table was signed by the members." Certain members who were absent on August 2 signed at a later date. As a matter of fact, several Signers were not members of Congress on July 4, and a few were not authorized by their states to vote for independence at that time.

There were contemporary manuscript copies of the final draft and of earlier drafts, each of which played its part in the final wording itself. Manuscript copies of the Declaration in its final form were of many kinds. Perhaps those written in unknown hands which appear periodically on the market are least significant, although none may be considered unimportant. The degree of interest is in proportion to the fame of the writer who copies it. The William L. Clements Library at Ann Arbor, Michigan, for example, has two copies that were sent to Lord George Germain. Unfortunately, the identity of the man who took the pains to transcribe them is unknown. Equally unidentified was a copy recently sold at auction, which was included among the James McHenry papers. There is no telling how many of these unidentified copies may still be in hiding. So-called "authenticated copies" were issued by order of Congress early in 1777 to the various states. These, however, were *printed* in Baltimore by Mary Katherine Goddard, the only written portions being endorsements by Hancock, President of the Congress, and Charles Thomson, Permanent Secretary.

Unparalled in importance, perhaps, were the official manuscript copies sent to the various reigning monarchs of Europe. The one dispatched to Frederick the Great, written in an unknown hand but attested by the American Commissioners in Europe, Benjamin Franklin and Silas Deane, is now owned by Dr. Rosenbach. On November 8, 1776, Deane wrote to the Count of Vergennes, the French Minister of Foreign Affairs:

"In Obedience to the orders of the honorable Congress... I have the honor to deliver to Your Excellency the enclosed Declaration of Independence of the United States of North America, and to inform you that... I was assured that the Congress were unanimous in this important resolution . . . ."* The manuscript copy sent to France, † again in an unknown hand but believed to have been signed by both Hancock and Thomson, was preserved in the French Archives of the Ministry of Foreign Affairs at least up to the invasion of France in 1940, and may still be extant.

Concerning a third copy, signed by Franklin, Dr. Boyd wrote: "About the same time Franklin sent a copy to the King of Spain... and the Spanish copy was accidentally discovered in the archives of the Indies at Seville about ten or fifteen years ago. I understand this discovery was made by a Princeton professor, since dead, and that efforts to locate the copy in the archives of the Indies have failed."

Any of these three copies may be considered second only in value to the original drafts described by Dr. Boyd in his scholarly history, *The Declaration of Independence, The Evolution of the Text*, in which he not only gives the full details of the various drafts and related documents but uses splendid reproductions to illustrate his text. This definitive work was published by the Library of Congress in 1943, in conjunction with an exhibit of the drafts, to commemorate the two hundredth anniversary of Jefferson's birth.

The earliest document having a direct bearing on the Declaration which Dr. Boyd cites is George Mason's draft of the Virginia Bill of Rights, thought to have influenced Jefferson's own composition. The draft is included among the Library of Congress's collection of Mason papers. Three drafts of a constitution, the first of which Jefferson sent in 1776 to the Virginia Convention, and which contain his "first ideas," are also owned by the same library and included among its Jefferson papers. If these drafts are considered as one document—their substance is more or less identical—they collectively constitute

* See B. F. Stevens Facsimiles, No. 592.

† B. F. Stevens, *Chronological Index*, Vol. xxxix, Arch. Aff. Etr. E. U. 1:34.

the second document. The third document relating to the Declaration listed by Dr. Boyd is the Resolution of Independence handwritten by Richard Henry Lee. This Resolution was submitted to Congress on June 7, 1776 and adopted July 2. Jefferson, in making his own draft, so Dr. Boyd recounts, did not adhere to the exact terms of the Lee Resolution in the final words of the Declaration, but Congress restored them. The Library of Congress preserves the Lee original among its Continental Congress Papers.

The fourth document is a copy of the actual Declaration, written in longhand by John Adams from Jefferson's original draft. Adams is believed to have sent this copy to his wife. It is today preserved in the Adams family papers owned by the Massachusetts Historical Society.

The fifth document is Jefferson's rough draft of the Declaration itself which also is included in this statesman's papers at the Library of Congress. "This great document," Dr. Boyd declares, "represents the form in which Jefferson submitted it, together with all corrections, additions, and deletions made by Adams and Franklin, by the Committee of Five, and by the Congress." Commenting in a letter, he further wrote: "There are probably in existence some other drafts of the Declaration of Independence in Jefferson's handwriting and there certainly ought to be at least one floating around in Europe, but the copies in the brochure are the only ones that are known up to the present." Anyone who is fond of building autograph day-dreams can entertain himself with fancies of discovering this lost paper.

The sixth document is a copy of the Declaration made by Jefferson for, and originally sent on July 8, 1776 to, Richard Henry Lee. This copy was presented in 1825 by Lee's grandson to the American Philosophical Society of Philadelphia, which has treasured it ever since.

An unidentified copy of the Declaration, also in Jefferson's hand and referred to as "the Cassius F. Lee copy," is the seventh document in Dr. Boyd's listing. There is good reason to suppose that it is the one Jefferson sent to George Wythe, another Virginia Signer. It was first sold by Cassius F. Lee to Eliot Danforth, who sold it to Dr. Emmet, from whom the New York Public Library, now the owner, purchased it.

The eighth document, now among the Madison Papers in the Library of Congress, is another copy of the Declaration, made also by Jefferson for James Madison. It was prepared at a considerably later date—the spring of 1783—and was enclosed with a letter Jefferson wrote to Madison on June 1, 1783.

The ninth, and final, document Dr. Boyd describes is another unidentified copy of the Declaration made by Jefferson. The original attending circumstances and its provenance throughout most of the last century are still undetermined. Known as "the Washburn copy," it was presented by Mr. and Mrs. Alexander C. Washburn in 1893 to its present owner, the Massachusetts Historical Society.

Hazelton, quoting Charles Francis Adams, states that a copy of the final Declaration, in the handwriting of Franklin and similar to the one made by John Adams, had been discovered in England and was said to be at that time in the hands of an American gentleman in London. Dr. Boyd reports that he did not discuss this document because he was unable to locate it.

These nine documents—eleven if that Dr. Boyd lists as the second is considered as three rather than one—are of such preeminent historic importance that it is logical they should now all be owned by institutions. Actually the fewness of the drafts, of which there may have been others long since lost, had nothing at all to do with keeping full knowledge of the final form of the Declaration from the public. The earliest official printing of the Declaration was ordered by Congress on July 4, 1776, and is believed to have been made during the night of July 4-5 by John Dunlap of Philadelphia. These copies, sent out to the various committees of safety, the commanding officers of the American troops and others, bore only Hancock's name since the document had not at that time been signed by the other members of Congress. Thereafter it was quickly quoted in full in many publications and soon found its way into textbooks and all manner of historical and reference works.

Had other manuscript draft copies of the Declaration existed beyond those listed by Dr. Boyd, it is highly improbable that they could have eluded scholars and historians throughout the years. The extremely remote possibility that some new related paper may be discovered in our time explains why Dr. Jamieson, or any other librarian or dealer, undergoes no quickening of pulse when a letter arrives offering an original copy signed by all the Signers. Should this prove to be one of the 1823 Stone facsimiles, however, dealers and collectors are at least interested. It has its own individual value, both because of its rarity and because it may bear some additional and prizable signature of one of the original recipients. The earliest facsimiles of Jefferson's original draft, published at Charlottesville in 1829 and showing the corrections and interlineations, may also arouse interest. The autograph world entertains the hope that an item of this kind may appear on the market, yet it recognizes that this may occur only once in a generation.

Perhaps there is no other document equal in importance and fame to the Declaration of Independence except Magna Carta, granted by King John in 1215 and generally regarded as the "Charter of Liberties" upon which the social and political freedom of the British people is based. The original, now exhibited in the British Museum, bears the seal of the King, who could not write, and of a large number of the nobles whose insistence and threats forced the sovereign's acceptance. This document, according to a story that may be a romantic invention, published in the *Philadelphia Press*, would have been lost but for the keenness of observation of an antiquarian and collector of autographs. He visited his tailor and found the man about to cut up a piece of old parchment to be used for "measures." Examined, the parchment proved to be Magna Carta, and, after the necessary arrangements had been made, it was surrendered as property of the nation.

Many persons have been puzzled because there are two "originals" of Magna Carta in the British Museum. The two are not to be explained, however, as are the two skulls of Oliver Cromwell, one formerly shown in the Ashmolean Museum at Oxford, the other in Cambridge. The second, being comparatively undersized, was represented by a former exhibitor as "the head of Cromwell—when he was a boy." Instead, the Magna Carta pair in the British Museum collection are both original copies of the charter. Actually, numerous copies for distribution among the counties were made in 1215, and one was sent to each cathedral with orders that it be publicly read therein three times a year. The most accurate and complete, still preserved in Lincoln Cathedral, was brought to America and exhibited in the British Pavilion of the New York World's Fair in 1939-1940.

Facsimiles of much less note than those of the Declaration are always bobbing up in sales and are by comparison considerably more troublesome to the collector. Reproductions of letters or quotations of Emerson, Longfellow, Lincoln, Lowell and Mark Twain, among countless others, are almost as plentiful as daffodils in a florist's shop during spring. Most of these were unquestionably made with the sole purpose of providing an illustration of the handwriting characteristics of some well-known person. Particularly common are the friendly autograph albums in which some of the pages carried facsimile signatures of poets and authors, or even extracts from their best-known poems. These might be interspersed with blank pages, which the owner could plan to have signed by his friends and contemporary celebrities. Common sense again should point out that poets of vastly different periods could hardly all sign these leaves within the brief life span of one individual collector, nor would they all have used the same color and shading of ink.

Suspicion that there was an intent of fraud in a few cases of such facsimiles is warranted. This is true of a facsimile of a one-page folio letter written by Christopher Columbus from Seville, December 27, 1504, to Nicolo Oderigo, now preserved in the New York Public Library Manuscript Division. The original is in the Palazzo Municipale of Genoa, and a reproduction of it was included by Cesare de Lolis in his *Scritti di Cristoforo Colombo.** The facsimile owned by the New York Public Library,

* Reale Commissione Columbiana, Rome, 1594, pp. 246-247.

however, could not have been extracted from a copy of this book, for it is not only of similar size to that of the original manuscript but is carefully executed on old rag paper. Ordinary facsimiles, especially when issued by libraries, are rarely attempted on this type of paper, and consequently the authorities suspect an ulterior motive in the manufacture of the New York item.

Among facsimiles there must also be classified those reproductions of a signature made by hand-stamp. Unlike a printed signature, its impress is affected by an eradicator which causes the ink to fade. Whereas the printed facsimile is logically used on form letters issued in the thousands, it is inappropriate for large correspondences of a semi-private, private or other nature. The stamp, now usually rubber rather than steel, undoubtedly originated as an aid to the harassed executive, has proved most serviceable and has been resorted to by many, including Woodrow Wilson and both Presidents Roosevelt. Actually for some a stamp proved to be an even greater necessity. President Andrew Johnson, for example, had a badly crippled right arm, and it was a physical impossibility for him during his tenure to sign his name to the innumerable state papers, and military and naval commissions, which then customarily carried the president's signature. Accordingly, a perfect reproduction of Johnson's signature was made, and his secretary used the stamp thereafter on authorized occasions.

An original document signed by Andrew Johnson as President in his own hand has a definite value in today's market, but the same item, having instead the stamped signature, is unsalable. There may be some technical discussion of the authenticity versus validity of President Johnson's impressed signature. Certainly the official papers, which carried the stamp signature, whether affixed by the President himself or his secretary, are in every instance attested by a member of the Cabinet—either the Secretary of the State, Treasury, War or Navy department—when he certified to the genuineness of the signature over the seal of the United States. Despite this guarantee, collectors, since the signature is not handwritten, refuse to accept it as an authentic autograph and will never, if they are aware of it, include an example in their collections.*

However curious or sentimental this may seem, the fact remains that it is extremely difficult to distinguish the Johnson stamp and other stamps from an authentic ink signature. This is particularly true if the stamp is on vellum, as was the case with many commissions. The color of the ink pad is definitely the chief reason for the difficulty. Red and purple ink almost immediately suggest the stamp, but certain shades of blue and black are more realistic and convincing.

The market has not infrequently been visited by reproductions which in content are the same as the original but actually are facsimiles of forged copies of the original. Among the most outstanding instances of this type are the numerous reproductions of the Bixby letter, whose history is as extraordinary as the contents are well known. There are few Americans who are not familiar with its words, and many can quote them partially at least from memory. The letter, to which frequent references are made by the orator, the editor and many other writers, is as follows:

"I have been shown in the files of the War Department a statement of the Adjutant-General of Massachusetts that you are the mother of five sons who have died gloriously on the field of battle. I feel how weak and fruitless must be any word of mine which should attempt to beguile you from the grief of a loss so overwhelming. But I can not refrain from tendering you the consolation that may be found in the thanks of the republic they died to save. I pray that our Heavenly Father may assuage the anguish of your bereavement, and leave you only the cherished memory of the loved and lost, and the solemn pride that must be yours to have laid so costly a sacrifice upon the altar of freedom."

These words are practically universally accepted as those of Abraham Lincoln, and the many reproductions carry the date, "Executive Mansion, Washington, Nov. 21, 1864"; the address, "To Mrs. Bixby, Boston, Mass., Dear Madam"; and the con-

*Depending on the contents, such items have sold for $50.

clusion "Yours very sincerely and respectfully," followed by the signature "A. Lincoln." Librarians and experts in the autograph field have for many years accepted the fact that an original Lincoln-Bixby letter existed. The core of the authorities' question is: Was the Bixby letter originally an L. S. or an A. L. S.? Was it written in the handwriting of Lincoln at all? Was it even signed by him?

There is nothing in their position which throws any doubt on the fact that the words are Lincoln's. These superbly expressed thoughts, both from the standpoint of their nature and their phrasing, are as typical of him as are those of the Gettysburg Address. Equally certain are the authorities that all reproductions which have come forward have definitely been facsimiles of a forgery. The years have kept silence on this enigma, and perhaps it may never be solved.

Its history begins in September 1862, a few days after the Battle of Antietam, when Mrs. Lydia Bixby, a woman in her sixties, consulted General William Schouler, then the Adjutant-General of Massachusetts. She stated that one of her sons had been wounded, and she could not follow her wish to go to nurse him because she lacked the needed money. Her plea was successful—the necessary amount of $40 was provided by Schouler who had obtained it from John A. Andrew, the Massachusetts Governor. Within two years the grateful woman again called on General Schouler, and he reported to the Governor that she had then shown him five letters from five different commanding officers, each informing her of the death of one of her five sons.

The Governor was as deeply impressed as Schouler had been, and he had copies of the documents in the case made and sent them to the War Department, himself penning this endorsement: "This is a case so remarkable that I really wish a letter might be written by the President of the United States, such as a noble mother of five dead sons so well deserves." Washington replied with a request to Schouler for additional information concerning the names, regiments and other details of the Bixby brothers, which was furnished on October 12, 1864, after a lapse of time that indicated Schouler had probably had difficulty in obtaining the requested information. It is possible thereafter that Secretary of War Stanton himself took the papers to the President who, understandably enough since his reelection was so imminent, did not write until November 21.

His letter evidently was sent to Mrs. Bixby care of General Schouler, who personally delivered it to her on Thanksgiving Day and promptly released the text to the *Boston Transcript*, *The Boston Advertiser* and the *Army and Navy Journal* of New York. The original has never been seen since. Although Mrs. Bixby dropped out of sight, the records show that she resided in Boston and Providence, where her addresses changed repeatedly. Was the letter lost in consequence of one of these moves or did she destroy it? It is not known to be in any library or private collection nor is it among the Lincoln Papers in the Library of Congress nor possessed by the Massachusetts Historical Society.

In 1926, after exhaustive research on the Bixby letter, William E. Barton published *A Beautiful Blunder,** devoted entirely to the discussion of this much agitated subject. His title referred not to any mistake in attributing authorship to Lincoln but to the fact, which he well demonstrates, that Mrs. Bixby's story of the deaths of her five sons was, as Mark Twain would put it, "exaggerated." General Schouler's dossier on the Bixbys shows that Sergeant Charles had been killed at Fredericksburg, May 3, 1863; Corporal Henry, at Gettysburg, in July 1863; Private Oliver, before Petersburg, July 30, 1864; Private George Way, at the same time and place as his brother Oliver; and Private Edward had died of wounds at Folly Island, South Carolina. The record adduced by Mr. Barton is not quite so glorious. Only Charles and Oliver were killed as stated.

Henry had been captured on July 2 at Gettysburg, was imprisoned for a time at Richmond, somehow found his way back north, returned to his regiment, was honorably discharged in December 1864 and is recorded as having died on November 8, 1871. Edward, who had volunteered for the army, changed his mind and deserted in May 1862, returned to Boston, where

* Bobbs-Merrill Co., Indianapolis, Indiana.

he lived briefly with his mother, then wandered to Illinois and died of pleurisy on January 4, 1909. George Way Bixby, who dropped his surname, supposedly to deceive his wife whom he had deserted, enlisted, jumped bounty once or twice—a popular and profitable pastime during the Civil War—and was captured, not killed, before Petersburg. Mr. Barton quotes records which show that he had died in the prison of that town well after Lee's surrender, but one report states that he had deserted to the enemy at Salisbury, North Carolina.

Mr. Barton seemingly does not agree with the solution to the Bixby enigma which is offered by Dr. Nicholas Murray Butler in *Across the Busy Years.** This book describes an incident when John Morley, M. P., while visiting President Theodore Roosevelt in 1904, occupied a guest room in the White House. The English parliamentarian was so impressed by a framed reproduction of the Bixby letter hung in this room that while in Washington he mentioned his admiration to John Hay, formerly secretary to Lincoln and then Secretary of State. Hay promptly confided that he had written the letter himself, a fact which, he explained, accounted for its non-appearance among Lincoln's papers and the subsequent failure to produce the original. Morley, who had promised to guard the secret until after Hay's death, told the story in 1912 to Dr. Butler, when the condition had been removed, but in turn asked that it be kept in confidence until his own death. Where there is secrecy on matters which cannot be substantiated by records, suspicion is inevitable. Mr. Barton, apparently aware of the story, examined it and states clearly: "I have made diligent inquiry of the family of John Hay, and...they, who ought to know of this if anyone knows, profess to have no knowledge that supports such a claim."

The charges and countercharges, the speculations and uncertainties, which surround the Bixby letter might have little more than academic interest for the autograph collector were it not for the reproductions. Apparently the *Boston Globe*, of April 12, 1908, was the first daily newspaper to reproduce it.

* Vol. ii, pp. 391-392.

But on April 25, 1891, Michael F. Tobin of New York City, who sold pictures and prints, applied to the Librarian of Congress for registration of an "engraving" entitled "Lincoln's Letter," although it might more specifically have been called "The Lincoln-Bixby Letter." Soon thereafter Huber's Museum, located on East Fourteenth Street in New York, displayed what it claimed to be the original Bixby letter. Huber also sold reproductions of it, but in his copies, which obviously were not made from the authentic original, there were numerous variations in the formation of certain of the characters as well as variations from Tobin's copy. Did Tobin or Huber then write out in each case a rough copy of the wording, themselves forging the original of the reproduction or did they employ some clever handwriting copyist? The question can only be answered through a comparison with the original which was handed to Mrs. Bixby, and which seemingly she treated with little care. Were it now available, very many papers based on the forged facsimiles would disappear from the market where they have for over a half century plagued both customer and seller.

Not so famous as the Bixby letter, a lithographic facsimile of a forged copy of the Thirteenth Amendment has also played hob with some collectors in recent years. This facsimile, erroneously believed to be an original, carries signatures of Lincoln; his first Vice-President, Hannibal Hamlin; the Speaker of the House, Schuyler Colfax; the Secretary of the Senate, J. W. Forney, and numerous senators and congressmen. It was so skillfully executed that experts believed it to be an original forgery until they resorted to the ink-eradicator test, which revealed it for what it was—a facsimile of a forgery.

Many newspapers during the second half of the last century carried columns headed "Autography" or "The Science of Autography," as autograph collecting was then termed. These often were more informal than the "science" of the title implied. Besides news items and "shop gossip," they included reproductions of signatures and letters of the renowned. Edgar Allan Poe conducted such a column in *Graham's Magazine*, which he once edited. This activity of the poet is familiar to many, but not the fact that he himself collected autographs. Professor Thomas Olive Mabbott of Hunter College points out that Poe's collector status is proved by an advertisement *Graham's* inserted in the *Saturday Evening Post* of December 4, 1841. The advertisement called attention to its editor's column and added the promise that autographs of American writers were to be engraved "from Mr. Poe's unrivalled collection." The engravings naturally were to appear in the magazine as reproductions.

Ben Perley Poore, editor and proprietor of the *American Sentinel*, also wrote an "Autography" column for his paper, and in later years he ran a new section devoted to the same subject in *Gleason's Pictorial Drawing Room Companion* and other journals. Many of his reproductions are obvious forgeries. In fact, they are so numerous it is unbelievable that he himself should have been caught so repeatedly. It is more likely that when he wished to illustrate a certain letter and was unable to obtain a facsimile of it, he resorted to tracings of originals which, in turn, he reproduced.

Reprints or reproductions of old newspapers are not properly autographs, but certain examples appear on the market so commonly that they are occasionally handled by dealers. The New York Public Library issued an excellent brochure in 1931, "A List of American Newspaper Reprints," written by Joseph Gavit, formerly State Librarian at Albany. Among those in this list, which doubtless has been enlarged since, the two which are seen with a fair degree of regularity include *The Ulster County* [N. Y.] *Gazette* of January 4, 1800, and the *Vicksburg Daily Citizen* of July 4, 1863. These are a constant source of disappointment to many people, which is not the case with the *Boston News-Letter* of April 24, 1704; the *New York Morning Post* of November 7, 1783, giving Washington's farewell to the army; the *New York Herald* of April 15, 1865, or other less widely circulated newspapers, since they appear infrequently.

There were in 1930 over sixty known reprint issues of the *Ulster County Gazette* containing an account of Washington's death. Although these would add up probably to more than a million copies, not a single original was then known to exist. So numerous were the inquiries which the New York Public Library received from actual or prospective purchasers of this paper, that it issued in 1930 a special brochure compiled and written by Dr. R. W. G. Vail, the former Director of the New York Historical Society. Therein he described in detail, and reproduced in facsimile, the known reprints, of which the first, a memorial number, appeared in 1825. Obviously, since no copy of the original paper had been located, no facsimile of it then existed.

In the following year, Dr. Vail, once again under the auspices of the New York Public Library, issued another pamphlet, "The Ulster County Gazette Found at Last." An authentic copy, after one hundred and thirty years, had finally been acquired by the Library of Congress, and in April 1945, Dr. Vail further revealed that a second, now owned by the American Antiquarian Society of Worcester, Massachusetts, had since been found. He also stated that today more than one hundred reprints of the *Gazette* are known, the first facsimile undoubtedly having been made from the original soon after it had reached the Library of Congress.

Collectors who wish to determine authenticity of copies they may own of the *Gazette* will find that Dr. Vail lists differences, too numerous to be cited, which serve as ready guides. Important among them is the fact that a genuine original must have the following reading for page 1, column 4, line 1: "command the town; and notwithstanding." Again, the name of the paper must be printed in slanting italic type. The fact that copies are on rag paper is no assurance of genuineness since many of the reprints were made on that type of paper stock. Definitive information about how to distinguish this and other original newspapers from their later reproductions is provided in excellent one-page circulars, one for each of the well-known reproduced papers, which the Library of Congress mails to all inquirers.

Somewhat similar problems of distinguishing between originals and reprints exist in the case of the *Vicksburg Daily Citi-*

zen. Because of the unique circumstances of its issuance, many so-called reprints have been made of it. Vicksburg, then the one Mississippi Valley key fortress left to the Confederacy, had been besieged by Generals Grant and Sherman for many months before it dramatically surrendered on July 4, one day after the victory at Gettysburg. Starvation forced this capitulation, and the presses of the *Citizen* during the siege, like the Vicksburgers, had been fed on a strange diet. Lacking newsprint, its editor and publisher, J. M. Sword, had issued one-page editions on the reverse side of wall-paper.

When Union soldiers entered the deserted *Citizen* plant, they found type set for the issue of July 2, complete with the following humorous, yet resolute and defiant, comment: *"On dit.—* That the great Ulysses—the Yankee Generalisomo, surnamed Grant—has expressed his intention of dining in Vicksburg on Saturday next, and celebrating the 4th of July by a grand dinner and so forth. When asked if he would invite Gen. Jo. Johnston to join he said, 'No! for fear there will be a row at the table.' Ulysses must get into the city before he dines in it. The way to cook a rabbit is 'first to catch the rabbit'.... ."

Among the victorious Union soldiers evidently was one who had an equal sense of humor, for he wrote an addenda to the comment, which was headed simply "Note" and read: "Two days bring about great changes. The banner of the Union floats over Vicksburg. Gen. Grant has 'caught the rabbit'; he has dined in Vicksburg, and he did bring his dinner with him. The 'Citizen' lives to see it. For the last time it appears on Wall-paper! No more will it eulogize the luxury of mule-meat and fricasséd kitten—urge Southern warriors to such diet never-more. This is the last wall-paper edition, and is, excepting this note, from the types as we found them. It will be valuable hereafter as a curiosity." Type was then shifted and deleted to make room for this "Note," and the edition was run off on July 4.

The prediction of the "Note" was fulfilled. The Library of Congress, probably because of many inquiries, specially treated the *Citizen* in an information circular describing certain methods to distinguish the originals from reprints. The main difference between the two, aside from the fact that the reprints show variations in typographical errors, occurs in the design of the wallpaper. The circular details three distinct patterns used for the original edition.

On the other hand, Eric Morrell, formerly associated with the New York Public Library, who has made an exhaustive sixteen-year study of the *Citizen*, states that wall-paper of at least four different patterns was used. He explains also that the *Citizen*, printed by its regular staff, really appeared on July 2. Evidently the type was not broken up for use in the next issue. Two copies are known to remain of this Confederate printing but, since it is the "Note" alone which attracts collectors, little interest has been shown in the earlier issues of the *Citizen*. Of the original printed on July 4 by the Union soldiers, Mr. Morrell states that only about six are known to him. One of these is in the Chicago Historical Society, one in the New York Historical Society and one in the American Antiquarian Society.

Three additional varieties of the original of July 2 with the July 4 "Note" are known. Whether or not these comprise three separate and later issues, it is not yet certain. All appear on wallpaper of those designs identified with earlier issues. Likewise the type, with its numerous typographical errors, is unquestionably the same as in the original of July 4. Two of these issues may conceivably be the same, for they both have a muddy and dirty appearance. Furthermore, copies of each of them have been found with and without an advertisement on the reverse or wall-paper side listing the various services offered by the Parker Express Company. This advertisement, dated Vicksburg, July 15, 1863, and bearing the agent's name, F. T. Phelps, is so faint that whether it was impressed by type or hand stamp has not been determined. Mr. Morrell believes that whether or not these issues have the advertisement on the reverse, they may well have been printed at the same time. The fact that a few copies of these two issues have been found with a misspelled title, *Ctiizen* instead of *Citizen*, is believed accounted for by the probability that the work was the product of an inexpert printer, one who did not clean the dirty or ink-filled type and who replaced in reverse order letters which fell out as a result of un-cleaned type and shrunken furniture.

The last of these later issues is identical with the authentic original save that an underlined running head proclaims that it was "Printed on the original form for Daniel E. Jones, Vicksburg, Miss." This line, the bottom of which is only one-quarter inch above the top of the paper's printed outline form, if cut off, would make distinction from the original virtually impossible.

Some forty-nine different examples of spurious wall-paper copies, countless numbers of which may have been run off, have been located by Mr. Morrell. They may be divided into three groups. In the first are some twenty-eight different ones, reasonably identical in wording to the original but usually printed, at least in so far as the masthead is concerned, in different type and with numerous typographical errors as well as variations in letter spacing. No single one of these agrees in every detail with the original. The second group contains a prominent item in the fourth column entitled "Recent Federal Losses at Vicksburg," while the third group includes an item in the fourth column bearing the title "Little Coquette" to lend substantiation probably to an advertisement on the reverse side announcing a play by that name. A very considerable number of the spurious issues were designed for or used as a means of advertising everything from newspapers to baking powder and artificial limbs.

Not a newspaper, but as important a facsimile problem for collectors who wish to include an original in their Lincolniana, is Ford's Theatre playbill of April 14, 1865. On that evening Lincoln, while attending at Ford's Theatre a performance of "Our American Cousin," was shot by John Wilkes Booth. After the tragedy, various reprints were sold as genuine "assassination playbills," and they are still being sold as such today, often by persons who have themselves been deceived. Furthermore, these reprints have been picked up and reproduced in books and articles as "originals."

The circumstances surrounding the printing of the playbill

prior to the fateful performance contribute to the confusion. Dr. William R. Van Lennep, Curator of the Harvard Theatre Collection, calls attention to the fact that there were actually two genuine playbills used that April night in the theatre [Plate III]. The collection includes a complete run of Ford's playbills for the season 1864-1865, formed by the theatre's stage manager, John B. Wright, and an account in manuscript by Wright explaining why two playbills, and not one, were distributed to the audience. The printing was in progress when in the forenoon it was learned that the President intended to visit the theatre that night. Wright, on this word, ordered the printing suspended and certain changes made in recognition of Lincoln's presence. The remaining number were then run off.

Dr. Van Lennep stresses the importance of knowing the differences between these two genuine printings, if a collector is to avoid mistaking a reprint for an original. Mr. Wright, he points out, instructed the theatre printer, H. Polkinhorn, to insert in the program eight lines of H. B. Phillips' song, "honor to our soldiers," which had been set to music by William Withers, the theatre orchestra leader. This song was to have been introduced at a benefit the following night, but John T. Ford hastily decided that it should be sung in Lincoln's honor by the cast and the audience between the second and third acts. Actually, this plan was not carried through because Laura Keene, the star, was not ready to appear on stage at the set time, and the assassination occurred during the third act.

The first version, Dr. Van Lennep explains, is easily identified by the reading "Orchestra Chairs" in the first line under the heading, "The Prices of Admission," a six-line list which was kept in type and repeated at the bottom of the playbills without variation throughout the season. Forgeries read "Orchestra" and not "Orchestra Chairs." Two other distinguishing features of this first version are the reading "Night 196"—the 6 being sharp and distinct—and "Whole Number of Nights, 49 5"—with a full letter space between the 9 and the 5.

The foremost distinguishing feature of the genuine playbill, second version, is obviously the song, "honor to our soldiers."

By dropping the six lines of admission prices; resetting the three lines featuring the actors, John Dyott and Harry Hawk, into a single line; omitting from the cast the unassigned part of "Rasper, a groom," and cleverly respacing the lines giving the cast, Polkinhorn gained sufficient space directly beneath the cast to insert the song. Since a good many playbills had been printed before this change was made, both versions, according to Wright, were distributed among the audience that tragic night to save expense, and copies of both appear in his collection now at Harvard.

Recently George Ford, son of H. Clay Ford, treasurer of the theatre in 1865, informed Dr. Van Lennep that his father once told him the second version was "a fake," printed on Polkinhorn's press after the assassination. Dr. Van Lennep, however, accepts this version as genuine and considers Wright's account accurate. He argues very logically that since "honor to our soldiers" was not sung, "Why would anyone have gone to the trouble of inserting it in a forgery when it would have been easier to copy the playbill that does not contain the song?"

Perhaps H. Clay Ford had in mind still another playbill printed on Polkinhorn's press. Although mistaken time and again for a genuine bill, this third version appears to have been issued after the assassination and to be a forgery of the first version. It also bears at the bottom the imprint "H. Polkinhorn & Son, Printers, D street, near 7th, Washington, D. C.," and was run off printed in the same types as versions one and two. But Dr. Van Lennep notes that "the 6 in 'Night 196' is so blurred by the wearing of the type that it looks more like 1 or half an O"; that a lower case "v" is replaced by a capital in the line, "Buddicomb, a Valet"; that periods which occurred, one after "Miss" in the name "Miss. H. Trueman" and the other at the end of the line "For Twelve Nights Only." are omitted. The original version, further, has no punctuation after the line, "The Prices of Admission"; in the forgery the line ends with a colon. Finally, the latter reads "Orchestra" and not "Orchestra Chairs," the reading on the playbills throughout the season.

Once a collector, with these details before him, is enabled to differentiate the Polkinhorn's press forgery from the genuine playbills, he should have no difficulty in spotting any one of the number of facsimiles of the forgery which have appeared since 1865. Dr. Van Lennep provides assistance when he writes: "I have two of these before me, both produced by photo-lithography. The paper of one has a gloss to it that no genuine playbill (unless printed on silk or satin) possesses. When I run my finger over the backs of these bills, I feel no indentation, a sure sign that they are not from a printing press."

Further possibilities of confusion were added when a forgery of the forgery, evidently set up and printed on a different press, was issued. Anyone who carefully examines one of these supposed "originals" can very simply avoid mistakes. In the first place, many of the types are different from those used by Polkinhorn, although his imprint appears at the bottom. Also, the forger, misreading the blurred 6, gives a new reading: "Night 191." Then again, he could not resist "gilding the lily," for below the date he inserted three lines: "This Evening/ The Performance will be honored by the presence of/ President Lincoln."

Dr. Van Lennep lastly calls attention to still another forgery, which carries the imprint of "L. Brown." He explains: "This is more correctly termed a piracy than a forgery although it was undoubtedly issued after the assassination 'with intent to deceive'." Since it has the misreading, "Night 191," and the announcement of Lincoln's attendance, he concludes that it was printed from the "gilded" forgery, but on a different press. Should the printer's name be trimmed away, Dr. Van Lennep states that it can be readily distinguished by the omission of the exclamation point after the line "Benefit" and by the misspelling "originaly" in the line below Tom Taylor's name. Dr. Van Lennep concludes his description of spurious playbills by declaring that the Harvard Theatre Collection "also has a poor forgery of this bill whereon the misspelling has been corrected."

Reprints unquestionably, as well as facsimiles and reproductions, present problems sufficient to require a collector years to master, and this is no less true of the many kinds of manuscript copies of letters. In the first and most important category are those that were written, signed and mailed by the writer himself. Occasionally they are noted "copy" or "duplicate" or even "triplicate," and dealers make no distinction between the value of each and that of the original itself. There is a simple explanation for the seemingly strange fact that a man would trouble to write three identical letters and dispatch them. He actually embarked on this labor because during his time the mails were often poorly organized and attended by many threats of carelessness or theft either at sea or on the highways. It was more customary than unusual during the American Revolution, for instance, for a man to send several copies of an important letter by different routes, and at intervals, in the hope that at least one would reach its destination. Deane wrote from Paris on November 28, 1776, complaining to the Secret Committee of Congress that a letter containing its first announcement of the Declaration of Independence and its text had not arrived: "Your favor of the 7th of August last, covering a copy of yours of the 8th July, I received though the original never came to hand....To keep a proper intercourse with Europe, it is by no means sufficient to write a single letter....Duplicates of every letter should be lodged in every port, in the hands of faithful and attentive persons to be forwarded by the first conveyance to any part of Europe. Had this been practiced since my leaving America, instead of receiving but two short letters from you, I might have had intelligence every month. Let me urge you, from the danger our affairs have been in of totally miscarrying for want of intelligence, to pay some attention to this in the future."*

It was not an unusual event for none of several letters to get through. Such a mishap occurred in the correspondence of Benjamin Franklin, revealed in one of his L. S.s, dated from Passy, July 22, 1778, addressed to James Lovell, President of the Continental Congress, and acquired by the American Philosophical Society a few years ago. "I received your Favour of May 15,

* *The Revolutionary Diplomatic Correspondence of the United States*, edited by Francis Wharton, Government Printing Office, Washington, 1889, Vol. II, pp. 196-197.

and was glad to find that mine of Dec. 21 had come to Hand," Franklin wrote. "Mr. Deane's Brother writes that it was not signed which was an accidental Omission... . You mention former Letters of the Committee by which we might have seen the Apprehension of the Resentment of Foreign Officers etc. Those Letters never Came to Hand. And we on our Part are amazed to hear that the Committee has had no Line from us for near a Year, during which We had written, I believe, 5 or 6 long and particular Letters, and had made it a Rule to send Triplicates of each, and to replace those that We happened to hear were Lost, so that of some there were 5 Copies sent; And as I hear that Capt. Young is arriv'd who had some of them, I think it probable that one at least of each must have come to your hands before this Time...."

Franklin's precautionary measures, which were adopted basically for much business correspondence as recently as the period of submarine-infested oceans during World War II, were followed by John Paul Jones and many others of his day who habitually sent copies of their letters. Collectors, aware that a marked triplicate copy, made by one of these men, may be unique, are ready to pay the same price for it as for a letter which is not labeled "Copy." This, however, is not true of letter drafts made and kept by the writers for their files. Some may argue that an original draft, particularly if it is signed, should be even more valuable because these first and likely more spontaneous thoughts of the writer may have been, after studied judgment, drastically or even slightly revised before the final letter was actually sent. From a practical standpoint the debate has been settled by collectors themselves. They logically or illogically prefer the final text which was actually despatched by mail or messenger. Values have been set accordingly.

Unsigned drafts of letters have considerably less value than either a draft signed or the final text. Only when the draft is in the handwriting of an autograph-important person, and its contents are unpublished, will there be a demand for it and an upward impetus thereby given its price. Nominal value only is attached to drafts of letters not written nor signed by the principal but by a secretary, a clerk or an amanuensis. Despite the name signed to such a draft, to have value it must definitely have been signed by the possessor of that name. A failure to make this distinction can and does frequently cause considerable grief. It may seem superfluous to mention that a writer generally knows how to sign his own name. Admittedly, in some documents of the Colonial period, it not infrequently happened that a writer, possessed of little schooling, may have written his name in two or three different ways. Those who are sufficiently educated and worldly-wise to keep drafts for their records are not likely to be the type who misspell their names. When, therefore, in more modern times copies of manuscripts appear, in which the signature of a well-known individual has been wrongly spelled, the chances are that even the signature is a copy. So, for example, when a manuscript signed "Dolley Madison" in recent days came on the market there was reasonable room for doubt.

It is seldom that a letter marked "Copy" was not written and signed by a secretary or clerk unless the handwriting is positively identifiable as that of the principal. This is certainly true when on a manuscript there stands in parentheses next to the signature the word "signed." So obvious is this fact that one can only marvel when letters marked "(Signed)" appear at auction, as they continually do, and are catalogued as original A. L. S.s. Save in exceptional cases they are entirely worthless. The same truths apply to documents, such as land grants, printed usually on parchment with "By the President," and below this in fairly large type "By" at the left of a ruled signature line and "Sec'y" at the right. Examples when the secretary signed both the President's and his own name are very numerous. They occur, mainly, in D. S.s of Presidents Tyler, Taylor, Fillmore, Pierce, Arthur and Buchanan [Plate IV].

Collectors may also be trapped by another type of letter-copyist, who practiced because in his time the methods of communication were so scant. It was not uncommon for some local newspaper to print letters which were of such unusual interest that a reader acted on his wish that an absent friend should know their contents. The reader, then, would copy a published letter word for word together with its writer's name. Well intentioned as such a person was, he failed to foresee the menace he thereby unloosed for incautious collectors who years later would accept his copy as an A. L. S. of the true author.

Another exception in types of copies which are valued by the collector is found in the many examples of quotations in their own handwritings by famous authors or poets. On innumerable occasions, Longfellow must have written stanzas or verses from "Excelsior" or "The Psalm of Life"; Holmes of "Old Ironsides," and Bryant of "Thanatopsis." Unquestionably the original manuscript of any one of these poems would command a substantial price. Nevertheless, once the fact is established that a verse is just one of many subsequent copies made by the author himself, the price of these is generally uniform.

This market truth is applicable to the rather extreme example of Lincoln's Gettysburg Address, of which five copies written by Lincoln are known to be extant. Two are in the Library of Congress, one in the Illinois State Historical Library, and the fourth and fifth in Indianapolis and Baltimore where they are privately owned. Of the two in the Library of Congress, which were presented to it by the children of John Hay, one is the original which Lincoln composed in the White House and revised at Gettysburg itself. The story that the President wrote his immortal address on the back of an envelope while en route to the dedicatory ceremony is false. And so, too, is the story that the audience expressed its praise throughout and immediately after the address in the solemnness of silence. The perhaps less poetic fact is that each sentence provoked applause. Aside from the original Gettysburg Address manuscript, were the other four copies made by Lincoln himself to be offered simultaneously on the market, they each would assuredly command the same huge price. This supposition is not apt to become real in the case of the three library-owned copies, but conceivably either or both the copies now in Indianapolis and Baltimore may in future be sold either privately or publicly.

This and other examples of notable manuscripts, documents and letters which have been reproduced in one form or another indicate, at least implicitly, that where dishonesty is involved facsimiles and copies, like forgeries, are not based on unimportant papers. However complex the field of facsimiles may be, and the complexities are more apparent than real, the informed collector can easily avoid the well-marked common pitfalls. He needs only to know that somewhere there is an authority who can advise him to avoid those which are uncommon. When a motorist encounters a sign, "Road under repair; proceed at your own risk," he thereafter drives prudently. With the facsimile field marked, "Danger—this field is trapped," the collector cannot afford to be more rash.

CHAPTER VIII

Detection

NO one tribunal, devoted specifically to questions concerning the authenticity of handwriting or legal papers and whose decisions have recognized authority, has ever been set up in the United States. That the need for such a judicial body exists is evidenced, at least, by the court histories of many a disputed will. In not less than fourteen states of the Union the autograph will and testament of an individual, properly dated and signed by him even though not witnessed, is considered valid and takes precedence over any other prior will typewritten, signed and *witnessed*.

Implicitly these states admit that a person's handwriting should need no witness, and they recognize that such a will, written without intermediary, faithfully embodies the wish and direction of its author. In numerous cases, however, the need to prove the authenticity of a challenged handwriting is thrown into sharp focus. The establishment of some court, commission or bureau of final appeal, staffed in part by tested experts skilled in "the science of forgery," would go far toward bringing properly safeguarded opinion to bear. It could be designed to serve as a court of appeals for legal cases which have baffled courts not too well equipped to weigh the frequently conflicting testimony of witnesses. Courts cannot easily determine whether or not a witness, put on the stand as a modern handwriting expert, has a real or only an alleged knowledge.

Were some such body, staffed by experts in handwriting, paper, inks and all phases bearing upon the authenticity of manuscripts, established in the autograph field, it would be a tremendous boon to collectors and dealers alike. By it, the genuineness of items, doubtful or otherwise, could fairly and without fear of reprisals be duly considered, carefully examined and clarified once and for all. Its mere existence would forestall and curb the all too frequent hoodwinking of the innocent. It would bring

order to that type of confusion cited by Mrs. Gertrude Hills*
when she reports that letters, manuscripts, annotations and inscriptions of W. E. Henley, Sidney Colvin, Fanny Stevenson,
Lloyd Osborne, Isabel Strong and Thomas Stevenson have been
mistaken for that of the latter's son, Robert Louis Stevenson.

To differentiate the natural handwriting of an individual from
that of another is not too difficult a task for the adept, but to
detect forgeries is a very different matter, requiring greater alert-
ness, patience, study and skill. The professional expert, for instance, has at his disposal fairly well perfected, modern and
scientific devices, such as measuring instruments, light rays and
chemical tests with which he can make a thorough analysis of
all materials. The dealer-expert, on the other hand, is equipped
with the complementary advantage of long experience. In addition to a subconscious guiding instinct, he draws on a heterogeneous fund of information. Generally he possesses such a
photographic memory that without ever seeing the signature
he can recognize at a glance the handwriting of hundreds of famous men and women. He is, moreover, familiar with those personal affectations which led them to select a particular type,
color and size of paper, a particular kind of ink or a thick or thin
pen. He knows certain eccentricities which distinguish an individual's script—the size of strokes, how letters are looped, how
"t's" are crossed and "r's" formed, how words are spaced and
many other revelatory features. This is a special knowledge,
gained by years of handling thousands of miscellaneous letters,
which even the professional expert does not have. That each one
can happily supplement the work of the other is obvious, and
on many occasions they have pooled their resources.

The average collector realizes that he need not attempt to
equip himself similarly, but he nevertheless must learn a few
basic and comparatively simple rules which will serve to keep
him on the alert and prepared for unpleasant eventualities.
A proper knowledge of paper and its development and uses
throughout the centuries is the first prerequisite in any study of

* *Robert Louis Stevenson's Handwriting*, privately printed by the Edwin J. Beinecke Collection, New York, 1940.

forgeries. This is not necessarily the case with vellum, on which forgeries are rarely attempted, nor with papyrus, which all but forces the forger into a crudeness easily recognized. The well-advised autograph collector will read up on rag and later varieties of paper made of wood pulp and other materials. An analysis of these is in many instances the surest means of detecting a spurious autograph.

Rag paper, which is reputed to have been known in Spain during the tenth century but not made there until 1150, was, prior to 1861, the only material in regular use for book and writing paper.* Wood pulp began to come into use about 1860. For the most part, newspapers previous to the year 1868 were all rag; those between 1868 and 1880 were mixtures of straw, rag and chemical wood fibres. Other materials used in the latter part of the nineteenth century with approximate dates were paper made of rag with soda pulp, used from 1845; of esparto—a Spanish and Algerian grass—or of esparto mixed with rag, or of esparto mixed with soda wood, from 1861. Papers made of wood reduced to pulp by chemical process were only in use from 1860.

With these brief facts before him, a collector needs no expert to tell him that a letter purported to have been written by Richelieu would not be on paper made of wood pulp; that Napoleon, despite his Egyptian sojourn, did not use papyrus, and that Lazarus either before or after his resurrection, would not have written on rag paper. In fact, little rag paper dated before the fifteenth century appears in the autograph market today. Manuscripts of earlier periods are almost invariably written on parchment.

Rag paper itself is of two kinds, the "laid" and the "wove." The difference between them, if known, will often help to expose a forgery. "Laid" rag paper can be recognized simply by holding up to the light a sheet of paper dated prior to the nineteenth century. Lines spaced about an inch apart and generally running vertically can then be discerned. These are called chain lines. Between them light and dark striations, caused by the laid wires of the mould, appear horizontally. The paper was pro-

*Julius Grant, *Books and Documents*, Grafton & Co., London, 1937.

duced by the use of a mould which left certain impresses from its wiring and in some instances from the wooden supports under the chain wires. These and other factors serve as identification or water-mark of a kind just as the individual markings on a fired cartridge can be identified as having come from a particular firearm. This mould method of production, which required the material to be handshaken in the process, necessitated the use of a "laid" pattern in most early papermaking. Such a product, whether heavy or light in weight, was extremely strong and durable.

The use of the "wove" type of mould, which was first known in China, was rediscovered by John Baskerville sometime prior to 1757.* Although "wove" paper appeared in Europe between 1750 and 1760, it was not used to any appreciable extent in America before 1800. Held to the light it is quickly distinguishable from "laid" paper by the complete absence of both chain and laid lines. Progress in the science of paper manufacture as well as resulting reduced costs inevitably led, for all ordinary purposes, to the abandonment of the more expensive hand- for the cheaper machine-made product, and the "wove" pattern became more common than the "laid." As is so often the case in this type of substitution, an immediate change in durability was noted. Machine-made paper is usually more fragile and more easily torn than hand-made. There are, however, hand-made papers of doubtful quality. Whether made by hand or machine, the lasting and enduring tendencies of a paper rest largely upon the raw materials employed and in the treatment of the materials previous to being actually made into paper.

In comparison to papers of later make, average quality rag paper is stronger than average quality wood-pulp papers. Each, if of good quality, can withstand considerable rough handling. "Laid" rag papers of the fifteenth century, such as were used in letters and documents signed by Ferdinand and Isabella of Spain, are often as strong and unworn as they were on the day they were first used. On the contrary, much modern paper, and in

* R. B. Haselden, *Scientific Aids for the Study of Manuscripts*, Oxford University Press, 1935, p. 9.

particular the ground-wood paper used for newspapers, has demonstrated both its fragility and its tendency, even after a year, to oxidize and turn yellow and brittle. Recognizing this fact, The *New York Times*, The *New York Herald-Tribune*, the London *Times*, and The *Chicago Tribune*, among others, have printed rag-paper copies of their editions, which are earmarked for libraries.

The expert, if not the collector, also adds to a knowledge of the type of paper employed that of the type of letter sheet in general use at various periods in history. He very soon learns that in the fourteenth and fifteenth centuries he must expect to find manuscripts almost exclusively written on long, narrow strips of parchment. In the fifteenth century the rag paper used was generally folio size, and this continued up to the latter half of the eighteenth, when it was rivaled by the quarto. Octavo then was rarely used, and, evidently, only when other sizes were lacking. It is notable, too, that vellum in larger sizes became more and more the vogue, and, in later centuries, the double or giant folio was not uncommon. The folio size is still employed today for commissions, diplomas and formal documents of a related nature.

Much of the paper used in America prior to the Revolution came from Great Britain. After peace was declared, the United States imported this commodity in less and less quantity. Quarto sheets came into more general use, save for legal documents, and, as the new country developed the refinements of life, new niceties in paper for private correspondence, such as gilt edges and tinted stock, were made generally available. From 1840 to 1860 a blue—known as "Lincoln blue"—correspondence paper was especially favored. Lincoln himself used it for many of his legal pleadings, and it is probably for this reason it is referred to as "Lincoln blue." At approximately the same time, the octavo threatened to supplant all other sizes, and it is still preferred in private correspondence. Business letters have been chiefly for many years, and are today, on quarto.

These generalities concerning paper and size must not be regarded as excluding definite variations in the quality of paper used at different periods and in different countries. During the French Revolutionary and Napoleonic era, for example, paper was apt to be a rag, very fine and thin, but nevertheless strong. England, during the reign of George III, used a coarse, cheap grade of rag paper, particularly for her official documents. This cracks easily and dries out rapidly. Nor was the rag paper used in Revolutionary America possessed of strength and durable qualities. In addition, the ink then available was so highly acid that it bit through the sheet on which it was used. The paper available in Southern states during the Civil War was of even poorer quality—wood pulp was at a premium, and such substitutes as cornhusks had to be found—and was so thin and fragile that it rapidly crumbles and deteriorates unless it is kept under careful conditions, including the proper degree of temperature and humidity.

These facts about paper are not entirely unknown to forgers. When they have such knowledge, they take what precautions they can to prevent detection. The more expert among them necessarily find themselves limited on this score, since it is not an easy matter to come by the appropriate paper. Some, less resourceful, use old scraps of torn paper or paper with ragged edges. Whether this is naturally aged or faked, they face the added difficulty that authentic letters are seldom found written on soiled and ragged fragments. The men and women of the period were too meticulous in a social life whose formality was particularly noticeable in all matters pertaining to correspondence. They then would no more have thought of using for a letter, paper which, however small, was not neat, than a person would today think of writing a formal invitation on the typewriter. The incautious or audacious forger dismisses, also, the fact that the crinkled edges of an authentic, time-worn sheet of paper cannot be imitated, a condition which age alone can bring about.

There are not many forgers who are conversant with accurate details about water-marks. Some may know what water-marks should appear, but may not be able to obtain the correct paper. If they proceed with the forgery on another type, their only hope is that they can find purchasers who are ignorant of the fact that water-marks may be a contributory means of dating material. Actually, some water-marks, besides being extremely ornate, carry a date. Others omit elaborate crowns, rampant lions or fleurs-de-lys and give only symbols, or perhaps the name of the manufacturer.

The custom of using water-marks dates from the thirteenth century, and in Europe these were registered. Charles M. Briquet's *Les filigranes—dictionnaire historique des marques du papier dès leur apparition vers 1282 jusqu'en 1600,** which lists some sixteen thousand early water-marks, with illustrations, dates and other descriptive matter, is very helpful in authenticating much paper of foreign manufacture. No similar work even partially covering water-marks of American origin has ever been compiled, but Dr. Dard Hunter in *Paper Making, the History and Technique of an Ancient Craft,*† lists fifty books on water-marks. These works give excellent indices to the age of paper, yet at first glance determination of this from water-marks is not always positive. For one thing, a few manufacturers, taking pride in the fact that their firms are long established, even today continue to use the same water-mark originally adopted perhaps a century or two ago. Scientists, however, have provided certain safeguards by which distinctions may be made. By photographing water-marks and noting their positions in relation to chain lines, a close approximate date can be obtained.

Obvious misuses of water-marked paper will, of course, betray a forger, but, by and large, the dealer depends on his knowledge of other factors. This position is supported by Dr. Hunter, Curator of the Dard Hunter Paper Museum of the Massachusetts Institute of Technology and the leading American authority on paper, who writes on April 11, 1945: "In our own work in judging paper, we do not rely upon water-marks to any extent as they are so misleading. The only way to determine the age and origin of certain papers is to arrive at the knowledge by the fibers, beating methods, moulds, etc. Through a study of these

* Paris, 1907. Four Volumes.
† Alfred Knopf, New York, 1943.

methods, it is possible to give the date and place of making of any paper whether it is water-marked or not." Nevertheless, if a forger is careless to the point of using a water-marked paper that came into being long after the alleged writer's death and it is so dated, it is not necessary to explore further to establish the fraud.

The majority of forgers give less attention to water-marks than to the imitation of inks, but in this, too, they can rarely fully insure themselves against discovery. Those whose task it is to detect forgeries classify ink into groups—the carbonaceous, the iron-gall and the aniline. The first, made of finely ground carbon or some similar substance as soot or lampblack, were extremely stable, very permanent and, if properly compounded, did not attack the paper. Iron-gall inks, which are likely to be acid, will often do so and will also noticeably affect the color of a paper if it is a dyed stock.*

In the aniline group of inks, there is the black, which in permanence is considerably inferior to a good iron-gall and will smudge easily in water. It, however, does not attack the paper. Other inks made from a wide variety of aniline dyestuffs share this advantage, but, since they do not hold their color and will run, are not recommended for records of a permanent nature.

The collector who arms himself with this information about inks must then learn the periods at which he can expect to encounter them. Carbon inks are the most ancient, and the transition from them to iron-gall did not take place until about 1020. It was not until the year 1836, according to Julius Grant,† that in England the practice of mixing a coloring matter with iron-gall was inaugurated. In America this custom prevailed at an earlier date, and coloring matter on rare occasions has been noted as early as the Revolutionary period. The color was imparted by the use of natural indigo at first, but synthetic indigo, introduced in 1861, came into common use in 1880. Thereafter, other synthetic aniline dyestuffs (whose presence in some cases aids considerably the dating of inks) were employed.

* Julius Grant, *op. cit.*, pp. 115, 117.
† *Op. cit.*, pp. 41, 43.

When natural indigo, a pigment dye which is fast in color and does not run nor affect the paper, is added to iron-gall, the resulting ink retards oxidation and makes it more permanent. Instead of indigo, logwood was mixed with iron-gall by H. F. Lewis around 1763 in the vain hope that the compound would have the required durability. Although indigo was known to have this quality about the middle of the sixteenth century, curiously enough its use in England was prohibited in Elizabethan times, and the ban was not raised until the reign of Charles II.*

Since indigo is easily identified in an iron-gall ink, if it is found in an ink used on an autograph prior to 1836, the expert's conclusion as to unauthenticity must be guided by his knowledge of its exceptional rarity and his consideration of dates and countries and their respective customs. Happily, various chemical tests can be applied to this and all types of inks to determine age and the further fact whether the ink used on a particular autograph is of the same period as the paper or the date written on the paper.

It should not be surprising that the older inks, which are in reality of a blackish-brown hue, should fluoresce darkly, while indigo-colored inks throw off a bluish tint. To the eye, inks used prior to and about 1836, showing little sign of deterioration or oxidation, appear to be a dark brown shade, which in some cases is almost black. This color tends to fade with time to a lighter shade of brown, which forgers have rarely successfully imitated. The iron filings, chimney soot, oak galls and other substances they use result generally in a washed-out, pale reddish-brown tint. This an expert recognizes at once. In recent years, a variety of forgeries, some done in washed-out blue tints, others in a deep reddish brown, have appeared on the market. Seemingly the forger responsible, realizing that the washed-out color would not pass, decided it was wiser to try a fresher looking type. Cosey, on one or two examples, used the dark brown inks in which items of David Garrick, Francis Bacon and Thomas Paine have also been written. Whether the autographs

* *Op. cit.*, p. 35.

of these three men are old or modern forgeries is uncertain, but there is no question that they are forgeries.

For those who in judging inks are not in a position to resort to scientific tests, the application of plain water gives valuable information. The iron-gall, including those mixed with natural indigo, neither blur nor smudge when wet, which is not true of those inks to which synthetic indigo has been added. Papers written in these more modern inks cannot even be exposed to dampness or moisture without being affected to some degree. It is true that some firms continue to manufacture the old types of ink, and writers still use it on modern paper. In the case of such ink, it is not always possible for any but the scientifiic expert to determine its age. But no letter dated before 1860 would have been written with the new aniline dyes. If, therefore, the ink of a letter claimed to have been written by John Jay or Benedict Arnold or Paul Revere or any of their contemporaries should run, the autograph's spuriousness is safely proved.

Obviously, in using plain water to determine whether an autograph's ink will run, one must be circumspect. The corner of the suspected item may be tested with a small drop of water, applied with anything as small as a toothpick and only to a minute fraction of a character. This procedure, carefully followed, will reveal the type of the ink. Inks prior to 1860 may not only be wetted, but may remain under water a considerable length of time and suffer no disintegration independently of the paper itself. The forgeries in the roll of signatures of the Signers, which Mr. Benjamin challenged,* were betrayed more quickly by the fact that their ink had run under the water test than by any other method.

When paper, acting in a manner somewhat similar to that of a blotter, unduly absorbs ink, there is cause for suspicion. A good grade of freshly manufactured paper, of any period, is rarely soggy. Ink used on it leaves a fine, clean impression. This same paper in aging, however, and especially if subjected to dampness and mildew, becomes readily absorbent. Ink of a later date, when applied to it, tends to spread in being absorbed,

* See Chapter VI, pp. 108-109.

but it will for this very reason not run. The effect differs widely in appearance from the clearly defined pen stroke made by the original signer at a time contemporary with the publication of the printed material or not too long thereafter. Forgeries may often be spotted because the fraudulent overlook these facts.

The non-absorbent qualities of freshly manufactured paper were indirectly stressed in a story carried by newspapers on the day of Franklin D. Roosevelt's death. A woman painter who was with the President just before he was stricken described how, when she arrived, Mr. Roosevelt was at a card table signing many papers. His secretary, standing by, would not blot each wet signature but spread them out to dry. The President jocosely referred to these papers as "his laundry." Questioned at a later date about the reason for this, William D. Hassett, White House secretary, stated that there was no rule against blotting the President's signature. The governing factor was whether or not it was practical to blot the signed document. It is not practical in the case of parchment, as the ink would be completely taken up by the blotter. Again, since many official papers are photographed by the Federal Register of the National Archives for their records, an ink signature, which new paper does not readily absorb, is best left to dry without blotting. It will show up better in the photograph. Mr. Roosevelt, aware of this fact, for ten years had turned to the use of the darker more ineradicable India ink in signing government documents.

India ink and printer's ink are somewhat similar in appearance and present many difficulties to collectors. The former is generally used by artists and cartoonists in their professional work. Besides Mr. Roosevelt, it has occasionally been adopted by others, among whom may be cited Eugene Field, who often used it when copying out his poems. Because it is uniform in shade and closely resembles printer's ink, its use may cause the item to be mistaken for a facsimile. The only apparent difference between the two lies in the fact that India has a sheen, whereas printer's ink has a dull finish. Printer's ink, which the collector encounters in facsimiles, is often mistaken for original ink by the inexpert. Fortunately, there is a final test that may be applied to determine the authenticity of an item suspected of being a facsimile. It is ink eradicator, a test which is infallible, except with India ink or printer's ink. The eradicator is a strong chemical, and, when applied to other types of ink, regardless of age or color, will cause them to fade out at once. This effect is balked by India ink or printer's ink.

In using an ink eradicator, great caution should be exercised. Since it is apt to leave a bleached spot that varies in degree with the quality and age of the paper, and so causes a disfigurement, it should be applied to the most inconspicuous part of the autograph. It is best, therefore, not to use the stick that accompanies the eradicator, which is thick, but, as in the case of the water test, the much smaller toothpick or some other tiny blunted instrument. Always, too, the drop of moisture should be dried off at once with a blotter. Because a stale eradicator will remove neither old nor modern ink, only the fresh solution should be used in such tests.

Fortunately, facsimiles have certain very definite characteristics which, when known, help in their detection. The ink, besides having a dull finish, is usually all one color and thickness with no visible variations in shadings. If closely examined or held under the magnifying glass, there will be breaks in the characters where the ink has not been properly absorbed by the paper. In original writings, the flow of the pen is uninterrupted. Although the ink may at points become fainter when the ink supply in the pen is low, no breaks in the continuity of the characters can be observed unless the supply is exhausted. Longfellow provides a curious exception to this rule. Whether due to his particular handwriting characteristics or to the quality of ink he used, which in many cases rapidly faded, the fact remains that his writing shows definite breaks. His letters, nevertheless, like all authentic original letters, will show areas of darker or lighter shade. Varying degrees of wetness, or dryness, of the pen or quill, plus the heavy or light pressure of the writer, result in thicker or thinner strokes, fainter or darker shadings. Facsimiles, except in rare cases, totally lack such features.

When the imaginative build up romantic pictures of our forefathers inditing letters, they summon up a picture of a white wigged or hair-powdered gentleman or lady complete with the quill pen and the antique ink-well. The novel and the screen delight in these bits of picturesqueness but overlook the fact that the steel pen was invented as early as 1780. Quills were not displaced, of course—there are some today who still affect their use—but it may be quickly determined that letters between 1780 and 1850 were written with steel pens. The ultropaque microscope reveals this immediately. Forgers often use a steel pen to create an item supposed to be written at a time when only quills were known, but sometimes they outwit themselves by reversing the process.

The microscope and both infra-red and ultra-violet rays are available today for the most exact tests of details in manuscripts and letters which are not visible to the naked eye. By means of the ultra-violet rays, it is now possible to ascertain whether ink has been superimposed upon pencil or whether a letter has been written and later punctuated and corrected. Alterations, additions and erasures become immediately apparent under various types of scientific scrutiny. It is useful to know that, although documents dating back to the sixteenth century have been found bearing penciled notations, the commercial manufacture of pencils was not perfected until 1795, at which time they came into general use. The Faber family had unsuccessfully attempted their manufacture as early as 1760.

Many forgers first trace in pencil the letter they propose to copy and then, either with a pen or camel's-hair brush, cover over and retrace these pencilings, which are finally erased with care. Despite all precautions, the most crafty cannot remove the minute grooves made in the paper by the stroke of a pencil nor the faint remains of its marks. This fact goes to illustrate why "Antique" Smith, Count Alberti and others of the notorious and more skilled forgers scorned the cruder methods of tracing and depended entirely on their own remarkable caligraphic skill.

The latter could only serve them in good stead if they were prepared to evade all other methods of detection, among which, in addition to the tests of paper and ink, is the form of an auto-graph text. There was, for instance, in the seventeenth century, a fixed form for charters, deeds and certain legal and official documents, and the expert is familiar with those typical of given periods. Again, there are telltale features to many scripts, as the "Court Hand" which was in vogue in England about the seventeenth century. This, due both to the unusual method of shaping characters and to the practice of abbreviating extensively, could not even be read by the people as a whole. Scriveners, it was alleged, made something of a racket of it. In any event, its use was made illegal in 1735.*

The peculiarities of style in penmanship were certainly not limited to one period of English history, nor to any one country. No less today than in the past, people develop a handwriting with distinctly national characteristics, so that the penmanship of the French is noticeably different from that of Americans, and the British from both. The Italian is a pointed script, and each letter of a word, although carefully formed, is frequently disconnected from its fellows; the British is at once recognizable because it is unusually small, cramped, rather irregular but neat; and the American is less regular still, inclined to sprawl and to be marked by bold strokes. The French is the most illegible—small, irregular and badly formed. The nationality of a writer can in many cases be quickly recognized by the type of penmanship, just as it is usually possible to differentiate a woman's from a man's handwriting. Lavater maintained that the vivacity of the French, the delicacy and suppleness of the Italian, the slowness and strength of the Dane, the German and the English could be read in the script of each.

These generalities are less applicable to letters written prior to 1750, since the majority of messages of an important nature were only signed by their senders after having been indited by a secretary or scrivener. The greater universality of education thereafter changed this situation, and from the mid-eighteenth century until the invention of the typewriter in 1867 and the beginning of its general use in 1874 again reversed the situation,

* *English Law Reports*, 5th Geo. II, c. 27, and 6th Geo. II, c. 14.

the majority of letters were written by the one who signed them. From the typewriter age back through the Revolutionary days, it was more the exception than the rule to find a letter, other than one of an official nature, written by a secretary.

Longhand, even for letters of an official nature, was used by the Presidents of the United States and by all officers of their Cabinet departments except the Treasury. This is evidenced by the fact that L. S.s of Jefferson and John Adams, and even of Lincoln, are actually far rarer than their A. L. S.s. Perhaps the etiquette of those days required that the individual write his own letters, or perhaps the privacy of a letter seen by no one but themselves and their correspondents was a reflection of America's recently won independence. In any event, the introduction of the typewriter and its almost universal use today brought about a new secretarial situation which had a great bearing on women entering into the business world. The contemporary American has no alarms about his privacy and feels as safe—the cynical might say safer—in entrusting affairs to a confidential secretary as to his wife. The handwritten letter is becoming more and more rare, save for intimate and very private matters, and it is not at all likely that its day, which required leisure among other things, will ever return.

This condition does not do away with the need for those skilled in authenticating a particular handwriting, whether it be one of a person now living or long since dead. The autograph dealer or expert in such matters depends entirely upon his past experience and the combination of the many and varied informative points he has picked up throughout his career. Every writer, for instance, has certain idiosyncracies. Nine times out of ten, one may cross his "t's" in a certain way, but he will do something quite different for the tenth. The forger is apt to scrutinize carefully the general characteristics of a penmanship he proposes to imitate—how the "t's" are crossed, the "p's" pronged, the "e's" looped, the capitals formed, and the writing sloped and similar points—but, omitting the equally typical quirks, he is often betrayed by the very uniformity of his imitation. More scientific methods are used by institutions which have available modern instruments for measuring script itself. By means of these, the slope and size of individual characters in an authentic autograph can be noted side by side with one which is suspected of having been forged.

It is the handwriting itself, however, which in all instances must be examined if forgeries are to be surely detected. For this purpose, photographs or facsimiles are of small value. R. B. Haselden writes on this point in his excellent pamphlet, *Scientific Aids for the Study of Manuscripts*: ". . . photography of manuscripts cannot take the place of direct visual examination . . . photography tends to make handwriting seem more current and to confuse the sequence of strokes . . . . No authoritative conclusions regarding a manuscript can be based on the examination of any known form of reproduction thereof; the original must always be consulted." In thorough agreement with this statement, no dealer can be found who, without seeing the original, will authenticate or make a final offer for an autograph on the basis of a photostat, photograph or facsimile. Haselden, who makes no exception in regard to the perhaps over-emphasized merits of microfilms which some libraries claim to prefer to original manuscripts, further comments: "Make it a rule, if possible, to transcribe from the original document and not from photostats or photographs; otherwise mistakes are apt to occur."*

Some who have autographs to sell frequently wish to do so by showing photographs. They are obliged to handle the transaction by mail, since they live nowhere near dealers and are not willing to entrust their possessions to the postman. Were the dealer to evaluate and buy under such circumstances, he would run many risks. A typical example is that of a photostat which arrived in a dealer's office, sent by an owner who believed an offer would be immediately forthcoming. According to the photostat, the original was a most important Lincoln item—an A. L. S. in which the President quoted from and discussed his Emancipation Proclamation. The dealer, keenly interested, but prudently alert, insisted on seeing the original. When it arrived,

* *Op. cit.,* pp. 58, 69-70.

many factors not shown in the photostat soon became evident and justified his caution.

The paper of the original was not that customarily used by Lincoln, although it could have passed as proper to his period. The ink corresponded with that of the date, and the writing seemingly was his. Yet it was tremulous, and never before had this characteristic appeared in the hundreds of Lincoln letters and documents which the dealer had examined. Suspicion aroused, an eradicator was applied to the ink in a small inconspicuous portion of the letter. The result was surprising and illuminating—the visible ink disappeared, and into view came printer's ink which naturally resisted the testing solution. It was then proved that someone had secured a good photostat of a fine original Lincoln A.L.S. and traced the entire writing over in ink. The owner stated that he had bought it from a book dealer in the West at a price which was overly respectable. Its only rather dubious value was as curious testimony to the ingenuity of the dishonest.

The source of his purchase might in itself have provided a clue to suspicion, for the provenance of an item, plus the circumstances of sale, also play their parts in the detection of a spurious item. Collectors, at times ignorant of the details, will overlook the very obvious. The expert, however, in addition to readily apparent factors, puts together stray bits of information like the pieces of a puzzle. It is hardly more than common sense, when purchasing a letter for more than a medium-low price, to verify the dates of birth and death of its signer and to know or obtain some salient details of his life and work. Clever as a forger may be with his pen, he may slip as a historian. He may parallel the experience of another who was detected because he forged a letter of Lafayette dated from a small town in America in the month of March 1779, when Lafayette himself had already sailed homewards and had resumed residence in his native France. This historical fact needed to be known, but, had the forger not so slipped, he would still have been uncovered by the additional fact that the date recorded by him appeared on paper which had only come into use during the following century.

For the expert, this latter lapse was as much a give-away as would have been the case had the letter been dated subsequent to Lafayette's death.

Exceptional instances may be quoted when the charge of forgery cannot be raised even if a signature appears on a document dated after the signer's death. No neat trickery is involved. The documents concerned are usually printed forms with signatures. There are in existence, for example, a considerable number of authentic signatures of Washington Irving written on an acknowledgment-of-gift form used by the Astor Library, an acorn of the New York Public Library. As its president, Irving signed a large quantity of these forms in advance, and very likely some frugal secondary official continued to use and date them for weeks after Irving's demise.

In the same category is an Emerson item the story of which is somewhat more startling. The great American writer, who providently looked ahead as Irving did, had signed blank forms in his capacity as chairman of the Concord Library Committee. Future acknowledgments of library gifts were then to be written above his "R. Waldo Emerson." The distinguished essayist died on April 27, 1882, and, at his burial three days later, the sermon was preached by the Reverend E. A. Horton. A copy of this oration was presented to the library by a well-known resident of Concord. This worthy citizen received in return a letter addressed personally to him which read as follows: "The Library Committee gratefully acknowledges the receipt from you of Mr. Horton's sermon on Ralph Waldo Emerson as a gift to the Concord Free Public Library. R. Waldo Emerson." This authentic Emerson signature was highly prized by its recipient. *The Collector** comments: "It has been the rare fortune of some men to read their obituaries. It has been the privilege of but few men to acknowledge the receipt of funeral sermons preached in their honor."

Another outstanding example of date discrepancy which does not affect the genuineness of a signature, concerns one of William Henry Harrison, inaugurated as President on March 4,

* Vol. v, November 1891, p. 33.

1841. His signatures of presidential date are extremely rare, for, on March 27, he contracted pneumonia which resulted fatally on April 4. The authenticity of his signature on a ship's paper dated March 29, when he was undoubtedly too ill to be bothered with such a routine matter, is not questioned. Harrison, compelled by existing laws to sign the numerous papers which served as passports for all vessels departing from American ports, had simply done the chore before he was fatally stricken, and a clerk had filled in the necessary data on the signed blank.

A similar explanation doubtless holds good in another case of an unusual autograph, described in *The Collector*.* It was an old ship's paper in the usual form, employing four languages, bearing the great Seal of the United States and signed by Lincoln and his Secretary of State, William H. Seward. The document, certified by Jeremiah Pease, Collector, and Joseph T. Pease, notary, was issued at Edgartown, Massachusetts, but was strangely dated August 7, 1865, nearly four months after Lincoln's assassination. New blanks signed by President Andrew Johnson apparently had not then been supplied the Edgartown office.

Conceivably, an authentic A.L.S. could carry a date which is after its writer's death, since one can imagine the possibility of a man in 1868 absent-mindedly dating a letter 1869, a year he never saw because death anticipated him. Yet there has been no known instance of such an error, and the correctness of date of an A.L.S. remains unchallenged as a means of unmasking the forger. More probable is the error made by T. Francis Knox, English nineteenth-century author, who in a far-off mood one day dated a letter February 28, 1581. Here, naturally, the paper, ink, handwriting, all point to an obvious mistake.

Another factor which aids in dating certain letters is furnished by postal markings, about which average collectors know little or nothing. Some forgers are well equipped in this regard and have cleverly executed their imitations. When stamps are used, a reliable philatelist can readily advise if it is a proper one. He will know, of course, that Great Britain was the first country to use adhesive postage stamps, invented by Postmaster Rowland

* Vol. xxix, June 1916, p. 85.

Hill and introduced in the first week of May 1840. Britain was also the first to apply postal hand-stamps on letters, a practice which was begun in 1661 by Henry Bishop, then head of the British Postal Service. He ordered that a postmark, which gave only the month and day in a small circle and which quickly came to be called "Bishop's mark," should be hand-stamped on all mail so that this "cancellation" would reveal to the addressee the time consumed in transit.

In France, the second country to adopt postmarks, hand-stamps were first known around 1695. These were the straight-line type and improved on Bishop's data by adding the city or town name of the letter's orgin. France facilitated its postal service greatly when Louis XIV expended great sums for the improvements of his kingdom's highways and roads. That highways and roads in Germany and Italy long afterwards remained few and poorly maintained perhaps explains why postal markings were not known in Germany until 1720 and in Italy until 1740.

Boston saw the first post office in Colonial America opened in 1693, but hand-struck postal markings were not used until Benjamin Franklin, on becoming Postmaster General of the Colonies in 1753, in due course of time ordered their fixation. The earliest known American hand-stamped letter is dated 1756 and shows, with others that followed, a cancellation very similar to the Bishop's mark plus a straight-line town or city designation. The small circle then used was first known to have been succeeded in New London about 1792 by the now current type of circle postmark with town name. It was not until 1842 that adhesive stamps were used in America, and this was by private mailing companies. In 1845, some forward-looking postmasters, in New York, Providence and St. Louis, issued adhesive postage stamps on their own authority. The first postage stamps authorized by Act of Congress appeared in the United States in 1847. Those who are deeply impressed by their ownership of letters dated prior to the postage-stamp era, yet bearing postal markings, should not overlook the fact that approximately from 1753 to 1847 all letters, unless delivered by hand or special messenger or private mail companies, carried hand-stamps or some hand-written official notations. The authenticity of these can logically be better vouched for by stamp specialists, experts in their fields, than by the autograph dealer. These specialists, in many instances, have been able to show that the forger has extended his activity to the imitation of postal markings for better camouflage.

Of course, since he takes up his illegitimate activities for profit, the forger is more interested in A. L. S.s, particularly in those of fine content by eminent men and women, than in documents. If the original of what he copies can be bought for a small sum, it is hardly worth his while to bother copying it. Where important letters are concerned, however, he resorts to all manner of guile to lend verity to his deception. It is not uncommon for forgeries to be dressed up in an antique frame, backed with wood and interlined with a newspaper contemporary with the letter. The story generally goes that such an item has hung in the owner's home for several generations, and the simulated age of the letter apparently supports this claim. The expert can quickly determine that the appearance of the reproduction has been faked by the application of some such fluid as tobacco juice, coffee or tea, all of which generally give a splotchy look. Paper in aging naturally turns an unimitable buff shade. Authentic letters, actually framed over a long period of time, will accordingly darken where exposed, but that portion protected by the frame itself changes more slowly and sometimes almost not at all. A definite line of demarcation between the surface of an autograph exposed to sunlight and the protected margin may be noted. In the case of spurious items it will be found that the forger has invariably stained the entire sheet. To determine this, it is wise to remove the suspected item from its frame. This step should be taken as a routine precaution by the collector not only to guard against forgeries but also because the glass in the frame, catching certain reflections of light, often makes it impossible to ascertain whether an item is a facsimile or the reproduced photograph of a letter.

Always in the case of manuscripts that are known to be rare, it is further advisable to compare the handwriting with reliable examples of printed facsimiles wherever and whenever possible. In such comparisons, hesitancy in the writing should be particularly looked for, or any one of the many telltale signs. Reference books for this purpose may be found in the majority of large libraries, particularly Charles Geigy's *Facsimiles of Famous Personages*,* and the excellent catalogues, in which many rare handwritings are reproduced, published by Alfred Bovet and Albert M. Cohn. Facsimiles reproduced in magazines cannot be relied upon because these have a very high percentage of inaccuracies. In obtaining authentic material for checking handwriting, librarians or heads of manuscript divisions will gladly refer the inquirer to the proper sources.

This study, however helpful, must be only one of many steps the novice must take to protect himself against possible trouble. Other precautions may be necessary, as more than casual knowledge is required to baffle the forger. Always there are certain danger signals which the collector, who habitually adopts a mild attitude of suspicion, can often see clearly. He should be initially skeptical of the authenticity of any letter excellent in contents or of any A.L.S. of an eminent historical personage if it is offered at a nominal price. Such an autograph may have been stolen or, more likely, is not genuine. The forger caters to the collector's supposed covetousness for a fine item, backed by a natural desire to obtain a bargain. The gambler's instinct—and greed traps more victims than ignorance—prompts the conclusion that five, ten or twenty-five dollars can be sacrificed on the chance that a rare item may prove genuine. Not the gambler, but the forger, who has once more played his old game, is the one who usually wins out. Cosey, quoted in the New York *Sun* of November 27, 1941, adds his own testimony: "You see, I never impose upon innocence; only upon greed. Of course, I never could do any business with really first-class dealers because if a thing is good they'll pay you full value for it, but only after they have investigated it. But the second raters, they'll take your eyeteeth. That makes it fun to deceive them."

* Rudolf Geering, Basle, 1925.

CHAPTER IX

The Hidden Signature

HOWEVER well versed some people may be in two of the three "R's"—reading and 'rithmetic—it is obvious that a large percentage never mastered, or quickly forgot, 'riting. Since the latter's purpose is to communicate, its chief virtue should be clarity. Nevertheless, many whose penmanship ranges from bad to impossible remain quite unperturbed by it, and, when it is called to their attention, are apt to retort that "all famous people" are poor penmen. This statement is a half truth, but not an accurate generalization.

Horace Greeley, who has been perhaps most often cited as the "horrible example" of the illegible penman, once sent a manuscript to the pressroom containing the statement "Virtue was its own reward." The compositor, after long labor over his deciphering, returned the proofs translated: "Washing with soap is wholly absurd." One of Rufus Choate's hurried letters to a client was mistaken for an architectural drawing of the plan of a house. Leopold Stokowsky's signature, among present-day puzzlers, defies recognition. The handwriting of other eminent men and women who have taken as little pains with the second "R" have caused similar difficulties for readers of every age.

It might semi-seriously be asserted that the autograph collector needs to acquire some of the abilities people devote to cross-word puzzles. The identity of a writer is often hidden not only because of illegibility but also due to the use of paraphs, pseudonyms and titles. Like the cross-word puzzle addict, the collector advances in experience and self-confidence as he becomes familiar with the intricacies of uncovering concealed facts. This specific knowledge may well lead to his acquisition of an unusually fine autograph item which has been overlooked by those who could not determine its authorship.

Because the ability to write, whether well or poorly, is an index to literacy today, there is a tendency to regard a signature in its narrowed meaning. Curiously enough, a signature need not be made up of letters of the alphabet, but can as well consist of anything used to denote authorship or approval of a letter, manuscript or document. All that comes into the category of the sign manual, for example, is a true signature.

Of alphabetless signatures, probably the earliest form is that which consisted of a cross or circle made by a person in lieu of spelling out his name. The name itself was always written by a scribe, and the sign manual appeared just over or across it. When the medieval age was succeeded by later eras, the practice of writing "his mark," with the cross or circle between the two words, was adopted. This usage is still followed today and for the same reason that prevailed in past epochs—the signer did not know how to write. Formerly, however, the sign manual was not at all limited to the poorly circumstanced, and document after document of the eleventh, twelfth and thirteenth centuries will show good examples of such signatures.

In those days education was not as highly regarded as it is today, and more often than not monarchs themselves were innocent of penmanship. A document, which was highly valued when it recently appeared on the market because it was dated in the first years of the twelfth century and signed by Henry I of England and members of his household, showed that none of this royal group could write even their own names [Plate V]. Pizarro, who conquered Peru about four centuries later, executed his signature by means of two little racquets, carefully drawn, about an inch high and an inch apart. His unvarying use of this double paraph served to identify him more than the totally illegible signature appearing between them. They, more than the signature, are recognized as his rightful autograph and have been valued in the thousands.

Pizarro's more artistic method of signing was followed by devices of other Spanish Conquistadores and was paralleled by the various symbols used by chiefs among the American Indians. Many Colonial deeds, dealing with treaties or land grants and sales, show that the chiefs of the Bear or Fox or Turtle tribes adopted for their personal signature a small drawing of their tribal insignia and executed these in crude yet quite recognizable fashion. It is interesting to notice the difference in knowledge of writing among the Indians as shown in their autographs. Thayendanegea, or Joseph Brant, who participated in the Cherry Valley Massacre in the Revolutionary period, was among the first to become fluent in the English tongue. He had been educated partly at Eleazar Wheelock's school, which later became Dartmouth College. Yet when Big Warrior, chief of the Creek Nation, addressed himself to the Governor of Georgia in the early years of the last century, he could do little more than laboriously draw his initials, "B. W."

The paraph, identical in purpose and akin to the sign manual in certain aspects, has its own individual and peculiar characteristics. Its use, which was especially popular in the eighteenth century, did not arise from ignorance of writing but was rather a more precise or faddish development. Always uniform with each individual using it, the paraph may consist of a curious swirl of the pen or an intricate flourish which, when it stands alone, is quite meaningless to the untrained eye. To the experienced collector, however, it is as much a full signature as is a "John Hancock."

The French were very fond of the paraph, and many letters of the eighteenth century, fluent and gracefully worded, have been signed in this cryptic manner. The paraph appears always at the bottom of the page in place of the alphabetized signature, and, on occasions, is also found at the top of the first page near the date line. Besides its distinctiveness, it allowed the writer to remain incognito save to the initiate, a fact that might have had certain advantages should the letter have been intercepted. Possibly for this reason, among others, royalty was especially given to its use, but it was by no means limited to them. Mme. de Maintenon, first the favorite and then the wife of Louis XIV, and Mme. de Staël, who so hated Napoleon, consistently signed their letters with paraphs [Plate V]. Louis Philippe, last of the French kings, may also be said to have followed this custom, for, although he generally signed his initials, he ran these so inextricably together that the result is more properly described as a paraph.

A variation of the paraph is the unchanging series of flourishes and curlicues added to a fully lettered signature. Charles Dickens practically always used such a distinctive accompaniment to his signature [Plate VI], and the paraph of President James K. Polk was a flourish immediately under and about the full length of his name [Plate VI]. The flourish appears whether he signed an official document, a letter or even an album. Many others who have adopted some similar twirl seldom vary once they start to use it.

In Mexico, the paraph used in connection with the signature was called the rubric and was legally considered of greater importance than the name itself. In fact, Mexican law made the rubric or flourish the essential part of the signature,* and no signature was legally recognized unless it had some such mark, even though it were no more than a simple straight line. The name might be printed or written in another hand, but it became the true signature only upon the addition of the rubric by the one taking responsibility for the letter or document. One might sign another's name on any paper without being guilty of forgery, but Mexican law held as a serious offense the forging of any rubric.

A few persons, for reasons not always known, have chosen to sign themselves in a fashion that needs some elasticity of definition to be described as either a paraph or a rubric. Of this number was James McNeill Whistler, who frequently affixed not a name but a delicately drawn butterfly [Plate VI]. How this practice of his began is possibly explained in a letter he sent to a close friend, who had retired for quiet to the country. "You shall not take this occasion to forget us altogether," he wrote, "so I, for one, knowing from tradition, that others, distinguished under the same conditions of isolation, made for themselves pet companions in their retirement of plants and inferior animals . . . send you a butterfly that you shall cherish as an emblem of hope and joy."† That Whistler, too, cherished the emblem for this significance may have led to his continued use of this now

---

* Cf. article by Reverend Arthur H. Noll, *The Collector*, Vol. 1. No. 6, February 1888, p. 3.
† Original in possession of the author.

famed butterfly signature. Ernest Seton Thompson adopted a drawing of a bear's paw, but always with his fully signed name.

Experience alone can teach collectors to recognize paraphs, since they are not explained, as was the sign manual, by the accompanying identification written by a scribe or clerk. Those, therefore, who are not equipped with adequate knowledge of this method of signing should not discard letters, particularly those of French origin, that conclude with some cabalistic curlicue or design. The writers may be men or women of note, and their letters of considerable value.

Reasons can be advanced to account for the use of abbreviated fashions of signing, but those which underlie a practice prevalent during the eighteenth century cannot be easily explained. In that day, many men and women repeatedly wrote letters and never bothered to sign their names at all. Inadvertence, as was the case in the letter to which Franklin referred when he wrote to James Lovell,* is not the answer. Since royalty was particularly addicted to this omission, it might be argued that majesty thus asserted itself, yet the custom was then as common as the use of the paraph, and unless one attributes an extraordinary egotism to many writers of the period, the practice remains inexplicable. Nothing is surely known of how the recipient was expected to determine his addresser's identity.

There are circumstances under which a writer deliberately omitted signing letters for reasons which were imperative due to the exigencies of war. Foremost in this category are those by spies who could rely on their addressees to identify them by other means than a signature and who took the natural precaution that this would not betray them to the enemy should such a letter fall into the wrong hands. During the American Revolution many others, not spies, adopted the same caution and dispatched unsigned letters. A notable example is a letter which Colonel Thomas Rodney, in command of the Delaware Militia, wrote to his brother, Caesar, a Delaware Signer and then a member of the Continental Congress. In this letter from Shamany Creek, two miles from Bristol, Pennsylvania, written on the eve

* *Cf.* Chapter VII, pp. 137-138.

of Washington's crossing the Delaware River, he enumerated in detail the disposition of the forces under him and in the neighborhood on that date. Continuing, he requested his brother to care for his family should he be killed and concluded: "It may for aught I know, be my fate to fall among the American Worthies. When and if it should so happen, to my God and to your Friendship I Commit the Charge of my Affairs, my Wife and my Children, whom I hope you will always remember with a brotherly tenderness. But don't leave Betsey know I am so near the Seat of Danger. It may give her many groundless apprehensions and much Uneasiness, in her present situation. I would not have her alarmed on my Account."

Pseudonyms, in similar manner, provide their own hurdles in any accurate determination of the identity of a writer. The difficulty is easily surmounted if the signer is in the literary field, for the parade of poets, dramatists and authors given to writing under assumed names is well known. In some instances pen-names are more readily recognized than given names. Many who are conversant with literature are familiar with George Sand, yet may not recall that the novelist was really Mme. Amandine Lucile Aurore Dudevant, née Dudin. On the other hand, few are unaware that Samuel L. Clemens signed himself more often than not as "Mark Twain"; that Charles Lamb chose "Elia," and Charlotte Brontë preferred the more masculine-seeming "Currer Bell." Less well known is the fact that Louisa M. Alcott, when writing her blood-and-thunder thrillers, used the *nom-de-plume* "A. M. Barnard"; that the humorist, "Artemus Ward," was Charles F. Browne; that Harriet Beecher Stowe occasionally signed herself "Christopher Crowfield" when writing articles for "House and Home Papers" published in the *Atlantic Monthly*, and that William Makepeace Thackeray sometimes assumed the name "W. M. Tomkins."

The use of pseudonyms cannot always be accurately described in terms of vagaries any more than can the use of an alias, which, after all, is a less polite form of pseudonym adopted for a distinctly different end. Pseudonyms have been used from time immemorial, and the collector must be concerned with them. He scarcely need be bothered with aliases unless these were used by autograph forgers. His solicitude, in such an event, is not with the forgers' own autographs, but rather with the knowledge of their operations necessary to avoid becoming one of their victims.

The pen-name was particularly employed in the American Revolutionary and post-Revolutionary periods when politics played a vital role in the lives of patriots and Tories alike. Prejudice ran high and, perhaps in order to continue freely expressing their opinions in print, it was advisable on occasion that real identities be concealed. Newspapers of the day contain letters signed "Pacificus," "Novanglus," "Pericles," "Brutus" or other classically derived appellations. Collectors seeking autographs of this period in time learn that any letter or manuscript signed "Pacificus," "Camillus," "Cato," "Lucius Crassus," "Phocion" or "Scipio" veils the fact that the writer is Washington's Secretary of the Treasury, Alexander Hamilton. "Novanglus" was chosen by John Adams in the years around 1775, and Colonel Thomas Rodney wrote repeatedly under the names of "Hermes" and "Pericles."

Stephen Simpson, the radical of the Revolutionary era, adopted "Brutus" as his pseudonym. "Andrew Marvell" frequently wrote "letters to the editor," but he was actually Arthur Middleton, a South Carolina Signer whose autographs in manuscript form are exceedingly rare. One instance after another can be cited, and this fact doubtless prompted various publications among which is an excellent book in two volumes by William Abbatt, *The Colloquial Who's Who—1600-1924.** Its subtitle, which indicates its value to the autograph collector as a reference, reads: "An Attempt to Identify the Many Authors, Writers and Contributors Who Have Used Pennames, Initials,

* Published by William Abbatt, New York, 1925. Other excellent reference books on this subject are: William Cushing, *Initials and Pseudonyms: A Dictionary of Literary Disguises*, New York, 1885; Samuel Halkett and John Laing, *Dictionary of Anonymous and Pseudonymous English Literature*, new and enlarged edition by James Kennedy, W. A. Smith and A. F. Johnson, London, 1926, 6 vols.; and Charles S. Stonehill, Andrew Block and H. Winthrop Stonehill, *Anonyma and Pseudonyma*, Second edition, London, 1927, 4 vols.

etc." In the majority of cases history has identified such writers, but the author of the famous "Letters of Junius," has still not been positively ascertained. He is generally believed to have been Sir Philip Francis, at one time a clerk in the British War Office. Although evidence today points to him, these important letters were earlier attributed to some forty different people.

On the other hand, the pseudonyms of Hamilton, Rodney and men of their day were an open secret to many of their contemporaries who first guessed and then verified their identifications. A modern parallel is "Pertinax," whose politically devoted column has appeared in the *New York Times*. Those who do not know need not inquire far to be informed that the writer in real life is André Geraud.

Letters signed "Sebastian Melmouth," might not be so easily recognized as those of Oscar Wilde. This pseudonym, the poet and dramatist chose to use when writing his friends after he had been released from Reading Gaol. He thought perhaps to eliminate any possibility of embarrassing them. On postal cards he went further and at times abbreviated the assumed name to "S. M." Collectors, who themselves specialize in literature, are more often better informed on this and similar points than dealers and the general autograph expert.

A case, whose uniqueness causes it to stand alone, is that of the Chevalier d'Éon, an adventurer in the France of Louis XV. This man involved himself so offensively in political intrigue that by royal command in 1774 he was oddly sentenced to wear woman's attire and to assume feminity in his signature as well as in his appearance. So extraordinary were the circumstances of his punishment and so amazingly did he play the part that many did not know his real sex until his death. Even as a "woman" he continued to exercise his brilliant skill as a fencer, and many a young cavalier fell before the swift blade of this skirted adversary amid the jeers of onlookers. In the days before he incurred royal disfavor, he repeatedly and quite legibly signed documents "Le Chevalier d'Éon," and just as often afterwards his signature appeared in the feminine gender, "La Chevalière d'Éon."

Unfortunately for both the autograph collector and dealer, there are many stumbling blocks to recognizing identity by titles. When, for example, a document or letter appears signed "Marlborough," it is not easy to ascertain which Duke of Marlborough, and, in solving such riddles, experience must necessarily play its role. Members of the English nobility, a very large class indeed, provide frequent obstacles to accurate identification because they omit from their letters those dates which would single out a particular holder of a title. The writer's identity may occasionally be ascertained, sometimes with certainty and sometimes only with probability, by a study of the paper and ink of a letter, which may suggest clues to the period of its origin. At times the contents may provide their own indices. There were numerous Earls of Guilford who signed "North," but the collector must determine which North, since only letters or autographs of the famous adversary of the American colonies, the second of the name, are desired.

Where dates are given the problem is not so serious, for the collector then need only determine of what generation the writer is a representative, and if he is the man whose autograph is sought. The Lords Chesterfield, whose family name was Stanhope, were as numerous as the Norths and cause equally great confusion. Their letters constantly appear on the market, although value is attached only to those written by the fourth Earl, 1694-1773, whose famous letters to his natural son were published in 1774 and whose autograph, closely resembling that of his father, can be verified only by its date. There are instances when the title, particularly if it was held by only one man, permits of ready recognition. No great historical knowledge is required to recognize any letter signed "Beaconsfield," as that of Disraeli, the prime minister whom Victoria made the earl of that title. Collectors must be better equipped, however, to ferret out the identity of another equally famous English historical character, known affectionately as the "Iron Duke." The victor of Waterloo not only signed his name differently at various periods in his career but also altered his handwriting. Late in life he signed himself simply with his title, "Wellington"; in the years before that title was bestowed, the same writing, with a few slight variations, appears with the signature "Wellesley," and as a young man, when his handwriting is radically different, he signed "Wesley."

The practice of using various names at different stages of one's life finds parallel in the autographs of English kings. Henry VII and Henry VIII could often not be bothered with signing even their five-letter name to official documents and, impatient by nature, abbreviated it to "Hy." This was written in such fashion that the signature seems almost like scroll work. Collectors are usually annoyed with themselves when they learn that by not recognizing such rare autographs they have missed fine opportunities. In contrast to these two sovereigns, Queen Victoria observed a greater formality in her private letters. She seldom signed her full name and frequently wrote in the third person—"The Queen regrets that she will be unable to attend..."—or affixed the initials, "V. R. I.," standing for "Victoria Regina Imperatrix." Her son, the popular Prince of Wales, signed himself "Albert Edward," but when he ascended the throne as Edward VII he varied this signature with the simpler "Edward," or to intimates "A. E." King George VI, before he took the crown, used his actual first name, Albert, and even did so later in private correspondence. His brother and predecessor, Edward VIII, later the Duke of Windsor, signed "Edward" on official documents, although he was said to be known almost exclusively as "David" to his friends.

Titles among nobles of the French *ancien régime*, have their thickets of Bourbons, d'Orléans, Montpensiers and similar families noted throughout the greater part of French history. There are also difficulties in the Napoleonic era which because of its plethora of titles and honors is full of confusion, particularly to those who form sets of the Emperor, his marshals, and his family. One hazard does not exist; the titles given so freely and generously during the First Empire were not handed down to the second generation as profusely as the British.

Napoleon's autographs are of unusual interest because of the variations he used in his signatures. The earliest known form, the

Italian-style "Buonaparte," was used up to February 29, 1796. On February 23 he was appointed General-in-Chief of the Army of Italy. His new rank perhaps caused him to drop the non-French spelling. Thereafter until his coronation, he used the French form, "Bonaparte," and finally as Emperor he formally signed "Napoleon"—autographs which are rare and coveted—or more hastily "Napol," "Nap" or "N." His full A. L. S.s, of extreme rarity, are generally signed "N. B." even during the imperial period. Of the various forms, "Buonaparte" is the rarest, followed by "Napoleon." Letters and documents signed "Bonaparte" or with any of the abbreviated forms are quite common and command more nominal prices.

Very much more of a feat of memory for the collector is involved in connection with the Napoleonic marshals. These were given titles in some cases as flowery as the stationery of the period with its elaborate vignettes and decorative headings. And they, who found themselves newly in the ranks of nobility, quickly became as fond of using their titles as the English hereditary duke, earl or lord. Andre Masséna, reputed the most brilliant of Napoleon's aides, accordingly might at varying times sign himself Masséna or the Duke of Rivoli or Prince of Essling. Marshal Ney might choose his family name or vary it with either Prince of Moskowa or Duke of Elchingen. Bernadotte, so long as he uses his family surname, is not difficult, but there are not many who would know that an autograph is his when he signs as the Prince of Ponte Corvo or even Carl Johan, the name he took when he ascended the throne of Sweden as Charles XIV. Marshal Marmont, who was rewarded with the title of Duke of Raguse, provided a new word in the French language, "raguser," which translated means "to be treacherous." Few were closer to Napoleon than Marmont, yet he was the first to desert the imperial cause. Unless all such titles are known, there is little other clue to the identity of these marshals' autographs. Their writing is not easily recognizable since in their day the L. S.s predominated.*

* For full list of Napoleon's marshals and of his family and immediate relatives, alphabetically arranged by title, see Appendix, pp. 279-282.

Napoleon's immediate family seemingly delighted even more in their titles. A veritable thesaurus is needed to penetrate the maze. The Emperor's sister, Caroline, who married Marshal Murat, with great relish signed herself, however temporarily, as Queen of Naples, and in later life as the Countess of Lipona. Joseph, during his occupancy first of the Neapolitan and then of the Spanish throne, might sign himself either "Joseph" or "Joseph Bonaparte" or he might prefer the Count of Survilliers, a title he used during his incognito travels in America and his residence in Philadelphia and Point Breeze, New Jersey. This last title his wife did not share with him, as she never visited American soil. Lucien varied between Prince of Canino or of Musignano, or Count of Casali. Josephine herself, unless one knows her history before the First Empire, during which she signed quite simply, "Josephine," might escape detection should one of her autographs appear with the name "Lapagerie-Bonaparte," or "Josephine Beauharnais," or with variations of her maiden name "Marie Joseph Rose Tascher de la Pagerie." Also the collector needs to know that Napoleon's mother, Letitia, customarily signed her letters either "Madame" or "Madame Mère."*

Such vagaries have their own interest as have those which characterized sovereigns of other nations. In Spain, for example, from early days to the abdication of King Alphonso in 1931, her kings and queens habitually did not use Christian names or the royal names they assumed when signing official papers. The form was "*Yo el Rey*" (*I, the King*) or "*Yo la Reyna*" (*I, the Queen*), a custom particularly confusing but fortunately limited to the Spanish royal house. Due to a sameness of penmanship style, passed on from century to century, it is extremely difficult to identify their autographs except by the date. Also the date alone must govern in those countries where kings of the same name follow each other as do the Louis' of France. Their signatures, too, bear close resemblance to one another [Plates IX, X].

Another complication is presented by these French sovereigns. In professional circles it is well known that the kings par-

* *Ibid.*

ticularly and the queens of France rarely signed their official papers. Instead documents were signed by the royal *secrétaires de la main*, whose handwritings closely resembled that of their principals [Plate VIII]. Differentiation is extremely difficult. This is particularly true of Marie Antoinette and her *secrétaire*. Not infrequently documents were also signed both by the king or queen—especially by Louis XVI and Marie Antoinette—and his or her secretary. In such cases the secretary always countersigned at the bottom of the page. Occasionally, when the secretary both countersigned and wrote the monarch's signature, a pen stroke or one-pronged arrow was drawn from the former to the latter. The "pointer" was at times omitted when the monarch signed personally and the secretary countersigned. These secretarial procedures tend to explain the low prices fetched by documents of Louis XIV, Louis XV and Louis XVI. When the authentic royal signature is verified values are doubled and tripled.

To unravel the eccentricities of certain of the presidents of the United States, special knowledge is likewise needed. It is easily conceivable that a collector might regard as valueless an autograph of Hiram U. Grant, of Stephen G. Cleveland, or of Thomas W. Wilson, yet these would be instantly recognized were their signatures written out Ulysses S. Grant, Grover Cleveland and Woodrow Wilson. Each of the three chief executives dropped his first name at some period of his life. Grant is known to have done so on leaving West Point. Although he later added the Simpson, in time even this he abbreviated to "S." The autographs of all three when signed with their early full names are exceptionally rare and command good prices.

The variations in methods of signing his name by one writer present problems which are companioned by other variations in the script itself. Generally speaking, it is not unusual for a man's handwriting to undergo changes in the course of his life. This normally is to be expected, but after the age of twenty-five, when certain characteristics have more or less become imbedded in penmanship style, differences are apt to be slight. It is the exception when an individual's script "suffers a strange sea change," and it is the rule that at least some recognizable similarities are present in both the slant and type of handwriting no matter how many years have elapsed.

John Adams, Massachusetts Signer and the second president, is an outstanding exception, for at different periods throughout his entire life there were complete changes in his script. When more than a hundred of his letters were offered in the auction sales of the Biddle papers in 1943, the differences between his various handwritings were so startling that a beginner not familiar with autographs might easily have doubted their authenticity and credited them to an amanuensis. Adams at times used large letterings with bold signatures; at others these characters were small, irregular and cramped, and again, more typically when late in life he was going blind, these were medium sized and tremulous.

The early handwriting of George Washington is also totally at variance with his later script. When he was a surveyor working for Lord Fairfax in Virginia, he used a straight and pointed, up and down style, and his signature is entirely different from his later easily recognized and usual one. As he grew older he changed to a broad, running hand, which remained characteristic almost up to the Revolutionary years. At this period and until his death, his handwriting was very legible, round, not unlike copperplate in its perfection and always notable for neatness and precision. These qualities were manifested even in his drafts which also were executed meticulously under circumstances when those of another man might have been hastily scribbled [Plate XXXI].

There is no explanation for the variations in Adams' and Washington's autographs, but in the case of Sir Walter Scott, an explicit reason existed. When a young man, he served as apprentice to the *Signet* and, since one of his duties was to copy out innumerable legal papers which required legibility above all, he logically adopted a straight up and down, legal calligraphy that was unusually distinct. For ordinary purposes, his handwriting, familiar to many collectors, was irregular, pointed, small, running and fairly difficult to read.

William Makepeace Thackeray was not so plausibly moti-vated. He continually used two completely different scripts and at times resorted to both in the same letter [Plate VII]. One was running, pointed, up and down; the other was backward and squarish. Apparently no more than whim guided him in his choice between the two. It is probable that a similar dexterity with the pen prompted men less honest than Thackeray to forg-eries. However this may be, it is nonetheless true that autographs of Thackeray himself have frequently been cleverly forged.

Not whim but necessity has on occasion obliged a man to change his calligraphy. Horatio Nelson, the great hero of the British Navy, is a case in point [Plate XVIII]. He lost his life at the Battle of Trafalgar in 1805, only eight years after he had lost his right arm at Santa Cruz. Previous to this casualty he cus-tomarily signed himself "Horatio Nelson," and wrote a fine, flowing, pointed, fairly large hand. Nelson autographs of this period are rare. One year after Santa Cruz, he was again in com-mand of his ship and in a few months had administered a serious defeat to Napoleon at Alexandria, for which victory he was cre-ated Baron Nelson of the Nile. His left-handed script, irregular and back-sloping, is invariably associated with his new signature of "Nelson and Brontë," and autograph letters so signed, being more common, are less valuable than his earlier ones.

About the period of the American Revolution and somewhat earlier, among American writers particularly, there seems to have been a fad of writing letters in one script and signing in an-other completely different one. Those who have seen handwrit-ten letters of Thomas Jefferson or John Paul Jones will recall the diminutive, neat characteristics of style in the contents' script contrasted to the large, elaborate and carefully executed signatures. In the case of the President the difference is so great that the body of many of his letters has been attributed to his daughter who on occasion was his secretary [Plates XI, XII]. That at times she did write out his letters for him, submitting them for his signature, and that her writing did in some respects resemble his, cannot be denied. But for one who has once seen the two scripts side by side no confusion can exist.

In considering variations in the handwriting of one individual, the collector must make sure that the autograph is neither a forgery nor a copy in the hand of another person, and such assurance cannot always be obtained from listings in auction catalogues, which not infrequently fail to distinguish between such copies and originals. For the expert, the problem of detecting a forgery is strangely enough not half as serious as that of distinguishing between an L.S. and an A.L.S. of the same individual. This is particularly true during the Revolutionary period when secretaries were not only commonly employed, but also actually took pains to imitate as best they could the calligraphy of their principals.

In the majority of cases the signature appended to an L.S. will be in a different colored ink from that used by the secretary in the text, however slight the variation in shade. Or the pen strokes may be heavier or lighter in the signature. Normally a letter that has been dictated is written if not the day before, at least several hours previous to the signing. The ink used for the signature, coming most likely from a different bottle, may be darker, and the pen used may have had a finer or thicker point. There is another clue in the fact that instinctively one who writes an entire letter and signature signs more or less symmetrically and at least parallel to the last line. This fact more than any other frequently aids in distinguishing between the A.L.S. and the L.S., since in the latter it is difficult to affix a signature absolutely parallel to a text written by another. An added clue may also be found in those cases where the letter includes the commonly used terminal phrase "Respectfully yours." If the signature below overlaps the tails of the "p" and two "y's," it is safe to say the letter is probably an L.S. However pressed he may be for space, the A.L.S. writer will prefer to reduce the size of his signature in order to avoid writing over his own line above.

Obviously the need to distinguish between the A.L.S. and L.S. is important for reasons of evaluation if no other. In this connection, it is likewise necessary to know that the value of an L.S. may be considerably raised through association. The writer of the body of an L. S. may very possibly be one who is important in his own right, as has occurred with certain L. S.s of Samuel Huntington, Governor of and Signer from Connecticut, which were signed by him but penned by William Williams, another of the Connecticut Signers.

Many of Abraham Lincoln's L. S.s provide notable examples. Lincoln, who invariably signed official documents with his full name, as required by law, just as invariably used the shortened form, "A. Lincoln," in his correspondence. Among his several secretaries were John G. Nicolay, who later became editor of the Chicago *Republican*, a publisher and author, and John Hay, who served as Secretary of State under both Presidents McKinley and Theodore Roosevelt. In this capacity Hay directed peace negotiations following the Spanish-American War, influenced the world powers to declare publicly for the "open door" in China and signed the Hay-Pauncefote Treaty and others concerning the acquisition of the Panama Canal Zone by this country. Both men collaborated in the writing of a massive biography of the president they had served as private secretaries. In those instances, when they penned Lincoln L. S.s, their own identities warrant mention. So, too, in the case of the L. S.s written by Mrs. Lincoln, who at rare intervals assisted her husband with his correspondence. Due to the scarcity of these, values are markedly affected upwards. However unusual such letters may be, an L. S. or an A. L. S. of Lincoln signed with his full name would be even more unexpected. Actually it is believed that only a few signed in this fashion are in existence.

Association values also are attached to many of Washington's L. S.s. The first President is known to have employed during the war years at least thirty-one aides and secretaries, probably the most prominent of whom was Alexander Hamilton. Others were Robert Hanson Harrison, later distinguished as a jurist, who in 1789 declined Washington's appointment of him as a justice of the United States Supreme Court; Edmund Randolph, who became Governor of Virginia; Jonathan Trumbull, who was elected Governor of Connecticut; Richard Varick, mayor of New York; James McHenry, who rose to the rank of major general and later took over the Secretariat of State under John Adams, and Thomas Mifflin, who was president of the Pennsylvania Provincial Congress. Still other aides reached distinction in many fields, but the more prominent ones at least merit special mention when Washington L.S.s are listed, and theirs were the hands which penned the contents.

The knotty questions which revolve around the determination of autograph authorship also include unsigned pages of manuscript or unsigned drafts of letters. These may go unrecognized for years, yet, if the handwriting is that of a distinguished person, any item in this category may have marked value of its own. Of definite and great importance would be any presently undiscovered manuscript page, however battered, of a speech which Washington wrote in longhand. He first planned to deliver this at his inaugural in 1789 or as his first address to Congress, but he agreed with his friends that it was too long and so wrote the short inaugural address that was subsequently delivered. Dr. Sioussat of the Library of Congress, who states that the manuscript of the discarded address was sixty-two pages, wrote that "only sixteen entire pages (eight sheets) and portions of eight other pages (four fragments) are now known to exist. The Library of Congress, I am sorry to say does not own any of the original draft. . . ." The Library, however, possesses photostats, and the text of known pages and fragments is published in *The Writings of George Washington from the Original Manuscript Sources*, 1745-1799,* which cites the list of their owners.

Jared Sparks, the historian and biographer of the President, committed a serious offense when he broke up this great manuscript which, on finding it had no official existence, he took upon himself to parcel out page by page, even by portions of pages, to his friends and admirers. He had done this on other occasions, specifically in that of the Washington "Diaries." It is extremely doubtful that the carefully composed address will ever be completely recovered. Washington had numbered each page himself, and some of those preserved bear Sparks' initialed state-

---

* Edited by John C. Fitzpatrick, Bicentennial Edition, Government Printing Office, Washington, Vol. xxx, pp. 296-308.

ment that the handwriting is Washington's. Knowing these details, should the collector come across a quarto page, 9 by 6½ inches, of the President's handwriting, he could easily verify his suspicion that it might be one of the missing sheets. Unfortunately, however, some of these, if extant, may be in the hands of those who do not have the remotest idea of their identity, value and importance to historians.

Not all unsigned manuscripts are of comparable importance, and many are of little or no value. Yet the wise collector never consigns to the waste basket any autograph manuscript which he cannot readily identify either because he does not immediately recognize its author or because it is unsigned. He prefers to wait until he can consult the expert, dealer or librarian. Innumerable instances can be cited to demonstrate the soundness of this policy. One dealer after another has held autographs for months and years until he can devote sufficient time for the necessary research to clear up the mysteries of their authorship. Mr. Benjamin repeatedly took pleasure in recalling the not infrequent occasions when for nominal sums he acquired manuscript poems of Shelley or unsigned letters of Beethoven because they were unrecognized by others less familiar with handwritings.

Today in the Talbot Collection of Georgetown University Library is a highly prized A. L. S. which had been shunted between dealers before one discovered that it was by Leonardo di Porto Maurizzio, a great Franciscan missionary Saint of the eighteenth century. In the same collection is an L. S. whose scrawled signature defied interpretation by one examiner after another. The letter was dated from Milan, addressed to a high churchman, and dealt with ecclesiastical affairs. It was eventually rescued from "innocuous desuetude" by an expert who noted on its reverse side the remnants of a rather flattened seal which visibly read only "meus." Under the magnifying glass, two other letters appeared and made "romeus." From this clue, which was dovetailed with others, it was finally conclusively established that the signature was written by the Cardinal and Saint, Carlo Borromeus.

Such autographs carry their own moral and remind one of the story told about Lon Chaney, the late Hollywood actor, who was famous for the variety and success of his many unusual character parts. A visitor to the cinema capital was on the point of crushing a spider with his foot when an official prevented him. "Don't step on it," he warned, "it may be Lon Chaney!" This admonition can rightly be paraphrased for any who come across autographs—"Don't destroy it. It may be a Queen Isabella or Jefferson, a Whistler or a Henry VII." To this could be further added, "Don't destroy but subject it to the closest examination by yourself or some authority." By the very nature of things there is available no list of valuable autographs lost because what they concealed was not known. Could such a list conceivably be compiled, it would undoubtedly be long and ever growing, and, at least for the collector, appalling.

CHAPTER X

The Strange Case of Button Gwinnett

WHEN a person reads that an item listed as an autograph of Button Gwinnett sold for $51,000 in the pre-depression period, and that another in early 1945 brought $150, he may well rub his eyes. The name, Button Gwinnett, unquestionably is a magic one in the autograph world, and there are many who, not even faintly interested in collecting, know that any Gwinnett autograph offered for sale is certain to make market history. These people are somewhat baffled, however, and inevitably question why there should be the vast difference in prices and why someone better known does not top the price list. At best Gwinnett means little more to them than that he was one of the Signers.

If prompted to inquire at greater length, they would find that biographical data about him is scant. For example, the famous eleventh edition of the *Encyclopaedia Britannica* does not mention him. And yet Gwinnett, around the time of the one hundred and fiftieth anniversary of his death, was actually making history—history in the autograph world. As a result he won encyclopaedia recognition. The fourteenth edition of the *Britannica* and the *Columbia Encyclopaedia** include him, although each devotes only thirteen lines in all to his biography. Both emphasize that he is best known for the lofty prices commanded by his autographs.

Collectors in general realize that the market value of Gwinnett's autographs is based on their great rarity in the face of a long-existing and extensive demand. Gwinnett's sole claim to fame otherwise is that he signed the Declaration of Independence. His autograph is needed to complete sets of the Signers. How many there are of those who would "give their eye teeth" for an authentic Gwinnett signature, and yet know but one detail of his career, cannot be ascertained. Nevertheless, collectors, from a very practical standpoint, should know certain circum-

* Columbia University Press, New York, 1935.

stances of his life. His biography, by Charles Francis Jenkins,* was the first written and fully based on all available material. Mr. Jenkins, former president of the Historical Society of Pennsylvania, included a descriptive guide to the then known documents bearing Gwinnett's unusually characteristic signature and reproduced several of them. For this and other reasons his book, since its publication in 1926, has continued to be regarded as the most authoritative work.

In Gwinnett's otherwise ordinary life there were two points of drama. The first was his participation in the history of the Declaration of Independence; the second, less than a year later, was his untimely death from a dueling wound in May, 1777. He was born about 1732 in England where, after receiving a good education, he engaged in merchandising in Bristol, before he emigrated to South Carolina to continue that business first in Charleston and then in Savannah. In 1765,† he purchased a nearby island plantation from Thomas Bosomworth, and Mr. Jenkins explains that " 'Button Gwinnett, late of Savannah, Merchant', became 'Button Gwinnett of the Island of St. Catharine, Esq. ' "

"Had Gwinnett not been overwhelmed with debt, much of it dating back to his commercial and shipping enterprises, he might have become a successful planter," Mr. Jenkins continues. "To work his plantation, man his sawmills, and conduct his shipping, hands were needed, and by the purchase of a large number of Negroes, probably all on credit or with borrowed funds, Gwinnett created additional debts which soon began to trouble him. The claims of merchants in Liverpool, Bristol, Pensacola, and St. Croix were placed in the hands of attorneys in Savannah, who tried to collect what was due. Embarrassed and harassed, he embarked on a course of borrowing from a new creditor to pay off an old one."

Meanwhile Gwinnett had further trouble. This came from trespassers and poachers who were killing and carrying off his hogs and cattle and who also were liberally helping themselves to the fish and oysters from his creeks and shores. Still he found

* *Button Gwinnett*, Doubleday, Page & Co., Garden City, N. Y., 1926.
† *Op. cit.*, p. 36.

time somehow to take over public duties. About 1767 he was commissioned Justice of the Peace for the parishes of St. John and St. Andrews, and in 1769 the voters of the former parish elected him to the Commons House of Assembly scheduled to meet in Savannah on the last Monday of October. No quorum was present on that day. Evidently the duty of attending legislative session was regarded more strictly than in our times, for Mr. Jenkins records that "by the end of the week, Gwinnett and two other members had not put in an appearance and the Speaker was directed to issue a warrant for their arrest."[*] The warrant was quashed when Gwinnett appeared later with the excuse of illness. Once he took his seat, he was made chairman of some of the Assembly's committees and a member of others.

The Assembly reconvened the following December, and Gwinnett, who had not arrived by February 20, again was ordered arrested, and one Thomas Lee was sent to "bring him in." Before this could be done, Governor James Wright dissolved the Assembly, and its members dispersed. "When Lee and his prisoner arrived in Savannah, there was no one to whom to deliver him, and no one to compel Gwinnett to pay the costs as was usual when a member was brought to the House." Gwinnett returned to his plantation to wrestle with his financial tangles, which "required all his time and effort."[†] It is natural, as Mr. Jenkins reveals, "with his creditors clamouring for payment, with his goods seized and sold by the provost marshal, with hurryings to and from Beaufort, Charleston, and Savannah in a vain effort to stem the tide of disaster...he would have little time and less heart for public affairs."

Five years elapsed before he again resumed such activities. Meanwhile, Gwinnett had taken up timbering, and records show that some of his frequent petitions for good pine land had been answered with various grants by the Council. Revenue from this source provided no solution to his financial involvements. "Gwinnett's affairs," so Mr. Jenkins concludes this chapter of the Signer's life, "came to a climax in February, 1773, when his

[*] *Op. cit.*, pp. 48, 49.
[†] *Op. cit.*, p. 65.

creditors were rounded up under the leadership of Alexander Rose of Charleston and Robert Porteus of Beaufort. They bought St. Catharine's for £5,250, and proceeded to use the proceeds to pay off the debts...Beyond this date, Gwinnett's relation to the actual ownership of St. Catharine's is not clear. Under some arrangement with the new owners, he continued to make the island his home, and on his death his personal property and slaves were located there."*

It is known definitely, however, that in 1775, when the clouds of the approaching Revolution were black and heavy, Gwinnett began again to take active part in politics and became noted for his warm support of the American cause. Logically, he was more and more in the public eye, and logically, too, he was appointed on January 20, 1776, a delegate to the Continental Congress. As such in the summer of 1776 he established his autograph fame even if many historians thereafter label him only as "one of the Signers." Had Gwinnett enjoyed a long life, perhaps more of his autographs would have been preserved, since his duties in Philadelphia had made him outstanding in his adopted Georgia. In February 1777 he was appointed a member of the State Government and elected president of the Provincial Council on the death of Archibald Bullock. But Gwinnett was militarily ambitious, and he was eager to secure the commission of brigadier-general of the Continental Brigade then being levied in Georgia. Instead this post was given to General Lachlan McIntosh. Whatever were the circumstances of the appointment, Gwinnett was bitter, and his bitterness was at least partly responsible for his challenging McIntosh on May 15, 1777, to a duel. McIntosh left Gwinnett mortally wounded on the field.

These biographical notes may give some clues but do not in themselves thoroughly explain why Gwinnett autographs should be so rare. They do bear heavily on a continuing series of events that began in the autograph world as early as 1894. They also provide some explanation for the sale of a Gwinnett at the fantastically high price of $51,000, and another at the ridiculously disproportionate figure of $150. "For many years, there has been

* *Op. cit.,* pp. 49, 50.

a question of the authenticity of much of the Button Gwinnett material offered for sale," wrote Forest G. Sweet of New York, noted authority, expert and dealer in Americana. "This doubt has been reflected by the refusal of many dealers to handle it, and the small fractional prices it has realized when sold as compared with recognizably authentic Gwinnetts. Fortunately certain research has definitely settled the status of a large number of alleged Gwinnett A. D.s." Documents and manuscripts catalogued as Gwinnett autographs have repeatedly appeared for sale either privately or at auction. Always they have aroused considerable discussion, revealing how divergent are the opinions concerning them. Several items offered for sale have been of unquestioned authenticity, and no one has challenged this fact. Other autographs, and these are not few, have caused heated and protracted debate, and even today opinions are probably still as varied as they were formerly.

The core of the difficulty in a number of cases can be summed up in the question: Did Gwinnett ever serve as the secretary to James Wright, Governor of Georgia? This was raised in 1894 at the Stan Henkels sale, April 24-26, in Philadelphia, when the papers of Colonel Charles Colcock Jones, including Gwinnett items, were sold at auction.

"Before the sale," Mr. Benjamin, who bought one of the listed Gwinnetts, wrote in *The Collector*,* protesting at some of the circumstances, "the buyer has two or three days to inspect the autographs, but this does not afford sufficient time, nor are there adequate facilities for passing on the genuineness of the rarer pieces. A dealer can only do this when he has the autographs in his office and brings all his authorities to bear on it. A case in point was the alleged Gwinnett MS., No. 644, sold at Philadelphia in April last. Colonel Jones was almost the only source from which Gwinnetts have come, and it was only fair to presume that what he said was Gwinnett was genuine. I am free to say that I have never seen more than a few lines by Gwinnett. . . .

"When this autograph was offered at the sale, Simon Gratz,

* Vol. vii, June 1894, pp. 97-98.

of Philadelphia, the highest expert on Revolutionary autographs, spoke up and said, 'I am willing to guarantee that.' Thus with Mr. Gratz openly and Colonel Jones apparently backing the autograph, it seemed safe to buy it, and I did so. This MS. was an attestation drawn by someone who was secretary to James Wright, the Governor of Georgia. It was in the same handwriting as the alleged Gwinnett No. 363, which was written by the secretary of James Habersham, [Acting] Governor of Georgia. So that this Gwinnett secretary must have held office under two governors. I also bought the latter specimen, and on taking them to my office put them to a thorough examination, as I guarantee all autographs bought on order, and quite a considerable sum was involved.

"I hunted up all other documents I had in stock signed by James Wright and James Habersham, and was delighted to find that they were all in the same hand as these alleged Gwinnett specimens—so that I was suddenly rich in Gwinnett. This exaltation did not last long. I found all these documents were signed by Thos. Moodie, as secretary to both Wright and Habersham. Then I hunted out some MS. of Moodie, and, sad to say, the hand was the same as Gwinnett's. Either Gwinnett had written Moodie's MS. and signed Moodie's name, or, what was quite plain, all of the specimens were written by Moodie.

"There is no record whatever of Gwinnett ever being secretary to any governor, and indeed in 1769 to 1771, when these documents were written, Gwinnett was a planter far away on the island of St. Catharine. So Mr. Gratz was plainly wrong for once. Colonel Jones was apparently wrong, but there seems no reason for saying that he ever claimed them to be Gwinnetts. They lacked his usual description at the bottom in red ink. I asked his son if Colonel Jones had ever claimed No. 363, and a third alleged Gwinnett, to be Gwinnett, and Mr. Jones said he had never heard his father say so, and declined to guarantee it. ... I promptly returned No. 363 and No. 644 as bogus, and sent one of my Moodie-Wright documents as proof. Mr. Henkels declined to receive them back for a time, but finally did so."

The Gwinnett item that sold for $51,000 was a D. S. with signatures of Gwinnett and several other fellow Signers. This, plus the fact that the item's date is 1776, explains in part the evaluation. The $150 item dated 1770 was not signed by Gwinnett but was listed as being in his handwriting. The handwriting is identical with that on similar documents owned by the New York Public Library, dated October 30, 1766 [Plate XIII], November 19, 1770, March 6, 1771, May 6, 1771, and September 30, 1774, and on one dated May 15, 1770, which is owned by the firm of Walter R. Benjamin Autographs and insured at one dollar and fifty cents ($1.50) [Plate XIV].

The Library's five documents are official in nature, and all but the one dated May 6, 1771, are signed by James Wright, as Governor, and Thomas Moodie, Deputy Secretary, of the State of Georgia. The odd one is signed only by Moodie. The authorities in calendaring these documents at the close of the century listed them under James Wright and Thomas Moodie, not under Gwinnett. Since even at that time Gwinnetts were highly valuable, the authorities would hardly have made a blunder that up to this day has not been corrected. Those that have appeared on the market are also official papers—affidavits, petitions and similar documents. Some, like those in the Library, are both handwritten and signed by Moodie in addition to Wright, and others are handwritten but are signed only by the Governor.

All the Library documents and those offered for sale were issued most probably from the State Office. The contention of those who believe them to be genuine Gwinnett autographs presumably is that he was a secretary or clerk in the Governor's office. This must be examined. There is no question that James Wright, appointed Royal Governor of Georgia in 1764, remained in office until June 1775. Ella May Thornton, State Librarian of the Georgia State Library, asserted in 1945 that James Habersham, who was the Secretary of State from 1754 to 1775, also served as Acting Governor from 1771 to 1773 in Governor Wright's absence. From 1773 to 1775, Habersham did not fill any state office actively. He had gone to New Jersey for his health and died there in August 1775. These facts certainly go far to explain why Thomas Moodie, as Deputy Secretary of State, should sign with the Governor many of the petitions and documents issuing from the latter's office and ordinarily co-signed by the Secretary.

Could Gwinnett then have served in that capacity for Governor Wright? Had he done so he would necessarily have been thus engaged from October 30, 1766, to September 30, 1774, the dates of the New York Public Library's documents. Gwinnett's career obviously rendered such an arrangement impossible. His personal affairs so demanded his attention that he neglected his legislative duties and incurred arrest. The Governor would scarcely send a man with a warrant on a search if the guilty party were actually working in the State Office. Nor, had Gwinnett been able to devote the time and absent himself from his plantation, would it have been in character for him to engage himself at the meagre salary paid in those days for such work. He was debt ridden, but he dealt in comparatively large sums, and he would have looked for more than a drop in his financial bucket.

Mr. Jenkins, questioned about the alleged Gwinnett documents, wrote in March 1945: "I do recall that the only specimen, so far as I know, that has any writing in Button Gwinnett's handwriting, is his will...at the J. Pierpont Morgan Library, but I have no information regarding Moodie. I agree... that Gwinnett was not a secretary to either Habersham or Wright. On the contrary, my recollection is that they were political enemies, they representing the City party and Button Gwinnett being distinctly of the Country faction allied with Lyman Hall."

The full Gwinnett A.L.S. owned by the Morgan Library [Plate XV], and a document in the possession of the Yale Library [Plate XVI], both of unquestioned authenticity, can be compared with the Moodie-Wright documents, signed by both men and claimed to have been written by Gwinnett himself. The A.L.S. shows that Gwinnett's handwriting differs radically from that alleged to be his on the challenged A.D.s. The Yale document is one of the several mortgages Gwinnett gave on St. Catharine's Island. Although the body of the document is in an unknown hand, the deed is dated April 24, 1770, and was recorded "Georgia Secretary's office Book Q, p. 464 & 465 9 May, 1770. Thomas Moodie, D. Secy." On it both the signatures of Gwinnett and Moodie appear. It is interesting to note that several authentic Gwinnetts are listed as D. S.s by the Library of Congress and the New York Public Library. Could they justifiably record others in their possession as A. D.s both institutions would hardly be expected to overlook such a detail—one that would unquestionably enhance the value of their holdings.

The problem of the alleged Gwinnetts has troubled collectors for more than fifty years. With the facts before them, they may draw their own conclusions.

CHAPTER XI

Confused Identities

THERE is a certain uniqueness in the questions presented by alleged Gwinnett autographs due more, perhaps, to wishful thinking than anything else. Another type of confusion, different in its origin, has governed autographs of another category and caused untold difficulties for collectors and dealers. It is rather neatly summed up in the story of a man who applied for work as a gardener and stated that his name was Poe. The lady who interviewed him facetiously asked, "Would you be any relation of Edgar Allan Poe?" "Why," he replied, straightening up to the full haughtiness of his stature, *"I'm* Edgar Allan Poe." The confusion which occurs when two or more people have the same name is easily explained but not so easily removed. Identical names have been a problem in the autograph world from the first, but, when these are borne by contemporaries, difficulties become more serious.

A few years ago newspapers reported the first meeting of a newly organized society, the "Fred Smiths." One hundred eligibles attended, all with the same first and last name. Two people who have an even less common surname than Smith are frequently namesakes entirely by accident. They may live out their lives without ever coming in contact with each other. Design rather than accident, however, rules when namesakes belong to the same family. In one there has always been an Abigail, in another a Charles, and in a third a Zebebulon, and such names are passed down both the lineal and collateral lines. A clever writer might build up an interesting book on the whys and wherefores that influence parents in naming their children.

The autograph collector, fortunately, is not concerned with the great majority of such daily recurring cases. Nevertheless, he must guard against the many dualities that can lead him, if he is not careful, into troubled waters. It may occasionally happen when he may equally value the autographs of two John Does, but what he must avoid is securing the one when he actually wants the other. An ability to distinguish between their handwritings may often be the only means of finding the proper solution. If the two John Does lived in different periods, dates should serve to identify each. Despite this sure index, strangely enough, mistakes occur similar to the inclusion in sets of the Supreme Court Justices of autographs of a John Jay who was twelve when his grandfather, the first Chief Justice of the United States, died in 1829. On the other hand, if the two John Does were contemporaries for a good part of their adult lives, other indices must be studied.

Very few people realize that Abraham Lincoln had an Illinois namesake, "Abram Lincoln," a cousin from Hancock County [Plate II]. "The only confusion of identity," writes Dr. Paul M. Angle, Director of the Chicago Historical Society, "arose from the fact that this cousin...was also of the same name. Since he was a Justice of the Peace, some people have concluded that Lincoln, the President, held that office. He did not.... The Hancock County Lincolns were Roman Catholic and as a result members of that church have at times claimed that Lincoln, the President, was of this faith." Dr. Angle adds, "that claim was made at the Chicago Eucharistic Congress in 1926 but was refuted by [William E.] Barton in an article, 'Abraham Lincoln and the Eucharistic Congress'."*

The costliest mistake the autograph collector could make in confusion of identity would concern Thomas Lynch, Jr. His is a name to conjure with in the autograph world simply because he is the rarest of the Signers. The scarcity of his autograph is in part explained, as in the case of Button Gwinnett, by the fact that he lived only a short time after the momentous date, July 4, 1776. Unlike Gwinnett, however, he was preceded by a father whose letters also were sought by collectors. In addition, there was a Thomas Lynch, a New York City merchant, about whom little is known and who shared with the Signer handwriting traits that were characteristic of the period. Letters of the Signer's father [Plate XVII], who was born in South Carolina in 1727, are themselves extremely rare, although his signature may

* *The Outlook*, July 14, 1926.

often be found on the State's pre-Revolutionary paper money. An early and staunch advocate of Colonial resistance to England, he was sent as delegate from his State to the first and second Continental Congresses. Early in 1776 a stroke of paralysis prevented his further participation in public affairs. Late in the year he seemed well enough to attempt the journey homeward in company with his son, but at Annapolis, Maryland, a second stroke ended his life. A. S. Salley, secretary of the Historical Commission of South Carolina, in a letter dated August 28, 1944, makes the interesting point that "The elder Lynch was a delegate to Congress at the time that the Declaration was passed, and there is a blank space on the Declaration today for his name, but he died without being able to get around to Independence Hall and sign."

His son was born on August 5, 1749, in Prince George Parish, South Carolina, was educated at Eton and Cambridge and studied law in the Temple, London. Returning home in 1772, he managed a plantation on North Santee River, given him by his father, and showed actively his sympathy with the colonist cause. He was commissioned a captain in 1775 and set about recruiting his company in North Carolina. There he contracted swamp fever which still afflicted him when, on March 23, 1776, the Assembly of South Carolina elected him an extra delegate to the Continental Congress so that he might care for his father in Philadelphia. After taking his place in the Congress, the younger man impressed all with his earnestness and eloquence. His signing the Declaration was one of his last public acts, for his health continued to fail, and he returned to his home in the autumn. Still in the hope of ridding himself of the fever which dogged him, he sailed three years later for St. Eustatius in the West Indies. His ship was lost at sea.

Thomas Lynch, Jr., has not received as great publicity as Button Gwinnett, probably because fewer of his autographs have appeared on the market in recent years. There is only one full A. L. S. known to be extant. It is a part of the Thomas Addis Emmet Collection now owned by the New York Public Library [Plate XVII]. Salient points of its provenance are interestingly given in the following account written by Mr. Benjamin in *The Collector**: "Dr. T. A. Emmet is again in possession of his famous letter of Thomas Lynch, Jr. .... . Induced by the advice of some friends, Dr. Emmet sold this letter to me ... the highest price ever paid for a single letter. I subsequently sold the letter to Mr. Augustine Daly. Dr. Emmet repented of having sold the letter, and Mr. Daly with great kindness of heart returned it to him at cost. Mr. Daly and myself may take a certain amount of pride in having, even for a short time, been the owners of this famous and unapproachable letter. Dr. Emmet says that no amount of money will ever induce him to part with it again."

Excepting this letter, little more than signatures have been offered for sale. These have appeared in various forms, on documents and on the fly-leaves of books, signed "Thomas Lynch, Jr.," "T. Lynch, Jr.," and simply "Lynch" [Plate XVII]. When the Signer used the latter form, the necessity of distinguishing his autograph from that of his father or other Lynchs comes to the fore. If signatures are compared with that which is on the Declaration, the majority of them will be found to be shaky, whereas the fateful one is firm. At what period the tremor began has not been ascertained. In all likelihood it was due to the cumulative effect of his illness, for when he signed the famous document he was already a very sick man.

In recent years it was rumored that the State of South Carolina had an unknown quantity of receipts signed by Thomas Lynch, Jr., and that, as occasion arose, these signatures would be snipped off and auctioned. The story has been proved entirely false. The South Carolina Historical Commission, to the best knowledge of its officials, has owned only two of these receipts. Both were sold to acquire funds, the first for a World War Memorial building in which to house the State Historical Records; the second, for necessary equipment to maintain the records. The sales were authorized by two resolutions of the South Carolina General Assembly. The first Lynch-signed receipt brought $9,500 at the Anderson Galleries in New York on April 25, 1929; the second was sold for $3,500 on May 26, 1938,

* Vol. II, May 1889, p. 144.

at the American Art Association Galleries. In reporting the latter sale, the New York *Herald-Tribune* of May 27 mentioned, without giving its authority, that the item was the forty-ninth Lynch signature known.

Other documents signed by Lynch, including receipts, have appeared on the market. These may or may not have been included in the Historical Commission's original supply. Before the State records were placed under lock and key, Mr. Salley once again voiced the opinion that many persons had access to them, and removals of Lynch autographs, assuming the items had been present, would not have been impossible. Librarians have often mourned that, in the early stages of their institutions, their predecessors failed to lock all stable doors, and present officials know that during such laxness certain valuable horses were stolen.

A collector who pays the scarcity prices of autographs of Thomas Lynch, Jr., only later to discover that he has acquired the autograph of another Lynch, will obviously be seriously penalized. So, too, would he be should he make the same type of mistake in regard to Nathan Hale. The likelihood of this is very much reduced by the fact that any writing at all of the gallant young patriot spy is extremely rare and seldom appears on the autograph market. Mere signatures on documents bring high prices. Hale's short life, begun on June 6, 1755, was ended on the scaffold on September 22, 1776. The briefness of that life of twenty-one years, however, does not prevent confusion with an unrelated namesake who, a son of Jonathan Hale of Longmeadow, Massachusetts, was born there in 1742. He died in 1813, after a career in which he had studied theology and served as a Connecticut legislator for fifteen sessions. In his *Documentary Life of Nathan Hale,** George D. Seymour reports: "Several books containing the autograph of Nathan Hale, a native of Longmeadow, Mass., have misled collectors and led to serious confusion and paved the way, no doubt, to deception, since the autographs of the two Hales are superficially not unlike [Plate XIX]. ... Nathan Hale of Longmeadow ... studied divinity.

* Privately printed, New Haven, 1941, p. 405.

Hence the character of these four books, all of which are theological. Collectors will do well to bear this in mind when offered books alleged to contain the signature of the Patriot, one of the rarest that any collector of Americana can hope to secure."

Those who have been trapped by incorrectly identified autographs of Button Gwinnett, Thomas Lynch, Jr., or Nathan Hale would unquestionably suffer a serious financial loss. A lesser penalty would be visited on a collector who purchases an autograph signed George Washington in the mistaken belief that it is one of the President [Plate XXXII]. At a recent sale of miscellaneous manuscripts held in New York, there was included an item dated "United States, 1800 Apr. 2d," and signed George S. Washington. The middle initial is so run into the surname that it is almost unnoticeable. Collectors who know that President Washington died on December 14, 1799, even if they did not spot the discrepancy between his and George S.'s handwriting, would need nothing more. It is safe to assume that George S. Washington, who was sufficiently well off to own a wagon and old enough to hire it out, had prior to April 2, 1800, signed papers for an indefinite period of years. Certainly anyone with the bare minimum of historical knowledge could reasonably conclude that President Washington did not engage in the livery business after he retired from office. In addition, it should be noted that there were still other George Washingtons who were his contemporaries.

The contents of various purported Samuel Adams documents that have appeared on the market in recent years, like that of the George S. Washington item, were the red flag for experienced collectors. Yet a surprisingly large number of both collectors and dealers plunged ahead and sank into the bog. These documents actually are signed by an unknown Samuel Adams whose signature to a considerable extent resembles that of the noted Revolutionary patriot and Massachusetts Signer. The similarity, however, ends there [Plate XX]. Common sense should have demonstrated that the Samuel Adams who signed in acknowledgment of the receipt of wages for a day's labor or payments for carpentry or cooper's work could not have been the more fortunately circumstanced patriot, a well-born man of wealth, wide education and culture, who was to become Governor of Massachusetts. There was in his day still another Samuel Adams, a surgeon during the Revolution, who later pursued his career in Maine. To unravel any autographs of his from those of the Governor requires much closer attention and study.

The same is true in cases of autographs signed Charles Francis Adams. There are three prominent in American history. The first is the diplomat, 1807-1886. The second is his son, 1835-1915, a lawyer, a brother of the author, Henry Adams, and a financier and railroad official who rose to the rank of a brigadier-general of volunteers during the Civil War. The third is his grandson, who was Secretary of the Navy under President Herbert Hoover. The confusion generally exists only concerning autographs of the first two, a fact which might have been eliminated had the second added "Junior" to his name. If this designation, as well as that of "3rd" or "III," had been more universally adopted throughout the years, the task of determining which Adams was which would have been simplified.

The first Josiah Quincy, 1744-1775, of the three who established their places in history and also in the autograph world, used "Jr.," but none thereafter did. His father was of little renown, and the son's signature differs by using the abbreviation. Quincy, Jr., was well known for his activities as a pamphleteer in pre-Revolutionary agitations against England. His son, who could have designated himself as Josiah Quincy III, lived from 1772 to 1864, was the president of Harvard and author of a two-volume history of that college. He passed his full name on to his eldest son, born in 1802. This scion continued the family's literary traditions by writing a book, *Figures of the Past*, published in 1882, the year of his death. Both these Quincys, who might be labeled Josiah III and Josiah IV, served as mayors of Boston—the third from 1823 to 1828; the fourth from 1845 to 1849—a fact which further tends to trouble the autograph collector.

Confusion of this type is perhaps more frequent among the families of Massachusetts than those of any other state and began in the earliest Colonial days. John Winthrop, for instance, came to Massachusetts in 1630, was the first Governor of the new Colony and left a journal which furnished an extremely valuable contribution to America's first history. His namesake and son, who survived his father by twenty-seven years, landed in Massachusetts in 1633, led the group that settled Ipswich that year, subsequently colonized Saybrook, Connecticut and became Governor of the Colony, for which he obtained a new liberal charter in 1661. About the same period there were two Simon Bradstreets, one the Massachusetts Colonial Governor, 1603-1697, the other the learned Congregationalist minister, 1671-1741. Again there appear in the early eighteenth century two Jonathan Belchers. The first, born in 1682, was Colonial Governor of Massachusetts and New Hampshire in 1730 and Governor of New Jersey in 1747. His son, born in 1710, who became Chief Justice and subsequently Lieutenant-Governor of Nova Scotia, died in 1776, some twenty-one years after his father.

The name William Bradford, first famous in Massachusetts and later distinguished in other states as well, has appeared on many documents and caused numerous mishaps in identification. The first of the name, born in 1590, was he who sailed with the Pilgrim Fathers, signed the Mayflower Compact, served as the second Governor of Plymouth Colony and died in 1657. Another William Bradford, born in 1663, but of an unrelated family, also emigrated from England and settled permanently about 1685. He aided in founding the first paper mill in America in 1690 and established a printing press in Philadelphia. Subsequently he moved to New York, where he printed the first New York paper money in 1709, the first American *Book of Common Prayer* in 1710, the first drama written in the American Colonies in 1714, the first history of New York in 1727 and the first newspaper to appear in that town, the *New York Gazette*, in 1725.

This printing tradition was followed by his namesake and grandson, born in 1722, and heralded as the "patriot printer of 1776." He became a colonel in the Revolutionary Army and was wounded at the Battle of Princeton, while his own son, still another William Bradford, was serving as a lieutenant-colonel in the Pennsylvania Militia. The printer died in 1791, four years before his son, who had been a Supreme Court judge and had served for a year as Attorney-General in Washington's cabinet. To the many opportunities of confusing these William Bradfords must be added still another. A namesake descendant of the Plymouth Colony Governor lived from 1729 to 1808 and was chosen a Rhode Island delegate to the Continental Congress. He did not take his seat, but in later years was a United States Senator and Governor of his State.

Two Samuel Dexters, both Bostonians, must be kept separate. The first, 1726-1810, was a merchant and ardent patriot well before and during the Revolution, and an early patron of Harvard. His son, born in 1761, was a distinguished jurist who served as Secretary of War and of the Treasury in the cabinet of the first President Adams. He had studied law in the office of Levi Lincoln, who had a son-namesake. The first Levi, born in 1749, was an early patriot who went as a volunteer with the Minute Men to Cambridge. He was chosen, but declined to serve, as a delegate from Massachusetts to the Continental Congress. In 1801 he accepted Jefferson's appointment as Attorney-General and also served as Secretary of State *ad interim* under the same President. He took office in 1807 as Lieutenant-Governor of Massachusetts and became Acting-Governor in 1808 on the death of his predecessor. The latter fact may account for the reason he is so often confused with his son who was Lieutenant-Governor in 1823, and Governor in 1825. Nine times out of ten, autographs of the son, who lived from 1782 to 1868, are found in sets of Cabinet Officers instead of those of the father who properly should be represented.

Contemporary with the Hancocks and the Lincolns were the two James Bowdoins. The elder, in whose honor Bowdoin College was named, was also Governor of Massachusetts in 1785 and 1786, at the time of Shays' Insurrection, and had been chosen a delegate to the Continental Congress but was prevented from attending by his failing health. His son and namesake, born in 1752, was sent by President Jefferson in 1805 as Minister

Plenipotentiary to Madrid to settle the Florida Purchase and the limits of Louisiana.

Autograph collectors must likewise be on the alert to avoid mixing the John Nixons, one from Massachusetts, and the other from Pennsylvania [Plate XXIII]. The Bay Stater was born in Framingham in 1725, led a company of Minute Men at the Battle of Lexington, commanded a regiment at Bunker Hill and was named a brigadier-general on August 9, 1776. He further distinguished himself at Saratoga and survived until 1815. The Pennsylvanian was his junior by eight years but predeceased him by seven. His military career was also a prominent one, for he served as a colonel, was a member of the Committee of Safety of Pennsylvania and commanded the defenses of Philadelphia. In addition, he served with Washington's Army in New Jersey, at Valley Forge and until the end of the war, and is remembered for the fact that he was the first to read the Declaration of Independence to the people, assembled on the State House grounds on July 8, several days after its adoption.

Connecticut, next to Massachusetts, is the native State of those with duplicated names which cause autograph collectors the greatest difficulty. The Trumbulls, of a family that still remains prominent in State affairs, are the most troublesome in the Nutmeg State category. Of its autograph-noted members there were two Jonathans and two Johns. Both Jonathans, father and son, were Harvard graduates, and both were State Governors, one from 1769 to 1784, the other from 1797 to 1809. The father, who added further complications by occasionally signing the earliest form of his surname "Trumble," lived from 1710 to 1785. He was a close friend of Washington, and the fact that the President at times referred to him as "Brother Jonathan" is responsible for the later use of this phrase to describe a typical American.

The son was born in 1740, was appointed paymaster in the Northern Department of the Revolutionary Army, served as secretary and aide to Washington, was elected a member of Congress in 1789, became Speaker of the House of Representatives two years later and thereafter was elected to the Senate. He died in 1809. The signatures of both Jonathan Trumbulls are so similar in style that the only way to distinguish between them is to note that the father customarily signed "Jonth. Trumbull," and the son, "Jona. Trumbull" [Plate XXIV].

The first, who is never known, incidentally, to have signed himself as "Brother Jonathan," was father to the renowned painter, one of the two John Trumbulls. Washington, whom this son served as aide, sat for him a number of times. He is also distinguished for other work including his paintings of the Battle of Bunker Hill, the Death of Montgomery at Quebec, and the Surrender of Lord Cornwallis at Yorktown. He lived from 1756 to 1843. The other John, his cousin, was born in 1750 and made a career as poet, author and jurist. He was a leading member of the coterie known as the "Hartford Wits," but his fame is chiefly based on his epic poem entitled *McFingal* —a popular imitation of Samuel Butler's *Hudibras*—and on his association with Noah Webster in the latter's preparation of his dictionary. The writing of both John Trumbulls is very similar, but letters of the less famous poet are very scarce, whereas those of the painter are very common. The scarcity of one versus the fame of the other approximately equalizes the market values of their autographs.

Like the Trumbull family, the Wolcotts of the same State present problems, but to a lesser degree. They chiefly center around the Oliver Wolcotts, father and son, both of whom were Connecticut Governors, about which office there seems to have been something of "dynastic succession." The first Oliver, who lived from 1726 to 1797, is additionally distinguished by the fact that he was a Signer; the son, who was Secretary of the Treasury under Washington, was born in 1760 and died in 1833. Their handwritings are very similar, and autographs of the younger Wolcott, which are far less valued, are constantly found improperly included in a set of the Signers.

Connecticut also claims two Jared Ingersolls. Their autograph values are reversed, for it is the son's which outstrips the father's. The latter, 1722-1781, practiced law in Connecticut and underwent public censure because he distributed stamps in New Haven under the terms of the notoriously unpopular Stamp Act of 1765. The younger Jared, who lived from 1749 to 1822, was a friend of Benjamin Franklin and an eminent Pennsylvania lawyer. He served his adopted State as a representative in the Federal Convention and signed the Constitution of the United States in that capacity. He was in 1812 an unsuccessful candidate for the vice-presidency.

Connecticut's eastern neighbor, Rhode Island, had its own share of "doubles," prominent among whom are two William Ellerys, who are frequently confused. Again they were father and son. The elder, 1727-1820, whose autographs are distinctly more valuable because he was a Signer, also served as Chief Justice of Rhode Island in 1785. Autographs of the son, about whom little is known, are constantly taken for those of the father, an understandable fact since both served as Collectors of the Port of Newport. In addition, their signatures, which regularly appear on import certificates and custom-house papers, bear such a close resemblance to one another that, despite the clue of dates, autographs of the son are often found in sets of the Signers. There is one means of making a distinction: the elder Ellery, signing as Collector, wrote "William Ellery Coll.," running the words somewhat together; the son signed similarly and added "Jr.," but he too practiced running words together, so that the "Jr." has been unfortunately overlooked in many cases [Plate XXXV].

Another Rhode Islander of note was Nathanael Greene, second in command to Washington during the War of Independence. This general, who spelled his name Nathan*a*el and not Nathan*i*el, had a cousin of the same name who lived in East Greenwich, Rhode Island. Repeatedly at public sales, letters purporting to be autographs of the distinguished soldier have been sold. Experts at once recognized them as written by the cousin and not by the general who drove the British out of South Carolina. The signatures of the two Greenes bear a certain resemblance to each other, but when examined together can quickly be differentiated [Plates XXI, XXII]. Unfortunately, the existence of this cousin to the general is not well known, and in consequence any Nathanael Greene signature written at that period is usually assumed to be that of the Revolutionary hero.

Autographs of the cousin are quite valueless; those of General Greene, although his letters are far from scarce, are held at good prices because of his prominence in American history. Besides these two Greenes, there were two William Greenes in Rhode Island. Father and son, both were Governors of the Colony, the elder from 1743 to the time of his death in 1758, and the son from 1778 to 1786. The latter, who lived from 1731 to 1809, was also Chief Justice of the Colony.

A name which was undoubtedly as common as leaves on a tree, as it still is today, is John Brown. Only three important contemporaries in Colonial America need to be considered by the autograph collector. They were from Rhode Island, Massachusetts and Virginia, and each was chosen as a delegate to the Continental Congress. The Virginian alone attended. The Rhode Islander, who lived from 1736 to 1803 and was a wealthy trader and merchant, anticipated the War of Independence when he instructed the captains of his ships to carry powder as freight on their voyages back to American ports. By this foresight he was able to supply the army at Cambridge when it had been reduced to four rounds. In after years he laid the cornerstone of the first building of what is now Brown University, which he generously endowed.

The Massachusetts John Brown, born in 1744, served with distinction as a Revolutionary officer, having been with Ethan Allen at the capture of Fort Ticonderoga and with General Horatio Gates when Burgoyne surrendered at Saratoga. Colonel Brown was killed by the Indians in 1780 as he was marching up the Mohawk Valley to relieve General Philip Schuyler. John Brown of Virginia, who was born in 1755, moved to Kentucky where, after he had played a prominent part in having that State admitted into the Union, he was elected to the United States Senate. On his death in 1837, he was the last survivor of the Continental Congress. The letters of all three Browns, distinguished in their achievements and position if not in their names, are very rare. Perhaps the best means of identifying their autographs is by studying the contents, the towns from which they were written and the dates. If necessary, the historical societies of the various states will provide facsimiles of their handwritings for purposes of comparison. A fourth John Brown, of Osawatomie, 1800-1859, was unquestionably more famous than any of his three namesakes, but his autographs present no problems.

Among New Yorkers, the George Clintons, both of whom were governors, are frequently confused. Their dates, however, should identify them easily, since the second was only twenty-two when the first died in 1761. The elder, who was no relation of the younger, was born about 1686 and served as Governor of New York Colony from 1743 to 1753. He belonged to the English nobility, and his son, Sir Henry Clinton, is far better known because he commanded the British forces in New York during the Revolutionary War. The second George was born in 1739 and served as Governor of the State from 1777 to 1795 and again from 1800 to 1804. He also served as Vice-President of the United States under Jefferson and died holding that office under Madison in 1812. Letters of the first Governor are very scarce and fairly expensive. Those of the second, and certainly more notable, are not uncommon and more reasonable in price. His documents appear with great regularity on the market and have only moderate value.

The same British-American pattern of duplication in the Revolutionary period is provided by the Howes. Actually there were three—two British, one a general and the other a vice-admiral; and one American, also a general. Letters of all three are fairly rare, but those of General Robert Howe, who commanded the North Carolina troops at the defense of Charleston, are most desired. This officer had a distinguished military career not at all marred by the fact that he was courtmartialed for his inability to defend Savannah. Allegedly surprised by the enemy there, he was tried but was honorably acquitted, later joined Washington on the Hudson and again served with ability. Vice-Admiral Richard and General William Howe, brothers who both customarily signed only their surnames, figured prominently in the reduction of Long Island and New York City. The latter had gained earlier fame since he was in command at the siege and capture of Louisburg, at the attack on Quebec and the capture of Montreal during the last French-Indian war paralleling the Seven Years' War in Europe. In the Revolution itself again he commanded at Bunker Hill and was further engaged at the Battle of Brandywine and the capture of Philadelphia.

The New York Robert R. Livingstons also contribute their worry to autograph collectors, inasmuch as the famous Chancellor of the State is frequently confused with his father. The senior Robert R. Livingston, a distinguished jurist, member of the Stamp Act Congress and a bitter opponent of the Act, died at the outbreak of the Revolution in 1775. The son, born in 1746, was one of the original five men to draft the Declaration of Independence and later administered the oath of office to Washington when he was inaugurated as first President. Letters of the younger Livingston are more common than those of his father, but the demand for the latter being greater they bring higher prices.

Another New Yorker, Benjamin F. Butler, may be mistaken for an unrelated namesake. Both were distinguished lawyers. The New Yorker, Attorney-General under both Presidents Jackson and Van Buren, was born in 1795 and died in 1858. The other, who lived from 1818 to 1893, was Governor of Massachusetts and prominent as a major-general of volunteers in the Union Army. This same military rank was also held by John A. Dix of New York, who was Secretary of the Treasury under President Buchanan and was Governor of his State from 1872 to 1874. When he died, another John A. Dix, who served rather inconspicuously as New York Governor from 1910 to 1912, was only nineteen. The difference in their dates should aid in distinguishing their autographs, but examples of both are neither rare nor more than nominally valued.

Were the Caesar Rodneys of Delaware confused, an unwary collector might suffer to a worse extent. The first, who lived from 1728 to 1784, was a Signer and a member of the Continental Congress, and, in his later years, like "Brother Jonathan" Trumbull, changed the spelling of his surname from Rodeney. Of the three Delaware representatives, two—George Read and Thomas McKean—were tied in voting to approve the Declaration of Independence, and, since Rodney later cast the deciding vote when that of his State's delegation was needed, he is reputed to have cast the vote which decided the Declaration's adoption. The Signer's namesake was his nephew, the son of his brother Thomas, who was a member of the Continental Congress. The nephew, Attorney-General in Jefferson's cabinet, was twelve when his uncle died, and, in addition, he signed himself Caesar A. Rodney. However, he was so accustomed to run the middle initial into the "R" of his surname that his signature is frequently mistaken for that of the Signer. When this occurs, and Caesar A. Rodney's autograph is included in sets of the Signers, ignorance of the dates of the two men is generally responsible.

The fact that there were two Gunning Bedfords, cousins, both from Delaware and both members of the Continental Congress, gives cause for frequent embarassment, a situation which was recognized by the younger, who signed himself "Jr." [Plates XXXIII, XXXIV]. The elder, born in 1742, became Governor of Delaware after serving as a colonel and being wounded at the Battle of White Plains. Bedford, Jr., born 1747, served as aide to Washington and later, a delegate to the Federal Convention, signed the Constitution of the United States. He had survived his cousin by fifteen years when he died in 1812. The autographs of neither Gunning Bedford are common, but those of the younger are very much scarcer and are in greater demand to complete sets of Signers of the Constitution.

Autographs of one of New Jersey's Signers, Richard Stockton, who lived from 1730 to 1781, need to be studied for their dates, since his handwriting closely resembles that of his namesake son, the United States Senator, who lived from 1764 to 1828. There is little demand for, and small value to, autographs of the son, but the elder Stockton's are scarce and bring good prices. Because of this fact, occasionally the son's A. L. S.s will turn up with the date line carefully clipped off in an effort, no doubt, to pass off the son for the father.

Another Signer from New Jersey, John Hart, had a namesake from Lancaster County, Pennsylvania. The signatures of the two men are sufficiently alike to prove troublesome. Those of the Signer, who lived from 1708 to 1780, are repeatedly encountered on the paper money issued by the Colony in 1776. But his A. L. S.s are exceptionally rare. The Pennsylvanian, a member of the local Committee of Safety, frequently wrote on political subjects, and, fortunately for collectors, his letters are generally dated at "Octoraro." Many of them, too, were written after the Signer's death. Much concerning the less famous Hart, including the dates of his birth and death, remains unknown. The Signer is sometimes further confused with John De Hart, a New Jersey lawyer and also a delegate to the Continental Congress, whose writing is quite different.

Four other Signers, John Penn from North Carolina, Charles Carroll from Maryland, George Ross and George Taylor, both from Pennsylvania, need to be watched as to their autographs to avoid mistakes in identities. Penn, who is high on the rare Signer list, may be confused with William Penn's eldest grandson [Plate XXV]. The Signer, who lived from 1740 to 1788, was born and practiced law in Virginia before he moved in 1774 to Williamsboro, North Carolina. After serving as a delegate to the Provincial Congress, he was repeatedly sent to the Continental Congress. Aside from the fact that he served from 1780 to 1781 as a member of the North Carolina Board of War, little is known of him thereafter. The grandson of the founder of Pennsylvania inherited from his father in 1771 life use of a quarter of the proprietary rights in the Colony and served as Colonial Governor. In 1777 he was held a prisoner on parole. He was never found guilty of any overt act against the American cause and was left to spend quietly the remainder of his life, aside from a few years abroad, at his country estate, "Landsdowne," on the Schuylkill, near Philadelphia.

The Signer Carroll, who always designated himself as Charles Carroll of Carrollton, is easily distinguished from his cousin Daniel, a Signer of the Constitution, to whom his contemporaries referred as "Daniel Carroll of Rock Creek," but who himself signed his name simply "Daniel Carroll" [Plate XXVIII]. Both, however, are apt to be confused with various namesakes in their large and noted family. Born in 1737, Charles Carroll of Carroll-

ton had outlived all other Signers when he died in 1832. Besides
long service in the Continental Congress and a three-year term in
the United States Senate, he, with Samuel Chase and Benjamin
Franklin, was a member of the American Commission fruitlessly
sent to persuade Canada to join the Revolution. He lived in semi-
retirement after 1801, and his last public act was to participate
in 1828 at the formal ceremony which marked the opening of
construction on the Baltimore & Ohio Railroad, the first in America. Daniel, 1730-1796, was his cousin, a Maryland delegate to
the Constitutional Convention of 1787, and, as one of her United
States Senators, took active part in ceding to the Federal Government that Maryland territory on the Potomac's north bank
which became the District of Columbia.

Charles Carroll, the Signer, may be confused first with his
father, who lived from 1702 to 1782 and designated himself as
"of Doughoregan"; second, with his father's relative, Charles
Carroll of Duddington, also later known as of Carrollsburg; and
lastly with Duddington's son, who died in 1820 and was known
as "of Bellevue." To make the necessary distinction between the
two Daniel Carrolls of the period, it must be known that Charles
Carroll of Duddington and Carrollsburg had a son baptized
Daniel. This second Daniel, 1764-1849, is not to be mistakenly
identified with his uncle-namesake who was active in Maryland
politics. Like his father, this Daniel used "Duddington" to distinguish himself and was commonly referred to and generally
signed "Daniel Carroll of Duddington Manor" or "Daniel Carroll of Dudn." [Plate XXVIII]. Active in the shipping trade and
a director of the Washington Canal Co., he inherited the mano-
rial lands where the Capitol and many of the Federal buildings
are now located.

George Ross, the Pennsylvania Signer, who lived from 1730
to 1779, practised law in Lancaster, Pennsylvania, was an active
patriot for many years and was particularly interested in Indian
problems. He was a delegate also to the Provincial Congress,
as well as the Continental, and in the years immediately thereafter was commissioned judge of admiralty. He must be kept
distinct from his son and also a much earlier George Ross, 1679-

1754, a prominent and peripatetic clergyman called by his contemporaries "a wandering star" because he traveled extensively in America and England [Plate XXVI].

George Taylor, by birth an Irishman, as a young man of twenty emigrated to America in 1736 and bound himself upon his arrival in Philadelphia to an iron manufacturer at Durham, Pennsylvania. Upon the death of his employer he married the latter's widow and became proprietor of the works. Early in the seventies, he was already taking an active part in political affairs. In 1775, he was sent to the Provincial Assembly from Durham, and the following year was chosen a delegate to the Continental Congress to replace one of the five Pennsylvania delegates who had hesitated to vote for the Declaration of Independence. In his new capacity, he not only voted for but signed the Declaration on August 2. He retired from Congress in 1777, and little is known about him from that time until his death in 1781. The few documents and letters of Taylor that have come on the market have usually been dated from Durham, and this fact helps to dissociate him from another George Taylor, also from Pennsylvania, who was signing papers about the same time, and about whom little is known. The wrong man, however, has repeatedly appeared in sets of the Signers, and collectors must be on their guard.

Among "duplicates" of the Revolutionary period should also be included the two Captain Stephen Decaturs, father and son, and the two Colonel William Butlers. Both Decaturs had distinguished naval careers, and, coincidentally, both served at different periods on the U. S. frigate *Philadelphia*. The father, 1752-1808, made a name for himself as a privateer in the Revolution and again at the time when war between the United States and France seemed imminent. His son, born in 1779 and killed in a duel with Commodore James Barron in 1820, distinguished himself on numerous occasions, particularly in the Mediterranean during the Tripolitan War and other expeditions which aided in opening up the Barbary Coast. Of the Colonel Butlers, one lived from 1759 to 1821 and was a noted South Carolinian and delegate to the Federal Convention. During the War of

1812, as Major-General of Militia, he commanded the South Carolina troops for State defense. The other colonel, whose birth date is unknown but who died in 1789, served for a time as aide to General William Alexander, Lord Stirling, won considerable renown by his exploits during the war and destroyed two Indian villages in retaliation for the Wyoming Valley Massacre in Pennsylvania.

Then there were the two John Armstrongs, father and son [Plate XXVII]. The elder was born in 1725 and died in 1795. He fought in the French and Indian Wars and, as brigadier-general in the Continental Army, commanded the Pennsylvania Militia at the Battles of Brandywine and Germantown. His son, 1758-1843, was a Revolutionary colonel, an aide to General Horatio Gates and the author of the first of the two" Newburgh Letters," which incited the army at the close of the war to seek satisfaction and justice from Congress. Madison appointed him his Secretary of War in 1813. Letters of his father are very rare and command a substantial price; his own are quite common and bring considerably less, although prices may vary according to the interest of their contents.

During the Revolution, the Lee name appears time and again. There were two Charles Lees [Plate XXX]. The one, a major-general and for a time second in command to Washington, was suspected of treachery at the Battles of Trenton and Monmouth and was eventually court-martialed. He was born an Englishman in 1731, and, making war his vocation, had served under several masters in various European wars before he finally sought his fortune in America. He acquired estates in West Virginia where he retired after his disgrace and died there in 1782. The other, his unrelated namesake, was born in 1758, a member of the noted Virginia family. A distinguished jurist, he served as Attorney-General under Presidents Washington and the first Adams, and, at one time, was Aaron Burr's counsel at the latter's famous trial for treason. This Charles Lee died in 1815.

His brother was Henry Lee, whose dates are 1756 and 1818, and who was affectionately nicknamed "Light-Horse Harry" by the young cavalrymen under his command. His most famous son was the Confederate General Robert E. Lee, but it is a son Henry, the author and historian, born in 1787 and living until 1837, with whom he is most frequently confused. Autographs of "Light-Horse Harry," who became Governor of Virginia, are of somewhat greater value than those of Henry, Jr. The older Harry's relatives, Francis Lightfoot Lee and Richard Henry Lee, who were also notable in American history, provide no stumbling blocks in the autograph world.

This is not at all the case, however, with the Benjamin Wests, of whom there were three contemporaries, all distinguished. The most famous, perhaps, was the painter, 1738-1820, who resided a great part of his life in England and became the president of the Royal Academy, of which, with Sir Joshua Reynolds, he was one of the founders. The second Benjamin, born in 1746, established himself as a lawyer in Charlestown, New Hampshire, and was chosen a delegate from that State to the Continental Congress, but declined the honor. He died three years before the painter and four years after the third Benjamin West, a Rhode Island astronomer, who was born in 1730. Letters of the painter are in greater demand than those of the other two, yet none of the three Wests' autographs command high prices.

About this same time there were two John Fitchs, the one a simple man who used bad grammar and had difficulty with his spelling; the other an educated person, one in authority who wrote fluently and with ease [Plate XXIX]. Of the two, the first is the more important. This John Fitch, 1743-1798, volunteered his services as a gunsmith for the American forces and endured the hardships of Valley Forge. He was later to be famed as the inventor of the steamboat in 1785, many years prior to Fulton's claim to this achievement. The second John Fitch, 1749-1840, a fourth or fifth cousin, served as Deputy Commissary General of Issues during the Revolution. Letters of the inventor are extremely rare and high priced, whereas those of his cousin, though also not common, sell for considerably less since they are not in great demand.

General Henry Dearborn, 1751-1829, who served as colonel in the Revolution and Secretary of War under Jefferson, is repeatedly confused in the autograph world with his son, Henry A. S. Dearborn, thirty-two years his junior, who died in 1812. The younger Dearborn made a name for himself in the War of 1812, as a brigadier-general in command of the defenses of Boston Harbor. Both Dearborns held office as Collectors of the Port of Boston, the son succeeding the father in that position. Autographs of the latter are much more sought, but those of Henry A. S., who ran his initials close together with his surname, are often mistaken for letters and documents of his father.

Still others who cause trouble are the two John Pickerings. The first, a New Hampshire member of the Continental Congress and Federal Convention, dates from 1737 to 1805; the second, a Bostonian by birth, 1777-1846, was a distinguished philologist. Of their autographs, those of the former, because rarer, are in greater demand. There were also the two Richard Peters, one the uncle of the other. The elder was born in 1704 and died in the year of Independence. He was a noted clergyman, secretary to a succession of Pennsylvania Governors and a founder with Benjamin Franklin of the Public Academy which grew into the present University of Pennsylvania. His namesake nephew, 1744-1828, was a Revolutionary patriot and represented Pennsylvania at the Continental Congress. Letters of neither command high prices, but the elder's are rarer than those of the younger.

The name, Return Jonathan Meigs, may sound unique today, yet there formerly were many who bore it. Of them, three must be disentangled. The first, born in 1734, was the noted Revolutionary colonel who accompanied General Benedict Arnold on the expedition to Quebec and who subsequently fought elsewhere both brilliantly and daringly. After the war he became one of the earliest settlers in Ohio and was appointed Indian Agent to the Cherokee Nation in 1801. He died in 1823, two years before his son, who had been named after him. The younger Meigs, born in 1765, had accompanied his father to Ohio and settled in Marietta. Noted as a jurist, he was elected Governor of the State in 1810 and later served as Postmaster-General under Madison and Monroe. The third Return Jonathan Meigs, born a grandson of the Revolutionary colonel in 1801, died toward the end of the century. He has little claim to fame, but, because he served as Special Agent to the Cherokee and Creek Indians in 1834, his autographs are sometimes mistaken for his grandfather's by collectors who fail to verify dates. The autographs of the Meigs, father and son, are not common, but neither are their prices prohibitive.

Those who form sets of the Signers of the Constitution find it necessary to differentiate between the John Blairs, father and son. The elder, 1689-1771, as Acting Governor of Virginia, showed a spirit of toleration that was unusual for his day. It is the letters of his son, however, which are extremely rare. They are in great demand by collectors because he fits into various categories and sets. Born in 1732, the younger John Blair became a distinguished jurist and, an early patriot, was chosen a delegate to the Federal Convention. In that body he, Madison and Washington were alone among the Virginia delegates to vote the adoption of the Constitution. Washington in later years appointed him a Justice of the United States Supreme Court, a position he held when he died in 1800. All too often letters or documents of his father are found in sets where his are wanted.

It is curious, although the handwritings of Presidents of the United States should be familiar to experienced collectors, that the fourth, James Madison, should be confused with one of his contemporaries. The President was born in Virginia in 1751 and died in 1836. The other James Madison, also a Virginian, born in 1749, became a Protestant Episcopal bishop and the president of the College of William and Mary, and died in 1812. It is not generally known that the Chief Executive was named after his father and at one time actually signed himself "Jr." A cataloguer in a recent auction sale, seeing the name "James Madison, Jr.," on a letter, jumped to the conclusion that it had been written by the President's son and was therefore valueless. Others, too, unfamiliar with the President's signature and ignorant of the fact that at one time he usually signed himself with the "Jr.," failed to recognize the A. L. S. It was accordingly neither listed nor mentioned in any way. Actually it was of major importance both because of its date and contents. It had been written on the very day that the Assembly of Virginia, on June 25, 1788, ratified the Constitution of the United States. Besides announcing this fact and giving the exact number of votes for and against the question, Madison noted that only two members had been absent, and these had been divided in their opinion. He added that recommended amendments would accompany the act of ratification.

Discovering the confusion of identities that occurs between American and American, and American and British, the collector cannot properly conclude that difficulties are confined to men of English-speaking countries. Unquestionably the greatest tangles due to identical name sharing occurs among the members of the French National Assembly during the years of the first French Revolution. Collections of sets of their autographs, doubtless given impetus by Carlyle's famous *History of the French Revolution*, have long been popular, and the problems involved have been perplexingly numerous because many of the Assembly had the same surname and invariably signed without the given name that might have differentiated them.

One of Napoleon's noted marshals, François Joseph Lefebvre, Duke of Danzig, whose letters or documents are highly desirable, is a case in point. Robinet's *Dictionnaire Historique et Biographique de la Révolution et de l'Empire, 1789-1815** lists not less than fourteen Lefebvres, some of whom hyphenated this surname. Another name to be conjured with in this same group is that of Berthier, of whom there were four, all of them contemporaries. Louis-Alexander Berthier, Prince of Neufchatel and of Wagram, 1763-1815, is the one most in demand, as he was Napoleon's marshal. A younger brother, Caesar Berthier, 1765-1819, rose to the rank of General of Division and distinguished himself at the Battle of Marengo. Both brothers served in America under Rochambeau. The third Berthier was Victor-Leopold, 1770-1807, who served under Bonaparte in Egypt and also became a General of Division. A fourth Berthier, 1745-1832, likewise bore the Christian name of Alexander, making things even

* Librairie d'Education Nationale, Paris, n. y.

more complicated. Apparently he was no relation to the others. He, too, was a general and served in the armies of the Revolution and Empire.

The name Kellerman is still another to be examined carefully. In this case there are two men who must be kept distinct. François-Christophe, first Duke of Valmy, 1735-1820, was Napoleon's marshal. His writing is fairly large and pointed. His son, who varied the name only slightly to François-Étienne, also bore the title of Duke of Valmy, the second in line, and dates from 1770 to 1835. He was a famous cavalry leader and rose to be a lieutenant-general. His writing is smaller and quite different from that of his father.

Occasionally in their autographs one or two of the many Assembly "duals" considerably added to the signature the name of the district he represented—one deputy Merlin signed himself "Merlin de Th."; another deputy Merlin, from Douay, always signed "Merlin d.d." Two other delegates, both members of the Committee of Safety, were known as Prieur de la Marne and Prieur de la Côte d'Or. Of the fourteen Leclercs listed, General Victor Emmanual Leclerc's autographs are most sought after by collectors because of his career both in France and in San Domingo. He was Napoleon's brother-in-law, having married Pauline Bonaparte, and later he governed the West Indian island where he died in 1802. Robespierre is another troublesome name of this French Revolutionary period, and Auguste-Bon-Joseph is very often mistaken for Maximilien, the famous leader of the Jacobins. Although both men signed themselves briefly "Robespierre," letters of the elder are far more in demand and of much greater value than those of Auguste, who was commonly known as "Robespierre le Jeune." The latter served as a member of the National Convention during the Reign of Terror, his career having been sponsored by Maximilien. The devotion of the two brothers to each other was exemplified in their death on the guillotine the same day. Auguste, hearing of Maximilien's execution sentence, requested the honor of ascending the scaffold with him.

If it should be noted that these various instances of duality of names concern only men, the fact is not difficult to explain. In the first place, although daughters are just as frequently named after their mothers as sons after their fathers, women even in this Lucy Stone era change their names on marriage. It is also unusual for autographs of women to be collected. There is one notable exception which may be specially cited—Eliza Parke Custis and her younger sister, Eleanor (Nellie) Parke Custis, who was Washington's adopted daughter. Both women were children of John Parke Custis, son of Martha Washington. On March 20, 1796, Eliza married Thomas Law, a man considerably older than herself. This fact may have played its unfortunate part, for they were separated in 1804 and formally divorced in 1811. At the latter time, Mrs. Law resumed her maiden name and took to signing herself "E. P. Custis." It was in this manner that Nellie, prior to her own marriage in 1779, had also signed. Her autographs, which are quite rare, are much sought after by collectors, while her sister's are nominally valued. There are times when autographs of the two can be properly attributed by examining their dates. Otherwise it is important to know that the one-time Mrs. Law had a pointed, irregular script, and Nellie Custis used a neat, squarish and small style of writing.

The question of which autograph belongs to what writer is necessarily asked in the field of literature, which also has its crop of name duplications. There were, for example, two Thomas Paines who were living in the late 1700's. The one, by far the more famous, was the author of *The Age of Reason*, *Rights of Man* and the pamphlet, *Common Sense*, which did so much to arouse the colonists to a sense of British injustice and a desire for independence. Collectors need not go into all the details of his stormy career, but should know that after the war he sojourned briefly in England, then went to France where he was widely hailed and made a member of the National Assembly. After he had been imprisoned by the French and barely missed the guillotine, he returned in 1809 to America to die in abject poverty. The other Thomas Paine, the son of Robert

Treat Paine, a Massachusetts Signer, was born in 1731 and gained some note as a writer of popular lyrics. To avoid being confused with the then notorious author of *Common Sense* he changed his name in 1801 to that of his father. Prior to that time, there remains the danger of mistaking the two Thomas Paines; subsequently it is necessary to distinguish between the son, who died in 1811, and the father. Few collectors are even remotely interested in the poet, but letters of the other Thomas Paine are in great demand, and when the contents are good they command very high prices.

The Channing family of Boston produced two William Ellery Channings, both men of literary distinction. The elder, 1780-1842, a clergyman known as the "Apostle of Unitarianism," was an intellectual leader among his contemporaries. His nephew, 1818-1901, was the associate of Emerson, Thoreau and Hawthorne and a poet of some renown. Of the two, autographs of the poet are in greater demand, but those of neither have unusual value.

Another poet of the last century, Richard Henry Dana, is apt to be confused with his son, both because of their overlapping dates and because of their position in the literary worlds of their day. The father, 1787-1879, was a lawyer and as well a miscellaneous writer and author of *Buccaneer and Other Poems*. The younger man, far more famous because he wrote *Two Years before the Mast*, the still classic sea story, was born in 1815 and died in 1882. The elder Dana is almost forgotten as a writer by the modern generation, which accounts for the fact that his autographs do not provoke any demand comparable to that for his son's.

The autograph history of the Danas somewhat resembles that of two French writers of the same name. These are Alexander Dumas, *père*, and Alexander Dumas, *fils*. The first, born in 1803, was the author of *The Three Musketeers*, *The Count of Monte Cristo* and other like romantic novels. He died in the year that marked the end of the Second Empire, while his son lived on to 1895. Dumas, *fils*, born in 1824, made an equally illustrious name in the field of drama, his work including the classic *La Dame aux Camelias*, the play which was shaped into a libretto for Verdi's opera, *La Traviata*. In former years the demand for the son's autographs exceeded that for his father's, but today the situation is reversed. Letters of both can now be obtained at a reasonable figure.

Dumas' authorship of *The Three Musketeers* also stimulated demand for autographs in another quarter. The novelist had taken his leading character, d'Artagnan, from life, using for model a seventeenth-century Count d'Artagnan, Charles de Baatz de Castlemore. The great paucity of his signatures, which might be used for purposes of comparison, made it even easier for his autographs to be mistaken for the near valueless writings of a Count d'Artagnan, Pierre de Montesquieu, who lived a generation or more later.

Among the literary of more recent times, the two Robert Bridges and the two Winston Churchills pose certain problems. Robert Bridges, the English poet laureate, 1844-1930, must be differentiated from the American author of the same name. Again the writing of the great English Prime Minister of our own day must not be mistaken for that of the similarly named American who wrote *Richard Carvel, The Crisis* and other historical novels.

Alfred Tennyson, the poet, may be confused with his son, Hallam, a difficulty which was precipitated when the former was made Baron Tennyson in 1884 and took to signing himself simply "Tennyson." This practice was followed by his son, who became the second baron. The latter, Governor and Commander-in-Chief of South Australia, was born in 1852 and died in 1928. The poet laureate had died in 1884.

The two Henry Wallaces, father and son, of whom the former had a middle initial "C" and the latter a middle initial "A"—letters difficult to distinguish in script—must also be differentiated. The younger, Vice-President during Franklin D. Roosevelt's third term and Secretary of Commerce under President Truman, held one post in common with his father. Both served as Secretary of Agriculture; the elder under President Harding from 1921 to 1924, and the younger during the first two terms of the Roosevelt administration, from 1933 to 1940.

Countless other examples of duplication of names undoubtedly exist. Many are unknown, and others, known, are fortunately of little concern since the autographs they involve do not appear on the market save infrequently. New instances, however, crop up plentifully. When they do they may cause trouble in similar degree to those duplications which have been cited because they are a potential danger to the unprepared autograph purchaser. This roll-call is not all inclusive, yet it may serve to suggest the pitfalls of confused identities.

A. M. Broadley in his *Chats on Autographs** refers to his happening on two Oliver Cromwells, two Horace Walpoles, two Charles Dickens' and two Sarah Siddons'. In the majority of autographs by those of the same name, the prices involved embrace a range which is not sufficiently wide to cause more than a dent in the careless buyer's bank account. When the error, however, involves the payment of a substantial price for a wrongly attributed autograph, the plea of "poor-judgment" on the part of a dealer will not exonerate him. Collectors may make mistakes, and often do, but they are not expected to be as familiar with the areas of confusion as are the dealers. For the latter circumspection is obviously necessary above all because they must place their guarantee on any manuscripts handled and sold.

In all matters bearing on confused identities when the collector himself is uncertain, he is best advised not to give himself the benefit of the doubt. A dealer may on occasion choose to gamble on an item and buy it in order to do research. Such a motive is not altogether altruistic, but, should he find himself wrong, the results of his time and effort at least serve to insure others against future blunders. To gamble with his own funds is naturally his own affair, but to gamble with those of a customer is quite another matter. When representing a client, the reputable dealer cannot afford to take chances. Should he do so and later be proved wrong, his reputation will deservedly suffer.

* T. Fisher Unwin, London, 1910.

CHAPTER XII

The Importance of the Collector

WINTER lay heavy over Washington during the first year of the Civil War. The capital, which was then more a large town than a city, had been habituated to strange sights. New recruits from New England, from the North Atlantic States, and from what was known as "the West" milled about the once quiet streets. Generals, cabinet members, those who were the great leaders of the Union, even the President himself in stovepipe hat could be seen almost any day hurrying up and down the White House steps. In the tense months of 1861, many events and the appearance of many distinguished men, which would normally have aroused interest, caused little stir among Washington residents. Anything could be expected. The backflow from the first Battle of Bull Run had prepared them, and subsequent activities had quickly taught that the war would not be over in a few months. Individually, they had their more serious affairs. Many were grimly concerned with the war itself, others with the daily problems of living in a war-disrupted world. It was no time for sidewalk spectators.

Dr. Thomas Addis Emmet, then only a young man, but possessed of that interest which later made him one of the greatest collectors of old manuscripts in America, braved the cold blasts on Pennsylvania Avenue one wintry day. Snow was falling, and the streets were blanketed so that the heavily laden sleighs which were gliding silently past seemed almost spectral. The drivers shivered and huddled in their thick cloaks, the straining horses pulled on their traces and massive hogsheads jostled and bounced. A horse slipped on an icy stretch and fell to his knees. Young Emmet's attention was attracted. The driver jerked sharply on the reins, managed to raise the struggling animal to its feet and, leaping from his seat, went forward to examine and steady the frightened horse. Meanwhile, the young man idly noted that the barrels contained half-torn bundles of papers. One yellowed sheet became detached, was caught by the wind and swiftly blown down the avenue. A second loosened, then a third, and both were swept away. Dr. Emmet's curiosity was fully aroused. The appearance of the paper seemed unusual, for it did not resemble ordinary scrap paper. He reached out and grabbed a handful, nodding to the driver as he did so. The latter only shrugged. Pointing in the direction of the Potomac, he indicated by a gesture that the load was to be dumped and that he himself was indifferent to the whole matter.

Dr. Emmet, turning to shelter the papers against the wind, unfolded an old manuscript. He whistled in his amazement. What he held was a letter in George Washington's well-known handwriting. His quick examination of the others revealed letters written by Jefferson, Hancock and a number of the nation's early leaders and patriots. Looking up in dismay, he watched as the long line of sleighs started up once more and moved toward the river.

Then, spurred by indignation, he hastened to the Capitol to inquire there why so very many documents written by those prominent in America's founding were being destroyed. An apathetic official informed him. Thousands of soldiers were being quartered upon the City, and the problem of feeding these men had become acute. Space for kitchens had been commandeered throughout Washington and had proved inadequate. Necessity demanded the use of the Capitol. Under the great front square were vast chambers and vaults, lined with shelves that were stacked high with the original manuscript records of the Colonial and Revolutionary periods. The Army appropriated these rooms to install temporary ovens for the baking of bread, and the papers, haphazardly crammed into hogsheads, were cleared out for what was considered, according to military efficiency, the most practical destination—the river.

Dr. Emmet, whose interest in autographs dated from boyhood, was never able to forget this experience, and out of it grew his serious resolve to collect historical manuscripts. With the comparatively few papers he had salvaged that morning in Washington, he began. Years later the New York Public Library acquired from him a set of the Signers of the Declaration of Independence, then in its completeness an astounding and valuable series; a draft of this great document, written entirely in the hand of Jefferson; a full autograph letter, the only one known to be in existence, signed by Thomas Lynch, Jr., the Signer from South Carolina, whose single signature today is rated amongst the rarest items for the collector; a collection of the generals of the Revolution; and the extra-illustrated set of Benson Lossing's *Field Book of the American Revolution*. Dr. Emmet spent many years in hunting, gathering and preserving documents, manuscripts and letters which in many instances gave lost information and threw new light on previously unrecorded American history. He saw, too, as others did after him, that his early Washington experience was not an isolated incident to be explained and excused by the upheavals of the Civil War.

Realizing the contribution the study of the past can make to the present, the average person is apt to be mildly indignant when he first learns about the various causes of lost records. The responsibility for their preservation, however, he decides is not his. Actually, it is the individual duty of no one person or official or institution in any one country; yet librarians and private collectors, who are more acutely aware of the value of these records, voluntarily assume this responsibility. They, together with the historian, the biographer and the historical novelist, know through direct experience that history, which so frequently has turned on a small and apparently trivial episode affecting the lives of nations and countless men and women, is more extensively unwritten than written. They realize that the key to an epoch is lost with that epoch's records, and that the unearthing of one letter, one document, or one deed, of little interest to the amateur, may radically change what has always been considered true.

War, any war, is of course the greatest destroyer of historical documents, but such destructions are unfortunately repeated in times of peace. Americans have read how European archives, one after another—the archives at Monte Cassino, the Ateneo de Manila, the National State Archives of Naples and the Columbaria Library at Florence—were destroyed during World War

II. They could not pause to grieve then, when grief over the loss of human life was paramount, but they were apt to exclaim: "Things like that do not happen over here. We take care of our records, wartime or no." In the majority of cases, this is true where the records are officially guarded. But no further back than 1907, a "peace year," the Civil War Washington loss was almost repeated in New York City, and the order for destruction was again given by officials.

At that time, as now, the Barge Office of the Port was situated on the Battery. Its attic was filled with records, and included among them were many documents signed by Washington, Jefferson, Madison, Adams, Monroe and others of the Presidents. In addition, there were countless invoices, import certificates, ships' papers, extensive correspondences of the Collectors of the Port of New York, then rapidly becoming the most important in the world. For its vast business more space was needed, and government authorities, intent on clearing out the attic accumulation, sold the entire contents, about one hundred and forty tons in all, to a junk dealer.

Mr. Benjamin, who had then been engaged in the manuscript and autograph business for twenty years and had gathered an extensive and historically invaluable stock, heard of the sale. Hastening to the Battery, he found the junkman and his assistants loading the purchase into large wicker baskets and burlap bags. A necessarily rapid examination immediately convinced him of the importance of the papers. Only by promising to pay for the manuscripts item for item, rather than by pound, did he arrange that the junkman would send the greater portion of the papers to his office. For months afterwards, the sifting-out process, which required careful examination of each paper, continued while each week new deliveries of baskets and bags were made. Mr. Benjamin described this episode—one of the most notable of his career—which added tremendously to his stock, in a copy of *The Collector*,* the still-existing publication founded by him in 1887. He commented that at this same period more than a dozen other custom houses in various of the

* Vol. LI, February 1937, p. 38.

country's ports were swept clean of the majority of their records.

A failure on the part of the officials to recognize the importance of historical records and letters is not the only cause of destruction. This is clearly illustrated by a letter written in 1937 by Frederick Coykendall, a Trustee of Columbia University, which throws a light at second-hand on the history of the Lincoln era.

"I was much interested," he wrote, "in your article in the last number of *The Collector*, 'Autographs in Retrospect'... Horace G. Young... told me the following: He was an intimate friend of Robert T. Lincoln, the son of Abraham Lincoln, and he and Mr. Lincoln were accustomed to spend part of each summer together. A few years before Mr. Lincoln's death, Mr. Young... found Mr. Lincoln in a room surrounded by a number of large boxes and with many papers scattered about the floor, and with the ashes of many burned papers visible in the fireplace. Mr. Young asked Mr. Lincoln what he was doing, and Mr. Lincoln replied that he was destroying the private letters of his father, Abraham Lincoln. Mr. Young at once remonstrated with Mr. Lincoln and said that no one had any right to destroy such papers—Mr. Lincoln least of all.

"Mr. Lincoln replied that he did not care, and intended to continue his destruction—since the papers he was destroying contained the documentary evidence of the treason of a member of Lincoln's cabinet, and that he thought it was best for all that such evidence be destroyed. Mr. Young told me this incident just a few years before Robert Lincoln died. I wonder how much history was lost because of this remarkable action."*

Mr. Coykendall continued the story in another letter written two months later: "The publication of the incident in *The Collector* has had an interesting aftermath .... While dining at the house of Dr. Nicholas Murray Butler... reference was made to the article in *The Collector* whereat Dr. Butler said: 'I remember the incident well for I was there at the time. Mr. Young came over to my hotel greatly agitated, and told me of Mr. Lincoln's action. The following morning I went to see Mr. Lincoln and

* Vol. LI, April 1937, p. 61.

told him he had no right to destroy such papers. There was still one trunk full of papers not destroyed and I persuaded Mr. Lincoln to send that trunk to the Congressional Library.' "*

This Mr. Lincoln actually did, but, in sending the trunk in 1923 to the Library of Congress, he stipulated that its contents were not to be examined until twenty-one years after his death. Mr. Lincoln died in 1926, and his wish has since been faithfully followed. Repeated requests to use the material for Lincoln biographies reveal that historians are alert to the importance of this trunk's contents. Yet when it was first received in Washington, the Librarian of Congress so casually regarded the new acquisition to the Lincoln material already housed in the Library that he briefly disposed of it in his 1923 report: "These papers," he stated, in reference to the entire collection, "have been in the Library as a deposit since 1919, but no announcement was permitted until the gift was completed by Mr. Lincoln." Meanwhile, the Library's previously acquired Lincoln papers, according to the report, had been "used by Mr. Nicolay and Mr. Hay in preparing their *Life of Abraham Lincoln*. The collection, having been examined closely by such competent writers may contain little unpublished material calculated to change estimates of men or matters." The Librarian's conclusion apparently was also applied to the subsequent and last Robert Lincoln contribution.

In 1937 Mr. Coykendall again wrote, "A friend of mine who saw *The Collector* tells me that he has in his possession a letter from Gideon Welles, who you remember was Secretary of the Navy under Lincoln, to his wife. I did not see the letter so cannot quote, but the substance is: Lincoln is dead. I hope his papers have been destroyed for there is rank treason in the Government. This seems to fit in strangely with the remarks of Robert Lincoln and Mr. Young.

"Again—Mr. Robert Levi Todd was one of Lincoln's most intimate associates. Lincoln wanted him to take a place in the Cabinet but he refused; however, he remained Lincoln's close

* Dr. Butler corroborates Mr. Coykendall in his Autobiography: *Across the Busy Years*, Scribner, 1939, pp. 375-376.

adviser—somewhat the same as Colonel House to President Wilson. Todd's Lincoln papers were left to a man named Todd Gentry, who later on destroyed all of the papers...These persistent and repeated stories of the destruction of Lincoln papers and the suggestion of treason surely suggest that there is some foundation for the idea of treason in Lincoln's cabinet."

Additional evidence that these important letters may point to treason was brought forward, in May 1945, by Dr. John J. Meng, Assistant Professor in the Department of Political Science, Queens College, who wrote: "The Assistant Chief of the Manuscript Division at the time Robert Todd Lincoln entrusted his father's papers to the Library was the late Dr. John C. Fitzpatrick. I recall hearing Dr. Fitzpatrick on a number of occasions state that 'the full and true story of the Lincoln administration will never be written until these papers can be used.' He further implied quite clearly that he believed they would demonstrate that there were treasonable activities going on in Lincoln's official family during the course of the Civil War." It is obvious that when the trunk of Lincoln papers arrived at the Library, it would not have been stored unpacked. The rapid effects of mildew and other diseases affecting paper are too well known to the authorities to allow them to be careless in such matters. It is not improbable that Dr. Fitzpatrick, who in his official capacity would have had access to the collection, might well have glanced through it. Certainly he spoke with the authority of one who had seen and knew the papers' contents.

The treason, about which there have been so many hints, has been suspected for a number of years and alluded to by historians and biographers.* If the idea of Mr. Coykendall and Dr. Fitzpatrick is correct, obviously Robert Todd Lincoln's destruction was dictated by the hope that the families or relatives of the guilty party or parties might not suffer through such revelations. The truth cannot finally be ascertained until the collection is made available in 1947 or at a date thereafter which the Librarian may determine at his discretion.

Modern readers are thoroughly familiar with accounts of

* See Otto Eisenschiml, *Why Was Lincoln Murdered?* Little, Brown and Co., Boston, 1937.

official papers being destroyed because those in whose care they were, like Mr. Lincoln, did not wish them to be made a part of history. "Legation employees were busy burning official papers" is a frequent sentence in newspaper reports at a time when the breaking of diplomatic relations between two countries appears imminent. On the eve of an invasion of a capital, it is quite usual that the government order destruction of papers rather than permit its state department documents to fall into the hands of the enemy.

A graphic account of just such action during the 1940 invasion of France is described by Samuel Flagg Bemis, Professor of Diplomatic History, Yale University:* "The Germans were advancing rapidly toward Laon. Premier Paul Reynaud told Ludwig Oscar Frossard, Minister of Information and Propaganda, that the highest military authorities would not guarantee the security of the French capital after midnight. Functionaries of the French foreign office were then summoned at dawn and ordered to destroy the archives of the ministry. In the first article of the new newspaper, *Le Mot d'Ordre*, Frossard described the destruction of the records: 'The *Quai d'Orsay* seemed prey to a veritable fury of destruction. Enormous masses of documents were hurled out of the windows and burned on the lawn. Hundreds of curious spectators gathered on the banks of the Seine to view the lamentable spectacle. A huge cloud of smoke arose from the garden of the *Quai*. There was such haste that a fire broke out [presumably in the building itself] and it was necessary to call out the firemen.' This is what the French did themselves. There is no telling what the Germans may have done since then to any remaining documents."

The most casual student of history realizes how very differently crucial periods of the world might appear today had authentic records survived. One of the mysteries of the life of Mary, Queen of Scots, which centers around the murder of her husband, Henry, Lord Darnley, might be solved had the famous Casket Letters been preserved. There were eight letters and a sequence of irregular sonnets said to be addressed by Mary

* *American Historical Review*, July 1944.

to the Earl of Bothwell. The nature of these documents—whether authentic, forged or partly forged and partly genuine—has been the theme of much discussion. If they were authentic throughout, they afforded perfect proof of Mary's complicity in the murder of her husband so that she might be free to marry Bothwell. When Queen Elizabeth brought Mary to her trial and death, the Casket Letters played an important role, but they were never produced, were repeatedly challenged by Mary, her adherents and historians later, and were certainly destroyed, presumably by her son who later became James I of England.

Man and his wars have played dominant roles in the destruction of historical records, but they have been abetted by floods, fires and other catastrophies of nature. Minor natural causes have also played their parts, for papers, improperly stored, have been ruined by rot, mildew and worms. Again, records are discarded due to inevitable changes resulting from varied tastes and interests of men and women of new generations, who are indifferent to the value of papers owned by them or in their care. In England, after the sequestration of the imperial estate of the East India Company to the Crown, the new masters of India House, removing their office to Westminster, made a clean sweep of the Company's records. Although some of these papers are known to have survived, and indeed a few have appeared at auctions since, a vast portion of the records of the Indian Navy disappeared forever.

G. Birbeck Hill, in his *Talks about Autographs*,* reports that the letters which Boswell, the biographer of Samuel Johnson, received from many of the most eminent men of his time were destroyed by his executors. Boswell's own correspondence with his friend, William Johnstone Temple, was sold for waste paper, and only a small portion of it, found being used as wrapping paper by a butter-man, was recovered and published. During the French Revolution of 1848, the *Hotel de Ville* in Paris and other buildings were ransacked, and a tremendous volume of papers, letters and documents, dealing with the first Revolution of 1789 and the Napoleonic period, was destroyed, and the balance lost

* Houghton, Mifflin & Co., 1896, p. 12.

to the French Government. The history of a very remarkable bound volume pertaining to the first French Revolution, which mysteriously found its way to the American market and was sold in 1929, might conceivably be traced back to that day. The volume contained fifty vellum sheets, each being a decree issued by the National Assembly, all signed by Louis XVI and comprising orders that related to the removal of taxes on salt and certain foods, the emancipation of Jews, the cancelling of bridge tolls and similar other long-disputed and democratically vital measures.

Many old court houses in the South were emptied of their contents during the Civil War, and it was said by contemporary witnesses that the path of the Union forces could be traced by following the old family papers strewn along the road. Among American librarians and in the autograph and manuscript trade, it is generally known that a vast number of the papers of the War Department in Washington were discarded. The understanding is that these were ordered burned, but that the person who was to have done this, appreciating more than his superiors their value and significance, chose to preserve them. Of these, many items have repeatedly appeared at auctions and in dealers' catalogues for several decades, and today are scattered in institutions all over the country.

Even now the general public's ignorance of the value of old manuscripts is surprising, and similar wholesale destruction still goes on. Within the past ten years many tons of material, unexamined and unquestionably including important and unknown historical facts, have been destroyed in the same heedless fashion which caused the burning in the nineties of the papers of Samuel Huntington, Governor of Connecticut and Signer of the Declaration of Independence. Late in the 1930's some forty tons of papers from the Philadelphia custom house were sold to various purchasers for a few hundred dollars. The sale was in accordance with an act of Congress permitting the Archivist of the United States to make recommendations for the disposal of "useless papers." Unfortunately, however, it was the Treasury Department and not that of the National Archives which decided what was to go. The list of papers to be disposed of, all dated after 1910, was sent to the Philadelphia officials at a time when they were extremely busy, and, in addition, they were only given a few hours in which to execute the order. The clerks responsible for the checking and removal of the papers hurried through their task and were careless in the bargain. Consequently, wrote Dr. Boyd, who was at the time Director of the Historical Society of Pennsylvania and who attended the sale and bought some of the papers, "they threw into one great mass practically everything they could lay their hands on, and I myself saw one document as early as 1743 in the mass of forty tons."

Librarians and collectors are today gravely concerned over the destruction of the written word and are most anxious that an ever-increasing public become conscious of the value that is inherent in manuscripts and letters. Through them, the traditions of the past may be safeguarded. Were a person to own a letter of Stonewall Jackson or Lafayette or of a statesman, king, queen or any other of the easily recognized famous, he would normally understand that it has a value. But he might not know that the correspondence of little-known individuals may prove of equal importance in throwing light on a particular era. Gideon Welles, who figures in the Coykendall-Lincoln correspondence, wrote a letter to his wife in which he speaks of "rank treason in the Government," and hopes that Lincoln's papers were destroyed upon his death. The letter, otherwise of small value, provides a clue for the historian-detective to track down.

Family papers may also frequently furnish information that to scholars is indispensable for a proper study and appreciation of a given period of the past. A letter describing the day-to-day details of her life by the wife of a pioneer in California during the '49 Gold Rush may prove a great "find" for a novelist writing of that period. Such books as Kenneth Robert's *Oliver Wiswell*, which so intimately describes Revolutionary Boston, New York and many other American cities; Margaret Mitchell's *Gone with the Wind*, with its detailed account of Georgia, during the Civil War; Elizabeth Page's *Tree of Liberty*, Thackeray's *Henry Esmond* and *The Virginians*, and James Fenimore Cooper's *The Last of the Mohicans* could never have been so graphically written had not their authors had access to original manuscript sources, from which they derived their material.

The biographer of Alexander Hamilton inevitably must record the fatal wounding of the first Secretary of the Treasury in a duel at the hands of Aaron Burr at dawn, July 11, 1804. The story can be told dryly. It could be given its full drama were the writer to consult the collection presented in 1945 by a private collector to the N. Y. State Historical Association at Cooperstown, New York. This fine group of some forty-five items comprises the original letters of Hamilton to Burr and those of his seconds to Burr's seconds, original drafts of Burr's letters in reply and of Burr's seconds, and the pardon granted by Governor D. D. Tompkins of New York to William Peter Van Ness for acting as Burr's second at a time when dueling was outlawed. The "other side of the fence" correspondence—what the Hamilton group received, originals taking the place of drafts, and drafts instead of originals—interestingly enough, is preserved in the New York Historical Society of New York City.

A failure to consider the term autograph in its professional sense may possibly explain why the announcement of a historical society's or library's acquisition of an autograph collection is given such scant attention by the public, yet in the academic world the collection may quickly become the honey that attracts a horde of scholars. When the American Philosophical Society, whose library in Philadelphia has for many years housed a tremendously important and extensive collection of Benjamin Franklin papers, purchased for some twenty-two thousand dollars the Franklin-Jackson letters at a London auction sale in January 1945, the fact went practically unheralded. These thirty-three unpublished signed autograph letters, covering the years of Franklin's life between 1753 and 1767, when he was American Agent for the Colonies in London, were addressed to Richard Jackson, a Member of Parliament. To the historian or biographer so fine an acquisition by the Society makes the library an imperative for all research on Franklin or his period.

Something of the same importance was quickly attached to the Illinois State Historical Library at Springfield, when its Lincolniana was made available; to the William Henry Smith Memorial Library at Indianapolis with its President William Henry Harrison papers; and to the Hayes Memorial Library of Fremont, Ohio, which specializes in all material relating to President Rutherford B. Hayes and his contemporaries. Also in this category, among many other institutions, is the University of Louisville Library, where are deposited various private papers of the late Supreme Court Justice Louis D. Brandeis, who was so actively engaged in the Zionist movement that its history in America and Palestine cannot adequately be written until his letters are open to the researcher.

Today, when the means for the collecting and disseminating of news have been so intensified, it is easy to reason that the present era's history is being written in a white light of publicity from day to day. A few may claim that in the year 2000 there will be no need for scholars to consult records and letters when an appraisal of our time is made. Anyone who stops to consider, however, will quickly realize that it may be years before he can have access to much secret information of actions and events and their controlling factors. The true history of the momentous Teheran and Yalta Conferences between Churchill, Roosevelt and Stalin is more veiled now than the agreements by which Poland was first partitioned between Germany, Austria and Russia. Certain published documents have contributed to the story, but very much of it is still contained in private reports and letters. No one of these may give a complete account. Each is a piece in a puzzle, and these pieces may even now be in the possession of individuals to whom some official wrote in great confidence. President Franklin D. Roosevelt showed his recognition of the fact that current history must await a much later day for accurate writing when he established a library at his home in Hyde Park for the housing of state papers. These, it may well be supposed, have been weeded out of such information as he did not wish, for personal or other reasons, to have become public property.

Mr. Roosevelt's decision is one of a growing list that points to the accelerating interest in autographs in America, an interest that lagged for many years behind Europe's, where this form of collecting has been popular for several centuries. It has often been said that there is only one collector of autographs in America to every thousand book collectors. The last forty odd years have brought a great change, and this ratio is becoming less and less disproportionate. Libraries specializing in regional material, historical societies and university collections have encouragingly multiplied, and through their expansion have drawn the attention of the public to the necessity of preserving old records. The quantity of these, hidden away in attics and basements, in offices and stores, forgotten, or preserved by those who look upon then merely as idle curiosities, is still very great. Librarians and collectors have shuddered at the thought of donations to paper-salvage drives, which in many cases may have been inspired by patriotic zeal but not governed by discretion. Such fervor led a woman to proffer for metal salvage an artistically wrought and irreplaceable Spanish iron balustrade that graced her town home. Her offer was rejected, but one could hardly visualize an enthusiastic salvage collector going through a bundle of old papers to determine which should be preserved and discriminating between the important and the unimportant.

Social, economic and business documents have also won new attention in recent years. In 1941 the New York Committee on Business Records was organized to impress upon the city's business men the importance of systematically preserving their records and making them available for research. Its organization and aims are described in a brochure by Thomas C. Cochran of New York University, entitled *New York City Records: A Plan for their Preservation.** The New York Public Library, which took over the more significant papers of the New York World's Fair Corporation, is also trying to prevent the destruction of the records of old business houses. The Library of Congress has begun the collection of all documents bearing on book publishing

* Reprinted from the article in the *Bulletin* of the Business Historical Society, June 1944.

in America, and a private collector in Boston is searching for any letters or material pertaining to the publishers Tichnor & Fields. Among the most valued collections owned by the American Antiquarian Society are the business papers of Isaiah Thomas, a famous printer of the Revolutionary period. The Scribner papers covering a full century are the most considerable collection of publishing records. In *Company Museums*,* Laurence Vail Coleman, Director of the American Association of Museums, lists eighty American and three Canadian business corporations which have properly valued their records and efficiently set about their preservation, some in recent years, others in the more distant past.

Correspondences which have been very recently written, are being written, and will be written in the immediately succeeding days may also have incalculable historic importance in the future. Often the private collector, equipped through long experience with both a special knowledge and an almost sixth sense of values developed by extended study, can ferret out and preserve that which may prove to have lasting value. He is, above all, a free agent in a sense that the librarian of an institution, who is circumscribed by many factors, cannot be. Most practically, the latter is restricted by his budget and by his duties themselves. These often do not permit him the time required to run down the material in which he may be wholeheartedly interested. He may read, for instance, that in Philadelphia certain documents are to be sold, but at a time when he cannot leave his post, or funds are not available. In similar instances, the private collector whose time is his own is in no way held back. He may travel anywhere for an objective.

Again, the private collector is often more the specialist than is the librarian. The latter's knowledge in the realm of autographs is extremely broad and frequently general, whereas the collector has narrowed his and focused it on a particular small area. Mrs. Hills, who assisted in gathering together the Beinecke Collection of Robert Louis Stevenson, is among the unquestioned authorities on that writer. Many librarians would bow to her

* The American Association of Museums, Washington, D. C., 1943.

judgment on Stevenson, yet she, in turn, would submit to their judgment on matters pertaining to the Revolutionary and Civil Wars or to the French First Empire. The private collector, then, is often the specialist among specialists.

He will also frequently have devoted himself solely to one subject—Sidney Lanier, Ethan Allen, Johannes Brahms—and have studied not only all available papers which have been written immediately by his "hero" but everything that pertains to him. The collector, accordingly, has at his fingertips an expert knowledge which few others are able to duplicate. It enables him quickly to determine the possibilities of new data being revealed, the likelihood that a particular paper may be extant and in the possession of some specific family or that "lost" material may crop up in a definite locality. Knowing very explicitly what he wants, he further is in the best possible position to "sleuth" or to explore in out-of-the-way places.

The autograph collector, perhaps more than any other, is better able to experience that joy in discovery which comes when he reaches the end of a long and difficult trail, or when he happens casually and unexpectedly on treasure he never knew existed. His interest and activity are similar in many ways to those of collectors in general. But his motives are superior to those of others who collect with no thought of contributing to cultural and historical progress. Autograph collecting leads him into lonely paths. Enthusiasms are not often readily shared. Yet, although his brothers may not be in his neighborhood nor in his own city, he has many scattered far and wide. These constitute a fraternity and one which he elects to join because he fully shares its cultural aims.

Illustrations

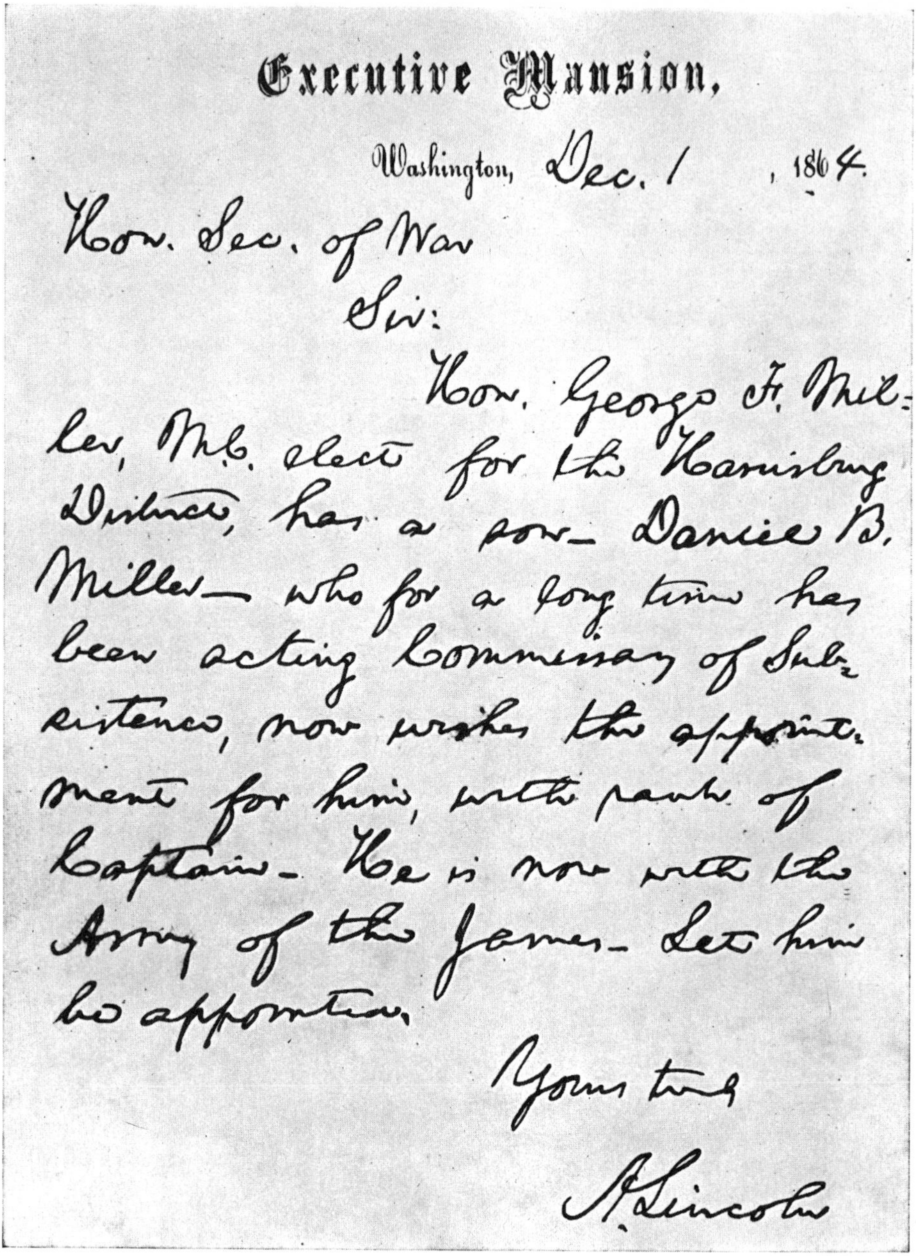

Executive Mansion,

Washington, Dec. 1 , 1864.

Hon. Sec. of War

Sir:

Hon. George F. Miller, M.C. elect for the Harrisburg District, has a son—Daniel B. Miller—who for a long time has been acting Commissary of Subsistence, now wishes the appointment for him, with rank of Captain.—He is now with the Army of the James—Let him be appointed.

Yours truly

A. Lincoln

PLATE I. PRESIDENT LINCOLN, HIS TWO SECRETARIES AND
HIS COUSIN NAMESAKE.

Plate I. A.L.S. of the Civil War President. To this letter he used "A. Lincoln," which he invariably signed in preference to his full signature legally required on official documents. See p. 180.

Plate II. A. Last portion of A.L.S. of John Hay, Lincoln's secretary who later became Secretary of State under McKinley and Theodore Roosevelt, and whose handwriting is not infrequently mistaken for that of Lincoln. See pp. 38-39, 180. B. Last portion of A.L.S. of John Nicolay who, like Hay, was a Lincoln secretary, whose writing has also been confused with that of the President. See pp. 38-39, 180. C. Portion of the last will and testament signed by Abram Lincoln of Hancock County, Illinois, the Catholic cousin of President Lincoln. See p. 194. Reproduced from the original in the Hancock County Clerk's Office.

A

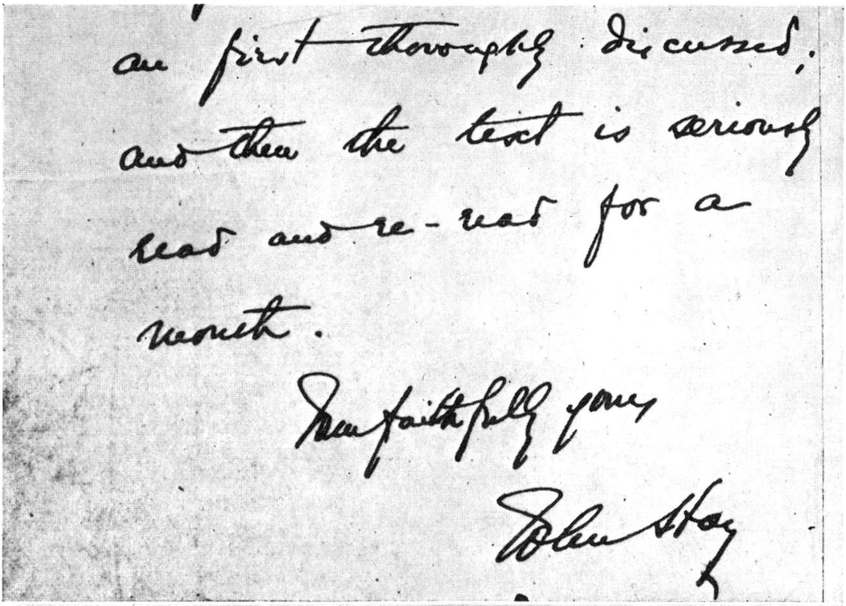

are first thoroughly discussed; and then the text is seriously read and re-read for a month.

Very faithfully yours,

John Hay

B

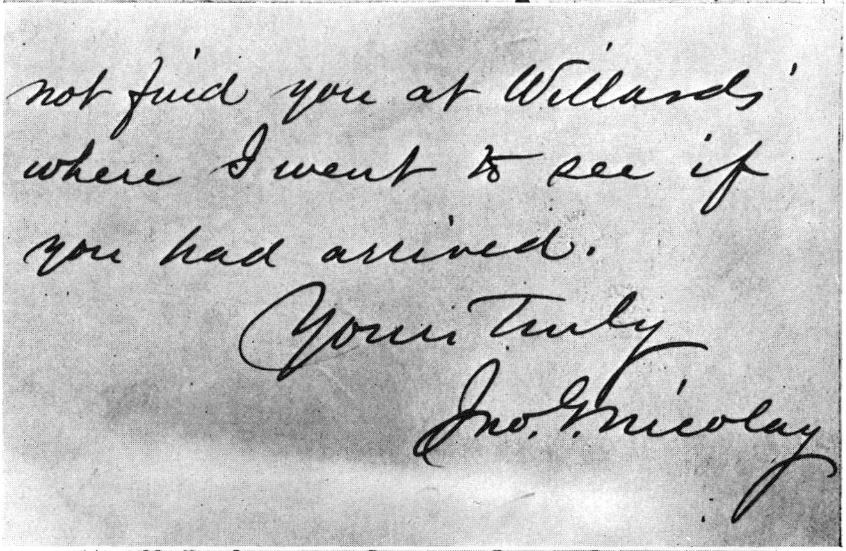

not find you at Willards' where I went to see if you had arrived.

Yours Truly

Jno. G. Nicolay

C

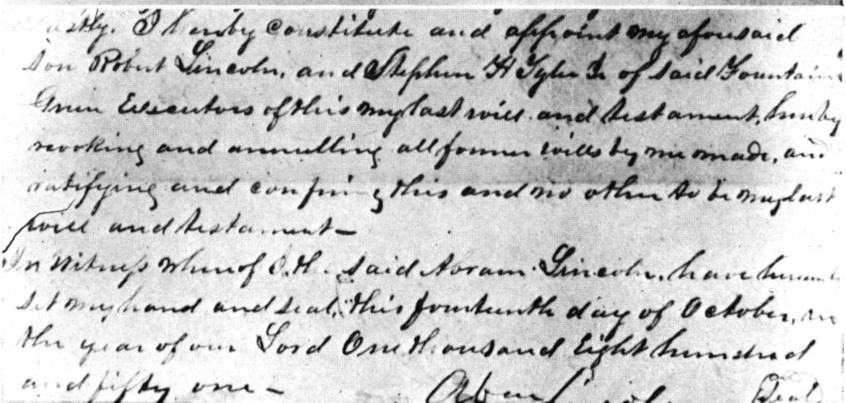

...astly. I hereby constitute and appoint my aforesaid son Robert Lincoln, and Stephen H. Tyler Jr of said Fountain Green Executors of this my last will and testament, hereby revoking and annulling all former wills by me made, and ratifying and confirming this and no other to be my last will and testament—

In Witness whereof OH. said Abram Lincoln have hereunto set my hand and seal, this fourteenth day of October, in the year of our Lord One thousand eight hundred and fifty one— Abr Lincoln (Seal)

PLATE II.

A   B

PLATE III.   THE FORD THEATRE PLAYBILLS.

These reproductions show the two different versions of the Ford Theatre playbill distributed on the night of Lincoln's assassination. See pp. 133-136. That on the left (A) was printed before it was known the President would attend. On the right (B) is the amended version.
The actual size of both, margins included, is 18 3/16″ by 4 7/8″. The original playbills belonging
to John B. Wright, Stage Manager of Ford's Theatre in 1865, are now preserved in the Harvard Theatre Collection, through whose courtesy they are here reproduced.

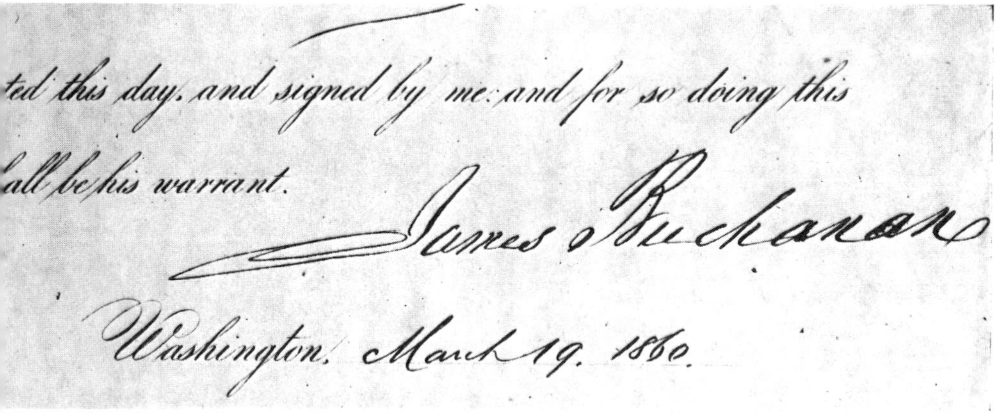

ted this day, and signed by me: and for so doing this
all be his warrant.

James Buchanan

Washington, March 19. 1860.

A

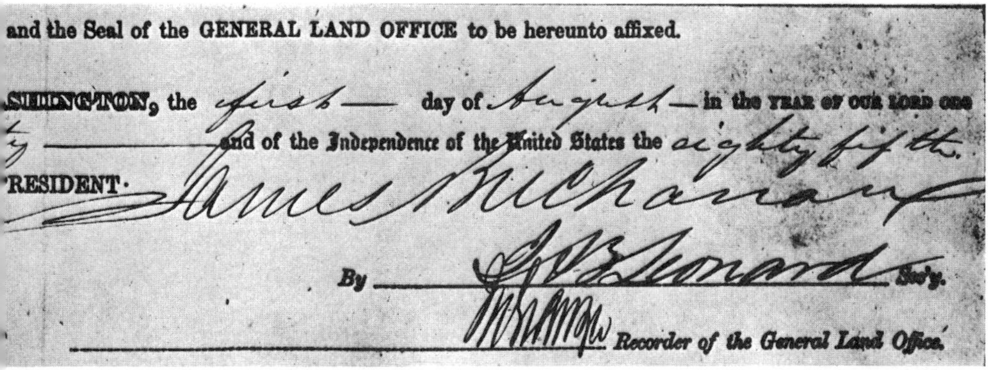

and the Seal of the GENERAL LAND OFFICE to be hereunto affixed.

SHINGTON, the *first* —— day of *August* —— in the YEAR OF OUR LORD one
ty —————— and of the Independence of the United States the *eighty fifth*.

RESIDENT: James Buchanan

By J. B. Leonard Sec'y.

—————————————— Recorder of the General Land Office.

B

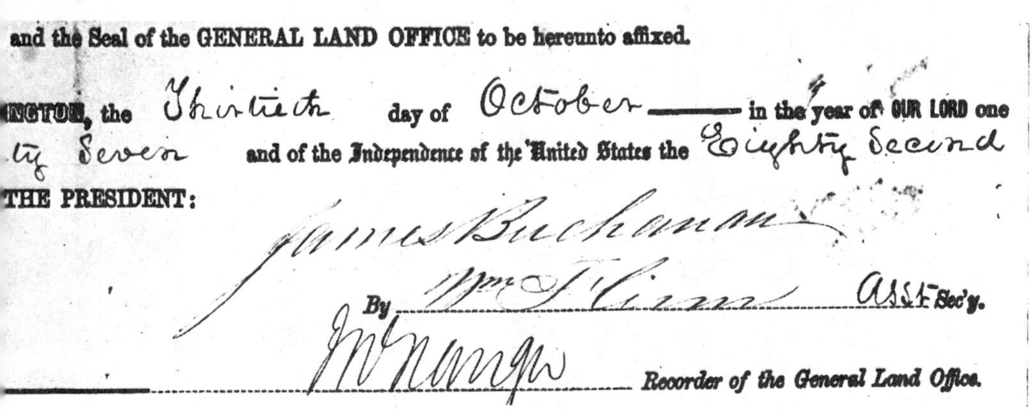

and the Seal of the GENERAL LAND OFFICE to be hereunto affixed.

NGTON, the *Thirtieth* day of *October* —————— in the year of OUR LORD one
ty Seven and of the Independence of the United States the *Eighty Second*

THE PRESIDENT: James Buchanan

By Wm Flinn Asst Sec'y.

—————————————— Recorder of the General Land Office.

C

PLATE IV.

BUCHANAN AND HIS IMITATORS.
(signatures reduced ⅓)

A. Authentic signature of President James Buchanan. B. Lower portion of document
signed for Buchanan by his secretary J. B. Leonard. C. Another by his secretary William
Flinn. In signing for the President, Leonard imitated as closely as he could the handwriting
of the President. See p. 139.

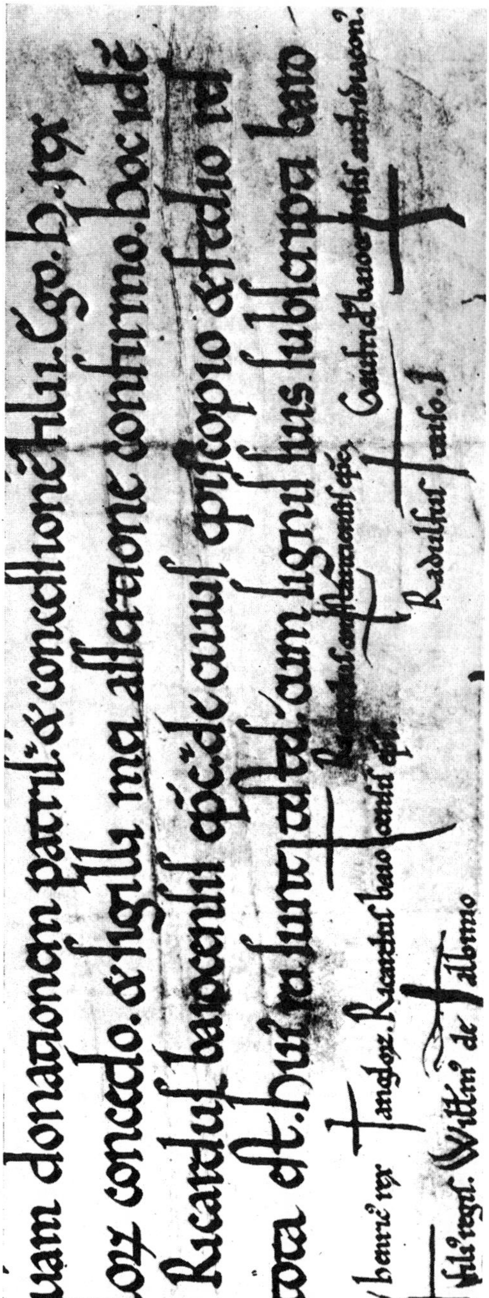

A 　　　　　　　　　　　　B

PLATE V.

SIGN MANUALS AND PARAPHS.

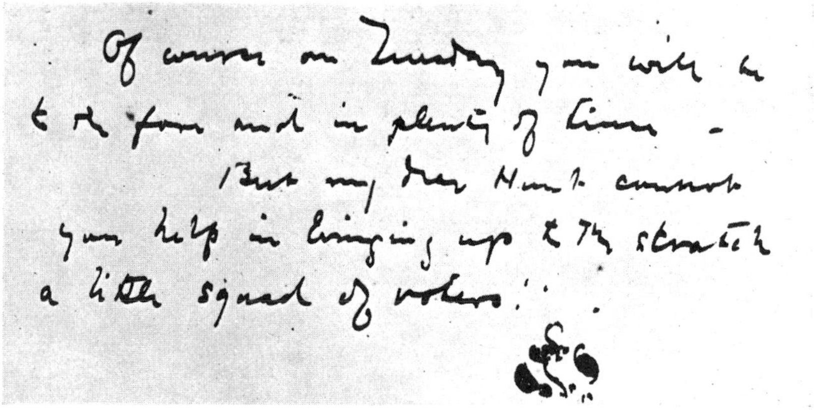

Of course on Tuesday you will be
to the fore and in plenty of time –
But my dear Hunt cannot
you help in bringing up to the scratch
a little squad of voters!

A

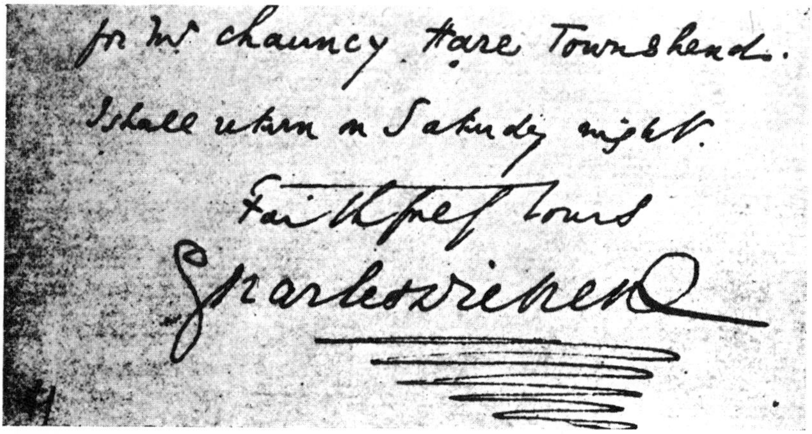

for Mr Chauncy Hare Townshend.
I shall return on Saturday night.
Faithfully Yours
Charles Dickens

B

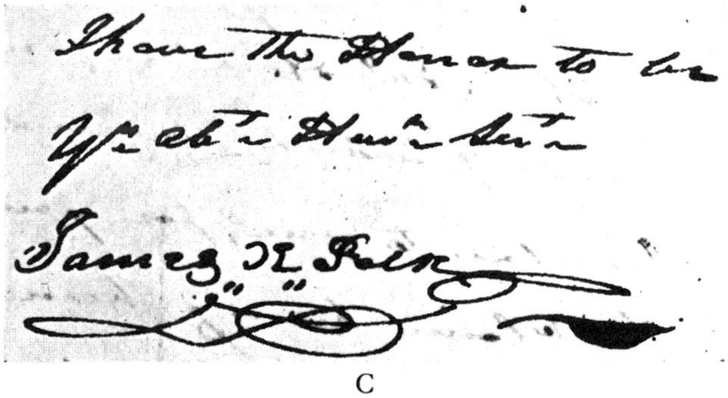

I have the Honor to be
Yr. obt. Hum. Servt.
James K. Polk

C

Plate VI.

Sign Manuals and Paraphs.

Plate V. A. Sign Manual of Henry I of England and his nobles. The King's is the first, following the text. See p. 165. B. Concluding portion of A.L.S. of Mme. de Maintenon, signed both in full and with repeated paraphs. See p. 166. It is most unusual for a paraph and handwritten signature to occur together.

Plate VI. A. A. Whistler A.N.S. with his butterfly signature. See p. 167. B. The rubric Dickens used with his signature. See p. 167. C. Rubric used by President James K. Polk. See p. 167.

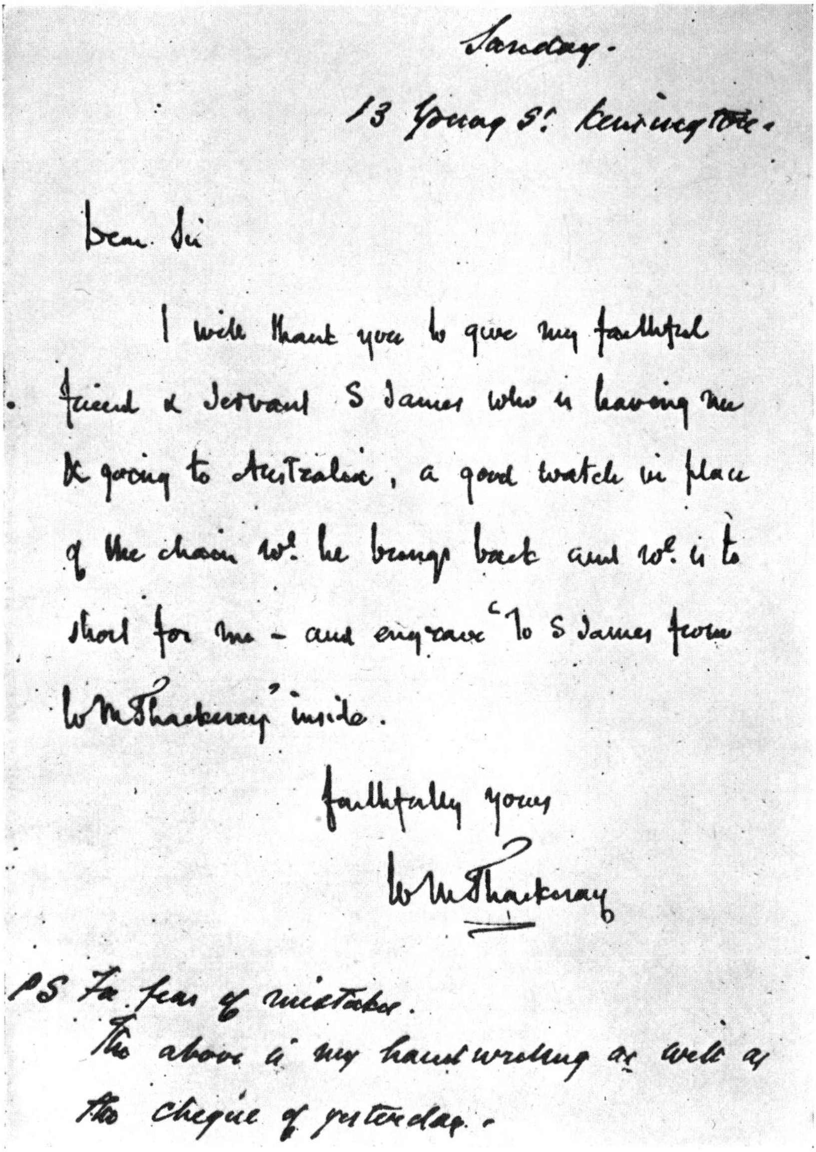

Sunday.

13 Young S.ᵗ Kensington.

Dear Sir

I will thank you to give my faithful friend & Servant S James who is leaving me & going to Australia, a good watch in place of the chain w.ᵗ he brings back and 10ᵉ. is to short for me — and engrave "To S James from W M Thackeray" inside.

faithfully yours

W M Thackeray

PS For fear of mistakes. The above is my hand writing as well as the cheque of yesterday.

PLATE VII.

THE IDIOSYNCRACY OF THACKERAY.

In this unique A.L.S., William Makepeace Thackeray not only used two different scripts but states that he does. See pp. 177-178.

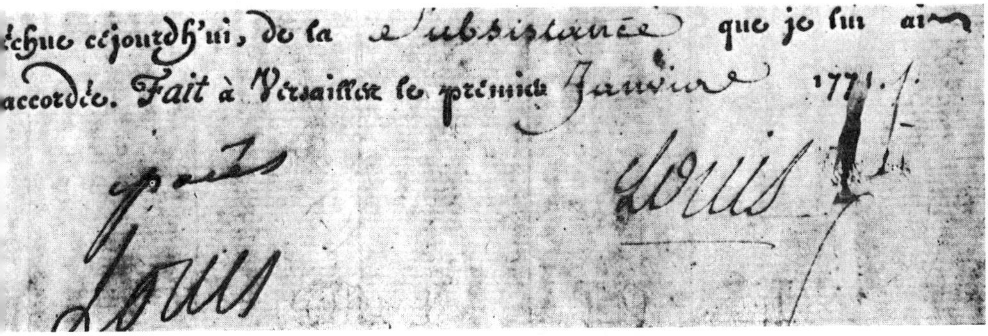

A

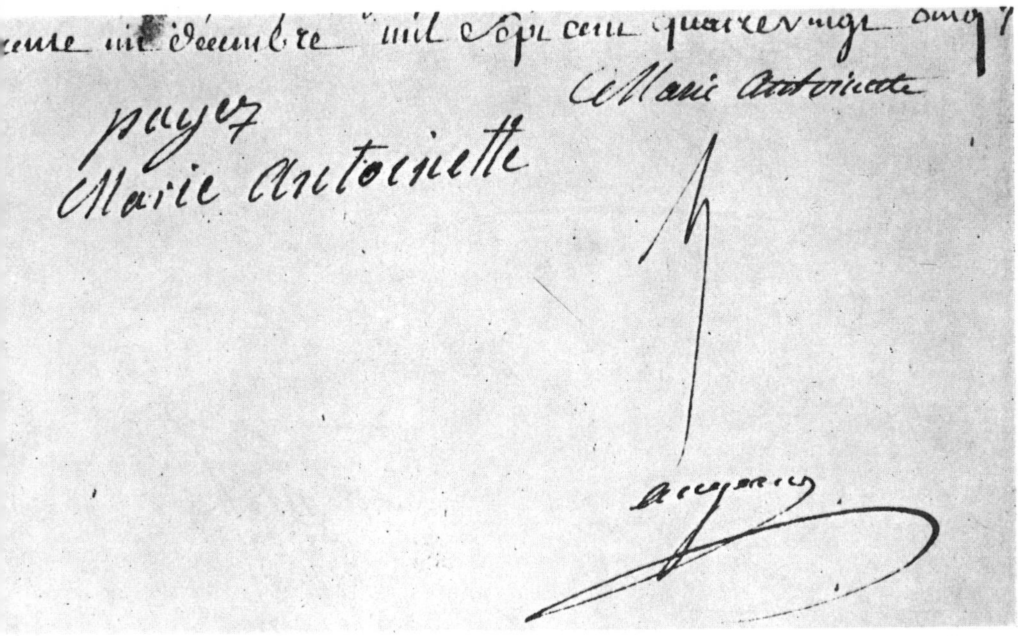

B

PLATE VIII.

AUTOGRAPH SIGNATURES OF FRENCH SOVEREIGNS.
(reduced ⅕)

A. D.S. of Louis XV. The King himself wrote "paiés" and "Louis" on the left; his *secrétaire de la main* signed "Louis" on the right. B. D.S. of Marie Antoinette. The Queen wrote "payez" and her name on the left; her *secrétaire* signed "Marie Antoinette" on the right and also his name below and from it drew upwards an arrow. See pp. 175-176.

PLATE IX.

AUTOGRAPH SIGNATURES OF FRENCH SOVEREIGNS.

A. Louis XI, reproduced by courtesy of The Pierpont Morgan Library. B. Louis XII. C. Louis XIII. D. Louis XIV. E. The Dauphin, Louis of France, son of Louis XV, who predeceased his father. F. Louis XVI. See pp. 175-176.

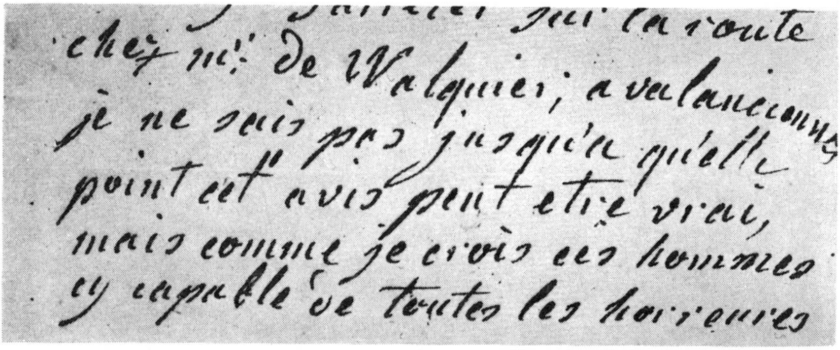

chez mr de Walquier, a valenciennes
je ne sais pas jusqu'a quelle
point cet avis peut etre vrai,
mais comme je crois ces hommes
cy capable de toutes les horreures

A

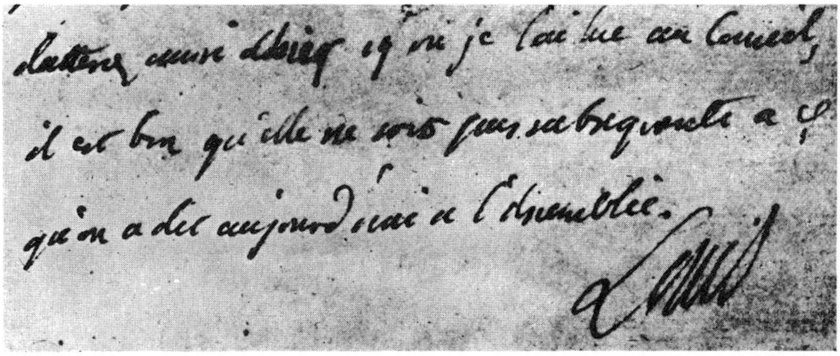

Louis

B

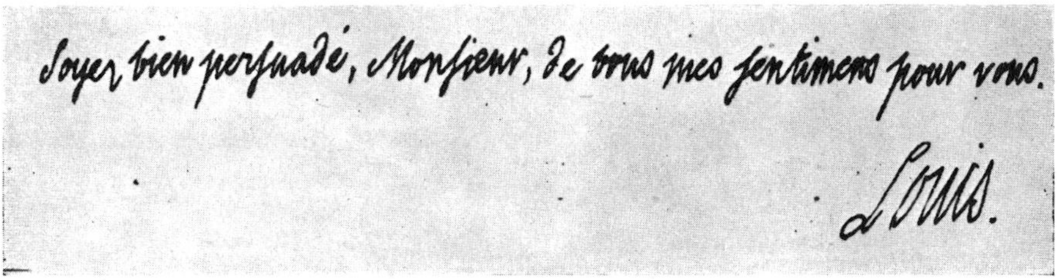

Soyez bien persuadé, Monsieur, de tous mes sentimens pour vous.
Louis.

C

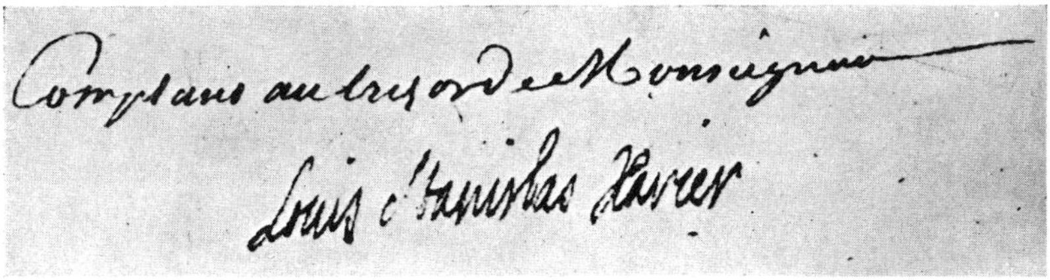

Comptant au tresor de Monseigneur
Louis Stanislas Xavier

D

PLATE X.

AUTOGRAPHS OF FRENCH SOVEREIGNS.

A. A few lines of the handwriting of Marie Antoinette. B. Lower portion of Louis XVI A.L.S. See p. 176. C. Louis XVIII's signature and a line of his handwriting. D. The signature Louis XVIII used prior to his reign.

it may be not deemed will pay you on application in consequence of a letter I write him this day. with respect to the glass 14. by 12 instead of 12 I square, I believe I must decline taking it, on account of the size, and it's not being 1½ thick, as in the high situation of my house, the winds make a very stout quality of glass necessary. as we have failed to finish our walls this season & consequently cannot cover in, we have time till the spring. or summer before this glass will be wanting, by which time you may perhaps be able to furnish me of the size & quality necessary. I am Sir

Your very humble servt

Th: Jefferson

180. panes = 270. feet @ .22.5 mills = $60.75
remitted before ———— 40.5
balance short remitted 20.25

PLATE XI.

THOMAS JEFFERSON.

Portion of Thomas Jefferson A.L.S. See p. 178.

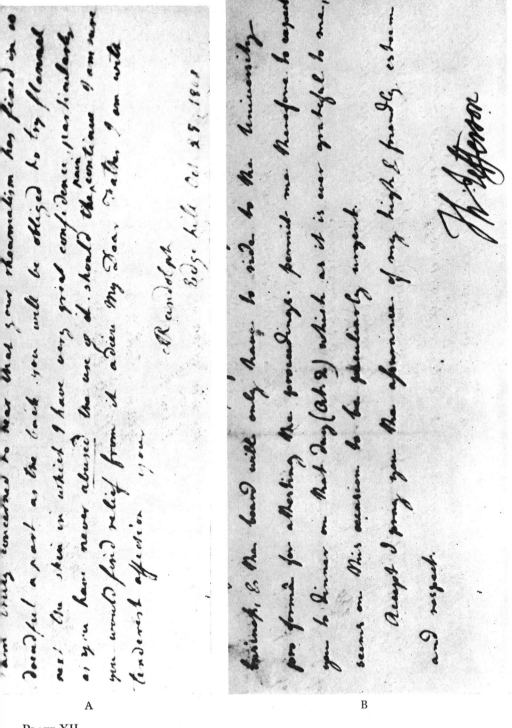

A   B

PLATE XII.   JEFFERSON AND HIS DAUGHTER-SECRETARY.

A. Portion of A.L.S. of Martha Jefferson Randolph. B. Portion of letter in the handwriting of Mrs. Randolph and signed by Thomas Jefferson. See p. 178. Both reproduced by courtesy of the Alderman Library, University of Virginia.

to be taken and also cause to be executed by the said Robert Baillie the Manual Bond also hereunto Annexed given by your Administrators, which is executed, with your other doings in the premises you are to return with all convenient speed to the Secretary's Office of this Province.

Given under my hand and seal at Savannah the Thirtieth day of October in the year of our Lord One Thousand seven hundred and sixty six and in the seventh year of the Reign of our sovereign Lord King George the Third

Ja. Wright.

Secretary Office
Certified by
Tho. Moodie D. Secry

PLATE XIII.   GWINNETT'S CONTEMPORARY—THOMAS MOODIE.

Lower part of A.D.S. of Thomas Moodie, who served as Deputy Secretary of Georgia when Gwinnett owned St. Catherine's Island. See p. 190. The document, also signed by James Wright, then Governor of Georgia, is reproduced by courtesy of The New York Public Library.

PLATE XIV.   GWINNETT'S CONTEMPORARY—THOMAS MOODIE.

Lower part of unsigned document in the handwriting of Moodie, with two lines of Governor Wright's script from which his signature has been cut off, now owned by Walter R. Benjamin Autographs. See p. 190.

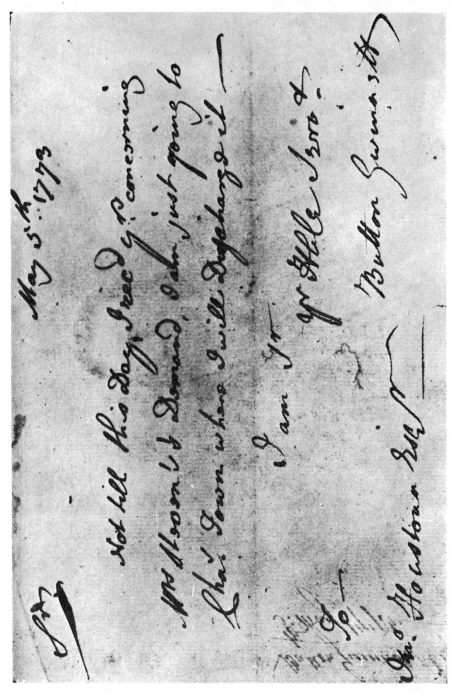

PLATE XV.

BUTTON GWINNETT.

An A.L.S. of the Signer from Georgia, owned by and here reproduced through the courtesy of The Pierpont Morgan Library. See p. 191.

A

B

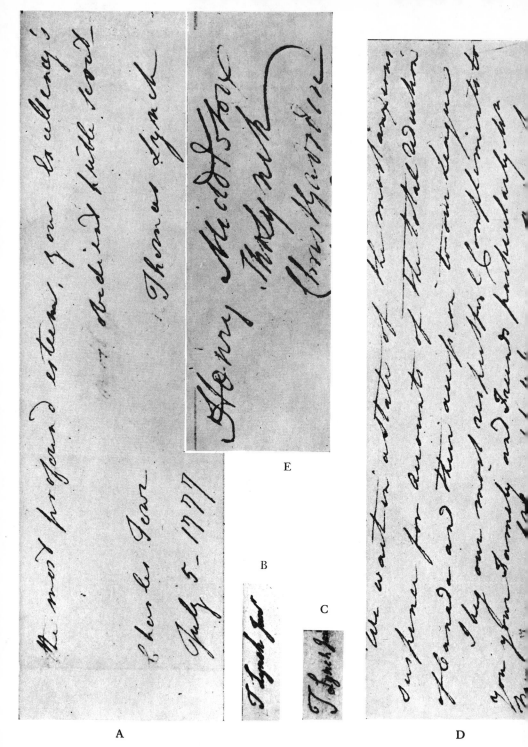

A

B

C

E

D

PLATE XVII.   THE THOMAS LYNCHS, FATHER AND SON.

A. The signature and concluding lines of the only known A.L.S. of Thomas Lynch, Jr.
B. Signature of Thomas Lynch, Jr., on the half-title page of David Hume's *The History of England*. C. The signature of Thomas Lynch, Jr., on title-page of Hurd's *Moral and Political Dialogues*. D. Portion of Thomas Lynch, Sr. A.L.S. E. Thomas Lynch, Sr.'s signature to an L.S. he signed with others. See pp. 194-197. The reproductions A, B, D and E are by courtesy of The New York Public Library.

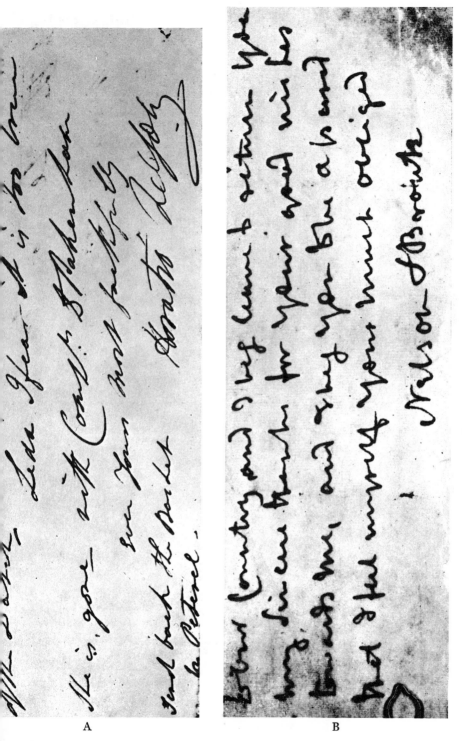

A   B

PLATE XVIII.   VARIATIONS IN NELSON'S HANDWRITING.

. Example of Admiral Nelson's script and signature before the loss of his right arm.
. Nelson A.L.S. written afterwards, with his left hand. See p. 178.

A   B

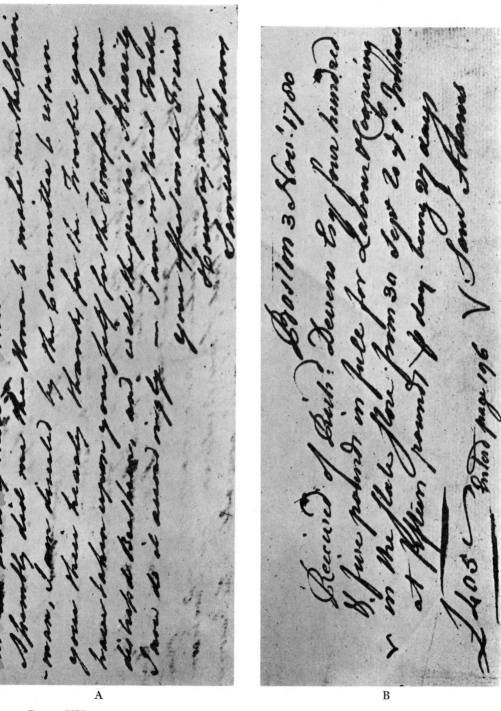

PLATE XX.

ADAMS—THE SIGNER AND COOPER CONFUSED.

A. Last portion of A.L.S. of Samuel Adams, the cultured Massachusetts Signer. B. An
A.D.S. of his unrelated namesake, who worked as a cooper in Boston. See pp. 198-199.

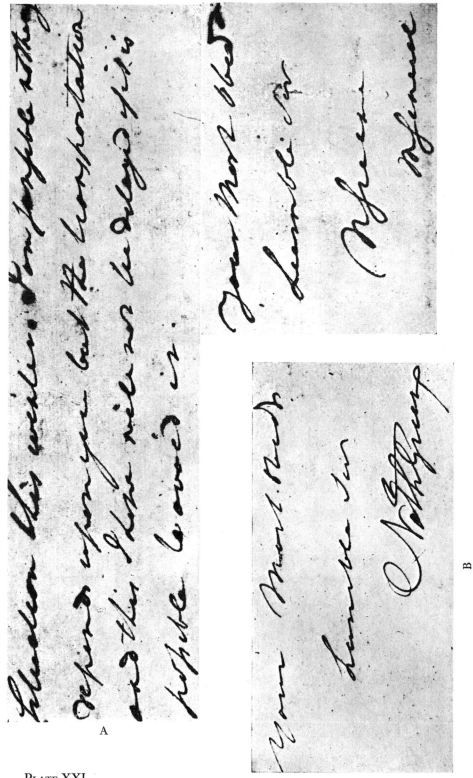

PLATE XXI.

GENERAL NATHANAEL GREENE'S DIVERSITIES.

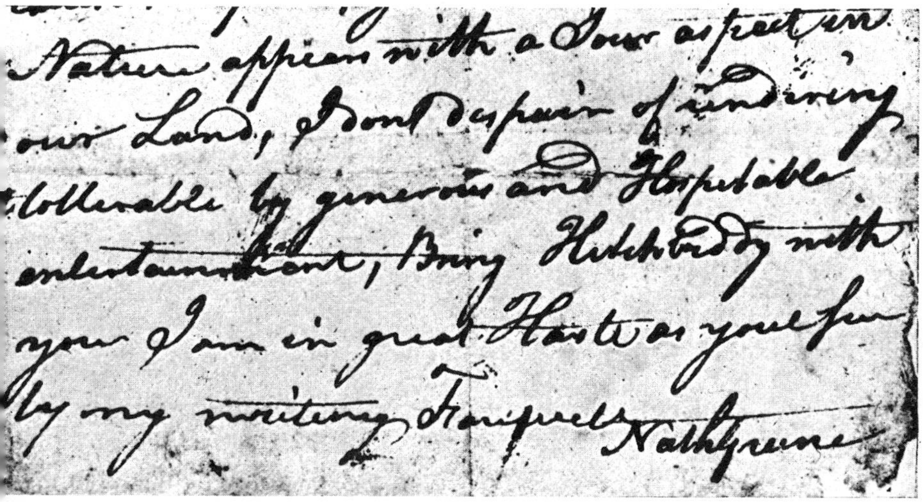

Nature appears with a Sour aspect in
our Land, I dont despair of rendering
tollerable by generous and Hospitable
entertainment, Bring Hitchbordy with
you I am in great Haste as youl perceive
by my writing Fairwell
Nath Greene

C

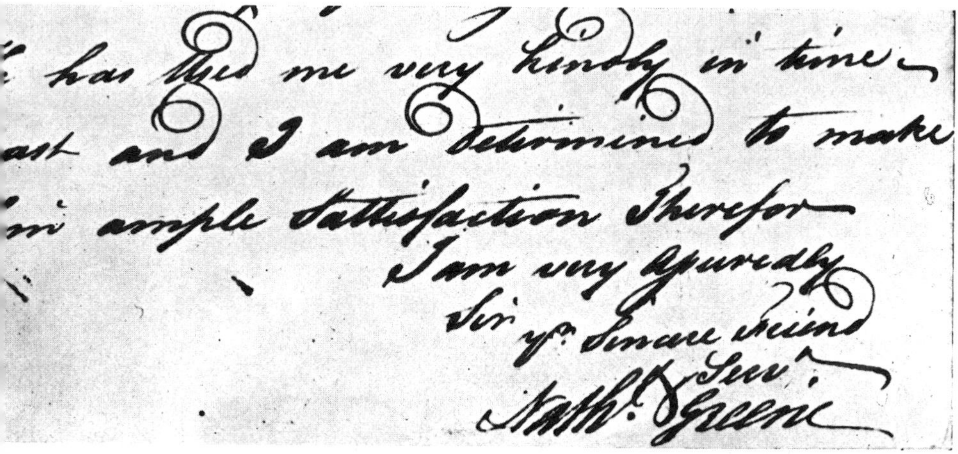

has used me very kindly in time
ast and I am determined to make
m ample sattisfaction therefor
I am very assuredly
Sir yr. Sincere Friend
& Servt.
Nathl. Greene

D

PLATE XXII.

GENERAL NATHANAEL GREENE AND HIS COUSIN.

Plate XXI. A. Last portion of a war-dated A.L.S. of General Nathanael Greene. B. Last portion of a post-war A.L.S.

Plate XXII. C. Last portion of a pre-Revolutionary A.L.S. In A, the General signed "N. Greene," with no space between the initial and surname; in B and C, it is "Nath. Greene," with the two words run together. D. Signature of the General's cousin of the same name. See pp. 204-205.

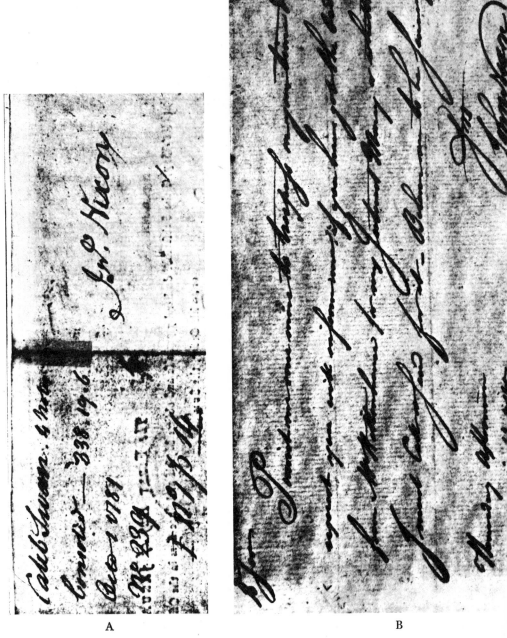

A   B

PLATE XXIII.

THE GENERAL JOHN NIXON AND THE COLONEL.

A. Document signed by John Nixon, Brigadier General in the Revolution. B. A.L.S. of John Nixon, Colonel in the Revolution, who was the first to read the Declaration of Independence to a public audience, on July 8, 1776, in Philadelphia. See p. 202.

A   B

TE XXIV.   Two Governors Trumbull of Connecticut.

A. Last portion of an A.L.S. of Jonathan Trumbull, whom Washington affectionately called
"Brother Jonathan." He served as Governor of Connecticut from 1769 to 1783. B. Last
portion of an A.L.S. of Jonathan Trumbull, son of "Brother Jonathan," who was an aide to
Washington and who served as Connecticut Governor from 1798 to 1809. See pp. 202-203.

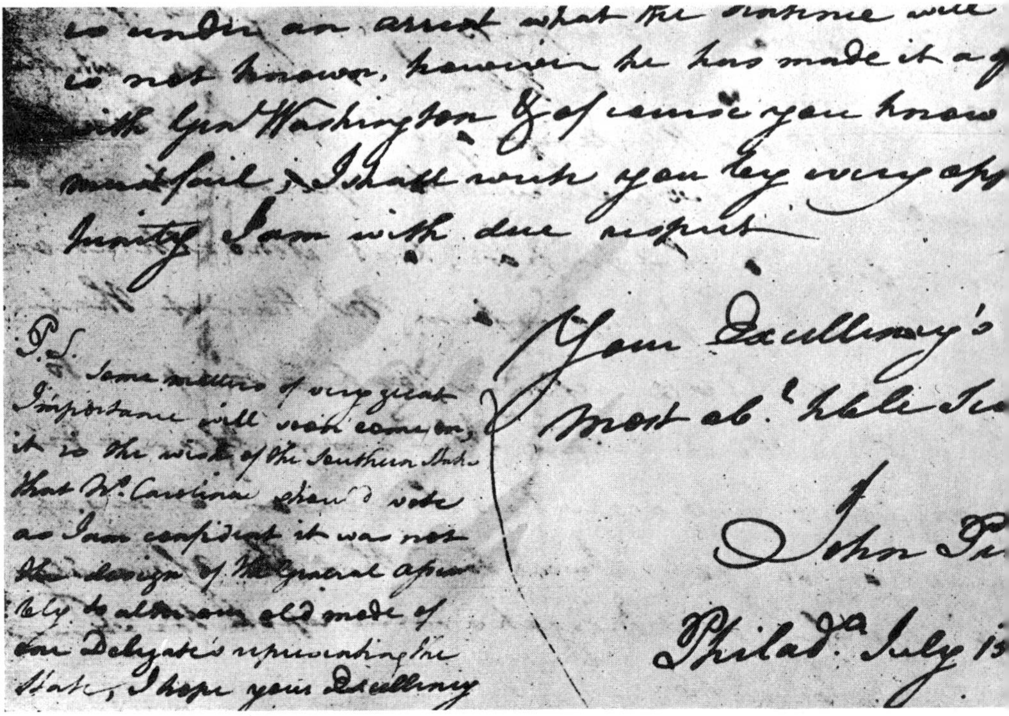

is under an arrest what the sentence will
is not known, however he has made it a
with Genl Washington & of course you know
must fail, I shall write you by every opp
tunity I am with due respect

Your Excellency's
most obt. Hble Ser
John Pe
Philada. July 15

P.S.
Some matters of very great Importance will soon come on, it is the wish of the Southern States that No. Carolina should vote as I am confident it was not the design of the General Assembly to alter our old mode of our Delegate's representing the State, I hope your Excellency

A

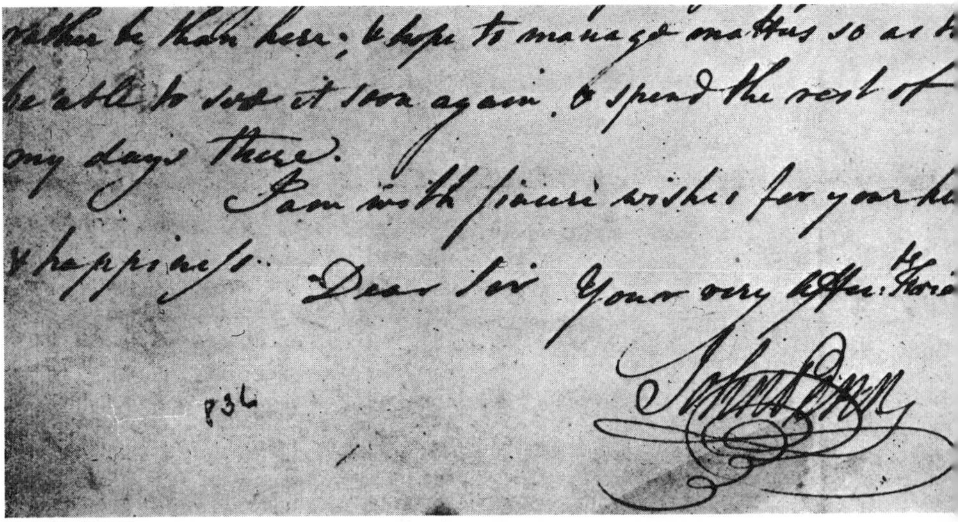

rather be than here; & hope to manage matters so as t
be able to see it soon again & spend the rest of
my days there.
I am with sincere wishes for your he
& happiness Dear Sir Your very affec. Frie
John Penn

P36

B

Plate XXV.

The John Penn Contemporaries.

(reduced ¼)

A. Portion of an A.L.S. of John Penn, the Signer from North Carolina. B. Portion of an A.L.S. of John Penn, Governor of Pennsylvania, here reproduced by courtesy of The New York Public Library. See p. 209.

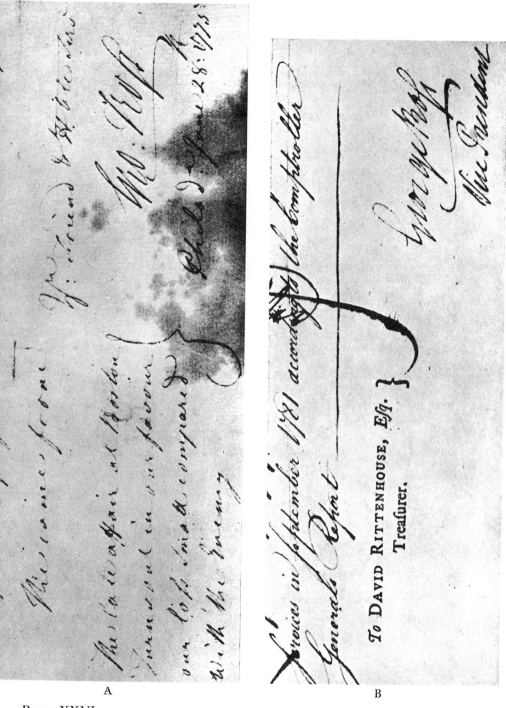

A

B

PLATE XXVI.

GEORGE ROSS—A SIGNER AND HIS SON.

A. Last portion of an A.L.S. of George Ross, the Pennsylvania Signer. B. Portion of a document signed by his namesake son. See pp. 210-211. Both A and B are reproduced through the courtesy of the Harvard University Library.

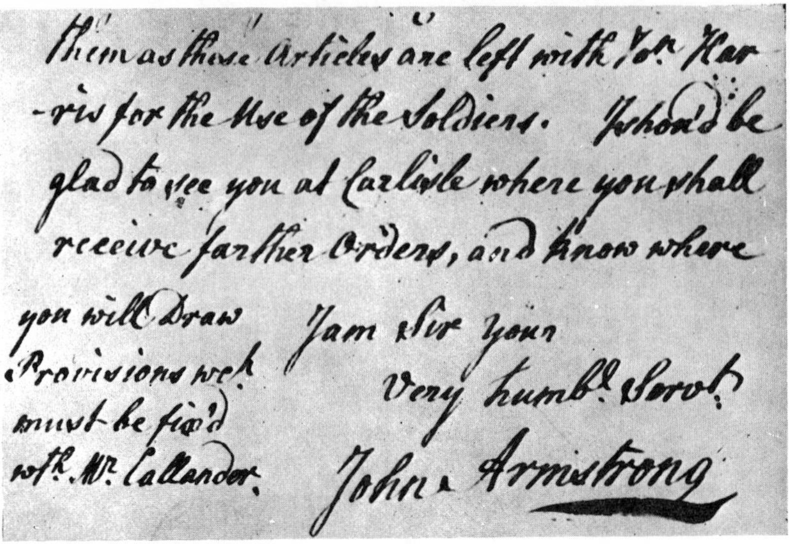

A

B

C

PLATE XXVII.   JOHN ARMSTRONG, SENIOR AND JUNIOR.
(reduced ¼)

A. Last portion of an A.L.S. of John Armstrong, the Revolutionary General. B. Last portion of an A.L.S. of his son, who served as a Colonel at the same time. C. Last portion of an A.L.S. dated 1823 of the son, who later served as Brigadier General in the War of 1812 and as Secretary of War under President Madison. See p. 212.

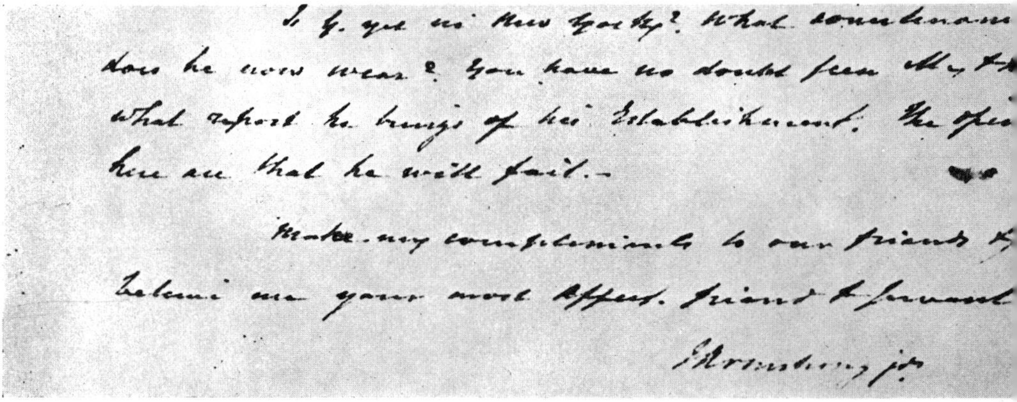

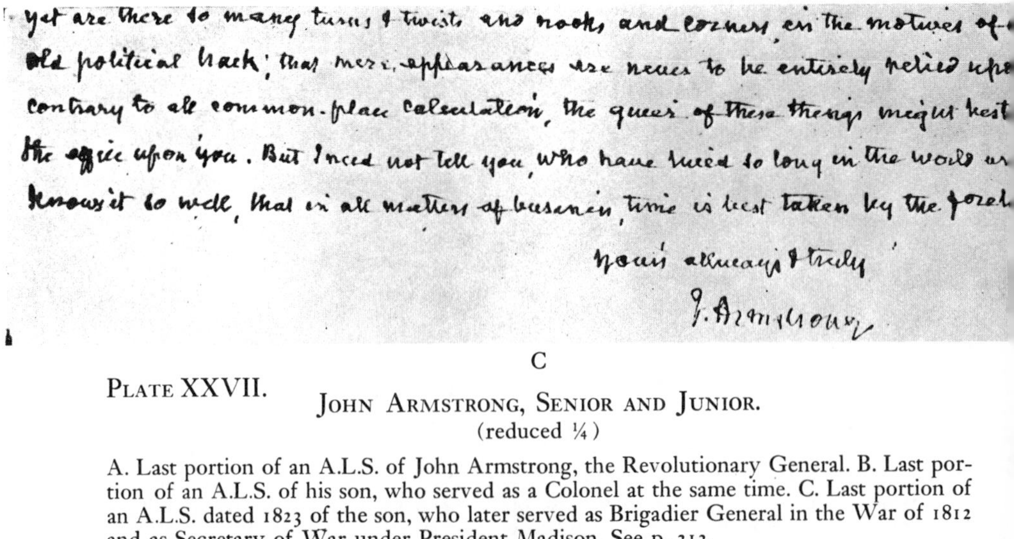

A   B

PLATE XXVIII.   TWO DANIELS OF THE FAMOUS CARROLL FAMILY.

A. Last portion of an A.L.S. of Daniel Carroll, the Signer of the Constitution, frequently referred to as "of Rock Creek." See p. 209. B. Portion of an A.D.S. of his nephew, Daniel Carroll of Duddington. See p. 210.

PLATE XXIX.   JOHN FITCH—THE INVENTOR AND HIS COUSIN.

A. Last portion of an A.L.S. by John Fitch, the inventor of the steamboat. B. Last portion of an A.L.S. of the inventor's cousin, John Fitch. See p. 213.

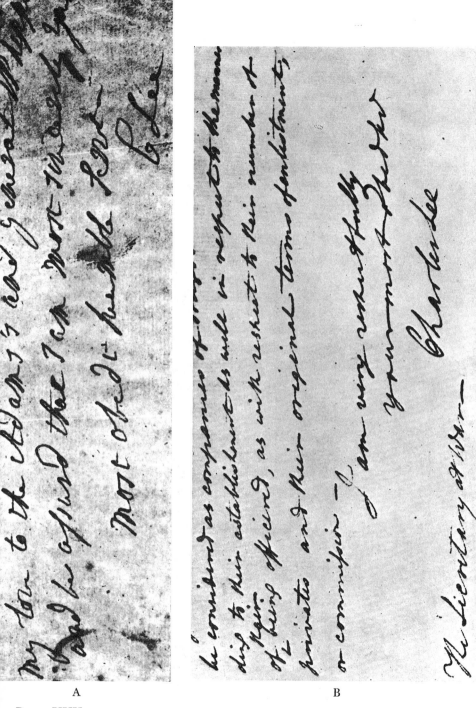

A   B

PLATE XXX.

THE UNRELATED CHARLES LEES.

A. Last portion of an A.L.S. of Charles Lee, British-born Major General in the Revolutionary Army, who was courtmartialed for treason. See p. 212. B. Last portion of an A.L.S. of Charles Lee, United States Attorney-General under Presidents Washington and Adams, brother of "Light-Horse Harry" Lee but not related to the Major General. See pp. 212-213.

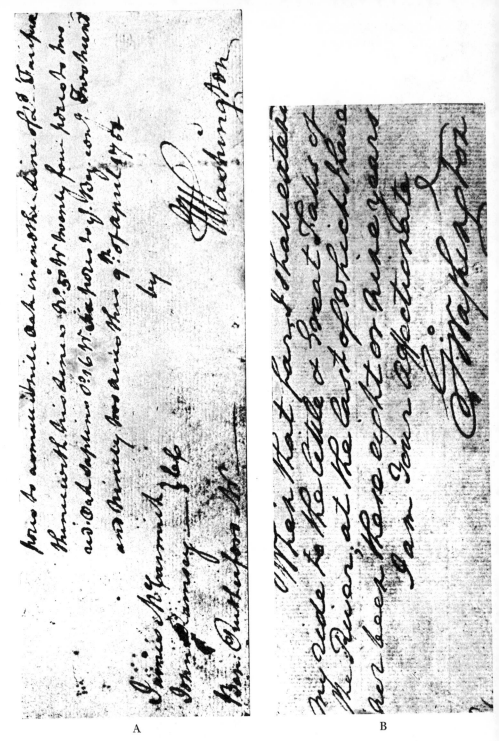

A   B

PLATE XXXI.   THE GEORGE WASHINGTONS.

Plate XXXI. A. Example of General George Washington's handwriting and signature as a young man of nineteen. See p. 177. B. His handwriting and signature in late life. See p. 177.

Plate XXXII. A.D.S. of George S. Washington, a contemporary of the first President. See p. 198.

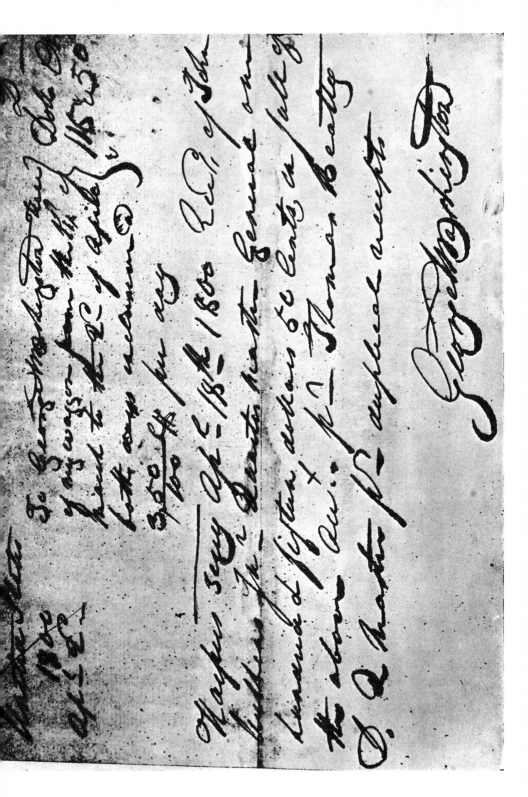

PLATE XXXII.

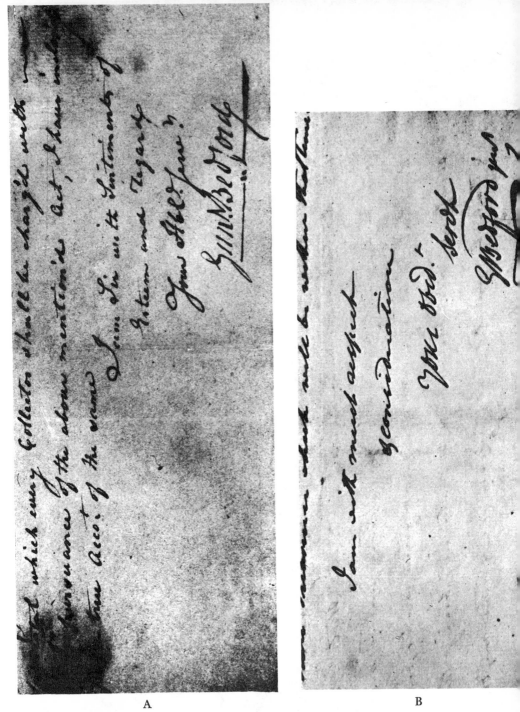

A   B

PLATE XXXIII.   THE TWO COUSINS—GUNNING BEDFORD.

Plate XXXIII. A. Last portion of an A.L.S. of Gunning Bedford, who represented Delaware in the Continental Congress. B. Last portion of an A.L.S. of his younger cousin, similarly named, who both served in the same Congress and also signed the Constitution as a delegate from the same State. See p. 208.

Plate XXXIV. Portion of a document signed by both men, who in the three illustrations are shown to have used rubrics. These three reproductions were made possible through the courtesy of the Public Archives Commission of the State of Delaware. See p. 208.

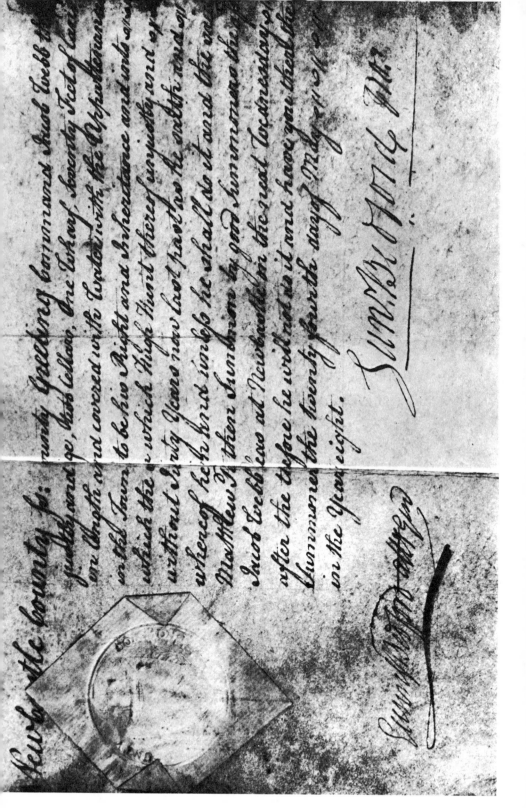

PLATE XXXIV.

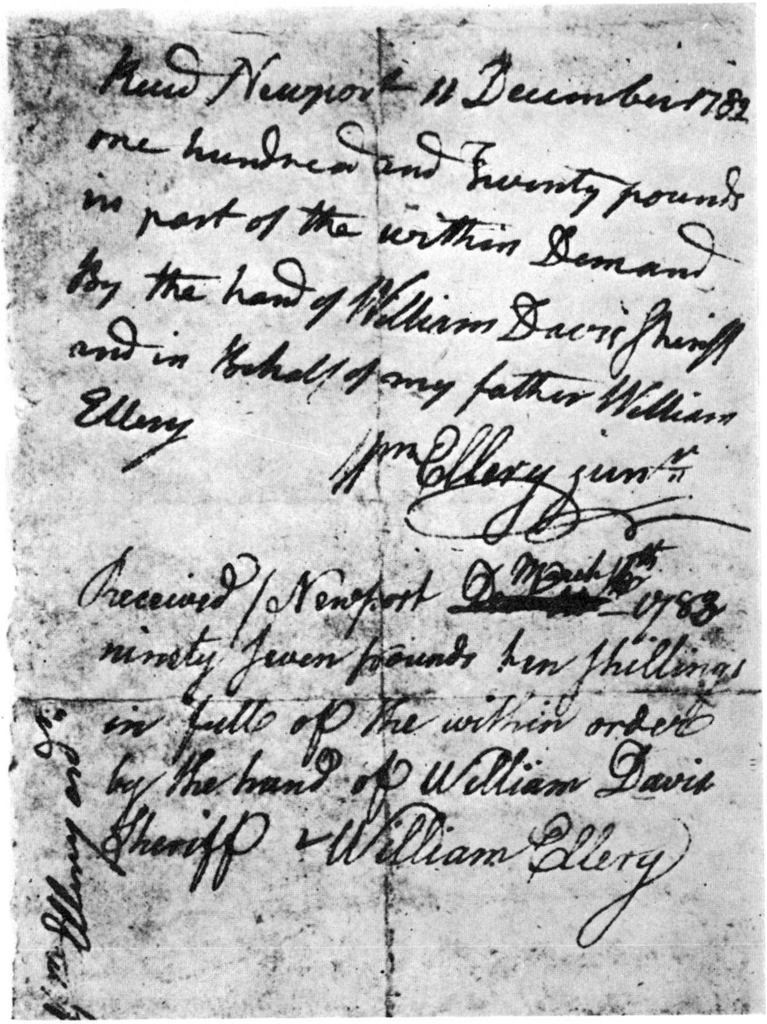

Recd Newport 11 December 1782
one hundred and twenty pounds
in part of the within Demand
By the hand of William Davis Sheriff
and in behalf of my father William
Ellery

Wm Ellery junr

Received Newport March 15th 1783
ninety seven pounds ten shillings
in full of the within order
by the hand of William Davis
Sheriff William Ellery

PLATE XXXV.

THE WILLIAM ELLERYS' SIGNED DOCUMENT.

The close similarity between signatures of father and son is shown in this document, unusual because it is signed by both. The elder William Ellery was a Rhode Island Signer; both he and his son served at different times as Collectors of the Port of Newport. See p. 204.

PART TWO

CHAPTER XIII

Care and Preservation

PROVERBIALLY the vaults of a bank are considered among the safest depositories for valuables. Frederick S. Peck, the noted Rhode Island autograph collector, believed this. With immense patience and at great expense over many years, he had acquired an outstanding collection including letters and documents of Myles Standish, Roger Williams, William Brewster and William Bradford, manuscripts of Revolutionary and Civil War importance and similar historic items. From these he selected and deposited in a Providence bank his two most prized possessions—a set of the Presidents of the United States and one of the Signers. Since the majority of the Signers' letters were handwritten and dated 1776, it was unquestionably one of the best in the country.

When the hurricane of 1938 struck the East Atlantic coast, the Providence River was turned into a torrent and quickly flooded many Providence streets and buildings, including Mr. Peck's bank. After five days, during which the waters barred any approach to the vaults, he had reconciled himself to the total loss of his collections. The river finally receded, however, and the sets were recovered. His distress was quickly turned to joy when he discovered that his autographs, carefully dried and cleaned, were none the worse for their wetting. The strong rag paper of Colonial times had not only resisted the effects of long submersion but the ink itself had neither run nor blurred.

Mr. Peck's unique experience would have been a most unhappy one had his collection consisted of letters written in modern inks and on modern papers. It proved beyond question that autograph materials of high quality can withstand even the catastrophe of a flood. For this reason, it is regrettable that good grade rag paper in common use in earlier centuries gradually came to be regarded as too expensive by letter-writers of a later generation. Manufacturers, of necessity, were obliged to seek a cheaper substitute. Paper made of wood-pulp and other materials, which cannot compare in durability, resulted, and on these the bulk of recent autographs are written. It is true at times that for important letters and documents a high quality stock is used, but the majority of every-day messages are on materials selected with little thought as to their preservation. Some, composed on the spur of the moment, are even on paper little better than scraps and often of the flimsiest consistency.

Fortunately librarians and autograph collectors, in assuming the task of preserving historical papers, are not starry-eyed dreamers who vaguely hope to correct this situation. While leaving to future generations the more difficult solution of how to preserve the modern and more perishable materials, they currently accept the responsibility for the proper care and preservation of their immediate manuscript possessions. Paper, properly handled, can last indefinitely if it is not exposed to fire, water and other obvious hazards. In addition, no matter in what condition letters are found, there is rarely if ever an occasion when something cannot be done to improve that condition and to strengthen the paper.

The average layman, unlike an institution, does not find it possible to use elaborate and multiple equipment suitable for the best protection of autographs—air-conditioning and ventilation; processes to insure against the inroads of insects, worms and mould; and the many devices used for ironing, washing, pressing and general handling. For him, the available means are few. Yet it is highly advisable that he should know what these are. All are based on that type of procedure which common sense itself indicates and begin with one simple rule—when an autograph is in good condition, it should normally be left alone. The average collector should also familiarize himself with the more complex and special means accessible to experts. He, then, will not permit autographs to deteriorate because he is unaware that certain types of repairs, even if beyond his own talents, are possible and under certain circumstances available to him through the resources of others.

When a document's material is mutilated or seriously damaged, there is little that can be done by an amateur, among whom the autograph dealer certainly lists himself. Major repairs are needed in such cases, and clumsy handling easily leads to greater damage. Nevertheless, experts almost unanimously agree that it is far better for a layman to make emergency or temporary minor repairs than to permit an autograph to disintegrate completely. Of such simple repairs the most common is that used to hold a sheet together to prevent further tearing or crumbling. For this purpose a gummed tissue or tape of the transparent type, white tissue paper, or better still the so-called Japanese tissue, may be cut in strips and applied with library paste at the point requiring treatment. They are recommended because each can later be harmlessly removed when a qualified person takes over permanent repairs. When using gummed tissue or tape, these should not be licked, as saliva has digestive juices which are injurious to paper. Any self-sealing tape, such as Scotch tape, should be definitely avoided. It leaves on the paper both an irremovable yellowish oily stain and a sticky residue which can only be dissolved with difficulty even by recommended solvents.

When paste is used in such repairs, some experts advise that it should be made on the day of its use.* It may be either of wheat or wall-paper paste mixed with water. To this may be added glycerine or sorbitolsyrup which helps to retain a certain amount of moisture and flexibility in the pasted sheet. A good quality library paste is also considered both satisfactory and harmless by other experts. Practically all agree that neither Japanese tissue nor any other should be used to cover an entire paper. None is as durable as silking, and all have the further disadvantage of obscuring the writing. Several decades ago it was a fairly common practice to varnish a color reproduction of a famous painting so that it might be mistaken for an oil. Whether any were fooled by this is another story, but, because the varnish also gave some protection from water and dust, the practice was picked up and applied by a few to autographs. It was quickly condemned by

* Detailed directions for making such paste and for its application, as well as numerous other excellent suggestions in regard to the repair and treatment of various kinds of paper, vellum, bindings, etc., are given by Harry Miller Lydenberg and John Archer in *The Care and Repair of Books*, New York, The R. R. Bowker Company, 1945.

experts. Under no circumstances should liquids made of varnish, shellac, drying oil or cellulosenitrate bases be used in any treatment of autographs.

The collector, who feels himself more or less forced to make emergency repairs, doubtless does not need to be told that his pound of cure would have been unnecessary had others before him taken an ounce of prevention. The tyro collector, however, can ill afford not to recognize the ounce he himself can take even in instances when autographs are in good condition at the time he acquires them.

No matter what their nature or condition, they should be kept as much as possible from light and from excessive heat or dampness. The rule applies equally to newspapers or any type of manuscripts. Papers become yellow and brittle if exposed to high temperatures for even short periods of time. Were a paper absent-mindedly put on a radiator cover or in direct sunlight and forgotten for a few hours, it might be irreparably harmed. On undue exposure to sun rays not only will papers dry out quickly, but the old-fashioned, highly acid inks of the iron-gall type will fade to a faint brownish color. Dye-base inks, recently developed for use in fountain pens, may fade out altogether, leaving no visible trace to the naked eye. Sun rays further accelerate the natural processes of time, and the best of papers become more quickly discolored and weakened in resistance. It is a fairly common, but unfounded, belief that glass, whether in a window or a frame, protects manuscripts from the harmful effects of direct sunlight. On the contrary, under certain circumstances glass, since it often intensifies heat, provides its own menace to the paper against which it presses.

The collector who exclaims against the summer's humidity rather than its heat would do well to think of his autographs in the same terms. An over-damp room encourages the growth of mould, a particular variety of which will cause a brown discoloration of the paper, called "foxing." Autographs should be kept in places where the atmosphere is neither overly humid nor overly dry. If the means are not available to insure these desirable conditions, the collector can from time to time resort to a simple bit of air-conditioning. To overcome dampness he can expose papers to the air, not the sun, on a dry bright day; or to overcome excessive heat and dryness, he can expose them on a damp or rainy day. Either can be done by opening file drawers or other containers for a few hours or by placing the material flat on tables.

Papers that have come into contact with water should be treated as soon as possible in order to prevent attack by mildew. None, in the first place, should be allowed to dry out in one mass because too frequently the sheets will stick to each other and become difficult to separate without damage. Each wet paper should be carefully lifted, put individually between white blotters and pressed. Then, when it is fairly dry, either a dry blotter or a sheet of paper should be placed over it, and the whole pressed with a warm, not a hot, iron. Frequently no further treatment is necessary. When using the iron caution must be exercised if seals are on the document in question, since these are thermoplastic.

Most authorities agree that the best possible method to keep autographs is to place them flat in fairly heavy paper folders. If, however, these folders are stood on end, one next the other, they should be arranged loosely so as to provide adequate ventilation yet at the same time tightly enough to prevent the documents from sagging, curling and possibly breaking within the folders. A safe rule is to store them on shelves never less than a foot from the floor, as this insures adequate air space and will give some degree of protection should the room be flooded.

Autographs should also be preserved as nearly as possible in their original state. They should always be completely flattened and never left folded, wrinkled or curled at the edges, since in this state paper, particularly if it is at all brittle, will eventually break along such creases or chip off. Nor should they be left within rubber bands or clips. Rubber rots, and almost everyone is familiar with the tell-tale brown stain it leaves. Both clips and pins, in corroding, leave their typical marks, and their rusting makes it difficult to remove them without the probability of tearing.

When a paper is folded, particularly if the folds are sharp and well defined, it is helpful first to dampen it—a process best carried out by spreading it in a very humid, warm room. A ready one would be a bathroom in which, with closed doors, a warm shower or tub has been allowed to run for a suitable time. Direct sponging or soaking in water is dangerous. Wet papers are very fragile and easily damaged. Also when ink is water soluble, as is the case with many modern ones manufactured for pen or typewriter, untold damage can be done. When more gently moistened, the paper may be ironed out after first placing it on a hard surface cushioned with white blotting paper, which serves to prevent the iron's edge from breaking the fragile edge.

Because irreparable damage may be caused by excessive drying out, many experts warn the inexperienced repairer against applying heat to a manuscript at any time. If the steamroom or any controlled humidity method is not possible, they suggest the material be laid out on a rainy day with windows opened so that the paper, properly sheltered from sudden gusts of wind or currents of air, may absorb moisture. As soon as the paper is sufficiently dampened, it should be hand flattened, next placed between sheets of blotting paper and then subjected to light pressure in a binder's press. In lieu of the latter, a heavy pile of books, their weight evenly distributed downward, will serve. Such pressure, rather than heat, takes more time than ironing but is undoubtedly a safer procedure.

For removing dust and other particles of foreign matter, it is recommended that every paper be brushed off with a camel's hair brush before it is put away in a folder. A piece of very soft silk may also be used, but in this case pressure must be avoided. Frequent handling of autographs is harmful to them. Aside from the danger of tearing, the moisture and unperceived dirt of hands may not only leave unsightly stains but also an acid residue which causes paper deterioration.

The removal of stains is always necessary before any attempt is made to reinforce or repair the paper itself. Pencil marks and superficial dirt are simply removed by means of the art-gum eraser. For other stains caused by grease spots, acids, paste and glue, the washing of the documents with water, a process which must be followed with utmost care, is suggested.

In these cases, the ink should be tested beforehand in some inconspicuous corner, and, if it shows any tendency to run, it may then be lacquered with a thin solution of cellulose acetate in acetone. When this coating has dried, washing, preferably with distilled water, may safely be undertaken. The residue is next carefully sponged off with absorbent cotton or soft cloth, and the paper rinsed in clean water. It should then be laid between clean white blotters and pressed either by a press-binder or with books. Finally the lacquer coating is removed by sponging the sheet with cotton dipped in acetone.

For other types of stains even greater amount of experience and judgment is required to select the perfect solvent or combination of solvents to be used in any specific case. In the normally recommended solvents most black typewriter inks or carbon impressions will unfortunately bleed. A starch-sizing treatment will minimize this effect, but such material must be very cautiously treated in any case. Occasionally ordinary inks will be affected by both water and solvents.

To remove stains of various types, the following solvents are suggested by Adelaide Minogue, Chief of the Cleaning and Rehabilitation Section at the National Archives in Washington:*

Stain	Recommended Solvent
Adhesive tape	Carbon tetrachloride or benzene
Duco-cement	Acetone
Glue (linen or glassine tape)	Warm water
Lacquer	Acetone
Oil	Carbon tetrachloride or benzene
Paint	Mixture of alcohol and benzene
Paste	Water
Rubber cement	Mixture of benzene and toluene
Scotch tape	Mixture of benzene and toluene
Shellac	Ethyl alcohol
Wax	Mixture of benzene and toluene

Caution should be observed when any of the chemicals are used, as many of them are inflammable and all are harmful to breathe. Each cleaning operation should be carried out in a well-

* "The Repair and Preservation of Records," Bulletin No. 5, National Archives, Washington, September 1943.

ventilated room and away from an open flame. At the same time Mrs. Minogue warns that the amateur should leave such work, wherever possible, to the expert. The former is too apt, by some accidental slip, to destroy the very sheet he seeks to preserve.

Stains caused by foxing, which shows in the spotty brown discoloration found on prints and documents that have been subjected to damp storage conditions for a considerable time, are difficult to remove. A bleaching treatment is required, and this somewhat drastic process always weakens the paper and fades any but carbon inks. When such stains occur over the writing, or between its lines, they are practically impossible to eradicate since the bleach cannot be kept from the script itself. In most cases the treatment, too, will blanch the paper where applied, and it is debatable whether stains or whitened spots are preferable.

To prevent that type of stain caused by the smudging of the carbon in a pencilled letter, experts suggest that it be treated with a fixative. Mrs. Minogue recommends that it be "sized" providing the paper itself is in good condition. This is done by dipping it into a thin starch or gelatin solution, after which it is subsequently dried and pressed. A sprayed lacquer of a suitable type may be used as an alternative, but this is much more expensive and more difficult to handle than the readily available starch. Such processes not only protect but, curiously enough, make pencil writing more permanent than ink. Ink fades when exposed to light, but pencil writings, treated by either tested method, neither smudge nor fade, a fact that may in future play its part in overthrowing the prejudice against the use of pencils in correspondence. Formerly the value of autographs would have been halved if they had been written in pencil, but today the new system of protecting and preserving them equalizes their value with others in ink.

There is another substance which is not uncommonly found to mar paper—sealing wax. When the wax is old it can be removed only by carefully scraping it off with a sharp knife after it has first been moistened by pressing between wet blotters. New wax can also largely be removed with a knife, and the last vestiges melted out by pressing the paper between white blotters with a gently used heated iron.

In some instances the removal of stains is of particular importance because their presence may hasten the deterioration of paper. To eliminate them is as much a precaution for its "health" as protection against over dampness. Paper, irrespective of the century of its manufacture, is not only affected by improper exposure to light, humidity and dryness, but is also subject to what might be called diseases. These are caused by fungi, and some claim by bacteria. Parenthetically, it can be stated that the perils of insects, rats and mice, which are in another category, are no less real and formidable if the proper precautions are not taken. Paper "diseases" are invited by a necessary process of manufacture called "sizing." This consists of immersing the fibres—cotton, linen, hemp or wood-pulp—in a bath of animal or vegetable glue, a substance which has somewhat the attraction for bacteria, fungi and other paper enemies that honey has for bees. It is also affected by temperature. Because of these facts some libraries fumigate their manuscripts and thereby kill all insect and mould life.

Many dangers to paper obviously come from sources foreign to it, but it often carries within itself another hazard. This is its own acidity, which for a number of years chemists have classed as one of the chief causes of brittleness found in many manuscripts. It results from chemical changes within the paper's substance and also from conditions of storage. For this reason, once stains have been removed, the strengthening or reinforcing of the paper should be delayed for an intervening process. Such a method has been adopted by experts after many experiments in recent years.

The potential harm of paper acidity and how to remove it is described by W. J. Barrow, Document Restorer of the Virginia State Library at Richmond, in a pamphlet issued in 1943.* He states that if a condition of acidity, the extent of which may be ascertained by laboratory tests, is permitted to remain, it not

* *Procedures and Equipment used in the Barrow Method of Restoring Manuscripts and Documents*, W. J. Barrow, Richmond, Virginia.

only continues the destruction of the paper but also contaminates and weakens any cellulosic material used to strengthen it. Calcium carbonate was found to have a stabilizing effect upon cellulose fibres and will neutralize acids absorbed by the paper at some future time. The solutions used are calcium hydroxide and calcium bicarbonate. Experiments further pointed to the fact that paper with high acidity was less stable under light than the same paper with low acidity. The conclusion was logically reached then that all documents should be treated for acidity before any restoration method was attempted. It follows also that the restoration process itself should be free of any factors that would tend to renew this condition.

One of the simplest and most helpful methods of protecting autographs is by means of sheets of cellulose acetate. They do not protect from the effects of light rays as is sometimes believed. A manuscript enclosed between them, if placed on exhibit under direct rays, advisedly should be safeguarded by some light filter. Today visitors to the Library of Congress who see the original draft of the Declaration of Independence, replaced on exhibition in 1945, may note how very faint and illegible the writing appears. According to Gaillard Hunt, quoting from the April 24, 1903, report of a committee of the National Academy of Sciences on the condition and preservation of the Declaration of Independence, "the wet press-copying operation to which it was exposed about 1820 for the purpose of reproducing a facsimile copy removed a large portion of the ink."* His statement was challenged by John C. Fitzpatrick, former Assistant Chief of the Manuscript Division of the Library of Congress.† Wherever the truth lies, no further risks, due to this or other causes, are being taken. A filter is now used to protect both the ink and parchment of this great document from the further harmful effects of light rays.

Celluloid sheets should not be confused with those of cellulose acetate, and under no circumstances should the former be used. Celluloid deteriorates and in doing so slowly gives off

* *The Department of State of the United States, Its History and Function* Department of State, Washington, 1914, p. 312.
† *The Spirit of the Revolution*, Boston, Houghton, Mifflin & Co., 1924.

fumes of nitric acid, which when absorbed by paper causes its early destruction. Papers of whatever make or period, kept in contact with celluloid, go entirely to pieces, and the ink quickly fades.

Mounting manuscripts that are written on only one side of a sheet is a method occasionally used to strengthen them but one not popular among collectors. This is understandable, since the acidity and other harmful factors of the stock employed for the mounting is often in time communicated to the manuscript under repair. The latter may also be stained as the result of the use of a poor quality paste. In older methods of framing, the documents were pasted on heavy board, a practice which was extremely bad since inevitably, as the cardboard dried out, the manuscript would do the same. Even the best expert today attempts with fear and trembling to separate such fragile and brittle paper from its backing. Not only is the paper apt to tear, but the ink often fades badly in the dampening process involved.

For the strengthening of entire sheets of fragile paper, or paper written on both sides that needs extensive repair, there are two available methods. One is called the crepeline,* the other lamination. The first consists of the application to a sheet of a thin layer of fine silk gauze, unfinished, unbleached and unstiffened. The gauze is generally applied to both sides since when only one is so treated the paper tends to curl. The bleached and stiffened old type of heavy quality crepeline, frowned upon by experts, is no longer used extensively. When the proper type and grade of silk are used the result is to leave the paper not appreciably stiffer than before treated. Its texture becomes practically invisible, the ink is only slightly obscured and meanwhile the whole paper is well reinforced.

Experts claim that the paste used in applying silk often makes the document more attractive to paper pests, and that over a period of twenty-five years or more the protective material itself deteriorates and adversely affects the paper. They accordingly recommend that documents so treated be examined from

* The various steps in this process are carefully described in Lydenberg and Archer, *op. cit.*, pp. 37-38.

time to time and, if necessary, re-treated. A few authorities also argue that, because the crepeline method does not protect paper from the evil effects of light, heat and acid gases, it is of little use as a preservative. Others counter with the perfectly sound statement that carelessness in the storage of autographs will hasten deterioration in any paper, and that rough handling will no more rapidly affect paper that has been silked than that which has been strengthened by any other known means. Silking, as is true of other methods, will unquestionably aid in preserving a document for an indefinite period of years if reasonable care is used in handling and storing.

Collectors generally prefer the crepeline to more modern methods endorsed by experts chiefly for the reason that the character of the paper itself is not changed. This is not true in lamination, in which the entire texture of the repaired manuscript is different from that of ordinary paper. Lamination is a method of repair by which transparent sheets of a thin flexible cellulose acetate foil, colorless and with a high degree of permanence, are applied to the two sides of a damaged paper. Their adhesion is effected by heating and pressing the thermoplastic foil into the pores of the paper by a steam-heated hydraulic or other suitable type of press, the writing remaining perfectly legible and clear. A modification of the process by the use of a sheet of high grade tissue on the outside of the foil has been found to produce a much stronger product than that laminated with foil alone,* but this at times tends to reduce the clarity of the writing.

Lamination was first adopted by the National Archives and is highly recommended by them. Although the foil will burn, it is not itself inflammable and is water repellent, relatively permanent, strong and resistant to fungi, insects and exposure to gases. It is therefore not only a method of reinforcing paper but also a means of preserving it. For these and other reasons many experts consider it has an advantage over the older silking and tissue methods of repair. Others, however, among whom is included John T. Washbourn, Chief of the Reading Room of the New

* Barrow, *op. cit.*

York Historical Society, voice practical objections to it. In a review of Mrs. Minogue's Bulletin* Mr. Washbourn states: "As long ago as 1936, Mr. Alexander J. Wall, our late director, collaborated with the National Archives in testing this method in comparison with others, and sent a sample document to be laminated in the National Archives shops. Our subsequent experience indicates that the silking method is far more practical. The document that was laminated has since broken in two where it was folded, whereas a document properly silked can be folded almost with impunity, the silk threads acting as a binder. We have silked manuscripts for the last twenty years and the documents have not shown any bad effects." Lamination, he continues, may have its advantages, but from a practical point of view he believes the silking of documents is more desirable. The objection has sometimes been raised that, under certain extreme conditions of heat, laminated paper might weld together into a mass. The National Archives, however, reports that it has found that such material is unaffected by temperatures below 250° F., and that sheets completely welded together by exposure to higher temperatures may be separated with acetone.

Lamination has further advantages in that its transparency permits the passage of ultra-violet and infra-red rays and so sets up no bar to photography. In addition, Mr. Barrow points out that "fiber and ink test of the type of which I am familiar can be made on documents laminated with either silk or cellulose acetate foil . . . . In order to make microscopic analysis of the fibers or chemical tests of the ink some portion of the cellulose acetate foil should be lifted and dissolved out of the paper with acetone."† It can therefore be noted that at any time, in order to make necessary tests, the protective coating can be partially removed from laminated paper. Naturally, to remove either silk, tissue or acetate foil is always difficult if the autograph was very much deteriorated before the protective process was employed.

Mr. Barrow reports interesting results of laminating paper

* New York Historical Society Quarterly *Bulletin*, Vol. xxix, No. 2, April 1945.
† Letter to the author, April 24, 1945.

after proper treatment for acid. "Upon subjection to accelerated aging tests," he writes in emphasizing the merits of lamination, "by baking for seventy-two hours at 100 degrees centigrade, it was found that the silked papers had lost 52 per cent of their folding endurance, those laminated but not treated for acid had lost 31 per cent, while those laminated with the acid neutralized had lost but 5 per cent and had no increase in acidity."*

Still another and somewhat related method recommended for the strengthening of paper is that of transparent sheeting with adhesive. This consists of the application to a damaged item of a thin sheet of foil, similar to that used in lamination, by means of an adhesive. The sheeting, gummed on one side in its manufacture, adheres to the paper under repair and, since the adhesive, made with a highly plasticized resin base, neither deteriorates nor darkens appreciably on exposure to light or heat, the sheeting affords excellent protection. It must be applied so that both sides of a damaged manuscript are entirely covered and a small margin left around its edges where the two sheets of cellulose join. Certain commercially offered articles of this type are Celluseal, Clearseal, Dulseal and Cometex. For documents of permanent value, lamination by means of sheets of foil with adhesive is not recommended by most authorities. It has been found that in time the foil is apt to peel off, and the adhesive remains attached to the manuscript. They therefore prefer lamination by means of foil without adhesive.

Such processes as lamination and those which are related to it are so new to collectors that there has been insufficient time for them collectively to reflect their judgment about the modern versus the old methods. For those who have a sentimental attachment to a manuscript in its original state, and who like the touch of the old paper, it is probable today that the market value of a laminated item might be considerably less than before it was treated. At the same time no proper test can be made since few laminated autographs have come on the market. Whatever the preference of collectors may ultimately prove to be, they must for the present still depend upon the older methods of re-

* *Op. cit.*

pair. Lamination is not as yet available to any but librarians who practically alone have access to the use of the elaborate equipment involved. This fact explains why until now few laminated items have been seen on the autograph market. Libraries, almost without exception, are rapidly becoming owners of any records of value, and they are seldom sellers.

All these methods of repairing naturally apply to those autographs written on paper and not on parchment, vellum or other writing materials. Nor do they apply to leather used in bindings. The aging of leather, just as in the case of paper when stored, is accelerated primarily by acid gases and improper conditions of light, heat or dampness. Bindings of leather, which encase autograph collections, should be lubricated periodically to preserve flexibility. If this is done, and once a year is recommended, the binding should remain strong and serviceable for a very long period. All librarians and collectors indeed recommend the safeguarding of original binding materials for their own sake, since in a number of cases these are of intrinsic value as works of art.

Parchment and vellum are like leather in many respects and benefit from careful handling, storing and an occasional lubrication with an oil preparation applied in small quantities. Although both are extremely strong and withstand considerable use without marked effect, little can be done to restore them once they have been damaged. They are extremely sensitive to changes in moisture content and tend to become stiff and brittle if exposed to dry air and to expand and wrinkle if damp.

Vellum or parchment that already has cockled or wrinkled or has been rolled or folded should be carefully flattened before storage. It should then be placed between damp white blotters or in a room of very high humidity until it has absorbed sufficient moisture to become soft and pliable. Next it should be spread between dry blotters and pressed for twenty-four hours. If after this treatment it still is not thoroughly dry, the blotters should be replaced with fresh ones, and the procedure repeated. Heat even in moderation, because it will cause considerable permanent shrinkage, must never be applied to accelerate drying of either vellum or parchment.

The use of organic solvents or of any kind of bleach to remove stains from parchment and vellum is likewise not advisable because these agents will stiffen the material and make it more brittle. It is scarcely worth while to attempt to patch holes or tears in sheep, goat or calf skins. The use of bits of parchment or cloth is of doubtful value in increasing the durability of a document, and they always make it more unsightly.

Silking is highly recommended for the repair of seals that may be partly damaged or in the process of disintegrating and which appear on parchment and paper deeds. The parts of the seal should first be carefully fitted together and held in place with a solution of Canada balsam in a mixture of benzene and toluene. Then, when the solvents have evaporated, the various fragments will be found to be firmly and invisibly welded. For storage or display purposes, the seal and its ribbon should be carefully supported to prevent strain on either the ribbon or the document's material.

Water should never be used by the amateur in trying to clean parchment, vellum or similar materials. None absorbs ink as does paper, and water is very apt to cause the ink to rub off entirely. Further, faded inks on such material cannot be restored by chemical means any more than they can on paper. In certain books on autographs, published in the not-too-distant past, frequent reference is made to such methods. However, most modern experts are unanimous in condemning as definitely destructive of the document all that have been attempted. They may temporarily bring out and make the ink more legible, but in a brief time this effect is lost, and the ink fades into a state generally worse than that before treatment. "Inks that have faded from age, oxidation, and exposure to light and water," Mrs. Minogue declares, "cannot be safely restored to their early brilliance by chemical means without seriously jeopardizing the strength of the paper and the ultimate permanence of the writing itself."*

Meanwhile, by the use of ultra-violet and infra-red rays, ex-

* Minogue. *Op. cit.*, p. 26.

cellent photographs revealing the full content of autographs may be obtained. The introduction of these rays, equipment for which is owned by many of the great institutions, has been a tremendous aid in deciphering otherwise unreadable papers or those that are faded, charred or impaired. The ultra-violet lamp causes certain materials to fluoresce, but it has no effect on various others. Where only one material of a document fluoresces—either the ink or the paper—the contrast thus produced makes it possible to read erased, faded or stained sections of a manuscript. Ink prepared from aniline dyestuffs (especially red ink), for instance, fluoresces strongly so that even when it is much faded it can easily be rendered visible. The ultra-violet rays also bring out invisible ink, often used in diplomatic correspondence. If neither material of a manuscript is affected by the rays it is sometimes possible to overcome the difficulty by moistening the reverse of the leaf with a solution of some strongly fluorescing substance such as anthracene in alcohol.

Again, the ultra-violet lamp causes materials to fluoresce with varying degrees of intensity in cases of papers and inks of different periods. Given a definite quality of paper or ink, it is often possible to ascertain under the ultra-violet, by comparison with a known authentic example, whether or not a document under consideration is the type common to the period and proper to the date it bears. Work and research along these lines is still in its infancy, but the results to date justify high hope that the verifying and authenticating of autographs of all ages will be greatly advanced.

By means of infra-red rays differentiations of ink which are apparent to the eye but which do not show on photostats can be revealed photographically. These rays also photograph writing which has been charred or which has been effaced by certain stains not affected by ultra-violet rays.

Microfilms are also invaluable as photographic records of historic autographs and manuscripts. Since they are only a fraction of the size of the original documents, they may be kept on small rolls and stored in the minimum of space. When papers show signs of disintegrating, or their inks are gradually disappearing, they may be photographed on microfilm before they lose their fairly good condition. When this is done, it is recommended that the reproduction be made before repairs to the autograph are undertaken because small bits of the original's material may be broken off and lost when it is being rehabilitated.

The fact that microfilms can be duplicated at will is a great advantage. Duplicates of papers which are of high value in the study of history have been made and distributed to institutions throughout the world while the original microfilm and the original paper remain in the hands of the latter's owner. Besides preventing complete loss of historically important facts, microfilms can serve as a means of identification in the case of theft and as proof of the existence of an item, forged or otherwise, even after the original has been destroyed. Photostats can serve the same end, but these are much bulkier than microfilms and, being loose, may more easily be lost. There is little doubt that had microfilms been made of great collections, such as have been recently destroyed in Europe, much still unknown historic information would have survived.

Had microfilms of the Casket Letters existed, the opinions of many historians of the Mary Stuart-Queen Elizabeth controversy might well have been changed. Microfilms would likewise have solved the mystery of the Bixby letter. The value of photocopying was fortunately recognized by some librarians before World War II. For instance, the British Museum entered into a pre-war agreement with the Clements Library of the University of Michigan under which many Museum items were microfilmed, and copies were sent to the library. Samuel Flagg Bemis, in reviewing *Guide to Material for American History in the Libraries and Archives of Paris*, compiled by Waldo G. Leland, John J. Meng and Abel Doysié,* expressed his gratification that the Library of Congress succeeded in getting "a great part" of these *Quai d'Orsay* documents "photocopied before the war." The copies of these records, he reports,† "are now available and

---

* *Archives of the Ministry of Foreign Affairs*, Carnegie Institution of Washington, Washington, D. C., 1943, Vol. II.

† *American Historical Review*, July 1944.

may even be consulted by inter-library facilities." This sharing of records obviates much travel formerly required of those doing historical research, travel that was often prohibitive in terms of time and expense.

It is apparent, then, that however complex preservation and care of old manuscripts may seem, there is always something the private collector can do to prevent his letters from disintegrating. Libraries obviously will care for their own. The collector, by one of the many methods available, can always stay progressive damage. If he fears to attend to his autographs himself, he can at least resort to the professional repairer. Laxity in this attention is unpardonable, the more so if the letters have definite historic significance.

CHAPTER XIV

How to Arrange

THE procedures to be followed by collectors in the arrangement of their autographs are not at all involved. Yet if these are haphazard, and the material is not properly kept for examination, either by the owner or by those who might otherwise be interested in it, the collection may suffer physically and proportionately lose in value. The jeweler recognizes that his gems can better be displayed against a dark background, and he usually has available on his counter a black or dark colored cloth. Autographs, too, can be shown to better and best advantage, and their full distinctiveness and importance enhanced. Each collection naturally has its own individualities and requires a little study to determine the best procedure for it. Whatever this may be, all collectors will recognize that the cardinal rule of arrangement is based on the proper guarding of autographs from damage.

With this in mind, the practice of pasting autographs on sheets of paper or in an album must at all costs be avoided. Unfortunately collectors, whether of signatures or costly A. L. S.s, who have resorted to this method are very numerous. Those who have done so are obviously ignorant of the fact that after a period of time any glue will badly stain the autograph and leave a brown mark which cannot be removed. The paper also deteriorates, and when an attempt is later made to detach the autograph from its backing it is not easy to do so without tearing. Immeasurable and irreparable damage has been done in the past to many fine autographs because their owners pasted them in this manner.

The collector who is taking his first steps in the field may plan initially to keep his acquisitions in a simple folder or a letter file alphabetically arranged. This will enable him to keep them safely and convenient for ready reference. The method is a good one, since his early purchases may cover items that fall into widely different categories, some of which he may subsequently wish to abandon. It provides for more permanent arrangement when at a later date his tastes have been confirmed, and his collection takes on sizable proportions. Many collectors with years of experience behind them continue to prefer the folder system.

Manila folders may be purchased at any stationery store for a nominal sum. The size of approximately fifteen by eleven is more generally used and will provide for the majority of manuscripts and hold the largest with comfortable margin. It is advisable at all times to keep the size of the folder uniform. When inserting the autographs in the folder or whatever the container may be, they should be opened up and placed flat. Letters, for example, obtained in the original envelopes in which they were mailed, ought to be removed and unfolded, the envelopes in which they came being carefully preserved, as the information they furnish may well have an important bearing on the letters themselves. An envelope may have a postmark and the full name and address of the original recipient, whereas the letter itself gives no date and begins "Dear Jane" or "Dear Sir." The business custom of including the formal details of address in the letter itself was usually followed by those writing personal letters in the past, but today this practice is seldom observed in the bulk of social correspondence.

The use of color in the folder method gives a bright touch. Paper of a good strong quality and of various shades may be bought and cut to size. The collector can then resort to a particular color for a special category—blue for Revolutionary generals, green for authors and poets, yellow for musicians—permitting him at a glance to file, or refer to, a particular item quickly. An advantage of this method is that material can be easily shifted from one folder to another. A collector, for example, who is forming sets both of the Presidents and cabinet officers, can transfer from the presidential to the cabinet folder a poor letter of such men as Jefferson or Madison, Monroe or John Quincy Adams, who served in both offices, and replace it with a newly acquired and more prized item.

The folder system can be slightly more elaborated by writing on the front cover the name of the person or persons whose autographs are contained in the folder and perhaps a few biographical references to the man's life and the period in which he lived. Clippings from newspapers, details concerning the circumstances under which the letter was written or the document signed, badges, curiosa—anything that relates to the individual whose autograph is represented—all add association interest. A typed transcript of the autograph, particularly one whose writing is not always quickly decipherable save by those familiar with it, is also a desirable addition. Some collectors type this transcript outside of or on the inside cover of the folder itself, but this can only be done when the latter is designed to hold no more than one autograph. The inclusion of a good engraving or print of the signer is always extremely effective. In this instance, as in the case of any printed material, it is necessary to guard against the danger of the ink of the autograph and of the items smudging one another. In old books the offset impression left on the opposite page by an engraving or print bound in with the book is familiar to many. This stain explains the presence, so often found, of the thin sheet of protective white tissue. To preserve autographs, sheets of very fine cellulose acetate foil may be obtained at artists' shops and cut to fold neatly over a manuscript. Foil sheets are very inexpensive and highly useful and will guard the autograph from dirt or print. When folders are of uniform size, they may often be neatly and snugly placed in a cloth case, affording protection against dust, which even modern steel files do not always give.

A more distinctive and attractive method of keeping autographs, having all the advantages of the folder system and added ones of its own, is that which involves the centering and hinging of each manuscript to a large sheet of good, strong quality paper —twenty-eight pound weight or more. Whatman paper with its deckle edge is particularly adaptable. A large sheet—15½ by 11½ —is preferably selected so that full allowance can be made for variations in the size of letter sheets, broadsides, vellum commissions and any other category which may be included. If the collector hastily chooses a smaller sheet for mounting purposes because this fits his first-acquired autograph, he will quickly find that other larger and even more desirable items will give him trouble. They cannot be hinged to a small sheet without folding, and this, of course, must be avoided whenever possible, since either paper or vellum will eventually crack when often folded and unfolded.

One great advantage in this mounting process is that the fingers need never touch the autograph. It is the heavy sheet which bears the wear and tear and the almost imperceptible dirtying caused by even the cleanest hands. The sheet used for mounting can always be replaced, but the autograph, once it has been stained by perspiration or smudged with dirt, cannot.

The collector himself may hinge autographs by using a thin strip of Japanese tissue and any good quality library paste or paste freshly made according to a special recipe recommended for this purpose.* Experts in the care and preservation of manuscripts strongly advise against the use of that type of gummy transparent tissue tape which needs no wetting. Before adopting any method of mounting, it is well for the collector to consult someone who is an expert on it or who has had long and sound experience.

Transcripts of letters may be hinged to a separate sheet of paper and immediately follow their originals. Or, in those cases when the original is larger than the transcript, one mounting sheet may be used, with the former vertically hinged on its left side, and the latter hinged so as to be beneath and hidden by it. By turning the autograph over, as one turns the leaf of a book, the transcript is revealed. To avoid an awkward or uneven appearance in such cases as that of a four-page octavo of considerable length, it is best to keep the transcript, which may be equally long or which may be written on a quarto page, on a separate sheet. The original autograph, it should be noted, is always centered, and the transcript is never hinged underneath it if the transcript is larger. This avoids the unattractive appearance which invariably results when the transcript juts out. The large white border around a letter is needed to set it off properly. If

* See Chapter XIII, p. 243.

this border is interrupted, or if the whole is uncentered, the effect is spoiled.

When letters, transcripts and other inclusions have been hinged and mounted on larger sheets of uniform size, a leather or cloth box of any desired color is frequently used by the collector, as in the case of folders. He can have his name, or a description of contents, stamped on the front and backbone, as title and author's surname are stamped on books. The box should be so sized that sheets will fit snugly into it, yet allowing a half inch for play. An ordinary box with cover is not practical for the same purpose, since, in lifting sheets from it, they may be creased or dirtied. To avoid doing this, the collector may use a box with cover in one piece, hinged on the left and with drop front on the right. The cover, when lifted from right to left, permits the drop front to fall down and the hand to slide under the sheets and withdraw them with ease. The depth of the box may be three, four or more inches, depending on the size of the collection or the preferences of the collector.

Because hinging involves a double thickness which makes a collection bulky, collectors customarily have all prints and engravings inlaid. Inlaying is to autographs what framing is to a picture. Only an expert or one highly skilled can do it properly. It provides a method by which both sides of a letter or manuscript are readily visible, and only a small fraction of its edge is covered by the framing heavy paper. The letter is contained in a sheet more or less as a window pane is enclosed in a puttied frame.

Some collectors prefer to inlay their letters as well as their prints. In the case of a folded four-page letter, it is the back sheet which is inlaid. The process, however, is not advisable for letters of eight or more pages. The reason is fairly obvious. In an eight-page letter, consisting of two folded four-page sheets, the back page of each folded sheet is inlaid on a separate sheet. There is no avoiding the possibility that the two may be separated, and one or the other lost. If the procedure of hinging rather than of inlaying such letters is followed, the second folded sheet is hinged immediately under and slightly to the right of the first folded sheet. The group and not the first page, then, is centered.

Collectors with whom inlaying was formerly very popular claimed that the system protected the edges of autographs from becoming frayed, a fact not always true, since inlaying for all but strong paper or that which has been strengthened, offers its own problems. Paper, in drying out or after a considerable a-mount of handling, tends to crack at the edges close to the inlay, and the latter eventually damages the autograph more than if the work had not been done. Strong paper alone can resist this wear. The majority of modern collectors in general prefer to keep autographs in their original state, not only for this practi-cal reason, but because of a taste—of course variable with indi-viduals—which frowns on any tampering.

The bound volume is still another method of keeping auto-graph collections. It is particularly attractive to collectors who form sets such as the Presidents or Napoleon and his marshals and are only interested in one specimen of each person. In bind-ing, inlaying is generally preferred to hinging, as the suction of air, when the leaves of the book are turned, may tear the old paper. Inlaid letters, which are better protected, are usually followed by an inlaid print, but transcripts, because they tend to make the volume too bulky, are frequently omitted. Undue bulkiness must be avoided, principally because the bound vol-ume, refusing to lie flat, will bulge ungracefully.

Such volumes may be simply bound or, if desired, may be dressed up with handsome, highly tooled leather bindings, silk doublures, ornate frontispieces, elaborate descriptions and other embellishments. Unquestionably striking and impressive as are the volumes, and however much a collector may pride himself on them, they cannot be used for autograph exhibition purposes, since only one letter can be shown at a time. If the binding it-self is displayed, obviously no letter can be seen.

Even those who are not collectors of autographs are at times tempted to purchase a volume of this kind because it is so hand-somely assembled. Bound sets of presidential letters and docu-ments, the most frequently formed, have been known to sell at a high figure. In the formation of this particular group, many collectors overlook what should be a cardinal rule in its arrangement—the leaving of blank sheets at the end of the volume. The failure to do so accounts for the fact that many collections, completed twenty or thirty years ago, conclude with President Taft or Wilson, Harding or Coolidge. The lapse is curious, since no American, unless he is convinced that the end of the world is just around the corner, ordinarily believes that the Chief Executive in office when he completes his set will be the last President of the United States.

The result of this seemingly unimportant omission of blank sheets in a presidential bound volume greatly lessens the value in later years. Collectors today, no matter how beautiful the binding or how important the letters, are not interested in purchasing a set which is currently incomplete and prohibits any additions. Because hinging or inlaying of an extra item can always be done easily by the expert, even after the book is bound, it is advisable always to include these extra pages. This procedure should be followed even in cases such as completed sets of the Signers, Napoleonic material or of any groups which are firmly limited to the past. There is always the possibility that an autograph which seriously merits inclusion may later be discovered. To place such an acquisition loosely in the front or back of the bound set is entirely unsatisfactory; the item itself may too easily be lost, it is not well protected and its importance is belittled.

Some few collectors who acquire a very remarkable item of exceptional interest adapt the bound volume method to it, binding it separately in equally beautiful form. Or they may bind it with accompanying prints and clippings, or they may place it in a handsome slip cover. Generally speaking, however, it is safer to keep such an item in a collection with other autographs. The owner, when his collection is all in one binding or one box, can better guard one than several, and thefts are more invited by a small, easily transportable case than by a weightier volume or container. The inclusion of the exceptional and rare piece in a group does not detract from it, but rather enhances the value of the other autographs with which it is associated. As a rule, it is not advisable to give individual items separate and elaborate arrangements.

Such advice is scarcely necessary for a collector who is so enthusiastic over his possessions that he insists on keeping them with him at all times. This type of enthusiast can find a practical method for his purposes by using a loose-leaf notebook easily available in larger stationery stores. Its leaves, made of cellulose acetate, and more accurately described as individual envelopes, are thin and transparent, and any autograph placed within them is clearly visible. The use of this system, as in the case of mounting or inlaying, affords ample protection against both dirt and moisture, and the autographs at no time need be touched by the fingers.

The notebooks can be purchased with leaves of varying sizes suitable for all requirements, and their pages may be removed or replaced or shifted to meet any exigency of arrangement. Since the use of cellulose acetate for notebook leaves is comparatively modern, its long-range effect on old paper has not been fully determined. In so far as is now known, it is harmless and gives splendid protection. Yet until time, which alone can provide final proof, has made its demonstration, the wise collector will take the precaution of checking at intervals on the condition of autographs encased in this manner. If they should show any tendency to become dried out or brittle, he should make other provision for their keeping.

Cellulose acetate notebooks are fairly reasonable. The price for each envelope varies from thirty-five to seventy-five cents, according to size, and certain manufacturers produce them with attractive edgings of various colors. Their use has one disadvantage when the collection is large. The binder will not hold more than approximately fifty envelopes, and the method may prove somewhat impractical and needlessly expensive if employed for an extensive collection. At the same time, for the collector who travels and who wishes to carry his collection in whole or in part with him, no cleaner, safer procedure can be found.

A simple album, rather than the envelope-type notebook, is

adequate for a collection of mere signatures. It is seldom practicable to arrange an album with one signature per page, and the majority of collectors prefer a large-sized book on which perhaps ten or more signatures will fit neatly. This gives opportunity to devote each page or group of pages to specific subjects and catagories. The signatures, whether on cards or small slips of paper, may be held in place by those devices familiar to the photographer and the stamp collector. A little study will reveal which of stamp stickers, corner tabs and any other method is best adapted, always with a view to keeping the signature from damage and making it readily detachable. Once the method is determined, since many signatures are almost illegible, the collector may want to print or type the name under the signature card, adding possibly some descriptive statement of identity.

For the casual collector, or the owner of a few letters who does not plan to acquire more, the album, too, can be well recommended. In it, tabs possibly take the preference. They not only hold the letter in place, but will not damage it. Even for this type of collector, the advice not to leave letters folded, and, above all, to remove them from their envelopes always holds good. The only exception may be made circumspectly in the case of vellum documents. If these are too large to be kept flat, they may be rolled on a cardboard tube. The collector who is willing to invest more than the price of an album may prefer, and is wise in, adopting the folder method.

A large number of collectors take greater pride in their manuscripts when these are framed with a handsome engraving, mounted and matted. They consider that such an entity gives distinctiveness to the room in which it is hung. Unquestionably, it draws attention to itself, but, like too many roses in one vase, often a single framed attraction is in better taste than half a dozen. It is obviously impractical to attempt to keep an entire collection in this manner, although one does occasionally hear of collections of two or three thousand framed items. Any who have wall space sufficient to accommodate such an accumulation may possibly be envied, but few would wish to bother with it. Actually, such collections frequently wind up stacked in a cellar or attic, where dust, dampness or excessive heat quickly works its damage.

When autographs are framed, they should never be hung so that the sun beats directly upon them. The intensity of sunlight will cause the ink to fade rapidly, and the paper will also oxidize and turn brown. These dangers are additionally present when letters that have been long in a family's possession are still kept in their original old frames. The custom formerly was to back the letter with wood, and, over the years, the wood, drying out completely, hastened the oxidation of the paper. If a long-framed manuscript is to be properly preserved, it should be removed from its wooden backing at the earliest possible moment. The frame itself may still be used, but the wood should be supplanted by cardboard. To this, however, the letter should never be pasted, as was also the unfortunate method of framers of another day. When the letter and cardboard are pasted together, the drying out of the latter hastens the same process for the other. To separate the two is a problem for the expert repairer, who alone can remove it with the minimum of damage.

There is one other method of autograph arrangement which was more popular from two to five decades ago than it is today, but which still holds interest and possesses fascinating points. This is a system known as Grangerizing, named after the Reverend James Granger, a British clergyman, whose chief claim to fame arises from his publication in 1769 of a lengthy tome entitled *A Biographical History of England from Egbert the Great to the Revolution*. The book was chosen by collectors of, and dealers in, prints as an ideal one to extra-illustrate, a process which can most briefly be described as involving the separation of a book's pages from its binding, interspersing them with many illustrations pertinent to the text and then rebinding the whole. From extra-illustrating with prints to extra-illustrating with autographs was a more or less natural step. Oddly enough, although the process was named after Granger, and he did own upward of fourteen thousand prints on his death, he never himself extra-illustrated any book.

The best example of Grangerizing as applied to autographs is unquestionably the famous Thomas Addis Emmet extra-illustrated set of Benson Lossing's two heavy volumes, entitled *Field Book of the American Revolution,* now among the prizes of the New York Public Library. The original books were taken from their binding and each leaf separately inlaid on a larger sheet. Between these leaves, wherever an anecdote or historic incident appeared in the text together with the name of a general or officer, an autograph letter of that man, dated as near to the period as possible and bearing on the subject itself if one could be obtained, was inlayed on a similar sized sheet and inserted. The entirety, which consists of hundreds of magnificent letters of the Revolutionary great, and mostly of war-year dates, was then permanently and elaborately bound.

Anyone who has attempted to read Lossing's somewhat ponderous, not always accurate, but on the whole vastly entertaining book will have some idea of the enormity of the task involved in assembling the set, which originally was two volumes, but, extra-illustrated, became ten. Dr. Emmet, who had above all the scholar's patience and persistence, fortunately also possessed unlimited funds. His invaluable compilation, in which Mr. Benjamin immeasurably assisted by locating many of its autographs, is a continuing reference for all dealers in old manuscripts, and particularly for those who specialize in Revolutionary material. From this, it can be argued that the extra-illustrating of Sandburg's life of Lincoln or Douglas Freeman's life of Robert E. Lee or of both is not beyond the range of possibility. For the first, the task would not be difficult, since letters of the Civil War period are fairly common, although none can predict how long this will continue. The same task for the Freeman book would present more hurdles, because Confederate autographs are far rarer than Union material of the same era.

What may be called a variation of Grangerizing is the simple insertion of an A. L. S. of an author in a copy of one of his books, preferably a first edition. The letter is usually hinged to the flyleaf. There are actually legions of collectors and lovers of old books who follow this practice. Unquestionably, a letter of Longfellow discussing *Evangeline,* which recently was sold at auction, would greatly enhance a first edition in which the poem appears. The same is true of the books of other poets and writers, or of scientists, military leaders or statesmen, even if the collector may prove over-optimistic in his hope to acquire a letter which discusses the book with which it is to be associated. Any good letter of a writer which is striking in contents and especially one which discusses the author's particular field, will serve to embellish the book and augment very much its market as well as sentimental value.

Methods of arranging autograph material are fundamentally limited but, like the primary colors, permit of numerous variations individually dictated by the collector's own taste. After he has undertaken the proper safeguards, what he considers the most attractive means of arrangement may be unusually distinctive, even unique. The basic methods, however, are simple and inexpensive. Possibly the majority may wish to keep them so; still others may decide to be more lavish. The man who throws himself into the planning of a new home derives equal pleasure whether it cost five, or fifty, thousand dollars. He does not remotely consider the study he devotes to blueprints as a chore; nor does the autograph collector who thoroughly enjoys the time he spends in planning or studying his collection.

TABLE OF APPROXIMATE DATES

Reproduced from Julius Grant's *Books and Documents; Dating, Permanence and Preservation,* through the courtesy of Grafton & Co., London, 1937.

7th century. The first bound books and introduction of quill pens.

863 The oldest printed book known (printed from blocks by Wang Chieh of Kansu, China).

1020 Beginning of the gradual transition from carbon to iron-gall writing inks.

1282 The earliest known water-mark.

1307 Names of papermakers first incorporated in water-marks.

1341 Invention of printing from movable type (by Pi Sheng) in China.

c.1400 Introduction of alum-tanned white pigskin bindings.

c.1440 Invention of printing from movable type in Europe (Johann Gutenberg, Mainz).

1445- Alternate light and dark striations in the look-through of paper
1500 due to construction of the mould.

1454 The first dated publication produced with movable type.

1457 The first book bearing the name of the printer.

1461 The first illustrated book (crude woodcuts).

1463 The first book with a title-page.

1465 The earliest blotting-paper; this is sometimes found in old books and manuscripts, and its presence may help to date them, although, of course, the blotting-paper may have been inserted subsequently to the date of origin.

c.1470 Great increase in the number of bound books produced, following the advent of printing; vellum and leather used principally.

1470 The first book with pagination and headlines.

1472 The first book bearing printed signatures to serve as a guide to the binder.

1474 The first book published in English (by William Caxton, in Bruges).

1476 The first work printed in England (by William Caxton).

1483 The first double water-mark.

1500 Introduction of the small octavo.

1500 Introduction of italics.

1536 The first book printed in America [in Mexico].

c.1545 Introduction of custom of using italics only for emphasis. Mineral oil and rosin first used in printing inks.

1560 Introduction of the sextodecimo.

1570 Introduction of the twelve-mo.

1570 Introduction of thin papers.

*c.*1575 The first gold tooling.

1580 Introduction of the modern forms of "i," "j," "u," and "v."

*c.*1580 The first pasteboards.

*c.*1600 Copper-plate illustration sufficiently perfected to replace crude woodcuts. Introduction of red morocco bindings.

1650 Wood covers (covered with silk, plush or tapestry) used for binding.

1670 Introduction of the hollander.

1720 Perfection of the vignette illustration.

1734 Caslon type introduced.

*c.*1750 The first cloth-backed paper (used only for maps).

*c.*1750 Gradual disappearance of vellum for binding and introduction of millboard covered with calf; or half covered with leather and half with marbled paper, etc. The first wove paper (Baskerville).

1763 Logwood inks probably first introduced.

1770 Indigo first used in inks (Eisler).

1780 Revival of the woodcut.

1780 Steel pens invented.

1796 The first lithographic machine.

1796 The first embossed binding.

1800 Blotting-paper in general use in England, following an accidental rediscovery at Hagbourne, Berkshire.

*c.*1803 Metal pens first placed on the market.

*c.*1816 Colored inks first manufactured in England using pigments.

*c.*1820 Linen canvas first used instead of parchment to hold the back of the book into the cover. Introduction of straight-grained red morocco bindings.

1820 The invention of the modern type of metal nib.

1825 The first permanent photographic image (Niépce.)

*c.*1830 The first linen cover.* Beginning of the era of poor leather bindings which have since deteriorated.

1830 Title printed on paper labels which were stuck on the cloth for the first time.

*c.*1835 Decoration by machinery introduced.

1836 Introduction of iron-gall inks containing indigo (Stephens).

1839 Invention of photography (Daguerre).

* According to Michael Sadlier's *Evolution of Publishers' Binding Styles* (1930), cloth was first used for bookbinding in 1821 and binding cloth generally available in 1825. The same authority places the first stamping on cloth in 1832.

1840   Titles first stamped on cloth.*

1845   Linen board cover in common use. At about this time it became usual to trim the edges of books, and the practice of binding in quarter leather declined.

1852   Invention of photogravure, leading to the development of lithographic etchings, color prints, line engravings, etc. (Fox-Talbot).

1855   Cotton first used as a cover for binding boards.

1856   Discovery of the first coal-tar dyestuff (Perkin's mauve), leading to the use of such dyestuffs in colored inks.

1860   Beginning of the custom of paring calf binding leathers to the thickness of paper.

1861   Introduction of synthetic indigo for inks.

1878   Invention of the stylographic pen.

1885   Invention of the half-tone process (F. E. Ives).

1905   The first offset litho press.

* *Ibid.*

	An II. 1793-1794	An III. 1794-1795	An IV. 1795-1796	An V. 1796-1797
1 vendém.	Sept. 22, 1793	Sept. 22, 1794	Sept. 23, 1795	Sept. 22, 1796
15 "	Oct. 6, "	Oct. 6, "	Oct. 7, "	Oct. 6, "
1 brum.	Oct. 22, "	Oct. 22, "	Oct. 23, "	Oct. 22, "
15 "	Nov. 5, "	Nov. 5, "	Nov. 6, "	Nov. 5, "
1 frimaire.	Nov. 21, "	Nov. 21, "	Nov. 22, "	Nov. 21, "
15 "	Dec. 5, "	Dec. 5, "	Dec. 6, "	Dec. 5, "
1 nivôse.	Dec. 21, "	Dec. 21, "	Dec. 22, "	Dec. 21, "
15 "	Jan. 4, 1794	Jan. 4, 1795	Jan. 5, 1796	Jan. 4, 1797
1 pluviôse.	Jan. 20, "	Jan. 20, "	Jan. 21, "	Jan. 20, "
15 "	Feb. 3, "	Feb. 3, "	Feb. 4, "	Feb. 3, "
1 ventôse.	Feb. 19, "	Feb. 19, "	Feb. 20, "	Feb. 19, "
15 "	Mar. 5, "	Mar. 5, "	Mar. 5, "	Mar. 5, "
1 germinal.	Mar. 21, "	Mar. 21, "	Mar. 21, "	Mar. 21, "
15 "	Apr. 4, "	Apr. 4, "	Apr. 4, "	Apr. 4, "
1 floréal.	Apr. 20, "	Apr. 20, "	Apr. 20, "	Apr. 20, "
15 "	May 4, "	May 4, "	May 4, "	May 4, "
1 prairial.	May 20, "	May 20, "	May 20, "	May 20, "
15 "	June 3, "	June 3, "	June 3, "	June 3, "
1 messidor.	June 19, "	June 19, "	June 19, "	June 19, "
15 "	July 3, "	July 3, "	July 3, "	July 3, "
1 thermid.	July 19, "	July 19, "	July 19, "	July 19, "
15 "	Aug. 2, "	Aug. 2, "	Aug. 2, "	Aug. 2, "
1 fructidor.	Aug. 18, "	Aug. 18, "	Aug. 18, "	Aug. 18, "
15 "	Sept. 1, "	Sept. 1, "	Sept. 1, "	Sept. 1, "
5e j. compl.	Sept. 21, "	Sept. 21, "	Sept. 21, "	Sept. 21, "
6e j. compl.		Sept. 22, "		

The last five days of the year were called "sans-culottides," and were observed

| An VI. | An VII. | An VIII. | An IX. | An X. |
1797-1798	1798-1799	1799-1800	1800-1801	1801-1802
Sept. 22, 1797	Sept. 22, 1798	Sept. 23, 1799	Sept. 23, 1800	Sept. 23, 1801
Oct. 6, "	Oct. 6, "	Oct. 7, "	Oct. 7, "	Oct. 7, "
Oct. 22, "	Oct. 22, "	Oct. 23, "	Oct. 23, "	Oct. 23, "
Nov. 5, "	Nov. 5, "	Nov. 6, "	Nov. 6, "	Nov. 6, "
Nov. 21, "	Nov. 21, "	Nov. 22, "	Nov. 22, "	Nov. 22, "
Dec. 5, "	Dec. 5, "	Dec. 6, "	Dec. 6, "	Dec. 6, "
Dec. 21, "	Dec. 21, "	Dec. 22, "	Dec. 22, "	Dec. 22, "
Jan. 4, 1798	Jan. 4, 1799	Jan. 5, 1800	Jan. 4, 1801	Jan. 5, 1802
Jan. 20, "	Jan. 21, "	Jan. 21, "	Jan. 21, "	Jan. 21, "
Feb. 3, "	Feb. 3, "	Feb. 4, "	Feb. 4, "	Feb. 4, "
Feb. 19, "	Feb. 19, "	Feb. 20, "	Feb. 20, "	Feb. 20, "
Mar. 5, "	Mar. 5, "	Mar. 6, "	Mar. 6, "	Mar. 6, "
Mar. 21, "	Mar. 21, "	Mar. 22, "	Mar. 22, "	Mar. 22, "
Apr. 4, "	Apr. 4, "	Apr. 5, "	Apr. 5, "	Apr. 5, "
Apr. 20, "	Apr. 20, "	Apr. 21, "	Apr. 21, "	Apr. 21, "
May 4, "	May 4, "	May 5, "	May 5, "	May 5, "
May 20, "	May 20, "	May 21, "	May 21, "	May 21, "
June 3, "	June 3, "	June 4, "	June 4, "	June 4, "
June 19, "	June 19, "	June 20, "	June 20, "	June 20, "
July 3, "	July 3, "	July 4, "	July 4, "	July 4, "
July 19, "	July 19, "	July 20, "	July 20, "	July 20, "
Aug. 2, "	Aug. 2, "	Aug. 3, "	Aug. 3, "	Aug. 3, "
Aug. 18, "	Aug. 18, "	Aug. 19, "	Aug. 19, "	Aug. 19, "
Sept. 1, "	Sept. 1, "	Sept. 2, "	Sept. 2, "	Sept. 2, "
Sept. 21, "	Sept. 21, "	Sept. 22, "	Sept. 22, "	Sept. 22, "
	Sept. 22, "			

as "Festivals" of Virtue, of Genius, of Labor, of Opinion, and of Rewards.

(continued next page)

	An XI. 1802-1803	An XII. 1803-1804	An XIII. 1804-1805	An XIV. 1805
1 vendém.	Sept. 23, 1802	Sept. 24, 1803	Sept. 23, 1804	Sept. 23, 1805
15 "	Oct. 7, "	Oct. 8, "	Oct. 7, "	Oct. 7, "
1 brum.	Oct. 23, "	Oct. 24, "	Oct. 23, "	Oct. 23, "
15 "	Nov. 6, "	Nov. 7, "	Nov. 6, "	Nov. 6, "
1 frimaire.	Nov. 22, "	Nov. 23, "	Nov. 22, "	Nov. 22, "
15 "	Dec. 6, "	Dec. 7, "	Dec. 6, "	Dec. 6, "
1 nivôse.	Dec. 22, "	Dec. 23, "	Dec. 22, "	Dec. 22, "
15 "	Jan. 5, 1803	Jan. 9, 1804	Jan. 5, 1805	
1 pluviôse.	Jan. 21, "	Jan. 22, "	Jan. 21, "	
15 "	Feb. 4, "	Feb. 5, "	Feb. 4, "	
1 ventôse.	Feb. 20, "	Feb. 21, "	Feb. 20, "	
15 "	Mar. 6, "	Mar. 6, "	Mar. 6, "	
1 germinal.	Mar. 22, "	Mar. 22, "	Mar. 22, "	
15 "	Apr. 5, "	Apr. 5, "	Apr. 5, "	
1 floréal.	Apr. 21, "	Apr. 21, "	Apr. 21, "	
15 "	May 5, "	May 5, "	May 5, "	
1 prairial.	May 21, "	May 21, "	May 21, "	
15 "	June 4, "	June 4, "	June 4, "	
1 messidor.	June 20, "	June 20, "	June 20, "	
15 "	July 4, "	July 4, "	July 4, "	
1 thermid.	July 20, "	July 20, "	July 20, "	
15 "	Aug. 3, "	Aug. 3, "	Aug. 3, "	
1 fructidor.	Aug. 19, "	Aug. 19, "	Aug. 19, "	
15 "	Sept. 2, "	Sept. 2, "	Sept. 2, "	
5e j. compl.	Sept. 22, "	Sept. 22, "	Sept. 22, "	
6e j. compl.	Sept. 23, "			

TITLES OF
NAPOLEON'S MARSHALS

Title	Name	Date Appointed
ALBUFERA, DUKE OF	LOUIS GABRIEL SUCHET	July 8, 1811
AUERSTÄDT, DUKE OF	LOUIS NICOLAS DAVOUT	May 19, 1804
BELLUNO, DUKE OF	CLAUDE PERRIN VICTOR	July 13, 1807
BERG, GRAND DUKE OF	JOACHIM MURAT	May 19, 1804
BRUNE, COUNT	GUILLAUME MARIE ANNE BRUNE	May 19, 1804
CASTIGLIONE, DUKE OF	PIERRE FRANÇOIS CHARLES AUGEREAU	May 19, 1804
CLEVES, GRAND DUKE OF	JOACHIM MURAT	May 19, 1804
CONEGLIANO, DUKE OF	BON ADRIEN JEANNOT DE MONCEY	May 19, 1804
DALMATIA, DUKE OF	NICOLAS JEAN DE DIEU SOULT	May 19, 1804
DANZIG, DUKE OF	FRANÇOIS JOSEPH LEFEBVRE	May 19, 1804
ECKMÜHL, PRINCE OF	LOUIS NICOLAS DAVOUT	May 19, 1804
ELCHINGEN, DUKE OF	MICHEL NEY	May 19, 1804
ESSLING, PRINCE OF	ANDRÉ MASSÉNA	May 19, 1804
GROUCHY, MARQUIS OF	EMMANUEL GROUCHY	April 15, 1815
ISTRIA, DUKE OF	JEAN BAPTISTE BESSIÈRES	May 19, 1804
JOURDAN, COUNT	JEAN BAPTISTE JOURDAN	May 19, 1804
MONTEBELLO, DUKE OF	JEAN LANNES	May 19, 1804
MOSKOWA, PRINCE OF THE	MICHEL NEY	May 19, 1804
NAPLES, KING OF	JOACHIM MURAT	May 19, 1804
NEUFCHATEL, PRINCE & DUKE OF	LOUIS ALEXANDRE BERTHIER	May 19, 1804
PERIGNON, MARQUIS OF	DOMINIQUE CATHERINE PERIGNON	May 19, 1804
PONIATOWSKI, PRINCE	JOSEPH ANTHONY PONIATOWSKI	Oct. 16, 1813
PONTE CORVO, PRINCE OF	JEAN BAPTISTE JULES BERNADOTTE	May 19, 1804
RAGUSE, DUKE OF	AUGUSTE FREDERIC LOUIS VIESSE DE MARMONT	July 12, 1809
REGGIO, DUKE OF	CHARLES NICOLAS OUDINOT	July 12, 1809
RIVOLI, DUKE OF	ANDRÉ MASSÉNA	May 19, 1804
ST. CYR, MARQUIS OF	LAURENT GOUVION ST. CYR	Aug. 27, 1812
SÉRURIER, COUNT	JEAN MATTHIEU PHILIBERT SÉRURIER	May 19, 1804
SICILIES, KING OF THE TWO	JOACHIM MURAT	May 19, 1804

SWEDEN, KING CHARLES JEAN XIV OF (CARL JOHAN)	JEAN BAPTISTE JULES BERNADOTTE	May 19, 1804
TARANTO, DUKE OF	ETIENNE JACQUES JOSEPH ALEXANDRE MACDONALD	July 12, 1809
TREVISO, DUKE OF	EDOUARD ADOLPHE CASIMIR JOSEPH MORTIER	May 19, 1804
VALANGIN, PRINCE OF	LOUIS ALEXANDRE BERTHIER	May 19, 1804
VALMY, DUKE OF	FRANÇOIS CHRISTOPHE KELLERMANN	May 19, 1804
WAGRAM, PRINCE OF	LOUIS ALEXANDRE BERTHIER	May 19, 1804

TITLES OF
NAPOLEON'S IMMEDIATE FAMILY AND CLOSE
CONNECTIONS BY MARRIAGE

Title	Name
AUSTRIA, ARCHDUCHESS OF	MARIE LOUISE
BAVARIA, PRINCESS OF	AUGUSTA AMALIA
BEAUHARNAIS, VISCOUNT OF	ALEXANDRE DE BEAUHARNAIS
BEAUHARNAIS, VISCOUNTESS OF	JOSEPHINE
BERG, GRAND DUKE OF	JOACHIM MURAT
BORGHESE, PRINCE	CAMILLE BORGHESE
BORGHESE, PRINCESS	PAULINE BONAPARTE
CANINO, PRINCE OF	LUCIEN BONAPARTE
CANINO, PRINCESS OF	ALEXANDRINE DE BLESCHAMP
CASALI, COUNT OF	LUCIEN BONAPARTE
CASALI, COUNTESS OF	ALEXANDRINE DE BLESCHAMP
CLEVES, GRAND DUKE OF	JOACHIM MURAT
EICHSTADT, PRINCE OF	EUGENE BEAUHARNAIS
EICHSTADT, PRINCESS OF	AUGUSTA AMALIA
FESCH, CARDINAL	JOSEPH FESCH
FRANCE, EMPRESS OF	JOSEPHINE
FRANCE, EMPRESS OF	MARIE LOUISE
GUASTALLA, DUCHESS OF	MARIE LOUISE
GUASTALLA, DUCHESS OF	PAULINE BONAPARTE
GUASTALLA, DUKE OF	CAMILLE BORGHESE
HOLLAND, KING OF	LOUIS BONAPARTE
HOLLAND, QUEEN OF	HORTENSE BEAUHARNAIS
ITALY, VICE-ROY OF	EUGENE BEAUHARNAIS
LEUCHTENBERG, DUCHESS OF	AUGUSTA AMALIA
LEUCHTENBERG, DUKE OF	EUGENE BEAUHARNAIS
LIPONA, COUNTESS OF	CAROLINE BONAPARTE
LUCCA, PRINCE OF	FELIX BACIOCCHI
LUCCA, PRINCESS OF	ELISA BONAPARTE
MADAME	LETITIA BONAPARTE
MADAME MÈRE	LETITIA BONAPARTE
MONFORT, COUNT OF	JEROME BONAPARTE
MONFORT, COUNTESS OF	CATHERINE OF WURTEMBURG
MUSIGNANO, PRINCE OF	LUCIEN BONAPARTE
MUSIGNANO, PRINCESS OF	ALEXANDRINE DE BLESCHAMP

NAPLES, KING OF	JOSEPH BONAPARTE
NAPLES, QUEEN OF	JULIE CLARY
NAPLES, KING OF	JOACHIM MURAT
NAPLES, QUEEN OF	CAROLINE BONAPARTE
NAPOLEON II	FRANÇOIS CHARLES JOSEPH
PARMA, DUCHESS OF	MARIE LOUISE
PIACENZA, DUCHESS OF	MARIE LOUISE
PIOMBINO, PRINCE OF	FELIX BACIOCCHI
PIOMBINO, PRINCESS OF	ELISA BONAPARTE
REICHSTADT, DUKE OF	FRANÇOIS CHARLES JOSEPH
ROME, KING OF	FRANÇOIS CHARLES JOSEPH
ST. LEU, COUNT OF	LOUIS BONAPARTE
SPAIN, KING OF	JOSEPH BONAPARTE
SPAIN, QUEEN OF	JULIE CLARY
SURVILLIERS, COUNT OF	JOSEPH BONAPARTE
TUSCANY, GRAND DUCHESS OF	ELISA BONAPARTE
WESTPHALIA, KING OF	JEROME BONAPARTE
WESTPHALIA, QUEEN OF	CATHERINE OF WURTEMBURG
WURTEMBURG, PRINCESS OF	CATHERINE OF WURTEMBURG

The above is only a partial compilation. A complete listing will be found in Albert Ciana's *Les Bonaparte.*

A SELECTED LIST OF REFERENCE WORKS

For the autograph collector, older reference books are just as useful as books fresh off the presses. *Appleton's* contains many biographies which had to be deleted from a more recent work such as the *Dictionary of American Biography*. On the other hand, Robert S. Henry's *The Story of the Confederacy* will have information which was not known to Benson J. Lossing.

I have omitted some sturdy work-horses of the reference library since most collectors are familiar with them. I have in mind *The Encyclopaedia Britannica; The Dictionary of National Biography* for British names; *Webster's Biographical Dictionary;* and *Webster's Geographical Dictionary. The Oxford Companion to American Literature* and its fellow volume, *The Oxford Companion to English Literature,* are excellent guides.

The great projects of issuing the papers of famous men afford enormous help to the collector. For historical research, there are such standard works as John Fitzpatrick's *Writings of Washington,* published in 1931-44, and *The Collected Works of Abraham Lincoln,* published in 1953-55. For literary reference, *Horace Walpole's Correspondence,* edited by W. S. Lewis, 1937-55, and *The Letters of Ralph Waldo Emerson,* edited by Ralph L. Rusk, 1939, are definitive studies of important correspondences.

In addition, I have found the following books helpful in day-to-day tracking down of information necessary to evaluate the vast volume of material which passes through my hands. Others could be suggested, but the ones I list are the most convenient and available.

A SELECTED LIST OF REFERENCE WORKS

Some Helpful Books for Checking Persons, Places, and Things

Appleton's Cyclopaedia of American Biography. Edited by James Grant Wilson and John Fiske. New York: 1886-1918. 6 vols. with 7th and 8th supplementary vols.

Atlas of American History. James Truslow Adams, Editor in Chief; R. V. Coleman, Managing Editor. New York: Scribner, 1943. With 147 plates.

Biographical Directory of the American Congress, 1774-1949. Washington: Government Printing Office, 1950.

Boatner, Mark Mayo, III. *The Civil War Dictionary.* With maps and diagrams by Major Allen C. Northrop and Lowell I. Miller. New York: McKay, 1959.

Cullum, George W. *Biographical Register:* Officers and Graduates of the U. S. Military Academy, From 1802 to 1867. Revised Edition, With a Supplement Continuing the Register of Graduates to January 1, 1879. New York: Miller, 1879. 3 vols.

Dictionary of American History. James Truslow Adams, Editor in Chief; R. V. Coleman, Managing Editor. New York: Scribner, 1940. 4 vols.

Dictionnaire Historique et Biographique de la Révolution et de l'Empire. (1789-1815). Paris: Librairie Historique de la Révolution et de l'Empire, n. d. 2 vols.

Encyclopedia of American History. Edited by Richard B. Morris. New York: Harper, 1953.

Encyclopedia of World History. Compiled and edited by William L. Langer. Revised Ed. Boston: Houghton, Mifflin, 1948.

Garros, Louis. *Itineraire de Napoleon Bonaparte, 1769-1821.* Paris: Les Editions de l'Encyclopédie Française, 1947.

General Register: United States Navy and Marine Corps, Arranged in Alphabetical Order, for One Hundred Years, (1782 to 1882). Edited by Thomas H. S. Hamersly. Washington: Hamersly, 1882.

Grove's Dictionary of Music and Musicians. Edited by Eric Blom. 5th Ed. New York: St. Martin's Press, 1955. 9 vols.

Harper's Encyclopaedia of United States History. New York: Harper, 1902. 10 vols.

Heitman, F. B. *Historical Register of Officers of the Continental Army during the War of the Revolution, April, 1775, to December, 1783.* Washington: Lowdermilk, 1893.

———. *Historical Register of the United States Army, from Its Organization September 29, 1789, to September 29, 1889.* Washington: National Tribune, 1890.

Henry, Robert Selph. *The Story of the Confederacy.* Illus. New York: Garden City, 1931.

International Cyclopedia of Music and Musicians. Edited by Oscar Thompson. New York: Dodd, Mead, 1939.

LaLanne, Ludovic. *Dictionnaire Historique de la France.* Paris: Hachette, 1872.

Lossing, Benson J. *Pictorial Field-Book of the Revolution.* New York: Harper, 1859. 2 vols.

———. *Pictorial Field-Book of the War of 1812.* New York: Harper, 1868.

———. *Pictorial History of the Civil War in the United States of America.* Philadelphia: McKay, 1866. 3 vols.

Metcalf, Bryce. *Original Members and Other Officers Eligible to the Society of the Cincinnati, 1783-1938.* Strasburg, Virginia: Shenandoah, 1938.

Pageant of America: A Pictorial History of the United States. Edited by R. H. Gabriel and others. New Haven: Yale University Press, 1925-29. 15 vols.

Phisterer, Frederick. *Statistical Record of the Armies of the United States.* Supplementary volume of *Campaigns of the Civil War.* New York: Scribner, 1883.

Books about Collecting

Broadley, A. M. *Chats on Autographs.* New York: Stokes, 1910.

Goodspeed, Charles E. *Yankee Bookseller.* Boston: Houghton, Mifflin, 1937.

Grant, Julius. *Books and Documents.* London: Grafton, 1937.

Hamilton, Charles. *Collecting Autographs and Manuscripts.* Norman: University of Oklahoma Press, 1961.

Hill, George Birkbeck. *Talks about Autographs.* Boston: Houghton, Mifflin, 1896.

Joline, Adrian H. *Meditations of an Autograph Collector.* New York & London: Harper, 1902.

————. *Rambles in Autograph Land.* New York: Scribner, 1913.

Madigan, Thomas F. *Word Shadows of the Great.* New York: Stokes, 1930.

Munby, A. N. L. *The Cult of the Autograph Letter in England.* London: Athlone Press of the University of London, 1962.

Rosenbach, A. W. S. *Books and Bidders.* Boston: Little, Brown, 1927.

Scott, Henry T. *Autograph Collecting.* London: [1894].

Stern, Edward. *History of the "Free Franking" of Mail in the United States.* Illus. New York: Lindquist, 1936.

———. "The Free Franking Privilege of the Presidents' Widows." *The Collectors' Club Philatelist,* January, 1944.

Storm, Colton, and Howard Peckham. *Invitation to Book Collecting, Its Pleasures and Practices, with Kindred Discussions of Manuscripts, Maps, and Prints.* New York: Bowker, 1947.

Wolf, Edwin, II, with John F. Fleming. *Rosenbach: A Biography.* Cleveland: World, 1960.

Important Facsimile Reference Books

Authors at Work. An Address delivered by Robert H. Taylor at the Opening of an Exhibition of Literary Manuscripts at the Grolier Club Together with a Catalogue of the Exhibition by Herman W. Liebert and Facsimiles of Many of the Exhibits. New York: The Grolier Club, 1957. With facsimiles of the manuscripts of forty-nine writers.

Autographic Mirror: Autographic Letters and Sketches of Illustrious and Distinguished Men. London: Cassell, Peter, and Galpin, 1864-66. 4 vols.

Autograph Leaves of Our Country's Authors. Compiled by John P. Kennedy and Alexander Bliss. Baltimore: Cushings & Bailey, 1864.

The Book of the Signers. Edited by William Brotherhead. Philadelphia: Brotherhead, 1861.

British Autography: A Collection of Fac-similes of the Handwriting of Royal and Illustrious Personages with Their Authentic Portraits. Edited by John Thane. London: Thane, [1793].

Catalogue of the Collection of Autograph Letters and Historical Documents Formed . . . by Alfred Morrison. London: Strangeways, 1883-97. 13 vols.

Charavay, Etienne. *Inventaire des Autographes et des Documents Historiques Composant la Collection de M. Benjamin Fillon*. Paris: Charavay, 1877-79.

————. *Lettres Autographes Composant la Collection de M. Alfred Bovet*. Paris: Charavay, 1885.

Ciana, Albert. *Napoléon, Autographes, Manuscrits, Signatures*. Genève: Éditions Helvetica, 1939.

————. *Les Bonaparte, Autographes, Manuscrits, Signatures*. Genève: Éditions Helvetica, 1941.

Geigy, Charles. *Handbook of Facsimiles of Famous Personages*. Basle: Geering, 1925.

Genesis of American Freedom, 1765-1795: A Selection of Original Documents from the Collection of Elsie O. and Philip D. Sang. Waltham, Mass.: Brandeis University, 1961.

Wise, T. J. *The Ashley Library, A Catalogue of Printed Books, Manuscripts, and Autograph Letters*. London: Printed for Private Circulation Only, 1922-36. 11 vols.

Current Periodicals

American Book Collector. Chicago: 1956–. Monthly.

Antiquarian Bookman. Newark: 1948–. Weekly.

Book Collecting World. Chicago: 1961–. Weekly.

Book Collector. London: 1952–. Quarterly.

Papers of the Bibliographical Society of America. New York: 1904–. (Quarterly since 1913.)

Index

A CATALOG OF SELECTED DOVER BOOKS IN ALL FIELDS OF INTEREST

CONCERNING THE SPIRITUAL IN ART, Wassily Kandinsky. Pioneering work by father of abstract art. Thoughts on color theory, nature of art. Analysis of earlier masters. 12 illustrations. 80pp. of text. 5⅜ × 8½. 23411-8 Pa. $2.50

LEONARDO ON THE HUMAN BODY, Leonardo da Vinci. More than 1200 of Leonardo's anatomical drawings on 215 plates. Leonardo's text, which accompanies the drawings, has been translated into English. 506pp. 8⅜ × 11¾. 24483-0 Pa. $10.95

GOBLIN MARKET, Christina Rossetti. Best-known work by poet comparable to Emily Dickinson, Alfred Tennyson. With 46 delightfully grotesque illustrations by Laurence Housman. 64pp. 4 × 6¾. 24516-0 Pa. $2.50

THE HEART OF THOREAU'S JOURNALS, edited by Odell Shepard. Selections from *Journal*, ranging over full gamut of interests. 228pp. 5⅜ × 8½. 20741-2 Pa. $4.50

MR. LINCOLN'S CAMERA MAN: MATHEW B. BRADY, Roy Meredith. Over 300 Brady photos reproduced directly from original negatives, photos. Lively commentary. 368pp. 8⅜ × 11¼. 23021-X Pa. $14.95

PHOTOGRAPHIC VIEWS OF SHERMAN'S CAMPAIGN, George N. Barnard. Reprint of landmark 1866 volume with 61 plates: battlefield of New Hope Church, the Etawah Bridge, the capture of Atlanta, etc. 80pp. 9 × 12. 23445-2 Pa. $6.00

A SHORT HISTORY OF ANATOMY AND PHYSIOLOGY FROM THE GREEKS TO HARVEY, Dr. Charles Singer. Thoroughly engrossing non-technical survey. 270 illustrations. 211pp. 5⅜ × 8½. 20389-1 Pa. $4.95

REDOUTE ROSES IRON-ON TRANSFER PATTERNS, Barbara Christopher. Redouté was botanical painter to the Empress Josephine; transfer his famous roses onto fabric with these 24 transfer patterns. 80pp. 8¼ × 10⅞. 24292-7 Pa. $3.50

THE FIVE BOOKS OF ARCHITECTURE, Sebastiano Serlio. Architectural milestone, first (1611) English translation of Renaissance classic. Unabridged reproduction of original edition includes over 300 woodcut illustrations. 416pp. 9⅜ × 12¼. 24349-4 Pa. $14.95

CARLSON'S GUIDE TO LANDSCAPE PAINTING, John F. Carlson. Authoritative, comprehensive guide covers, every aspect of landscape painting. 34 reproductions of paintings by author; 58 explanatory diagrams. 144pp. 8⅜ × 11. 22927-0 Pa. $5.95

101 PUZZLES IN THOUGHT AND LOGIC, C.R. Wylie, Jr. Solve murders, robberies, see which fishermen are liars—purely by reasoning! 107pp. 5⅜ × 8½. 20367-0 Pa. $2.00

TEST YOUR LOGIC, George J. Summers. 50 more truly new puzzles with new turns of thought, new subtleties of inference. 100pp. 5⅜ × 8½. 22877-0 Pa. $2.25

REASON IN ART, George Santayana. Renowned philosopher's provocative, seminal treatment of basis of art in instinct and experience. Volume Four of *The Life of Reason*. 230pp. 5⅜ × 8.   24358-3 Pa. $4.50

LANGUAGE, TRUTH AND LOGIC, Alfred J. Ayer. Famous, clear introduction to Vienna, Cambridge schools of Logical Positivism. Role of philosophy, elimination of metaphysics, nature of analysis, etc. 160pp. 5⅜ × 8½. (USCO)
20010-8 Pa. $2.75

BASIC ELECTRONICS, U.S. Bureau of Naval Personnel. Electron tubes, circuits, antennas, AM, FM, and CW transmission and receiving, etc. 560 illustrations. 567pp. 6½ × 9¼.   21076-6 Pa. $8.95

THE ART DECO STYLE, edited by Theodore Menten. Furniture, jewelry, metalwork, ceramics, fabrics, lighting fixtures, interior decors, exteriors, graphics from pure French sources. Over 400 photographs. 183pp. 8⅜ × 11¼.
22824-X Pa. $6.95

THE FOUR BOOKS OF ARCHITECTURE, Andrea Palladio. 16th-century classic covers classical architectural remains, Renaissance revivals, classical orders, etc. 1738 Ware English edition. 216 plates. 110pp. of text. 9½ × 12¾.
21308-0 Pa. $11.50

THE WIT AND HUMOR OF OSCAR WILDE, edited by Alvin Redman. More than 1000 ripostes, paradoxes, wisecracks: Work is the curse of the drinking classes, I can resist everything except temptations, etc. 258pp. 5⅜ × 8½. (USCO)
20602-5 Pa. $3.95

THE DEVIL'S DICTIONARY, Ambrose Bierce. Barbed, bitter, brilliant witticisms in the form of a dictionary. Best, most ferocious satire America has produced. 145pp. 5⅜ × 8½.   20487-1 Pa. $2.50

ERTÉ'S FASHION DESIGNS, Erté. 210 black-and-white inventions from *Harper's Bazar*, 1918-32, plus 8pp. full-color covers. Captions. 88pp. 9 × 12.
24203-X Pa. $6.50

ERTÉ GRAPHICS, Erté. Collection of striking color graphics: *Seasons, Alphabet, Numerals, Aces* and *Precious Stones*. 50 plates, including 4 on covers. 48pp. 9⅜ × 12¼.   23580-7 Pa. $6.95

PAPER FOLDING FOR BEGINNERS, William D. Murray and Francis J. Rigney. Clearest book for making origami sail boats, roosters, frogs that move legs, etc. 40 projects. More than 275 illustrations. 94pp. 5⅜ × 8½.   20713-7 Pa. $2.25

ORIGAMI FOR THE ENTHUSIAST, John Montroll. Fish, ostrich, peacock, squirrel, rhinoceros, Pegasus, 19 other intricate subjects. Instructions. Diagrams. 128pp. 9 × 12.   23799-0 Pa. $4.95

CROCHETING NOVELTY POT HOLDERS, edited by Linda Macho. 64 useful, whimsical pot holders feature kitchen themes, animals, flowers, other novelties. Surprisingly easy to crochet. Complete instructions. 48pp. 8¼ × 11.
24296-X Pa. $1.95

CROCHETING DOILIES, edited by Rita Weiss. Irish Crochet, Jewel, Star Wheel, Vanity Fair and more. Also luncheon and console sets, runners and centerpieces. 51 illustrations. 48pp. 8¼ × 11.   23424-X Pa. $2.50

DECORATIVE NAPKIN FOLDING FOR BEGINNERS, Lillian Oppenheimer and Natalie Epstein. 22 different napkin folds in the shape of a heart, clown's hat, love knot, etc. 63 drawings. 48pp. 8¼ × 11.   23797-4 Pa. $1.95

DECORATIVE LABELS FOR HOME CANNING, PRESERVING, AND OTHER HOUSEHOLD AND GIFT USES, Theodore Menten. 128 gummed, perforated labels, beautifully printed in 2 colors. 12 versions. Adhere to metal, glass, wood, ceramics. 24pp. 8¼ × 11.   23219-0 Pa. $2.95

EARLY AMERICAN STENCILS ON WALLS AND FURNITURE, Janet Waring. Thorough coverage of 19th-century folk art: techniques, artifacts, surviving specimens. 166 illustrations, 7 in color. 147pp. of text. 7⅞ × 10¾. 21906-2 Pa. $9.95

AMERICAN ANTIQUE WEATHERVANES, A.B. & W.T. Westervelt. Extensively illustrated 1883 catalog exhibiting over 550 copper weathervanes and finials. Excellent primary source by one of the principal manufacturers. 104pp. 6⅛ × 9¼.
24396-6 Pa. $3.95

ART STUDENTS' ANATOMY, Edmond J. Farris. Long favorite in art schools. Basic elements, common positions, actions. Full text, 158 illustrations. 159pp. 5⅜ × 8½.   20744-7 Pa. $3.95

BRIDGMAN'S LIFE DRAWING, George B. Bridgman. More than 500 drawings and text teach you to abstract the body into its major masses. Also specific areas of anatomy. 192pp. 6½ × 9¼. (EA)   22710-3 Pa. $4.50

COMPLETE PRELUDES AND ETUDES FOR SOLO PIANO, Frederic Chopin. All 26 Preludes, all 27 Etudes by greatest composer of piano music. Authoritative Paderewski edition. 224pp. 9 × 12. (Available in U.S. only)   24052-5 Pa. $7.50

PIANO MUSIC 1888-1905, Claude Debussy. Deux Arabesques, Suite Bergamesque, Masques, 1st series of Images, etc. 9 others, in corrected editions. 175pp. 9⅜ × 12¼.
(ECE) 22771-5 Pa. $5.95

TEDDY BEAR IRON-ON TRANSFER PATTERNS, Ted Menten. 80 iron-on transfer patterns of male and female Teddys in a wide variety of activities, poses, sizes. 48pp. 8¼ × 11.   24596-9 Pa. $2.25

A PICTURE HISTORY OF THE BROOKLYN BRIDGE, M.J. Shapiro. Profusely illustrated account of greatest engineering achievement of 19th century. 167 rare photos & engravings recall construction, human drama. Extensive, detailed text. 122pp. 8¼ × 11.   24403-2 Pa. $7.95

NEW YORK IN THE THIRTIES, Berenice Abbott. Noted photographer's fascinating study shows new buildings that have become famous and old sights that have disappeared forever. 97 photographs. 97pp. 11⅜ × 10.   22967-X Pa. $7.50

MATHEMATICAL TABLES AND FORMULAS, Robert D. Carmichael and Edwin R. Smith. Logarithms, sines, tangents, trig functions, powers, roots, reciprocals, exponential and hyperbolic functions, formulas and theorems. 269pp. 5⅜ × 8½.   60111-0 Pa. $4.95

HANDBOOK OF MATHEMATICAL FUNCTIONS WITH FORMULAS, GRAPHS, AND MATHEMATICAL TABLES, edited by Milton Abramowitz and Irene A. Stegun. Vast compendium: 29 sets of tables, some to as high as 20 places. 1,046pp. 8 × 10½.   61272-4 Pa. $19.95

THE RIME OF THE ANCIENT MARINER, Gustave Doré, S.T. Coleridge. Doré's finest work, 34 plates capture moods, subtleties of poem. Full text. 77pp. 9¼ × 12.   22305-1 Pa. $4.95

SONGS OF INNOCENCE, William Blake. The first and most popular of Blake's famous "Illuminated Books," in a facsimile edition reproducing all 31 brightly colored plates. Additional printed text of each poem. 64pp. 5¼ × 7.
                                                                22764-2 Pa. $3.50

AN INTRODUCTION TO INFORMATION THEORY, J.R. Pierce. Second (1980) edition of most impressive non-technical account available. Encoding, entropy, noisy channel, related areas, etc. 320pp. 5⅜ × 8½.   24061-4 Pa. $4.95

THE DIVINE PROPORTION: A STUDY IN MATHEMATICAL BEAUTY, H.E. Huntley. "Divine proportion" or "golden ratio" in poetry, Pascal's triangle, philosophy, psychology, music, mathematical figures, etc. Excellent bridge between science and art. 58 figures. 185pp. 5⅜ × 8½.   22254-3 Pa. $3.95

THE DOVER NEW YORK WALKING GUIDE: From the Battery to Wall Street, Mary J. Shapiro. Superb inexpensive guide to historic buildings and locales in lower Manhattan: Trinity Church, Bowling Green, more. Complete Text; maps. 36 illustrations. 48pp. 3⅞ × 9¼.   24225-0 Pa. $2.50

NEW YORK THEN AND NOW, Edward B. Watson, Edmund V. Gillon, Jr. 83 important Manhattan sites: on facing pages early photographs (1875-1925) and 1976 photos by Gillon. 172 illustrations. 171pp. 9¼ × 10.   23361-8 Pa. $7.95

HISTORIC COSTUME IN PICTURES, Braun & Schneider. Over 1450 costumed figures from dawn of civilization to end of 19th century. English captions. 125 plates. 256pp. 8⅜ × 11¼.   23150-X Pa. $7.50

VICTORIAN AND EDWARDIAN FASHION: A Photographic Survey, Alison Gernsheim. First fashion history completely illustrated by contemporary photographs. Full text plus 235 photos, 1840-1914, in which many celebrities appear. 240pp. 6½ × 9¼.   24205-6 Pa. $6.00

CHARTED CHRISTMAS DESIGNS FOR COUNTED CROSS-STITCH AND OTHER NEEDLECRAFTS, Lindberg Press. Charted designs for 45 beautiful needlecraft projects with many yuletide and wintertime motifs. 48pp. 8¼ × 11.
                                                                24356-7 Pa. $2.50

101 FOLK DESIGNS FOR COUNTED CROSS-STITCH AND OTHER NEEDLE-CRAFTS, Carter Houck. 101 authentic charted folk designs in a wide array of lovely representations with many suggestions for effective use. 48pp. 8¼ × 11.
                                                                24369-9 Pa. $2.25

FIVE ACRES AND INDEPENDENCE, Maurice G. Kains. Great back-to-the-land classic explains basics of self-sufficient farming. The one book to get. 95 illustrations. 397pp. 5⅜ × 8½.   20974-1 Pa. $4.95

A MODERN HERBAL, Margaret Grieve. Much the fullest, most exact, most useful compilation of herbal material. Gigantic alphabetical encyclopedia, from aconite to zedoary, gives botanical information, medical properties, folklore, economic uses, and much else. Indispensable to serious reader. 161 illustrations. 888pp. 6½ × 9¼. (Available in U.S. only)   22798-7, 22799-5 Pa., Two-vol. set $16.45

HOW THE OTHER HALF LIVES, Jacob A. Riis. Journalistic record of filth, degradation, upward drive in New York immigrant slums, shops, around 1900. New edition includes 100 original Riis photos, monuments of early photography. 233pp. 10 × 7⅞. 22012-5 Pa. $7.95

CHINA AND ITS PEOPLE IN EARLY PHOTOGRAPHS, John Thomson. In 200 black-and-white photographs of exceptional quality photographic pioneer Thomson captures the mountains, dwellings, monuments and people of 19th-century China. 272pp. 9⅝ × 12¼. 24393-1 Pa. $12.95

GODEY COSTUME PLATES IN COLOR FOR DECOUPAGE AND FRAMING, edited by Eleanor Hasbrouk Rawlings. 24 full-color engravings depicting 19th-century Parisian haute couture. Printed on one side only. 56pp. 8¼ × 11. 23879-2 Pa. $3.95

ART NOUVEAU STAINED GLASS PATTERN BOOK, Ed Sibbett, Jr. 104 projects using well-known themes of Art Nouveau: swirling forms, florals, peacocks, and sensuous women. 60pp. 8¼ × 11. 23577-7 Pa. $3.50

QUICK AND EASY PATCHWORK ON THE SEWING MACHINE: Susan Aylsworth Murwin and Suzzy Payne. Instructions, diagrams show exactly how to machine sew 12 quilts. 48pp. of templates. 50 figures. 80pp. 8¼ × 11. 23770-2 Pa. $3.50

THE STANDARD BOOK OF QUILT MAKING AND COLLECTING, Marguerite Ickis. Full information, full-sized patterns for making 46 traditional quilts, also 150 other patterns. 483 illustrations. 273pp. 6⅞ × 9⅝. 20582-7 Pa. $5.95

LETTERING AND ALPHABETS, J. Albert Cavanagh. 85 complete alphabets lettered in various styles; instructions for spacing, roughs, brushwork. 121pp. 8¾ × 8. 20053-1 Pa. $3.95

LETTER FORMS: 110 COMPLETE ALPHABETS, Frederick Lambert. 110 sets of capital letters; 16 lower case alphabets; 70 sets of numbers and other symbols. 110pp. 8⅛ × 11. 22872-X Pa. $4.50

ORCHIDS AS HOUSE PLANTS, Rebecca Tyson Northen. Grow cattleyas and many other kinds of orchids—in a window, in a case, or under artificial light. 63 illustrations. 148pp. 5⅜ × 8½. 23261-1 Pa. $2.95

THE MUSHROOM HANDBOOK, Louis C.C. Krieger. Still the best popular handbook. Full descriptions of 259 species, extremely thorough text, poisons, folklore, etc. 32 color plates; 126 other illustrations. 560pp. 5⅜ × 8½. 21861-9 Pa. $8.50

THE DORÉ BIBLE ILLUSTRATIONS, Gustave Doré. All wonderful, detailed plates: Adam and Eve, Flood, Babylon, life of Jesus, etc. Brief King James text with each plate. 241 plates. 241pp. 9 × 12. 23004-X Pa. $8.95

THE BOOK OF KELLS: Selected Plates in Full Color, edited by Blanche Cirker. 32 full-page plates from greatest manuscript-icon of early Middle Ages. Fantastic, mysterious. Publisher's Note. Captions. 32pp. 9¾ × 12¼. 24345-1 Pa. $4.50

THE PERFECT WAGNERITE, George Bernard Shaw. Brilliant criticism of the Ring Cycle, with provocative interpretation of politics, economic theories behind the Ring. 136pp. 5⅜ × 8½. (Available in U.S. only) 21707-8 Pa. $3.00

KEYBOARD WORKS FOR SOLO INSTRUMENTS, G.F. Handel. 35 neglected works from Handel's vast oeuvre, originally jotted down as improvisations. Includes Eight Great Suites, others. New sequence. 174pp. 9⅜ × 12¼.
24338-9 Pa. $7.50

AMERICAN LEAGUE BASEBALL CARD CLASSICS, Bert Randolph Sugar. 82 stars from 1900s to 60s on facsimile cards. Ruth, Cobb, Mantle, Williams, plus advertising, info, no duplications. Perforated, detachable. 16pp. 8¼ × 11.
24286-2 Pa. $2.95

A TREASURY OF CHARTED DESIGNS FOR NEEDLEWORKERS, Georgia Gorham and Jeanne Warth. 141 charted designs: owl, cat with yarn, tulips, piano, spinning wheel, covered bridge, Victorian house and many others. 48pp. 8¼ × 11.
23558-0 Pa. $1.95

DANISH FLORAL CHARTED DESIGNS, Gerda Bengtsson. Exquisite collection of over 40 different florals: anemone, Iceland poppy, wild fruit, pansies, many others. 45 illustrations. 48pp. 8¼ × 11.   23957-8 Pa. $1.75

OLD PHILADELPHIA IN EARLY PHOTOGRAPHS 1839-1914, Robert F. Looney. 215 photographs: panoramas, street scenes, landmarks, President-elect Lincoln's visit, 1876 Centennial Exposition, much more. 230pp. 8⅜ × 11¾.
23345-6 Pa. $9.95

PRELUDE TO MATHEMATICS, W.W. Sawyer. Noted mathematician's lively, stimulating account of non-Euclidean geometry, matrices, determinants, group theory, other topics. Emphasis on novel, striking aspects. 224pp. 5⅜ × 8½.
24401-6 Pa. $4.50

ADVENTURES WITH A MICROSCOPE, Richard Headstrom. 59 adventures with clothing fibers, protozoa, ferns and lichens, roots and leaves, much more. 142 illustrations. 232pp. 5⅜ × 8½.   23471-1 Pa. $3.95

IDENTIFYING ANIMAL TRACKS: MAMMALS, BIRDS, AND OTHER ANIMALS OF THE EASTERN UNITED STATES, Richard Headstrom. For hunters, naturalists, scouts, nature-lovers. Diagrams of tracks, tips on identification. 128pp. 5⅜ × 8.   24442-3 Pa. $3.50

VICTORIAN FASHIONS AND COSTUMES FROM HARPER'S BAZAR, 1867-1898, edited by Stella Blum. Day costumes, evening wear, sports clothes, shoes, hats, other accessories in over 1,000 detailed engravings. 320pp. 9⅜ × 12¼.
22990-4 Pa. $10.95

EVERYDAY FASHIONS OF THE TWENTIES AS PICTURED IN SEARS AND OTHER CATALOGS, edited by Stella Blum. Actual dress of the Roaring Twenties, with text by Stella Blum. Over 750 illustrations, captions. 156pp. 9 × 12.
24134-3 Pa. $8.50

HALL OF FAME BASEBALL CARDS, edited by Bert Randolph Sugar. Cy Young, Ted Williams, Lou Gehrig, and many other Hall of Fame greats on 92 full-color, detachable reprints of early baseball cards. No duplication of cards with *Classic Baseball Cards*. 16pp. 8¼ × 11.   23624-2 Pa. $3.50

THE ART OF HAND LETTERING, Helm Wotzkow. Course in hand lettering, Roman, Gothic, Italic, Block, Script. Tools, proportions, optical aspects, individual variation. Very quality conscious. Hundreds of specimens. 320pp. 5⅜ × 8½.
21797-3 Pa. $4.95

YUCATAN BEFORE AND AFTER THE CONQUEST, Diego de Landa. Only significant account of Yucatan written in the early post-Conquest era. Translated by William Gates. Over 120 illustrations. 162pp. 5⅜ × 8½. 23622-6 Pa. $3.50

ORNATE PICTORIAL CALLIGRAPHY, E.A. Lupfer. Complete instructions, over 150 examples help you create magnificent "flourishes" from which beautiful animals and objects gracefully emerge. 8⅛ × 11. 21957-7 Pa. $2.95

DOLLY DINGLE PAPER DOLLS, Grace Drayton. Cute chubby children by same artist who did Campbell Kids. Rare plates from 1910s. 30 paper dolls and over 100 outfits reproduced in full color. 32pp. 9¼ × 12¼. 23711-7 Pa. $3.50

CURIOUS GEORGE PAPER DOLLS IN FULL COLOR, H. A. Rey, Kathy Allert. Naughty little monkey-hero of children's books in two doll figures, plus 48 full-color costumes: pirate, Indian chief, fireman, more. 32pp. 9¼ × 12¼. 24386-9 Pa. $3.50

GERMAN: HOW TO SPEAK AND WRITE IT, Joseph Rosenberg. Like *French, How to Speak and Write It.* Very rich modern course, with a wealth of pictorial material. 330 illustrations. 384pp. 5⅜ × 8½. (USUKO) 20271-2 Pa. $4.75

CATS AND KITTENS: 24 Ready-to-Mail Color Photo Postcards, D. Holby. Handsome collection; feline in a variety of adorable poses. Identifications. 12pp. on postcard stock. 8¼ × 11. 24469-5 Pa. $2.95

MARILYN MONROE PAPER DOLLS, Tom Tierney. 31 full-color designs on heavy stock, from *The Asphalt Jungle, Gentlemen Prefer Blondes,* 22 others. 1 doll. 16 plates. 32pp. 9⅜ × 12¼. 23769-9 Pa. $3.50

FUNDAMENTALS OF LAYOUT, F.H. Wills. All phases of layout design discussed and illustrated in 121 illustrations. Indispensable as student's text or handbook for professional. 124pp. 8⅝ × 11. 21279-3 Pa. $4.50

FANTASTIC SUPER STICKERS, Ed Sibbett, Jr. 75 colorful pressure-sensitive stickers. Peel off and place for a touch of pizzazz: clowns, penguins, teddy bears, etc. Full color. 16pp. 8¼ × 11. 24471-7 Pa. $2.95

LABELS FOR ALL OCCASIONS, Ed Sibbett, Jr. 6 labels each of 16 different designs—baroque, art nouveau, art deco, Pennsylvania Dutch, etc.—in full color. 24pp. 8¼ × 11. 23688-9 Pa. $2.95

HOW TO CALCULATE QUICKLY: RAPID METHODS IN BASIC MATHEMATICS, Henry Sticker. Addition, subtraction, multiplication, division, checks, etc. More than 8000 problems, solutions. 185pp. 5 × 7¼. 20295-X Pa. $2.95

THE CAT COLORING BOOK, Karen Baldauski. Handsome, realistic renderings of 40 splendid felines, from American shorthair to exotic types. 44 plates. Captions. 48pp. 8¼ × 11. 24011-8 Pa. $2.25

THE TALE OF PETER RABBIT, Beatrix Potter. The inimitable Peter's terrifying adventure in Mr. McGregor's garden, with all 27 wonderful, full-color Potter illustrations. 55pp. 4¼ × 5½. (Available in U.S. only) 22827-4 Pa. $1.75

BASIC ELECTRICITY, U.S. Bureau of Naval Personnel. Batteries, circuits, conductors, AC and DC, inductance and capacitance, generators, motors, transformers, amplifiers, etc. 349 illustrations. 448pp. 6½ × 9¼. 20973-3 Pa. $7.95

SOURCE BOOK OF MEDICAL HISTORY, edited by Logan Clendening, M.D. Original accounts ranging from Ancient Egypt and Greece to discovery of X-rays: Galen, Pasteur, Lavoisier, Harvey, Parkinson, others. 685pp. 5⅜ × 8½.
20621-1 Pa. $10.95

THE ROSE AND THE KEY, J.S. Lefanu. Superb mystery novel from Irish master. Dark doings among an ancient and aristocratic English family. Well-drawn characters; capital suspense. Introduction by N. Donaldson. 448pp. 5⅜ × 8½.
24377-X Pa. $6.95

SOUTH WIND, Norman Douglas. Witty, elegant novel of ideas set on languorous Mediterranean island of Nepenthe. Elegant prose, glittering epigrams, mordant satire. 1917 masterpiece. 416pp. 5⅜ × 8½. (Available in U.S. only)
24361-3 Pa. $5.95

RUSSELL'S CIVIL WAR PHOTOGRAPHS, Capt. A.J. Russell. 116 rare Civil War Photos: Bull Run, Virginia campaigns, bridges, railroads, Richmond, Lincoln's funeral car. Many never seen before. Captions. 128pp. 9⅜ × 12¼.
24283-8 Pa. $6.95

PHOTOGRAPHS BY MAN RAY: 105 Works, 1920-1934. Nudes, still lifes, landscapes, women's faces, celebrity portraits (Dali, Matisse, Picasso, others), rayographs. Reprinted from rare gravure edition. 128pp. 9⅜ × 12¼. (Available in U.S. only)
23842-3 Pa. $7.95

STAR NAMES: THEIR LORE AND MEANING, Richard H. Allen. Star names, the zodiac, constellations: folklore and literature associated with heavens. The basic book of its field, fascinating reading. 563pp. 5⅜ × 8½.
21079-0 Pa. $7.95

BURNHAM'S CELESTIAL HANDBOOK, Robert Burnham, Jr. Thorough guide to the stars beyond our solar system. Exhaustive treatment. Alphabetical by constellation: Andromeda to Cetus in Vol. 1; Chamaeleon to Orion in Vol. 2; and Pavo to Vulpecula in Vol. 3. Hundreds of illustrations. Index in Vol. 3. 2000pp. 6⅛ × 9¼.
23567-X, 23568-8, 23673-0 Pa. Three-vol. set $36.85

THE ART NOUVEAU STYLE BOOK OF ALPHONSE MUCHA, Alphonse Mucha. All 72 plates from *Documents Decoratifs* in original color. Stunning, essential work of Art Nouveau. 80pp. 9⅜ × 12¼.
24044-4 Pa. $7.95

DESIGNS BY ERTE; FASHION DRAWINGS AND ILLUSTRATIONS FROM "HARPER'S BAZAR," Erte. 310 fabulous line drawings and 14 *Harper's Bazar* covers, 8 in full color. Erte's exotic temptresses with tassels, fur muffs, long trains, coifs, more. 129pp. 9⅜ × 12¼.
23397-9 Pa. $6.95

HISTORY OF STRENGTH OF MATERIALS, Stephen P. Timoshenko. Excellent historical survey of the strength of materials with many references to the theories of elasticity and structure. 245 figures. 452pp. 5⅜ × 8½. 61187-6 Pa. $8.95

Prices subject to change without notice.
Available at your book dealer or write for free catalog to Dept. GI, Dover Publications, Inc., 31 East 2nd St. Mineola, N.Y. 11501. Dover publishes more than 175 books each year on science, elementary and advanced mathematics, biology, music, art, literary history, social sciences and other areas.